LANDSCAPE, LAND-CHANGE & WELL-BEING IN THE LESSER ANTILLES

Sidestone Press

LANDSCAPE, LAND-CHANGE & WELL-BEING IN THE LESSER ANTILLES

Case Studies from the coastal villages of St. Kitts and the Kalinago Territory, Dominica

CHARLOTTE ELOISE STANCIOFF

© 2018 Charlotte Eloise Stancioff

Published by Sidestone Press, Leiden
www.sidestone.com

Imprint: Sidestone Press Dissertations

Lay-out & cover design: Sidestone Press
Photograph cover: C. E. Stancioff

ISBN 978-90-8890-586-5 (softcover)
ISBN 978-90-8890-587-2 (hardcover)
ISBN 978-90-8890-588-9 (PDF e-book)

This research has received funding from the European Research Council under the European Union's Seventh Framework Programme (FP7/2007-2013) / ERC grant agreement n° 319209.

This dissertation followed the Nexus Ethics Code and the Code of Conduct/Ethics of Leiden University.

DOI https://doi.org/10.17026/dans-x8w-cdqd

Contents

List of Figures	**11**
List of Tables	**15**
Acknowledgments	**19**
Preface	**21**
1 Introduction	**25**
1.1 Rural landscapes as microcosms of global land-use change	25
1.2 The imagined islands: framing the research in historical context	27
1.3 Aims and objectives of the research	31
1.4 Scope and structure of the research	32
2 Theoretical framework	**35**
2.1 Introduction	35
2.1.1 Landscape: from interaction to detached view	36
2.1.2 The Caribbean region as an imagined geographic space	38
2.1.3 Colonial expansion and the "exotic" environment	41
2.1.4 The environmental crusade: external perspectives on the Caribbean	45
2.2 Current landscape theory: research trends and directions	50
2.2.1 Landscape and the community	55
2.3 Socio-ecological systems: the origins and definitions of terms	56
2.3.1 The resilience within SES and a community	57
2.3.2 Connecting to well-being: the Ecosystem Services and cultural values	62
2.3.3 One concept of well-being	64
2.4 Landscape, community and well-being	66

3 Methodology — 67

Part I. Macro factors of a system: society and ecology — 67

3.1 Overall methods and approach — 68

3.2 Research principles: the socio-ecological indicators — 72
    3.2.1 The interview process and protocol — 72
    3.2.2 Interview analysis using socio-ecological Indicators: coding and the discourse network analysis — 74

3.3 Analysis of the land-use and the land-change — 77
    3.3.1 The historical land-change and community perceptions — 78
    3.3.2 The land classification — 79
    3.3.3 The preprocessing of data — 80
    3.3.4 Supervised and unsupervised classification — 81
    3.3.5 Accuracy assessment — 82

Part II. Micro factors of the local landscape context — 85

3.4 The coastal villages of St. Kitts: the study area and background — 86
    3.4.1 Integrating the ecological and community knowledge in land-change analysis: coastal erosion — 88
    3.4.2 Linking physical changes with community perceptions — 90

3.5 The Kalinago Territory, Dominica: study area and background — 91
    3.5.1 Integrating ecological and community knowledge in land-change analysis: community mapping and river degradation — 94
    3.5.2 Watershed management in the Kalinago Territory — 96
    3.5.3 Linking physical changes with interviews and surveys — 99

3.6 Final thoughts: challenges and partnerships — 100

4 The coastal villages of St. Kitts: the bitterness of sugar — 103

Part I. A recent history of the Kittitian landscape — 104

4.1 St. Kitts under British colonization — 104
    4.1.1 The impact of the sugar industry on historical land-use and society — 105
    4.1.2 Land after slavery — 106
    4.1.3 Shaping the landscape: independence and land — 108
    4.1.4 The collapse of the sugar industry in 2006 — 109

Part II. Landscape: use, modification and value	112
4.2 Multiple use of lands: analyzing the land-cover change	112
4.3 Resource conservation: the impacts of coastal erosion, rising sea levels and beach access restrictions	124
4.4 Shifting community: socio-cultural aspects of landscape change	134
Part III: The significance of fallow land: case study observations	136
5 The Kalinago Territory: Land for survival, land as a burden	**139**
Part I. A recent history of the Kalinago landscape	140
5.1 The Kalinago Territory and its historical background	140
5.1.1 The early European contact and the British occupation	141
5.1.2 The Kalinago Territory: land, power and politics	143
5.1.3 Shaping the current Kalinago Territory landscape	145
Part II. Landscape: use, modification and value	146
5.2 Multiple uses of the land: an analysis of the land-cover changes	146
5.3 Resource Conservation: Water Resources	165
5.4 Shifting community: the socio-cultural aspects of landscape change	172
Part III: The Kalinago Territory at a crossroads	180
6 Discussion and Conclusions	**183**
6.1 Discussion on the case study findings	184
6.1.1 Landscape change and community well-being	184
6.1.2 Synergies and antagonisms in access to land	185
6.1.3 Agricultural production and the effects of mono-cropping	188
6.1.4 The (re) positioning of individuals and community in a changing landscape	189
6.2 Innovation and implications of the methodology	191
6.3 Final conclusions	194

Epilogue	**199**
References	**201**
Interviews	240
APPENDICES	**243**
Appendix A The interview questions and the analysis of the Socio-ecological Indicator	**245**
A.1 Defining the research focus of coastal villages of St. Kitts: the socio-ecological indicators	246
A1.1 Percentages of the main and sub themes, the coastal villages of St. Kitts.	248
A.2 Defining research focus of Kalinago Territory: socio-ecological indicators	252
Appendix B Land-use/land-change results	**259**
B.1 Land-use/land-cover change of the coastal villages, St. Kitts	259
B.2 Land-use/land cover change analysis of the Kalinago Territory	263
Appendix C Micro factors methods applied to the coastal villages of St. Kitts	**269**
C.1 Survey questions, St. Kitts	269
C.2 Data distribution provided by the survey respondents, St. Kitts	270
Appendix D The micro factors methods applied in the Kalinago Territory	**273**
D.1 Survey questions, Kalinago Territory	273
D.2 Data distribution provided by the Kalinago Territory survey respondents	274
Appendix E Data results of the coastal villages of St. Kitts	**277**
E.1 Specific land class results of land-cover/land-change analysis	277
E.2 Survey results of the coastal villages of St. Kitts	282
E.3 Coastal erosion of coastal villages, St. Kitts	285

Appendix F Data results of the Kalinago Territory	**287**
F.1 Specific land class results of the land-use/land-change analysis	287
F.2 Kalinago Territory survey results	291
F.3 Watershed management of the Kalinago Territory	294
Summary	**295**
Samenvatting	**297**
Curriculum vitae	**301**

List of Figures

Fig. 1. St. Kitts and Dominica in the Caribbean region	26
Fig. 2. Key components in a landscape and their connection to human use; adapted from Liu and Opdam (2014).	60
Fig. 3. The multiple scales and influences on landscapes; adapted from Liu and Opdam (2014).	61
Fig. 4. Cultural Value Model, adapted from J. Stephenson (2008).	63
Fig. 5. Conceptual model of the linkages between the Cultural Ecosystem Services (CES) and cultural landscape approach; adapted from Tenberg et al (2012).	70
Fig. 6. The overview of the applied methodology in the case studies, merging qualitative and quantitative data.	71
Fig. 7. Case study settlement locations on St. Kitts.	86
Fig. 8. Macro and micro factors relevant to the coastal villages of St. Kitts case study.	88
Fig. 9. St. Kitts Coast Guard carrying out a shoreline survey (photo by author).	90
Fig. 10. The Kalinago Territory, Dominica.	92
Fig. 11. Macro and micro factors relevant to the Kalinago Territory case study.	93
Fig. 12. Cozier Frederick leading a community mapping workshop in Salybia.	95
Fig. 13. Marcus Philips and Asher Burton collecting GPS points during a land survey (photo by author).	96
Fig. 14. Maximum Likelihood Supervision classification of the coastal villages of St. Kitts, 2006.	113
Fig. 15. Maximum Likelihood Supervision classification of the coastal villages of St. Kitts, 2015.	114
Fig. 16. Total percentage of each land class regarding the gains and losses (2006-2015), the coastal villages of St. Kitts.	115
Fig. 17. Overall land class changes of the coastal villages of St. Kitts, indicating land cover modifications between and 2006 to 2015.	116

Fig. 18. Urban gains: contributions from other land classes, 2006-2015.   117
Fig. 19. Bare gains: contributions from other land classes, 2006-2015.   118
Fig. 20. Crop gains: contributions from other land classes, 2006-2015.   119
Fig. 21. Grass gains: contributions from other land classes, 2006-2015.   119
Fig. 22. Forest gains: contributions from other land classes 2006-2015.   120
Fig. 23. Empty sugar cane fields present an odd but beautiful landscape (photo by author).   121
Fig. 24. This chimney, a remnant of the sugar cane industry, still stands in the overgrown fields located at the foot of Mount Liamuiga (photo by author)   122
Fig. 25. Clearing the heavy overgrowth to create a path through now discarded sugar cane fields (photo by author).   123
Fig. 26. Village houses located very close to the water's edge (photo by author).   125
Fig. 27. Mean and standard deviations of the variables of coastal changes whereby 1 represents the negative and 4 the positive changes.   126
Fig. 28. Net Shoreline Movement (2006-2015) of the coastal villages, St. Kitts. Figure created with the aid of Julijan Vermeer.   129
Fig. 29. Visualized End Point Rate (2006-2015) of the coastal villages of St. Kitts. Figure created with the aid fo Julijan Vermeer.   130
Fig. 30. View from Horseback Ridge Road en route to the Kalinago Territory (photo by author)   147
Fig. 31. The Kalinago Territory expanse as observed from Horseback Ridge Road (photo by author).   147
Fig. 32. Maximum Likelihood Supervised Classification 2005, the Kalinago Territory.   148
Fig. 33. Maximum Likelihood Supervised Classification 2014, the Kalinago Territory.   149
Fig. 34. Percentages of the total land class type changes between 2005 and 2014, the Kalinago Territory.   150
Fig. 35. Overall land class changes in the Kalinago Territory, indicating the modification of the land-cover changes between 2006 and 2015.   151
Fig. 36. Urban gains: contributions from other land classes, 2005-2014.   152
Fig. 37. Bare gains: contributions from other land classes, 2005-2014.   153
Fig. 38. Low Vegetation gains contributions from other land classes, 2005-2014.   154
Fig. 39. Forest gains contributions from other land classes, 2005-2014.   155
Fig. 40. Perception of any hamlet, territory, land and changes as expressed by the respondents of the survey residing in the Kalinago Territory whereby 1 represents the negative and 3 the positive changes.   156

Fig. 41. Point category of plots: understanding the perception of changes of the variables: Hamlet, Land and Territory. ... 157

Fig. 42. Point category of plots: understanding the relationships between the perception of changes regarding the variables, Land, Territory and Hamlet, and the demographic factor of age. ... 158

Fig. 43. Overall perceptions expressed by the survey respondents regarding modifications to agricultural variables, whereby 1 represents the negative and 3 the positive changes. ... 160

Fig. 44. Joint category of plots: understanding the relationships between the perceptions of changes of the variables: Agriculture Production, Soil Fertility, Crop, Input Amount, and Water Resources. ... 161

Fig. 45. Mapping a field in the course of the Kalinago Territory land survey (photo by author). ... 164

Fig. 46. These undulating fields encountered in the course of the Kalinago Territory land survey reveal the variability of use and fallow (photo by author). ... 164

Fig. 47. Perceptions of changes to water resources overall as expressed by the survey respondents. ... 167

Fig. 48. Curve Numbers of 2005, the Kalinago Territory. ... 168

Fig. 49. Curve Numbers of 2014, the Kalinago Territory. ... 169

Fig. 50. Shifts in CN values as recorded between 2005 and 2014 in the Kalinago Territory whereby the numbers indicate a larger modification from the original low CN value (2005) to a higher CN value (2014). ... 170

Fig. 51. A canoe, being hollowed out and carved by hand from Gommier tree (Dacryodes excelsa) which was later sold outside the Kalinago Territory (photo by author). ... 174

Fig. 52. Drying reeds of the auro (u)man (Ischnosiphon arouma) plant to produce baskets (photo by author). ... 175

Fig. 53. Overall perceived community changes in the Kalinago Territory, whereby 1 represents the negative and 3 the positive changes. ... 176

Fig. 54. Joint category of plots: understanding the relationship between perception of the changes concerning the variables of Community, Education, Politics and Business. ... 178

Fig. 55. Desired changes as defined by survey respondents, the Kalinago Territory. ... 180

Fig. 56. Averages of the main themes, St. Kitts. ... 249

Fig. 57. Average percentages of the sub themes, St. Kitts. ... 250

Fig. 58. Graphical representation showing affiliation network of relationships between main themes and sub themes in St. Kitts case study. ... 251

Fig. 59. Percentages of the main themes, the Kalinago Territory.	254
Fig. 60. Percentages of the sub themes, the Kalinago Territory.	255
Fig. 61. Graphical representation showing affiliation network of relationships between main themes and sub themes in the Kalinago Territory case study.	256
Fig. 62. ISO land-cover classification 2006, St. Kitts.	259
Fig. 63. ISO classification of the land cover 2015, St. Kitts.	260
Fig. 64. ISO unsupervised classification of the land-changes 2006-2015, St. Kitts.	261
Fig. 65. ISO unsupervised classification of the land cover 2005, the Kalinago Territory.	263
Fig. 66. ISO unsupervised classification of the land-cover 2014, the Kalinago Territory.	264
Fig. 67. ISO unsupervised classification of the land changes 2005-2014, St Kitts.	265
Fig. 68. Water gains: contributions from other land classes.	267
Fig. 69. Land-cover changes to Urban 2006-2015, St. Kitts.	277
Fig. 70. Land-over changes to Bare 2006-2015, St. Kitts.	278
Fig. 71. Land-cover changes to Crops 2006-2015, St. Kitts.	279
Fig. 72. Land-cover changes to Grass 2006-2015, St. Kitts.	280
Fig. 73. Land-cover changes to Forest 2006-2015 St. Kitts.	281
Fig. 74. Extracted shorelines 1986-2015.	285
Fig. 75. Land-cover changes to Urban 2005-2014, the Kalinago Territory.	287
Fig. 76. Land-cover changes to Bare 2005-2014, the Kalinago Territory.	288
Fig. 77. Land-cover changes to Low Vegetation 2005-2014, the Kalinago Territory.	289
Fig. 78. Land-cover changes to Forest 2005-2014 the Kalinago Territory	290
Fig. 79. Watershed catchments, the Kalinago Territory.	294

List of Tables

Table 1. Ecosystem services; adapted from the Millennium Ecosystem Assessment (MEA)(2006).	61
Table 2. Determinant and constituents of well-being; adapted from the Millennium Ecosystem Assessment (MA 2005).	64
Table 3. Socio-ecological Indicators; adapted from van Oudenhouven *et al.* (2010) and UNU-IAS (2014).	75
Table 4. Selected imagery applied in the land-use/land-cover analysis.	80
Table 5. Land-cover reclassification, St. Kitts and Dominica	82
Table 6. Accuracy assessment St. Kitts and the Kalinago Territory.	83-85
Table 7. Socio-ecological system assessment and the main focus.	85
Table 8. Associated error types linked to the various types of imagery.	89
Table 9. Selected shoreline data, St. Kitts.	89
Table 10. Explored relationships applying the MCA.	100
Table 11. Total acreage changes of land class Urban	117
Table 12. Total acreage changes of land class Bare.	117
Table 13. Total acreage changes of the land class Crops.	118
Table 14. Total acreage changes of land class Grass.	118
Table 15. Total acreage changes of land class Forest	120
Table 16. Perceptions of changes in sea-level fluctuations at the coastal villages of St. Kitts based on gender.	127
Table 17. Perceptions of the coastal erosion at the coastal villages of St. Kitts based on age groups.	128
Table 18. Perceptions of the coastal erosion and the impact on quality of life on St. Kitts based on age groups.	128
Table 19. Total End Point Rate of the study area, 1986-2015.	130
Table 20. End Point Rate by village group of the coastal villages of St. Kitts.	131
Table 21. Perceptions of survey respondents of the sea-level fluctuations, based on village groups.	131
Table 22. Perceptions of survey respondents of the sea-level fluctuations on the quality of life, based on village groups.	132

Table 23. Perceptions of survey respondents of coastal erosion, based on village groups.	132
Table 24. Perceptions of survey respondents of coastal erosion on the quality of life, based on village groups.	133
Table 25. Krusal-Wallis test, relationship between village group and combined environmental changes of coastal erosion and sea-level fluctuations impacts on village group and quality of life.	133
Table 26. Total acreage changes of land class: Urban.	152
Table 27. Total acreage changes of land class: Bare.	153
Table 28. Total acreage change of the land class: Low Vegetation.	154
Table 29. Total acreage changes of land class: Forest.	155
Table 30. Discrimination measures of variables: Land, Territory, and Hamlet.	156
Table 31. Discrimination measures of variables: Agriculture, Soil Fertility, Crop, Input Amount, and Water. The filled-in cells denote the significant relationships.	160
Table 32. Discrimination measures of variables: Community, Education, Politics, and Business. The filled-in cells denote significant relationships.	177
Table 33. Complete list of interview questions asked during both case studies. Continued on next page.	245-246
Table 34. Socio-ecological indicators: the main theme and sub theme, St. Kitts. Continued on next page.	247-248
Table 35. Socio-ecological indicators and descriptions thereof, applied as codes for the interview analyses.	253
Table 36. ISO unsupervised classification Cross Tabulation Matrix 2006-2015, St. Kitts.	262
Table 37. Maximum Likelihood Classification Cross Tabulation Matrix 2006-2015, St. Kitts.	262
Table 38. ISO unsupervised classification Cross Tabulation Matrix 2005-2014, the Kalinago Territory.	266
Table 39. Maximum Likelihood Classification Cross Tabulation Matrix 2005-2014, the Kalinago Territory.	266
Table 40. Land class type: Water	267
Table 41. Survey questions asked on St. Kitts.	269-270
Table 42. Age distribution.	270
Table 43. Village distribution.	270
Table 44. Village group distribution.	271
Table 45. Occupation distribution.	271
Table 46. Distribution of the family living situations	271
Table 47. Survey questions asked in the Kalinago Territory.	273-274
Table 48. Data distribution of gender, age and hamlet.	274

Table 49. Distribution of the aggregated variables (recoded).	275
Table 50. Distribution of the aggregated variables (recoded).	275
Table 51. Distribution of the aggregated variables (recoded).	275
Table 52. Gender * Occupation Cross Tabulation	282
Table 53. Gender * Occupation Chi-Square Test.	282
Table 54. Gender * Sea Levels Change Cross tabulation.	282
Table 55. Gender * Sea Levels Chi-Square Test.	283
Table 56. Age (aggregated) * Coastal Erosion Effect on the Village Cross tabulation.	283
Table 57. Age (aggregated) * Coastal Erosion Effect on the Village Chi-Square Test.	284
Table 58. Age (aggregated) * Coastal Erosion Effect on the quality of life Cross tabulation.	284
Table 59. Age (aggregated) * Coastal Erosion Effect on the quality of Life Chi-Square Test.	284
Table 60. Descriptive statistics of water resources.	291
Table 61. Overall perception of changes to water resources.	291
Table 62. Water Resources * Age Cross-Tabulation	291
Table 63. Water resources * Age Chi-Square Test.	292
Table 64. Water resources * Gender Cross-Tabulation.	292
Table 65. Water resources * Gender Chi-Square Test.	292
Table 66. Water resources * Hamlet Cross-Tabulation.	293
Table 67. Water resources * Hamlet Chi-Square Test	293

Acknowledgments

Капка по капка – вир става – "Drop by drop – a pool is created"

Bulgarian proverb

The tangible achievement of this dissertation is clearly thanks to the efforts of many. Welcomed on both St. Kitts and in the Kalinago Territory not only as a researcher but also as a friend, I am indebted to these collaborators as they provided a rich background as well as an essential knowledge, ensuring the satisfactory completion of both case studies. The relationships that developed in the course of this process ensured as much a personal as a communal result.

The present research was made possible through the support of governmental ministries and local agencies. On St. Kitts, both the Ministry of Culture and the Department of Physical Planning and Environment (DPPE), and the National Trust, facilitated local introductions. Specifically, Graeme Brown was instrumental here both in the formulation and execution of the case study. Truly dedicated, he provides leadership and support in all aspects of community life. I will be eternally appreciative of his constant motivation and support.

In the Kalinago Territory (Dominica) the Ministry of Kalinago Affairs and the Department of Planning and Forestry were instrumental in providing information, introductions and data. Time spent here has led to numerous friendships. I will be forever grateful for the continuing support and innovative input provided by Cozier Frederick and Kimani Lapps. Two great community leaders, they are true role models to me in life and work. The research carried out in the Kalinago Territory became so much more meaningful thanks to our amiable partnerships.

Furthermore, I have met community members who provided insight, knowledge and friendship. On St. Kitts: Cameron Gill, Lucinda Philips, Perry Peats, Calvin Ferrier, Peraline Gables, Emile Davis. In the Kalinago Territory: Irvince Auguiste, Asher Burton, Marcus Phillip, Danni Auguiste, Diliane Darroux and Peter Sinnott. I hugely appreciate their work and the collecting of data. I also would like to thank Gweneth Frederick, Charmayne Frederick, Lawrence Tyson, Andy Francis, Chief Charles Williams, Henry Williams, Garrett Joseph, Faustolous Federdick, and Irvince Auguiste. And, needless to say, I am grateful to everyone in the villages of St. Kitts and the Kalinago Territory.

This PhD research is part of the ERC-Synergy NEXUS 1492 project directed by Prof. dr. Corinne L. Hofman and is funded by the European Research Council / ERC grant agreement n° 319209. Prof. dr. Corinne Hofman has given me great flexibility and trust in order to pursue my goal in this research. Through her knowledge of the region, established through working closely with community partners, Prof. dr. Hofman ensured that connections were made throughout the duration of my research. Furthermore, dr. Amy Strecker provided unparalleled aid and encouragement in understanding the subtleties of landscape research in her role as co-supervisor. Through numerous brainstorming sessions Amy Strecker, has been a guiding light in the research process, always providing support and patience.

Nexus1492 provided a platform for exchange and synergy with colleagues and disciplines. Much of the research development and analysis advanced through extensive collaborations with individuals in the Nexus1492 project. Notably, collaborations with Dr. Habiba (University of Konstanz), Arlene Alvarez, Eldris Con Aguilar, led to the development of a crowdsourcing platform for heritage and archaeological management, strengthening community ties. Moreover, Jimmy Mans and Samantha de Ruiter not only supported in field work but motivated me to do better research during field work. Being a part of such a large team, I will always be grateful for the humor and backing provided by my colleagues. Furthermore, the produced analysis and results would not be possible without Julijan Vermeer (Leiden University), Dr. Viviana Amanti, (University of Konstanz), as well as partnerships with external researchers, Emily A. Himmelstoss, (US Geological Survey), Erin Kennedy (Vrije Universiteit, Amsterdam) and Dr. Eric Koomen, Department of Spatial Economics (SPINlab, Vrije Universiteit, Amsterdam). It goes without saying that I must thank everyone in the Nexus1492 project, Ilone, Maribel, especially the Heritage Corridor, the ladies at Office B.211, Ivan and Jana. Whether it was during the intense moments of field work or just enjoying morning coffees, it is through our teamwork that I can convincingly state that the innovative ideas shared between us has led not only to better research but also to friendship. My warmest regards to Peter Richardus for his excellent and efficient editing of the thesis manuscript

Finally, the continuous support of my family and friends is impossible to describe only in words. Bri, Paula and Adelaide, you keep me laughing. The countless hours spent speaking over the phone to you Mom and Dad have preserved my sanity throughout these four years. Richard, thank your hours of editing and advice! Benoit, thank you for being my favorite Skype contact. Sam, Lou and Francis, how lucky I am to have such a wonderful Dutch family!

Preface

It is my belief that trajectories are rarely straight but rather a succession of seemingly random events that ultimately move you in a certain direction. For me, they led to the completion of this dissertation and began each summer when visiting my grandparents, or more specifically, my grandfather's garden. In the warmth of the late afternoon sun, he made a ritual stroll to admire the richness of the greens, pinks and reds. Watching him as a child, I often found these strolls boring and unnecessary. How ironic it is to realize that 20 years later, I would find myself repeating such strolls in the Kalinago Territory or in the coastal areas of St. Kitts accompanied by various local community members, admiring their bountiful crops, the vast vistas from their mountain grounds, or the fresh breeze rolling up from the coastline in the afternoon heat.

What this simple act reveals to me is that place and people are always connected. Indeed, the fact that understanding someone's relationship with the land around him or her often reveals even more. Returning to those afternoon strolls, in my experience, I was quickly exposed to three main elements of land I believe are developed further in this dissertation. The first element concerns history. Dig one layer down beneath the surface, and you will find the remnants of those that were there before. Dig deeper and you will find a trove containing all parts of human life – from the births to the burials, to the accumulated wealth and development, to the leftovers and trash. The landscape acts as a living artifact passed down from one generation to the next, making a landscape never untouched, but used and recycled.

The second element concerns ownership: what does it mean to have land? And why is land ownership so difficult to obtain for some? One may call it naïve to wonder about these questions, but for me, there has never been a simple answer. Ever since humans settled as agriculturists, leaving behind hunter gatherer ways of life, any land access or lack thereof remains an essential aspect of our society. Throughout history, we see the clash between those with and those without land. Aspects of the feudal system, colonization of the New World, landless workers movements (e.g., the Movimento Sem Terra, Brasil), or the environmental racism of today illustrate the diverse manners in which power always remains with those who have land.

The third element concerns identity. The land or our home, where we originate from, becomes a fundamental part of who we are. There is no shortage of examples that reveal the importance of one's homeland. The rituals and habits we develop are all shaped by our surroundings, which include not only our society but also the land. In today's world, where we see upheaval and unrest on a daily basis, individuals are constantly forced to pose the question of either staying or leaving one's homeland. Whether forced directly because of war, crime or disaster, or pressured subtly through indirect factors defined by economy and opportunity, an individual leaving his or her land also leaves behind part of one's self. The significance of this personal un-rooting reveals even more the importance of land. Through this experience that so many people have faced, the land left behind becomes an even stronger part of one's identity as it continually exists through memories, stories and heritage.

What makes these aspects of land or landscapes so fascinating is the fact they are rarely inextricable. Political or economic processes that lead to consequences regarding land access only reinforce one's identity. Or is it through one's own strong affiliation with the land that individuals fight for land access hereby influencing the political processes? Hence, when considering how to explain one specific element of land-use, I opine this is impossible without reflecting on the roots as well as the continued offshoots that create a landscape.

While finding myself exploring the characteristics of use, change and well-being, I was often disappointed in the result because the larger questions of identity, access and history remained shrouded. Nevertheless by means of multidisciplinary methods, including the GIS (i.e., a geographic information system applied to visualize, question and interpret data in order to understand relationships, patterns, and trends), remote sensing and environmental studies, I realized that the intersections of methods could unveil more information on the landscape.

Joining the Nexus1492 project was therefore a step in that multidisciplinary direction. The main objective of this project NEXUS1492 "investigates the impacts of colonial encounters in the Caribbean, the nexus of the first interactions between the New and the Old World[1]". Through interdisciplinary methods, it seeks to address the changing values and meanings behind the heritage of the Caribbean landscape – one that is rich, diverse, and dynamic. One exemplary aspect of the Caribbean heritage is its landscape.

First, we see almost immediately, within all island contexts, the direct impact of colonization. The exotic species of plants and animals imported to the Caribbean have forever changed the landscape. Or, we can consider the colonial elements of Caribbean towns, often with streets named after European streets. For example, on the island of St. Kitts, which the first case study presented in this dissertation deals with, the historical heritage includes the tomb of Sir Thomas Warner (1580-1649), who in 1624 established St. Kitts as the first successful English colony in the Caribbean. Or, in the Kalinago Territory, where the second case study presented in this dissertation was executed, the French patois still spoken today reminds us of the French history and settlement of Dominica before the formal British colonization in 1764. We can also observe perhaps one of the largest impacts: the creation of multicultural societies as the result of the forced labor, migration and enslavement of millions of men, women and children from Africa.

---

1 This dissertation is part of the project NEXUS1492, which has received funding from the European Research Council under the European Union's Seventh Framework Programme (FP7/2007-2013) / ERC grant agreement n° 319209

Second, as discussed above, land bears all the residues of such historical processes. If we consider that globalization began with the colonial encounter, then the current connection of land-use policies is even more evident. The Caribbean has remained a playground for both resource extraction and exploitation, even today with the impact of current trade laws and tourism industries. For example, the historic exportation of sugar, bananas or copra, as well as the current global trade laws (e.g., the General Agreement on Tariffs and Trade (GATT) continue to negatively affect the Caribbean. In both St. Kitts and Dominica, the collapse of the export of sugar and bananas due to a combination of factors, including trade laws, has greatly impacted small rural farmers.

Third, if we look into the indigenous dimension of the Nexus 1492 project, land remains a fundamental issue. A reminder of the violent past, the Caribbean presents us with a unique situation whereby, contrary to many settler societies which included indigenous ethnic groups, the Caribbean region reveals little contestation involving indigenous land and settler land. The reason for this is the fact that many members of the indigenous populations were either killed or had fled to new living places. Furthermore, when considering the case study of the Kalinago Territory, the policy of containment, or the formal distinction of the Kalinago Territory (formerly known as the Carib Reserve) by the British Crown, paradoxically ensured land security, preserving until today one of the few indigenous communities in the region. As a contrast, the case study on the coastal villages of St. Kitts never witnessed such land security, creating an entirely different context. This research, consequently, forces one to grapple with issues as land and history, and identity.

Returning to my grandfather's garden, as with everything, time only brings changes. The garden I have known has seen various forms through the years, depending on the weather, the season, and the motivation of my grandfather. However, what does not alter, is his connection to his garden. Often, when following someone around in their garden in the Kalinago Territory or in the coastal villages of St. Kitts, I realize that I am still trying to understand this connection. What causes my grandfather to return to his garden year after year? Or what brings so many community members in the Kalinago Territory to recount with joy their childhoods spent playing in the river or hiking through the mountains? Why do villagers on the Caribbean Sea side of St. Kitts retell the hours spent in their garden plots up on the cool mountain? Does something pull us back, making past experiences relevant today? Because they embody one's history, one's land access and one's identity, to me, these living practices are perhaps the most fundamental way to understand the relevance of land.

1

Introduction

1.1 Rural landscapes as microcosms of global land-use change

Rural landscapes are caught between local tradition and a rapidly modernizing world. While varying in isolation, geography and culture, rural landscapes are often the first to face direct, as well as indirect, impacts of land-use change due to land dependence, inaccessibility, poor national planning, limited resources, and vulnerability brought about by hazardous weather events (Adger et al. 2013; Shah and Dulal 2015). Such landscape modifications often degrade local ecological knowledge that individuals and communities acquire over time through interaction with their living environment. This important knowledge pertains to land-use, crop systems, agricultural productivity, ecological processes and important community heritage (Hong et al. 2013; Whyte 2013). When viewed from a global perspective, therefore, rural landscapes are situated at the interface where "food security, economic development, ecosystem conservation, and climate change converge" (Milder et al. 2013, 68).

One of humanity's central preoccupations is the study of how the physical environment has been used and altered through human agency (Goudie 2013; Kohler 1993; Bahre 2016). The impact of human endeavor upon landscapes is almost always an outcome that reflects, in some measure, both exploitation and conservation values. Landscapes transform as human beings utilize and modify their surroundings, leading to a change in ecological, social and economic processes (Berkes 1998; Binder 2013; Alliance 2010). Despite this co-evolution of human activity and ecosystems, a dichotomous view of nature versus culture developed as a dominant trope in much of the early academic literature and theoretical frameworks applied in economic policies, land-use planning and conservation (Descola 2005. Real "nature" was described as pristine or untouched by man (Lehtinen 2005). Such a prevailing perspective led to an overall disconnect between nature and culture, which in turn had implications for processes of colonialism, industrialization, and more recently, globalization.

However, the culture-nature dichotomy is no longer viewed as being a tenable way to approach land-use planning or conservation. First, the preponderance of environmental concerns without consideration of local populations has been largely discredited, not only by normative developments in law and policy, including environmental impact assessment, but also disciplines working in and

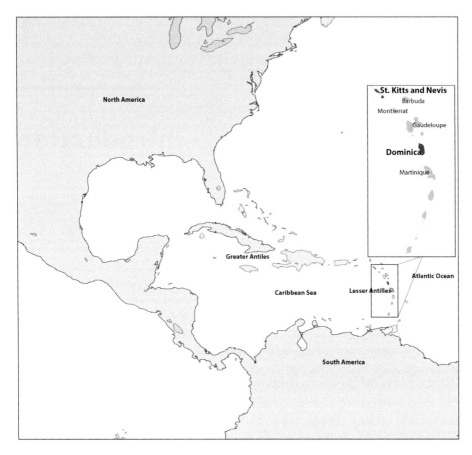

Fig. 1. St. Kitts and Dominica in the Caribbean region. Unless explicitly stated, all figures were created by the author using her own collected data, open access data, and/or data acquired through grants.

around land-use change, land tenure and heritage studies. Second, as global land-use change continues to occur at an unprecedented rate (WHO 2016; Yang 2013), the underlying roots, as well as the effects, of this change continue to be neglected. Understanding these landscape changes consequently remains a central question for sustainability and development.

This research assesses landscape change and its subsequent impact on cultural ecosystem services and community well-being on two island communities in the Caribbean: the coastal villages in St. Kitts and the Kalinago Territory, Dominica. Collaborating closely with communities in both case studies, the principle aim of the research was to ascertain: a) how landscape has changed, considering both anthropogenic and natural causes, in these two case studies since independence; b) how particular landscape change has led to transforming perceptions of local culture and values by the communities in both case studies; and (c) in an era of increasing awareness regarding not only climate change, but also the reality that countries that experience the most climate-related impacts are rarely the largest contributors, how individuals in these two case studies have positioned themselves in a changing landscape.

Seeking to contribute to the growing literature on the connections between land, community and well-being, this research uses as a guiding framework the theory of Socio-Ecological Systems (SES)[2] (Berkes and Folke 1998; Davidson-Hunt and Berkes 2003; Gunderson and Holling 2002; Oudenhoven *et al.* 2012; Oudenhoven *et al.* 2010; Walker *et al.* 2006). If we imagine a landscape or SES as a web of interactions between humankind and nature, then human intervention and ecological processes intertwine through use, degradation and cultivation. A sustainable, rural landscape is one in which human activity; land-use and ecological processes are in relative balance, meeting social needs while providing for sustainability in the future. By investigating how landscape change impacts ecosystems services, we can better understand how the values attached to certain places remain a central part of maintaining a sustainable landscape. Furthermore, the use of such methods provides insight into how individuals and communities respond to these changes.

Employing such a framework recognizes not only that landscapes are continually utilized and modified by human society, but also that these applications and modifications affect their capacity to provide the "ecosystem services" that sustain human life, in this case, in the coastal communities of St. Kitts and Dominica (Fig. 1). While geographically rural, these two case studies reveal the conundrum that so many rural communities find themselves in today as they negotiate the push and pull of globalized economies.

1.2 The imagined islands: framing the research in historical context

Before outlining the scope and aims of the research, a brief historical overview of the case study areas needs to be provided. Of course, one central element prevails in the discussion on the Caribbean region,[3] that of "islandness." A region imagined and re-imagined by outsiders, the Caribbean islands share commons threads from their historic connectivity, to the colonial creation of their exoticism and abundance leading to the pillage of natural and social resources, right up to the present, as a central location in the current global discussion on climate change, especially regarding vulnerability and adaptability.

Perhaps the most globalized place on earth (Klak 1998; Potter *et al.* 2004), the Caribbean is characterized by an intense multi-vocality, diverse histories, and abundant biodiversity. Rich in exchange since the first human settlements in 5,000 B.C (Boomert 2016; Keegan 2004; Keegan and Hofman 2017; Pagán Jiménez 2007; Pagán Jiménez 2011), this part of the world is a quintessential melting pot comprising cultural interaction and ecological modification. The first settlers of the Caribbean region encountered a sometimes hostile environment, leading to innovative approaches to nature-human relationships. Such settlements

---

2   The spelling of SES varies sometimes to social-ecological systems. This dissertation refers to the concept as socio-ecological systems.

3   Recognizing the fact that the boundaries of the Caribbean region are relatively dynamic and that they also concern the coastal areas of South and Central America, the present study refers mainly to the Caribbean archipelago as the two case studies were executed here.

of Amerindian communities created networks of exchange and trade across the islands (Hofman *et al.* 2007; Hofman and Hoogland 2011; Hofman *et al.* 2014; Pesoutouva and Hofman 2016; Samson *et al.* 2015; Siegel *et al.* 2013).

The arrival of the Europeans transformed the Caribbean region immensely and partly due to genocidal practices, the majorities of the Amerindian communities either disappeared or were forcibly assimilated into an ever-changing society (Forte 2006; Strecker 2015, 2016 Porter 1984). Ecologically, the islands became laboratories for invasive species arriving from Europe and beyond. Perhaps the most revealing element of the changing Caribbean landscape remains the connection between economics and society. To maintain and fuel the plantation economies of the 16th-20th centuries, the region witnessed the violent importation of enslaved Africans (ultimately plantation laborers) to facilitate the growth of a number of crops, including sugarcane, which in most instances were purely for export purposes. Such violent practices continue to shape people-place relationships in these islands, often experienced in the form of land exclusion or lack of access of future generations (Césaire 1939, 1972; Fanon 1963, 1967; Mintz 1975, 1984).

"Globalization," consequently, began with this dramatic meeting of societies[4] and has continually shaped the use of land on Dominica and St. Kitts from colonial times to the present day. The early colonization of St. Kitts led to the virtual erasure of any connection to its Amerindian past. However, many Amerindians were able to flee southwards to other islands located within the Lesser Antilles, including Dominica. As a result of the rapid colonization of other Caribbean islands, Dominica became a safe haven, not only for Amerindians who had been pushed out of their native homelands, but also for marooned slaves who founded villages high up in the mountains (Honychurch 1995).

From the 17th century to date, the Caribbean has served as a hub for resource extraction and exploitation by the Spanish, French, Dutch, Danish, British and United States. For example, the historic exportation of sugar during the Plantation Era completely re-shaped the indigenous pattern of land-use in the course of the first (colonial) wave of globalization, as plantation economy marginalized the traditional patterns of subsistence agriculture in favor of export crop specialization. On St. Kitts, the subsequent sugar economy and plantation society existed for more than 350 years, establishing the island as one of the most profitable colonies, not only for plantation owners, but also for the British Crown, all thanks to the quantity of sugar it exported (Dyde 2005).

From the 1960s on, the Caribbean underwent rapid change as many islands in the region experienced a combination of independence, free trade and the effects of modern globalization, including the impact of the General Agreement on Tariffs and Trade (GATT). Between the mid- and the late 20th century, the GATT facilitated not only certain preferential trade arrangements for Caribbean islands in the markets of their former colonial overseers, but also provided a level of prosperity which its inhabitants still remember. However, the burgeoning WTO

---

4 This thesis considers the brutality and long-lasting impacts of this meeting between European and Amerindian societies to be too significant to be referred to as merely a "colonial encounter", which it is sometimes referred to.

discontinued these agreements, undermining the traditional cotton, banana and sugar export industries of these islands, thereby limiting their competition in the global marketplace through the economies of a scale achievable on the mainland and much larger islands.

The fact that Dominica's rugged terrain did not facilitate the establishment of any large sugar estates during the Colonial Era (as was the case on St. Kitts) did not imply that the island evaded mono-crops and any dependence on foreign trade. Banana plants (aka Green Gold) were grown extensively throughout Dominica between the 1970s and the 2000s, bringing considerable wealth to the island, specifically to the uniquely and legally constituted indigenous space in the Caribbean, the Kalinago Territory. This affluence could not undo the dependencies established and was violated when foreign markets disappeared. Eventually, Dominica witnessed a financial collapse shortly after the preferential treatment for exported bananas, which occurred at the turn of the 21st century.

Prior to the Post-independence Era, which began in 1960's,[5] the British colonial government did little to foster any institutional or infrastructural development, leaving an arduous climb for newly independent Caribbean governments as they sought to establish effective self-governance structures[6]. Throughout the 1970s, numerous emerging Caribbean states ventured into fresh approaches and strategies with regard to governance as well as development (e.g., Cuba, Grenada). However, in many instances, power relations remained the same. For example, Grenada's New Joint Endeavour for Welfare, Education, and Liberation, aka the New JEWEL Movement (NJM) (1973-1983), never acquired any solid footing as the United States asserted dominance in the region (Conway 1998; Klak 1998). During the 1980s, the Caribbean region as a whole suffered an economic downturn, ultimately leading to a burden of debt owed to foreign governments.

The sugar and banana economies on Dominica and St. Kitts prevail as the most powerful examples of foreign modification of the landscape in these two case studies. Developing the relationship between land and labor, these two mono-crops influenced all aspects of life, accelerating each island's rural population into the thick of globalized markets, and ultimately devastating local economies and livelihoods (Potter *et al.* 2004; Rhiney 2016). Towards the beginning of the 21st century, the result left Dominica and St. Kitts bereft of any agricultural export markets, and, at the same time, unable to revert to the self-reliant, subsistence patterns of the past.

As Conway writes, "five hundred years of externally dominated incorporation into a succession of metropolitan empires" (Conway 1998, 29), has shaped a core/periphery relationship, evolving from the historic dependencies beginning with European contact, and subsequent colonization of the Caribbean region to current commodification of Caribbean landscapes. Such systemic land exclusion continues to be visible as a regional shift occurs towards a consumer economy, and tourism (Lee

---

5 Haiti and Dominican Republic declared their independence in 1804 and 1844 respectively.
6 Similar to other foreign powers in the Caribbean, the British still retain control on a variety of islands (Anguilla, Bermuda, British Virigin Islands, Cayman Islands, Montserrat, Turks and Caicos). However, the islands of Jamaica (1962), Trinidad & Tobago (1962), Barbados (1962), Bahamas (1973), Grenada (1974), Dominica (1978), St. Lucia (1979), St. Vincent (1979), Antigua & Barbuda (1981), St. Kits & Nevis (1983) are independent (Higman 1995; Higman 2010).

et al. 2015). Creating a binary economy, the emphasis on tourism has led to another exploitative foreign entity extracting Caribbean resources, as well as the continued decline of regional agriculture and local economies (Rhiney 2015; Rhiney 2016).

Within this Caribbean geography exists another looming issue, and that is the vulnerability of these Caribbean islands, and island communities in general (Berrang-Ford *et al.* 2011; Ford *et al.* 2006; IPCC 2007). Often described as "Small Island Developing States" (SIDS), the Caribbean region is "particularly vulnerable to the dangers of sudden environmental change because of their location within the earth's climate system" (Cooper 2012, 93).

Often labeled by their limitations or constraints, Caribbean islands are usually reliant on subsistence agriculture, may have scarce land resources, depend on non-normalized trade and are easily affected by global shifts or disasters (Centre 2011; Cooperative 2013). SIDS are considered more vulnerable than larger (island) countries due to (a) geographical and/or economic isolation, (b) a developing state status, and (c) the impact of historic colonial land-use policies which are still in place. Research suggests that SIDS will be among the first to feel the impacts of global economic policies or extreme weather events and climate change (Pelling and Uitto 2001; Saffache and Angelelli 2010; Scobie 2016). For example, a global sea-level rise of 1m. is predicted towards the end of the 21st century. For the islands of the Caribbean, this implies drastic impacts on livelihoods and Gross Domestic Product (GDP). In fact, it has been estimated that Antigua and St. Kitts will face costs of adaption ranging between 32% and 27% of the GDP (Shah and Dulal 2015). Moreover, between 1995 and 2004, more than twenty hurricanes were recorded at a mere 60 nautical miles off the Kittitian coast (Carter 2010b). Tropical Storm Erika (August 2015) resulted in death and destruction on the island of Dominica. Such events have already led to physical changes but also societal impacts. During the final revisions of this dissertation, Hurricane Maria (September 2017) destroyed the entirety of Dominica and much of the case study area of St. Kitts. Many places where this research was conducted were demolished. It is not an exaggeration to state that this hurricane will have lasting and costly impacts on Dominica and St. Kitts for years to come.

With such environmental vulnerability, disasters[7] become seemingly inevitable. But what do these statistics actually mean at a local level? Unsurprisingly, current perceptions and research geared toward islands often myopically place islands at

---

7   This research uses the following definitions: Hazard as the "potential interaction between a physical event (such as a hurricane or an earth quake) and a human system; an event that is potentially harmful to people and their assets and can cause disruption of daily activities" (López-Marrero and Wisner 2012, 133), Disaster: a "situation in which a hazard actually influences a vulnerable human system and has consequences in terms of damage, loss, disruption of activities, or causalities that are of such a magnitude that the affected people do not have the mechanisms to deal effectively" (López-Marrero and Wisner 2012, 133), Vulnerability as "being susceptible to loss, damage, injury. The characteristics of a person or group and their situation that influence their capacity to anticipate, cope with, resist and recover from the impact of a disaster" (López-Marrero and Wisner 2012, 133), Risk as "the coincidence of hazard and vulnerability" (López-Marrero and Wisner 2012, 133), and finally, Capacities as "the abilities of a person or group to take actions" (López-Marrero and Wisner 2012, 133). This can be through natural resources, physical resources and technology, economic resources, human resources, social resources, and/or political resources and institutions.

the forefront of the disaster paradigm, with impending danger from increased climate and environmental change. Throughout this research process and fieldwork in St. Kitts and Dominica, it remained important to reexamine the proposed inevitability of climate disasters experienced in small islands, considering once again the discourse behind climate change and development politics.

These two case studies share common threads, including initial Amerindian settlement, European contact and colonization, the slave trade and plantation economy, mono-crop agriculture, tourism, and the current attention to islands within hazard and vulnerability research. These elements continue to influence the present-day Kittitian and Dominican communities and landscapes, in turn influencing the re-reimagining and realigning of identities, whether that be Kittitian or Kalinago. The result leads to a complex web of interactions, making culture and nature inextricable. To understand this web, the essential yet dynamic relationship, that of land and individual or land and community, contextualizes the underlining complexities of identity, economy, politics and history within these two case studies. In doing so, the research reveals the diversity of interactions that occur from a local to global scale and back again, impacting land, community and, ultimately, well-being.

1.3 Aims and objectives of the research

To begin this investigation into modern landscape change and the subsequent impacts on rural landscapes, the following questions were asked:
a. How has landscape changed, considering both anthropogenic and natural causes, in these two case studies since independence?
b. How has particular landscape change led to transforming perceptions of local culture and values by the communities in both case studies?
c. In an era of increasing awareness regarding not only climate change, but also the reality that countries that experience the most climate-related impacts are rarely the largest contributors, how have individuals in these two case studies positioned themselves in a changing landscape?

As part of the ERC Nexus1492 project, which aims to examine the impact of colonial encounters on the New World, the choice of case study locations was somewhat guided by the geographical scope of the project itself. Established Memorandum of Understandings with the National Trust of St. Kitts and the Kalinago Council in Dominica ensured local government support for conducting research in these locations. Through this early introduction to the two islands, a desire to collaborate on the part of local communities became apparent from an early stage, ensuring that these case studies were possible. Kittitian and Dominican local knowledge proved paramount for the development of the research, and as a consequence, the direction of the research was collaboratively decided upon with community partners. The subsequent methodological planning and goals also included community input. The resulting research project contains community contributions in the form of early research planning, interviews, surveys, and community workshops. All results and produced data were not only shared but are formatted to sustain and provide for any future land management planning in these two case studies.

This dissertation follows a multi-disciplinary approach favored by the Nexus 1492 Project, by combining GIS/remote sensing, historical research and community collaboration to yield a composite picture of the physical and socio-economic causes, and consequences, of landscape and land-use change impacts on heritage and contemporary culture of these two case studies, coastal villages of St. Kitts and the Kalinago Territory, Dominica. (Bergamini *et al.* 2013; Buck *et al.* 2006; Oudenhoven *et al.* 2012; Oudenhoven *et al.* 2010; Suneetha and Pisupati 2009; Tebtebba 2008).

Using a multidisciplinary approach offers various ways of investigation. While GIS mapping offers powerful new tools to explore both current landscape as well as land-use patterns, looking further back in history requires more traditional techniques, as does understanding the socio-economic causes and the felt consequences of these landscape and land-use changes, old and new, for current inhabitants of these two case studies.

Beyond the utility and timeliness of this research, the overall goal from a personal standpoint was to provide tools to facilitate sustainable landscape management for community partners. Methods merged GIS/remote sensing with field interviews to provide insights into patterns of a land-human interaction. Incorporating these insights into tangible deliverables that community members- either local government or interested stakeholders- could use to promote sustainable development and community well-being.

1.4 Scope and structure of the research

The two case studies could be described by their history, small area, limited resources, growing populations, economic instability and, hence, their place within the larger Small Island Developing State (SIDS) discourse. However, such aspects apply a framework of commonality to these two case studies, erasing the unique position that these communities represent in terms of understanding land dynamics within rural communities, the perception and evolution of value and heritage, and finally the importance of wellbeing to resilience.

The characteristics of rural communities in the Caribbean again connect back to the historic context of plantation economies. Plantations dictated life on many islands, including the development of these communities. As all resources and infrastructure were attributed to the success of the plantation crop, these rural communities or "peasantries" were described as "embattled cultivators" (Mintz 1984, 6). Furthermore, the diversity of this region in terms of population reinforced the view that rural communities are central to the perpetuation, or creation, of uniquely local traditions. Caribbean rural communities have continued to face economic and development challenges as the economic focus of the island shifted towards tourism or other economic ventures, creating possibility for some but often leaving most communities excluded. Such an experience combined with environmental change forces adaptation, as past livelihoods no longer provide. Examples of this dilemma abound globally.

If we consider that landscape change is part of the human experience, then it will always be present, even during extreme events. However, returning once again to the notion of the inevitability of disasters occurring on such islands, this doomsday perspective fails to reflect not only the fact that catastrophes are never natural, nor unavoidable, but that they are often the outcome of human mismanagement (Kelman, Gaillard, *et al.* 2015; Lopéz-Marrero and Wisner 2012). Therefore, experienced environmental change, or potential disaster, must be considered within the context of broader global shifts, including social, economic and political processes and injustices, rather than attributed to the inevitability of local island vulnerabilities (Hewitt 1983; Lewis and Kelman 2012; Pelling and Uitto 2001; Wisner *et al.* 2012). Local Caribbean communities, just as other communities the world over, have lived with change in the past, making it more relevant to discuss their local experiences or resilience than merely their perceived vulnerability (Bankoff 2001; Bettini 2013; Kelman 2017; Kelman, Gaillard, *et al.* 2015; Kelman, Lewis, *et al.* 2015; Nicholson 2014).

The importance of the Caribbean region in general and these two case studies, in particular, is illustrated by the continual survival of communities from pre-Columbian times through colonization, to the current reformation and the re-shaping of these contemporary identities (Cooper 2012). Land-change analysis is a lens through which, by zooming in and out, allows us to understand the complexities behind historical and present-day socio-ecological dynamics. It will be ascertained to whether and what extent any land-change not only puts biodiversity at risk, but also impacts a rich heritage and culture. This fact as well as the reasons mentioned above illustrates the need for more research into land dynamics unfolding on such small islands. Both case studies will prove that landscape changes lead to disruptions of not only ecological processes, but also of customary practices and traditions which play an integral role in the community fabric, the shared heritage; in sum, the way the population sees itself, or the perceived well-being. Consequently, as a part of the Nexus1492 project, this dissertation reveals the importance of the past in ensuring a sustainable future.

This thesis is structured as follows: it begins with an introduction to the historic context of the Caribbean region (see chapter 2). The community collaboration made it clearer that the weight of history continues to affect current relationships with the land. Accordingly, chapter 2 provides not only an overview of the Caribbean colonial project and the degree to which it reshaped relationships between the land and the people, but also its continued and renewed impact on current Caribbean communities, ecology and land relationships. With such a unique history and continued cultural richness, these communities have never been complacent about their history. Understanding the relationship between land and community calls for flexibility as well as holism which is why the socio-ecological system (SES) was adopted as a guiding framework). In doing so, the approach links people to environment, instead of overemphasizing either humankind or nature. Focusing on current Caribbean land relationships as identified by the community collaborations dealt with in each case study, this approach utilizes cultural ecosystem services (CES) (a substratum of SES) to explore how landscape change impacts community well-being.

The theoretical underpinnings of chapter 2, understood through the historical and political context and reinforced through community collaboration, highlight the need for interdisciplinary methods. Accordingly, the methodology as presented in chapter 3 provides an overall approach to both case studies, as well as a discussion of the detailed methods applied to each individual case study in order to answer the main research questions. To ensure the applicability and relevance, the methods were not only dynamic but also constantly modified with the help of community advice and integration. Chapter 3 first addresses such diversity by breaking down the methods into macro factors of analysis, or by means of methods applied to both case studies, and then into micro factors of analysis which are applied only to a specific case study. These methods depart from similar goals but arrive at conclusions in varying ways depending upon the context of the case study. Because of the methodological structure, the two case studies, though unique, developed to include three main aspects: (a) the multiple usages of land and resources, (b) resource conservation, and (c) the socio-cultural aspects of land. The micro factors explore how these aspects differ in each case study setting.

Chapters 4 and 5 present the collaborative research findings of each case study, concerning the coastal villages of St. Kitts and the Kalinago Territory, Dominica, respectively. Both studies presented are dealt with in a complementary manner because of (a) shared colonial experiences, (b) dependence on industrial agriculture, and (c) community concerns of environmental degradation. While the experience of each case study is unique, Chapters 4 and 5 are structured similarly, revealing that despite their very different contexts, research issues and outcomes, many rural coastal areas continue to experience similar types of landscape change. Broad themes emerge from both chapters, highlighting once again the necessity of community collaboration throughout the entirety of the research process. In chapter 4, we explore the changing landscape of the coastal villages of St. Kitts, as a history of sugarcane production continues to influence how land is accessed. This isle's changing shoreline has begun to impact the low-lying villages more and more. In chapter 5, we consider the unique land access situation of the Kalinago, the only indigenous group in the Caribbean with a communally held land title. Here again, we assess the aftermath of industrial agriculture, which in this case concerns the banana trade, on the landscape. In addition, we look into the ensuing environmental effects on water management. Of course, as land and community are connected, chapters 4 and 5 deal with the ensuing societal effects of landscape changes on these island communities, revealing consequences in cultural practices, community interaction, and livelihood fulfillment or well-being. Finally, chapter 6 brings the unique situation of each case study into a broader light as it offers a discussion on the subsequent findings, while proposing innovative insights and directions with regard to the study of land change within rural landscapes and small islands. Once again we are reminded of the constant link between people, place, and the perpetual influence of global and local policies on our relationship with land.

2

Theoretical framework

Imperialism after all is an act of geographical violence through which virtually every space in the world is explored, chartered, and finally brought under control. For the native, the history of his or her colonial servitude is inaugurated by the loss to an outsider of the local place, whose concrete geographical identity must thereafter be searched for and somehow restored.

Said 1993, 77

2.1 Introduction

The changing nature of landscapes tells a deeper story of human ingenuity and environmental influences. These global land processes of human modification, and natural alteration, reveal broader trends in historic and socio-economic relationships with the land. As this research analyzes the impacts of land-change on cultural ecosystem services, it delves into the visible impacts to the landscape, as well as into the underlying factors of change that lead to ultimate disruptions in ecosystem services and well-being in both case studies.

Due to the Caribbean region's past, specifically the entrenched societal violence, the subsequent shaping of international trade and markets, and the profound connections to ecological imperialism as well as modern environmental thought, this theoretical chapter connects the colonial with the ecological, drawing inspiration from post-colonial eco-critiques (Deloughrey 2001; DeLoughrey *et al.* 2005; Gohrisch and Grünkemeier 2013) as well as literature and scholarly publications of the region (Glissant 1989; Harris 1970; Kincaid 1988, 1999; Walcott 1990).

Taking not from the field of political ecology as well as progressive contextualization, this approach seeks to "disentangle the ultimate, underlying causes of socio-ecological problems" (Hummel *et al.* 2013, 490) by understanding the local relationships of society and environment through the interactions of political and ecological processes that may operate at different temporal, organization and geographic scales (Hummel *et al.* 2013; Jolly 1994; Vayda 1983; Zimmerer and Bassett 2003). However, this research holds the historical regional context as deeply connected to present day human-nature relationships, societal processes and global networks. Therefore, by adopting such an approach, this dissertation seeks to challenge the colonial violence in the region by appreciating the local landscape for its relation to humanity, while highlighting "the universalizing impulses of the global" (DeLoughrey and Handley 2011, 28).

As discussed in chapter 1, the Caribbean's history leads to intertwining scales of geography, space and time. Manifested through historic land exploitation, colonization, forced migration and labor, and current trade processes, unbalanced land relationships exist in both Dominica and St. Kitts (Aiken & Leigh 2011). Each case study of this present research remains embedded within a complex web of environment, culture and community. In order to untangle these intricate relationships, this study examines specific examples of ecosystem services in each case study, progressively contextualizing the entirety of the landscapes, or Socio-ecological Systems (SES), as utilized by human communities, but also within the broader global context.

The present chapter proceeds with an investigation into landscape theory and associated discourses, paving the way for the applied theory in this research. As terminology never exists without precedence in meaning, a brief review of landscape as a term explores its place in various disciplines and its trajectory through time. This includes a survey of landscape and its historical roots, colonial practices in territorial expansion, as well as current applications in eco-critique and environmental literature. From such a broader outlook, the chapter will then focus on current considerations of the Caribbean environment and landscape. The historical roots of landscape, colonial impacts, external perceptions of the Caribbean and current environmentalism have alienated the most basic or most local level i.e., the community. How then to address this paradigm in each case study? This research seeks this answer by examining localized examples of community and their relationship to land. Defining the basis of land-use as through this localized example, this chapter discusses the definition of community and its place within this research. Hence, the notion of community grounds the research by providing the foundation for the subsequent holistic analysis. From this point of departure, chapter 2 presents a rationale for basing the research on Socio-ecological Systems (SES). SES approach allows comprehension of the cultural and environmental interactions in the subsequent case studies. As the research seeks to understand the impacts of land-change on cultural ecosystem services, the present chapter links environment, SES and ecosystem services. Finally, chapter 2 ends with a discussion on the importance of landscape and ecosystem services in the formulation of community well-being.

2.1.1 Landscape: from interaction to detached view

What is the relationship between gardening and conquest?

Kincaid 1999, 132

Regardless of this obvious co-evolution of human activity and ecosystems, a dichotomous view of nature versus culture developed as a dominant trope in much of the earlier academic literature and theoretical frameworks applied in economic policy, political theory, and land and resource management (Descola 2005). While no such nature has existed for some time, real "nature" was described as pristine or untouched by man. Such views of ecological processes as separate from mankind remained persistent, even as global environmental change continued. Often accompanied by social calamities and economic inequalities, we can consider, for example, the broader social and environmental impacts that accompanied the Green Revolution (Pingali 2012; Shiva 1991) or the increased deforestation of Rondônia (NW Brazil) following road construction throughout the region (Ferraz *et al.* 2005; Milikan 1992; Persoon and Simarmata 2014).

Examples such as these or the countless others of secondary effects on human and nature interaction due to landscape change reveal the dichotomy of nature and culture as irrelevant. The environment or nature and human agency respond to each other in complex ways, yielding often unintended and unforeseen effects. (Pelling and Manuel-Navarrete 2011, 11). Understanding the ebbs and flows of the natural and social divide and interaction can be encapsulated in a "landscape," or managed or cultivated space from which services are derived for the benefit of the manager or cultivator. This definition, while simple, will be expanded upon below to emphasize the fullness and multiple meanings of the term landscape.

From its early Germanic beginnings in 500 CE, the European concept of "landscape" represented an association with cultural processes, as it represented a human-engineered artifact (Jackson 1989; Olwig 1993, 1996, 2002), as the German word ladskipe/landscaef referred to a "clearing in the forest with animals, huts, fields and fences" (Taylor and Lennon 2012a, 22). Perhaps even more relevant in the case of this thesis, Olwig demonstrates how the term Norse landskapr and Germanic Landschaft referred to custom, interaction, and community justice in a particular space (Olwig 1996; Strecker forthcoming). However, between the 14th and 17th centuries, representations of landscapes in Renaissance art, the idea of a landscape evolved to represent more of something visualized rather than an enacted space (Cosgrove 1985). Western artists attempted to depict their surroundings as realistically as possible, or as a landscape (Milani 2006; Sassatelli 2006). Needless to say, this coincided with the European expansion into new lands as painters, botanists and geographers all brought back illustrations and objects. During the 18th and early 19th centuries, the popularity of French and English gardens and parks influenced the popularity of landscapes as being enclosed and managed areas. Among the 19th-century Parisian bourgeois, this perception concurred as more and more affluence allowed individuals to move into urban settings, resulting in less time spent outside or working on agricultural fields. The European townspeople did not seek to engage with the rural environment, but, rather, wished merely to view it (Green 1995).

Landscapes became distant scenes for viewing, not interaction. Perceived by society, a landscape represented the separation between the natural and human world where mankind was the center of the "ego-centric landscape" (Bender 1993, 1). This opinion led to the dichotomous problem of landscape as "a vehicle for nostalgia and so-called 'timelessness,' a value in which to take refuge from the 'progress' of a determinedly modern society" (Nys 2009, 74). In art, landscape painting represents the reproduction of a given moment for a given artist as pixels on a canvas, not the reality. It is an abstraction, creating an imagined reality with symbolized meanings that allows society to place itself within space and nature (Thomas 1993). Landscapes are more than a body of paintings "to be interpreted in historical context, but a body of cultural and economic practices that makes history in both the real and represented environment, playing a central role in the formation of social subjects as unreadable 'private' identities and determinately public selves figured by regional and national identity" (Mitchell 2002a, 2). Through the rise of urbanism, capitalism and the industrial society, a division occurred between the relationship of society and nature. Fewer people were engaged with the land in practical livelihood ways (Carrier 2003). Appreciating landscape in modern society "is characterized by the disengaged person, the flâneur, the tourist gaze. To put these together, the assumption is this: because people in modern societies no longer have a practical engagement with their surroundings, but instead see them in an abstract way, quintessentially that of the tourist gaze" (Carrier 2003, 6).

Rooted in European thought (Bieling *et al.* 2014; Olwig 1996), the term "landscape" re-emerged during the early stages of capitalism, thanks to European "aesthetes, antiquarians, and landed gentry-all men" (Bender 1993, 1-2). Even more so, "landscape is a particular historical formation associated with European imperialism" (Mitchell 2002b, 5). In Western societies, landscapes are only the perceived surface of the land whereas in other societies, they incorporate the spiritual worlds above and below (Bender 1993). Despite its association with representation in the visual arts, landscape is not only a "matter of internal politics and national or class ideology but also an international, global phenomenon, intimately bound up with the discourses of imperialism" (Mitchell 2002b, 9). In imperialism, landscapes were conquered or inevitable expansions of a mother colony evolving from urban city centers to natural and pure lands. The detached gaze of the European on her or his surroundings became increasingly stronger in the progressive colonial expansion from Europe into new and unknown landscapes.

2.1.2 The Caribbean region as an imagined geographic space

Sitting at the crossroads between the Old World and the New World, the Caribbean comprises a microcosm of diversity in ecology, language, history, culture and societies. The islands represent a unique meeting place of histories and interaction (Miller 1994; Géigel 2007), as the coastal and archipelago boundaries emphasize how the region has been "spatially and temporally eviscerated from the imaginary geographies of 'Western modernity'" (Sheller 2003, 1). While the complexities make a common Caribbean identity almost impossible to define as either a cultural or a geographic space (Premdas 1996), this dissertation provides an overview of a pan-Caribbean ideal proposed by many Caribbean scholars and others that remains fundamental to this dissertation, as it the case studies within a more familiar and regional framework (Géigel 2000; Ramos 2011; Vidal 2003).

To understand the Caribbean of today requires admission of the toll paid by so many islands in both body and land. This price of exploitation and extraction of Caribbean resources brought such wealth to Europe that modern life as we know it began with the spurring the Industrial Revolution. Such a truth often remains difficult to accept. For example, in many European maritime museums, little can be found regarding the dependence upon slavery (Pattullo 1996; Sheller 2003). And, as Caribbean scholars (e.g., Jamaica Kincaid, Derek Walcott, Edouard Glissant, Franz Fanon) note, the imagined idyllic beauty and outsider perception of the

Caribbean islands overshadows any real attention to both the creativity and significance of Caribbean societies (Braziel 2005; Glissant 1989, 1997; Kincaid 1988, 1999; Walcott 1990). The Caribbean has long been packaged and repackaged to fit the needs of external powers, forcing all genuine issues into the shadows. This disparity echoes Sheller's statement that "it is time to recognize its centrality in the making of 'our' modernity" (Sheller 2003, 203).

Any research in the Caribbean concerned with heritage, environment and community must be cognizant of the historical context, including the diverse creolization, plantation agriculture, violence, colonialism, export markets, and ecological imperialism (Crosby 2003; DeLoughrey *et al.* 2005; Ross and Hunt 2010) that left lasting marks on the Caribbean landscape. This context is even more important when considering the general lack of awareness of the importance of the Caribbean past in shaping modern economic and cultural relationships around the world. Whereas the region was by no means "discovered" by Christopher Columbus in 1492 at the onset of colonialism, the interaction between Amerindians, Africans and Europeans shaped not only the course of its history but also the way people perceived themselves within this history. The melting pot of the Caribbean, as with many other locations occupied by Europeans, was founded on the:

> *presumption that during the colonial period large parts of the non-European world were produced for Europe through a discourse that imbricated sets of questions and assumptions, methods of procedure and analysis, and kinds of writing and imagery, normally separated out into the discrete areas of military strategy, political order, social reform, imaginative literature, personal memoir and so on* (Hulme 1986, 2).

The Colonial Era throughout the world, including the Caribbean, witnessed the violent process "by which one nation extends sovereignty over another nation's territory and establishes either settler colonies or administrative dependencies between the host nation and the colonial metropolis. The displacement and administrative subjugation of indigenous populations often occurred as a direct result of this process" (Harrison and Hughes 2010, 237). Colonialism brought with it forms of government, ordinance, culture, divisions, affecting every possible aspect of life. In fact, while seemingly unconnected, colonialism, culture and heritage management are deeply intertwined:

> *The anthropological concept of culture might never have been invented without a colonial theatre that both necessitated the knowledge of culture (for purposes of control and regulation) and provided a colonized constituency that was particularly amenable to 'culture'. Without colonialism, culture could not have been so simultaneously and so successfully ordered and orderly, given in nature at the same time that it was regulated by the state. Even as much of what we now recognize as culture was produced by colonial encounter, the concept itself was in part invented because of it* (Dirks 1992, 3).

The experienced impacts to the colonized drastically alter everyday life. As Said explains in Orientalism. Western Conceptions of the Orient (Said 1978), the relationship between the colonizer and the colonized leaves the impression that the two differ, and even more so, that this discrepancy is entirely natural and not something socially constructed. Such a dichotomy presents the colonizer versus the colonized as "female versus male, emotional versus rational, nature versus culture, and in terms of the essential inferiority of the 'other' in every way" (Harrison and Hughes 2010, 237).

In the Caribbean, many aspects of life, altered by the radical changes brought by colonialism, continue to this day. When the Colonial Era ended in the late 20th century[9], no clear boundary or delineation occurred, only perpetuating the socio-political and cultural effects colonialism imposed on societies. As discussed by other researchers, unlike many other regions with post-colonial experiences, the Caribbean and Central America are unique in their position within global capitalism (Medina 1996; Pagán-Jiménez 2000) to such a degree that they "reproduce the globalizing tendencies that impose themselves at present, on a small scale, the geopolitical aforementioned make possible, by means of multiple factors, that these tendencies prevail and recreate themselves" (Pagán-Jiménez 2004, 202). Therefore, since the days of colonial contact with the Caribbean, a non-local and biased perspective has been applied to all aspects of politics, economics and social interactions within the region (Hauser and Hicks 2007).

Post-colonial theories emerged during the second half of the 20th century to describe, from the perspective of multiple disciplines, how individuals and societies deal with the demise of colonial rule (Harrison and Hughes 2010). This issue leads to new questions concerning identity and authenticity as the colonizer leaves behind a fragmented society which is usually much divided by means of arbitrary categories of class and/or race. Instead of accepting the variety of hybridizations formed during colonialism, an urge to establish a post-colonial identity can be observed, an urge often at the expense of alternative or competing histories. This phenomenon is often the outcome of the nationalistic, or nation building, pressures experienced by newly independent countries (Harrison and Hughes 2010).

In practice and experience, however, little has altered in many post-colonial situations. For example, when considering globalization, Lazarus asks whether "it represent[s] a complete break from the past or just an intensification and consolidation of the trends of modernity?" (Lazarus 1999, 18). This globalization merely led to a concentration of economy in certain areas, reminiscent of the colonial experience (Pagán-Jiménez 2004; Pagán-Jiménez and Ramos 2008). Apparently, "there is nothing very 'post' about post-colonialism; colonialism can't be left behind because cultures and environments have been transformed through these processes in ways in which communities and scholars are still trying to understand" (Ireland 2010, 3).

Historical biases stemming from the Colonial Era have shaped the terminology, discourse and understanding of both research as well as popular representations

---

9 As this research concerns case studies on Dominica and St. Kitts, this date refers to the end of British colonialism on these two islands. The end of colonialism in the Caribbean remains a contested issue, with many foreign nations still having control on a variety of islands.

concerning the human-nature relationship in the Caribbean region (DeLoughrey *et al.* 2005; DeLoughrey and Handley 2011; Ross and Hunt 2010). When considering the historical and present-day context, terms such as environment, community and heritage can be contentious if applied without reflection of their roots in the colonial past (Huggan 2008; Smith 2006). In any research, it is important to understand the roots and development of a particular theory or science. Research is neither executed within a vacuum, nor without any cultural or societal influences. (Gohrisch and Grünkemeier 2013; Madsen 1999; Stam and Shohat 2012). The framework on which this dissertation is based, seeks to acknowledge the loaded terms of "environment," "community," and "heritage" within the Caribbean region, by taking a trans-disciplinary approach that delves into the local complexities of each case study (Gohrisch and Grünkemeier 2013; Moran 2002).

2.1.3 Colonial expansion and the "exotic" environment

Plantation houses, sugar mills and garrisons dotting the Caribbean landscape stand as some of the final physical vestiges of European power. However, these visible artifacts are only some of the tangible ways that this region has been shaped not only by the social, cultural and economic violence of the colonial project, but also by the environmental effects. In fact, colonial history cannot be separated from its own "environmental history", as the European arrival in the New World forever shaped the future environmental trajectory (Crosby 1986).

While this profound and lasting encounter between Europe and the Caribbean impacted all aspects of society, this section (2.1.2) will address the historical factors from an environmental perspective, revealing that the change in capital was as much tied to the environment as it was to the economy. If we consider industrialization, and for that matter, capitalism within an ecological framework, it remains impossible not to consider the deep connections between environment, human use and economy. Such socio-ecological insights presented in Wallerstein's and Marx's critique of capitalism reveal the need for a "rethinking environmental transformations in world-historical perspective" has been proposed (Moore 2003, 309).

Prior to the colonial expansion into the Caribbean, Europe maintained a feudal agro-economy (Moore 2014) with little room for any expansion or development. The "socio-ecological limits of continued expansion" (Moore 2003, 313) in Europe were reached after exhausting agricultural lands, and increasing the number of emigrations. This led to the declining or stagnating of agricultural yields across Europe. However, the Caribbean and elsewhere in the colonized world, land was fertile and, according to the European, freely available. While the Caribbean was inhabited, European ideals with regard to nature and the "savage man" provided the philosophical, anthropological and legal leeway for the claiming of new territories (Roos and Hunt 2010).

Completely misrepresented and romanticized, the Caribbean was misconstrued as wilderness without human occupation. Contrary to evidence from the ethno-historical sources and the archaeological record, the landscapes that the European colonizers encountered had been transformed by social and trade networks by indigenous groups throughout previous the millennia (Denevan 1992; Hofman and Hoogland 2011; Hofman and Hoogland 2015). It has been hypothesized that c. 3,000,000

Amerindians inhabited the Caribbean when Christopher Columbus arrived (Denevan 1992). In 1492, the Americas were far from being a pristine landscape, but as de Las Casas famously described: "all that had been discovered up to the year forty-nine (1549) is full of people, like a hive of bees" (de Las Casas and Sanderlin 1971). However, the European perspective on indigeneity and indigenous groups reinforced the idea of a pristine landscape, inhabited by Jean-Jacques Rousseau's "noble savage," ultimately misrepresenting and idealizing the Caribbean indigenous groups. Such opinions coincided with the incorporation of indigenous knowledge systems into the European imagination as symbolic and idealized (Grove 1995, 3), remaking the Caribbean, incorrectly, as an empty land with only rich fertile soil.

European explorers reported on another kind of Caribbean world, a "proto-environmentalist Utopia" (Garrard 2007, 18), untouched and pristine, ripe for European exploitation. Many scholars note the Caribbean's reconceptualization as a tropical paradise (DeLoughrey *et al.* 2005; Gerbi 1985; Jaffe 2006). The Colonial Era marked a renewed interest in nature and empirical science. Europeans utilized, consumed and exported the newly encountered flora and fauna. Numerous European perspectives on Caribbean landscapes continue in contemporary descriptions, presenting acculturated and highly stereotypical images of nature (Wilke 2010). In literature and the arts, these tropical Gardens of Eden, lying peacefully in a warm, clear blue sea were exaggerated by all those who had travelled to the Caribbean, including explorers, botanists, planters, artists and writers (Jaffe 2013; Sheller 2004; Thompson 2006).

European claims to these ideal locations led to the emergence of the capitalist agro-economy, a transformation to be considered remarkable because it transformed the geography as well as social ecology of the Caribbean region and of Europe. Shaping not only the world market but also social hierarchy, this shift in agricultural production within colonial expansion occurred through four transitions described in Moore's article "The Modern World-System as environmental history? Ecology and the rise of capitalism" (Moore 2003, 311) as:

a. equalization across space as "through the production of a new geographical scale – the capitalist world-economy – Europe's leading strata brought together formerly isolated or only loosely articulated areas into a single division of labor." Subsequently Europe's smaller economies merged.

b. expansion across geographies into the Americas "was essential to the resolution of feudal crisis in a way favorable to capitalist development".

c. a process of divergence took place between the core and the periphery, "between eastern and western Europe and between western Europe and the Americas".

d. agro-ecological transformation as the "rise of capitalism was part and parcel of a radical reshaping of world ecology, whose most dramatic features were found in the new American and eastern European peripheries" – specifically the expansion of commodities, like sugar to zones in the periphery, like the Americas, was the decisive moment of world ecological recognition.

Nowhere better can we observe the effects of historical, economic, societal and environmental interactions of the New World Economy than the cash crop of sugar. First, the production of sugar and all subsequent monocrops further divided the

Americas and Europe by the insatiable need for manual labor to keep the plantation system afloat. With the expansion into the Americas came the uneven development between the two continents, reinforcing the notions of core and periphery, as land and human labor were taken at the expense of European conquest (Cumper 1954; Mintz 1975, 1985; Moore 2003; Sheridan 1973). Sugar, "reflected and instantiated capitalism's tendency to accelerate environmental degradation, to intensify exploitation of labor and land (human and extra-human nature), and to globalize these exploitative and transformative production systems" (Moore 2003, 347).

Second, sugar and the plantation system created an ecological crisis, hereby drastically altering the relationship with the environment. Competition and lack of knowledge about the fertility of the Caribbean soil led to the land being continually planted until the nutrients were depleted and the soil exhausted. This result only restarted the process of cultivation, with an increase of laborers and an expansion into new land (Mintz 1984; Moore 2003).

Finally, it goes without saying that sugar also led to the degradation of the worker. The wealth of the European colonizer only grew due to the forced and constantly replaced labor initially provided by enslaved Amerindians and later by enslaved Africans. Sugar, consequently, intertwined with ecology, politics, and economy. Indeed: "the rise of a capitalist world market created new pressures to push land and labor beyond sustainable limits" (Moore 2003, 351).

The expansion of the capitalist economy coincided with an ecological re or dering of the world, as the Caribbean environment was "radically altered in terms of human and botanic migration, transplantation and settlement" (DeLoughrey *et al.* 2005, 1). Core and periphery relationships, ecological destruction and the degradation of the worker, all led to an altered relationship between society and nature not only throughout the colonized Caribbean but also in Europe (Fanon 1963; Moore 2003; Wallerstein 2011). These transformations felt on both ends of the ocean changed interaction between nature and human beings alike, "as capital sought to simplify land and labor radically through monocultures and new specialized labor processes that transformed the laborer" (Moore 2003, 331). As the capitalist world order emerged through this time of colonization, so too did its impact influence the crystallization of western environmental attitudes. Ironically, as European use of these new environments[10] caused one of the most severe ecological upheavals to occur to date (DeLoughrey *et al.* 2015; DeLoughrey *et al.* 2005; Gerbi 1985), European ideas of conservation blossomed.

Other than the Caribbean archipelago, few landscapes were established and reestablished by such a powerful, capitalist driving force, crystallizing knowledge and use of the local environment (DeLoughrey *et al.* 2005; Glissant 1989). The Colonial Era resulted in a new way of knowing the world, thereby creating a category and order for everything in it, while subjugating the "other" (Fanon 1967; Mount and O'Brien 2013; Pratt 1992). As the colonial powers expanded into new territories, an environmental ideology evolved, leading not only innovation in the natural sciences, but also, subsequently, to influencing Europe's own understand-

---

10 In this instance, environment is used to encapsulate the natural geography of biota, fauna and flora encountered for the first time by European expansionists.

ing of the environment. Nature was to be improved, creating "enclosure at home and expansion abroad" (Drayton 2000, xvi). Imperialism, as with colonies in the Caribbean, brought about such a drastically altered landscape that colonialism can be understood as a cause of environmental degradation. It was noted that the local landscapes, particularly in the sugar producing areas, "provided an open invitation and laboratory in order to study the destruction of the environment, resulting from plantation farming" (Mount and O'Brien 2013, 2). As both destruction and beauty were witnessed in the Caribbean, European scientific thought was shaped immensely by phenomena witnessed here after the 15th century (Grove 1995). We read,

> *In sum, European Enlightenment knowledge, natural history, conservation policy, and the language of nature – the very systems of logic that we draw from today to speak of conservation and sustainability – are derived from a long history of colonial exploitation over nature, as well as the assimilation of natural epistemologies from all over the globe* (DeLoughrey and Handley 2011, 12).

Following colonial contact and subsequent settlement, the landscapes of the Caribbean took on a variety of meanings shaped by the elements of power, control, domination, and resistance. Colonizers incorporated an idea of the landscape as "empty landscapes especially through doctrines of terra nullius (un-owned land): denying Indigenous property rights, creating new planned colonial landscapes and mapping and laying territorial claim to Indigenous land" (Gosden 2004, 25-33). This was even more apparent in the Caribbean as it represented "an open frontier, where boundaries are notoriously fuzzy"(Trouillot 1992, 35).

The following phases of European landscape representation in the Caribbean have been identified (Sheller 2004, 37-38):

a. the 17th-century focus on the "productions of nature" as living substances with specific kinds of utilitarian value emerging from both the establishment of early plantations and the collecting practices of early natural historians.
b. the 18th-century "scenic economy" associated with the monoculture of sugar production leading tropical landscapes to be viewed with a "painterly aesthetic constructed around comparative evaluations of cultivated land versus wild vistas".
c. the 19th-century and 20th-century view of the landscape with "romantic imperialism", appearing after Emancipation, stressing the "untamed" tropical nature "constructed around experiences of moving through Caribbean landscapes and of experiencing bodily what was already known imaginatively through literature and art".

Currently, the perpetuated "exoticism" of the Caribbean exists within the profitable tourism industry. Upon review, we find unfortunate resemblances to colonial practices, for example, with the creation of the "exotic" in terms of environments and ascription of the "other" when considering the local Caribbean population. First, there is a striking similarity between colonial and tourist narratives concerning the beauty of the "destination," serving to reproduce geo-political myths. The landscape is once again appreciated through the tourist gaze, as tourism packages the most beautiful sites and vistas without revealing the actual reality of these islands. Instead, an island becomes a stage for the tourist. Second, beyond the exploitation of the landscape, these tourist landscapes often reproduce the idea of the "other" as the tourist consumer defines the price of cultural authenticity. As tourism has become the hegemonic economic power in the Caribbean, leaving few other employment options, many local residents must participate in a variety of often tangential roles for the entertainment of the tourist (d'Hauteserre 2006; Strachan 2002; Thompson 2006).

2.1.4 The environmental crusade: external perspectives on the Caribbean

Caribbean environmentalism is an environmentalism of everyday life.

Lynch 2006, 167.

As discussed above, European expansion into the Caribbean brought visible changes in the landscape, bringing an exchange of innovative perspectives and epistemologies in the sciences (Grove 1995). Ironically, the separation of nature and society continued with the development of European environmentalism, shaping subsequent human-nature relationships and much of the 21st-century environmental agenda (DeLoughrey and Handley 2011; Grove 1995). The destruction witnessed in the Caribbean informed the emerging disciplines of ecology and biology with the "discovery" of new species of plants and animals as well as the observed ultimate land degradation in the colonies. Rooted in this environmental degradation witnessed in the Colonial era, this present section (2.1.4) investigates further today's discourse of ecological sciences and their application as tools of power within the Caribbean (Mount and O'Brien 2013). With consideration of the above-mentioned relationships with colonial expansion, capitalism's separation of society and nature as well as its influence on ecological disasters, this section will briefly discuss the concept of "environmentalism" as a movement and as it is used in the Caribbean.

Although Christopher Columbus' arrival in 1493 CE at La Isabela (one of the first European settlements in the Americas) ensured that "the environmental fate of the Caribbean has been intimately connected to the political economy of the world system" (Lynch 2006, 159), the contemporary environmental international focus on the region has been limited. Views of pristine landscape have continued to blur the perception of the present-day Caribbean archipelago. As was ironically commented, "whether the prevalent trope is savage wildness or pristine innocence, the New World is overwhelmingly the realm of the natural. To even the most benign commentators, there is no culture or civilization worthy of mention" (Dash 1998, 29).

Of course, the importance of the Caribbean as an ecological center of biodiversity is without question. Widespread through academic research and the popular media, images of the Caribbean evoke ideals of biodiversity, vibrant coral and coastal ecosystems, and lush vegetation. (Aldemaro and West 2006; Hillstrom and Hillstrom 2004) The region remains one of the ecosystem hotspots of the world, making its relevance in environmental conservation easy to understand (CEPF 2010). However, the local current application of environmentalism requires an understanding of the historical context that developed environmental ontologies which continue to be applied today (Lipshultz 2004, 8).

As discussed above, concern for the environment, and eventually, the formalization of the philosophy, environmentalism[11], arose as the thrust into industrialization using raw resources from the colonies and machine power in Europe led to severe degradation of rural and urban centers. Due to the focus of this research, colonies experienced this degradation in the form of declining land productivity, and natural resources. Such reactions to this decline became official through legal means. While not new[12], the application of environmental conservation in the Caribbean can be seen in the first comprehensive forest-protection legislation, introduced in St. Vincent and Tobago in 1764. Dominica followed suit in 1765 (Grove 1995, 52). In fact, environmental degradation and subsequent conservation action in the Caribbean, led to a sustainable colonial forest reserve systems, revealing the rising popularity of the environmentalism conscience throughout the 19th century, environmentalism (Grove 1995, 54).

Jumping ahead to the 20th century, the environmental movement gained strength and popularity throughout the 1960s. Influenced by the socio-political context of the time, including the aftermath of World War II, social development and progress, and the Vietnam War (Nixon 2011), environmentalism developed through pure biology, devoid of human ecology (Nixon 2011; Sauer 2007). The ecological communities of the time, influenced by the popular epistemological view of a separate nature from society, provided an alternate formulation of related issues, replacing a focus on managing discrete resources with a focus on preserving ecosystems through the management of their multiple applications.

Between 1970s and 1990s, national environmental agencies became commonplace throughout the industrialized world (Haas 2016). Canonized by certain renowned publications by (often American) authors including Ralph Waldo Emerson, Henry David Thoreau, John Muir, Aldo Leopold, Annie Dillard, the environment, while glorified and protected, remained objectified and separate from societal use (Buell 1996, 2001; Glotfelty and Fromm 1996; Nixon 2011; Oelschlaeger 1991). Often approached by creating natural reserves or national parks, new ideas of environmentalism again reinforced previous notions of a pristine, protected or enclosed nature. Imagined as "wild" or unspoiled by human intervention, such landscapes, instead, reveal a conservation approach that is both a-historical and depoliticized. This environmental discourse removes human agency from the evolution of ecosystems (Buell 2001; Oudenhoven *et al.* 2010).

---

11   The term "environmentalism" is defined as "a theory that views environment rather than heredity as the important factor in the development and especially the cultural and intellectual development of an individual or group; advocacy of the preservation, restoration, or improvement of the natural environment; especially : the movement to control pollution" (Merrian-Webster 2018).
12   The term "conservancy" was first adopted in England during the 14th century with relation to the control of entire river basins e.g., of the River Thames (Grove 2002, 50).

Whereas environmentalism has expanded to broader domains and more inclusive definitions, the power behind the environmentalism discourse remains. First, one has observed "tremendous growth in size and numbers of environmental NGOs (Princen and Finger 1994, 1). Second, environmental NGO appear to have an essentiality within "world environmental politics itself" (Princen and Finger 1994, 1). Moreover, environmental NGOs remain powerful because of their lack of a bounded identity. They are at once not comparable to lobbyist groups, nor can they replace governments. The proliferation of environmental agencies however denotes the power of their role in influencing their environment (Fairhead and Leach 2003).

While not the case in all Caribbean nations, a common reality on many islands reveals an environmental agenda that is disjointed or disconnected from the particulars of local reality, (Atiles-Osoria 2014; Thomas-Hope 2013). Shaped by the global discourse and the historic context, the environmental agenda in the Caribbean is very much a foreign implantation, with little focus on local needs. Environmentalism in the Caribbean often involves environmental goals of international actors and NGOs, such as protection of the past (e.g., monuments, architecture) or elements within an ecosystem, such as the sea or coral reefs (Jácome 2006). While these are important sites and affected areas, this discourse ignores the social context of the local communities.

Environmental aid usually focuses on technical or financial assistance, creating little cooperation between national governing bodies and leaving little hope for any sustaining change (Jácome 2006). One concrete example of this is found on the island of Trinidad, where foreign environmental NGOs sought to expand the boundaries of a national park for tourism development (Fairhead and Leach 2003). Eventually, this park became a haven for crime, putting the surrounding local communities at risk. Examples such as this one reveals the issue of sustainability, as a there remains a lack of resources in regional and national governing, often causing environmental issues to be wrapped in politics, hereby again ignoring the local communities (Anderson 2002; Thomas-Hope 2013a, 2013b).

While environmental degradation and climate change impacts are real, unfortunately, much of the research and focus of the global community continues to emphasize the response of the tourism and industry sectors or to the eventual destruction of the Caribbean's natural beauty (Baver and Lynch 2006; Fairhead and Leach 1996, 2003; Thomas-Hope 2013b). In fact, much of today's Caribbean environmental literature deals mainly with risk assessment presented in economic terms of a specific sector, for example tourism. Whenever multinational hotel chain choses to build a marina on coral reefs located at such islands, capital outweighs environmental goals (Grove 2002). At any rate, the environmental discourse within and outside the Caribbean usually deals mainly with issues of biodiversity, nature conservation, marine environment and coral reefs. Such environmental concerns of natural origin reveal once again the persistence of the historical perspective of the Caribbean as an idyllic, pristine landscape (Jaffe 2013).

One factor influencing local control remains the complicated issue of land ownership and land rights. On a large number of Caribbean islands formerly under British rule, we still find "Crown Lands", vestiges of European in casu British monarchies, leading to confusing periods of land tenure and ownership after Caribbean independence, starting in the 1960s right up to the 1980s (Richardson 1997). The current situation implies that many of these plots of land are owned, but rarely used, by the government, often leading to little local regulation or passing of effective legislation in land management (Thomas-Hope 2013b). When considering the balance and distribution of land resources, such idle land sits as a harsh reality as Caribbean societies are rapidly developing and growing demographically. Therefore, integrating environment and development remains vital to build resilient Caribbean communities (Anderson 2002).

Local perceptions of the environment in the Caribbean differ drastically from the afore-mentioned focus on Caribbean environmentalism. Recent studies on Curaçao and Jamaica (Jaffe 2006, 2007, 2008, 2009, 2013) echo this sentiment (Ringel and Wylie 1979). Such authors agree on the fact that the environment is important for its beauty, but also for its utilization by mankind. There is a clear recognition of the degradation caused by human beings in the region and the possibly ensuing ecological catastrophes. However, nature and the environment in the Caribbean are instrumental to communities because of their natural resources. Nature is appreciated for its utilization rather than for its beauty. This relationship with the environment influences the way individuals value their surroundings. Understanding these specific, local relationships with the environment is elementary to bridging the gap between global environmental discourse and local realties.

How have these local and national environmental perceptions and policies been shaped by the global level context? Globally, environmental, non-governmental, or international and the public citizenry agencies have all acted in creating a business out of the environment or what it is held to be "environmental". Negotiations concerning the environment are comparable to business transactions (Agarwal *et al.* 1999). Groups (e.g., rural or indigenous communities, international organizations, NGOs or even national governments) produce varied opinions on nature and how it relates to them. Competing strategies on the management of nature are created on the basis of various knowledge systems (Escobar 1999; Oudenhoven *et al.* 2010).

Perhaps most obvious when picking apart the hierarchies of power found within the environmental movement, remains the relationship of the global environmental movement and marginalized communities (Nixon 2011; Rocheleau *et al.* 1996; Schlosberg 2013). Unfortunately, the above-mentioned phenomenon of the business of environmentalism often excludes rural and indigenous communities, even as the argument increases for their inclusion (Adams and Hutton 2007; Oudenhoven *et al.* 2010). This has frequently been the case in regions such as Central America, where a range of issues become embedded in the rights of landscape, or how "nature is not only an object of social struggle, but is also inextricably intertwined with the very voices that render the environment political" (Latta and Wittman 2012, 1). Previous research in the region reveals the ignored connections between land, politics, and livelihood with agency and recognition (Latta and Wittman 2012; Latta 2007; Postero 2007; Yashar 2005).

It may appear ironic that the exploitative colonial economic system provided the conditions resulting in the birth of the environmentalist spirit. Nevertheless, reflection on the current applications of environmentalism in former colonies provides a different picture. One might even go so far as to describe environmental politics as once again propagating core-periphery ideas because countries in the "Global South" often pay for environmental utilization, missteps, or needs of the "Global North" (Agarwal *et al.* 1999; Nixon 2011). Such examples reveal how environmental inequalities occur as an outcome of social inequality (Blowers and Leroy 1994; Harrison 2014), as political and social justice issues are manifest in environmental issues. Described as "slow violence", the power scales that exist within a landscape are perpetuated by means of the "unequal burdens of consumption and militarization imposed on our finite planet by the world's rich and poor, in their capacity as individuals and as nation states" (Nixon 2011, xii).

Therefore, the violence which ensues in such instances is not visible to the naked eye, remains slow in time and space, and is rarely considered hostile at all. Floods, hurricanes and fires are all examples of rapid, visible environmental destruction. "Slow violence" occurs in the aftermath. For example, communities located on the outskirts of manufacturing plants effected by polluted drinking water, or industrial agricultural export leaving behind degraded soils for the local population to deal with. On a global level, an example would comprise the climate change discourse. Despite the global evidence of climate change observed, the communities and locations which bear the brunt of impacts have contributed the least to this change. Slow violence consists of a merging of Galtung's notion of structural violence, or anything that constrains human life structurally, combined with Carson's notion of a long-lasting ecological change, or the delayed but subsequently tremendous impacts of the current environmental or development policies on the future ecological processes (Carson 2002; Galtung 1969).

While rarely immediate, the ultimate repercussions of slow violence distribute spatially in a pattern that impacts the poor, marginalized communities first (Nixon 2011). Taken one step further by N.E. Narchi, he describes an "environmental violence" that leads "stakeholders, by the active use of the power differentials, recurrently perform violent acts in order to maintain an established socioeconomic order and a deleterious attitude toward nature. Accordingly, this kind of violence occurs on multiple convoluted time scales in which structural, gradual, and immediate acts of violence intersect to perpetuate a hegemonic socioeconomic order" (Narchi 2015, 7).

In the Caribbean, the above discussion on the colonial expansion and subsequent radical restructuring of people and place throughout the islands reveals the centuries of environmental violence that has occurred. Current examples of a similar violence occur today whenever agribusiness, tourism and real estate encroach on local land, thereby exacerbating any continued deforestation, soil and coastal erosion in the limited space of island arena (Heuman 2006; Lynch 2006). These examples reveal how environmental violence rising from development, in the broad sense of the term, occurs at the expense of people's livelihoods and the continuation of their "cultural reproduction by appropriating, transforming, and destroying natural resources and the environments in which these are embedded" (Narchi 2015, 9) Consequently, to understand the Caribbean environment, one needs to acknowledge the colonial roots of environmental issues (e.g., land access, economic stagnation, and unequal access to land resources) and the perpetuated "greening" of the landscape (McLaren 2003; Nixon 2011; Rose *et al.* 2012).

2.2 Current landscape theory: research trends and directions

A landscape then is not devoid of its past, but a template of all past human interaction with nature. As discussed above, the notion of the landscape shifted through time from a substantive meaning to a more aesthetic appreciation. The colonial experience further alienated the connection of nature and human, leaving yet another imprint on how landscapes are experienced and visualized. However, this separation, and the quest for a truly "pristine nature" (i.e., untouched by human intervention) by popular environmental thought of the time remains futile. Our environment, landscapes, or however we chose to define it will always wear the mark of human intervention. Untouched natural geographies remain practically impossible to find on Earth (Oudenhoven *et al.* 2010). Observed in the archaeological record of the past, nature is profoundly altered by human agency. Such a binding of "history, culture and memory" (Bodenhamer 2007, 99) create the nature, environment or landscapes that possess physical attributes and mental significance. Never static, landscapes are intrinsically dynamic, representing less of an artifact or relic, and more of a process of continual construction and reconstruction (Bender 1993, 3). While the term "landscape" is itself contentious, evoking a variety of narratives regarding power relations, aestheticism, and environment (Bender 1993), the current landscape discussion tends to lean once again to the practical and functional role that landscapes once had (Kolen and Renes 2015; Olwig 1996; Strecker forthcoming). This changing definition of landscape will be discussed below.

Through time, the term "landscape" has gained and lost popularity. The term "cultural landscape" was introduced during the 1920s and 1930s by the Berkeley School of Latin American Geography. Its founder Carl O. Sauer (1889-1975) defined a cultural landscape as "fashioned from a natural landscape by a culture group. Culture is the agent, the natural area is the medium, the cultural landscape is the result" (Sauer 1925, 46). Despite this definition, the application and popularity of the term "cultural landscape" waned around the middle half of the 20th century. This occurred due to a transition within the discipline of geography towards mathematical and scientific approaches as popularized during the 1960s brought about by, for example, the "New Geographers" (Fowler 2001).

Cultural landscapes reveal the separation of culture and nature, as they were recognized as having an associated significance and history through human utilization, but nevertheless remained separated from nature. Such dichotomous perspective on the role of culture and nature within a landscape is visible in for instance the 1972 World Heritage Convention which classified natural heritage as a separate category (Committee 1992; Organization 2005). However, in publications entitled "Prospect, perspective and the evolution of the landscape idea" (Cosgrove 1985) and Landscape (Wylie 2007), the notion of cultural landscape has re-emerged yet again to encapsulate the cultural and natural dimensions within a landscape.

A cultural landscape arises from a merging of disciplines as well as from the recognition of the inherent dynamism and the value of socio-ecological interaction. This starting point has led to the assessing of diverse landscapes, while recognizing the vast human ingenuity. Whereas the cultural landscape provides a platform on which to visualize the human and environment relationship within the framework of this dissertation, it also presents a variety of issues to be dealt with. Firstly, the numerous historic and modern layers of the landscape discourse involve an inevitable tension involving power as well as ideology. A landscape is littered with not only social but also political, religious and economic values capable of excluding (Taylor 2012; Taylor and Lennon 2012b). As has been suggested, "any landscape is likely to contain all manner of ideological representations so that a description of its appearance must also logically be 'thickened' into an expression of its meaning" (Baker 1992, 4).

The above assessment is expanded upon as thus:

Ask not just what landscape 'is' or 'means', but what it does, how it works as a cultural practice. Landscape, we suggest, doesn't merely signify or symbolize power relations; it is an instrument of cultural power, perhaps even an agent of power […] independent of human intentions (Mitchell 2002a, 1-2).

Therefore, this broaches the issue of whether "landscape" as an originally Western or European concept may be applicable to all regions (Taylor 2012; Taylor and Lennon 2012a). In the case of the Caribbean, the landscape is embedded with the historic power struggle created for exploitative purposes. As discussed above, the European understanding and shaping of the pristine landscape evolved from the 15th-century expansion and domination. If we still view the Caribbean as a beautiful and idyllic place, we ignore the local condition of the Caribbean (Paravisini-Gebert 2005; Sheller 2003; Wylie 2007). This intentional disregard continues today as tourism, which is to be considered an economic driver in the region. While reaping the benefits of static beaches, it eliminates all elements of societal change and community development (Smith 2003; Taylor 2012; Thompson 2006).

A second issue concerns management. Antrop asks if "the scientific community of landscape researchers lacks interest or even competence to answer adequately specific questions in particular cases" related to "how should a particular piece of land be organized and shaped? What functions can be allowed? How severe will be the impact of a particular factor on the cultural values of landscape?" (Antrop 2006, 28). In the top-down approaches, any absence of consultation with local stakeholders can lead to little interest in conserving a landscape (Silverman 2010).

As noted above, an overall progression towards landscapes as participatory and substantive has gained momentum. This evolution of the term illustrates once again how applicable landscape remains in types of research, such as this thesis, that involve land, culture and community. Most reflective of the term's implementation on a wider European stage is the adoption of the Council of Europe's European Landscape Convention (ELC) (Council of Europe 2000). The ELC has acted as a catalyst to prompt further discussion on landscape and its relationship to people, democracy and human rights. Although an international instrument, the ELC focuses on local landscapes (Herrington 2010; Olwig 2015; Strecker 2012; Wall and Waterman 2018). However, once again, the ELC remains European in its roots and core. No international treaty or organization is comparable to it in scope and means of implementation from a Caribbean perspective.[13] Without such a tool utilized at a local level, the importance of local landscape management remains difficult to ensure in the local context (Antrop 2005).

How to manage a space that exists only in a dynamic state? Cultivated or used for other activities in order to support life, many cultural landscapes will continue to transform at an increasing pace and by means of innovative technologies. This observation suggests that managing a landscape must include accepting change (Lennon 2006; Lennon 2012). In addition, this diversification seems to be counter-intuitive because a definition of landscape includes the dynamic processes which take place between a society and an environment. Such dilemmas have already been encountered in the rice terraces of the Philippines. Here local people wanted to grow vegetables instead of rice as it was physically easier and economically more advantageous, or to move to an urban setting. However, this poses the real question: should local people be unwillingly kept in a traditional lifestyle so that the broader community can benefit from the protection of World Heritage values (Alpin 2007, 438).

Consequently, this separation of nature and society within the domains of cultural heritage or environment poses issue when considering a landscape. The strength of the landscape concept remains in its capacity to delve into human and environmental interactions while democratizing diverse cultural values. Landscape has become a tool to investigate alternative histories of agency and mobility, questioning the hierarchical historic perspective of the past (Anyon *et al.* 2005; Bender 1993). In the Caribbean for example, such use of the landscape has led us to rethink power relationships throughout colonialism (Hauser and Hicks 2007; Pagán-Jiménez 2009). Examples of these issues have been acknowledged in the Council of Europe's ELC, which recognizes the landscape as both natural and a cultural heritage that exists in rural, or urban settings, in water or on land, and as either ordinary or spectacular (Council of Europe 2000).

The ELC has indeed expanded the definition of landscapes in order to include not only extraordinary, but also ordinary landscapes. This fact has important implications because the nature/culture divide is no longer an issue in the definition. Moreover, the ELC moves away from specific points or sites as being relevant to entire landscapes. The aim of management, planning and protection of landscapes is not the "preservation or the freezing of the landscape at a particular point in its lengthy evolution" (Council of Europe 2000, 42). This statement includes the recognition that spatial development policies must "foster social, economic, territorial cohesion, the preservation of nature and the cultural heritage, an improved living environment and more balanced competitiveness of territory" (Council of Europe 2000, 2).

This acknowledgement has led to a shift in policy within the Council of Europe, moving away from past understandings of landscape as an abstract perspective to

---

13   The Caribbean Landscape Charter (CLC) captures several similar aspects regarding the ELC, including the linkage between natural and cultural aspects of the landscape (Caribbean Landscape Conservation Cooperative 2013). However, Caribbean government agencies or local authorities have rarely called upon the CLC as a form of landscape governance.

a more "holistic and communitarian notion" (Strecker 2012, 345). This point of view increasingly recognizes the moving parts within a landscape, not only its cultural or natural aspects or the human dimension, but also the economic, political, and developmental aspects that fit together in a spatial medium.

These diverse perspectives imply disagreement and critique of the term "landscape", a fact fully recognized within the framework of the present dissertation. For this reason, whenever this term is applied here, it hints at a flexible, continuous ecosystem based on human and natural interactions, influenced not only by the realities of the environment but also by the perspective of communities. As a system, a landscape comprises a series of exchanges created by inputs and outputs of politics, economics, belief systems and history. The outcome seeks to modify a landscape from an object observed into a process through which identities or heritages are formed and reinterpreted (Mitchell 2002a).

This present dissertation adopts the understanding of landscape as a system of everyday interactions, as stated by the ELC in the above-mentioned definition. The following dimensions of landscape are recognized. Landscape can be:
- regarded as a purely natural phenomenon, considering only the biophysical processes, leading to a physical interpretation;
- seen as an artifact of human and environment interaction, leading to an anthropogenic interpretation;
- often defined by its intangibility;
- or its cognitive understanding; understood as a totality of both natural and cultural dimensions, described by its socio-ecological interpretations (Angelstam *et al.* 2013).

Landscapes, shaped by human agency over the centuries, are currently valued for the qualities of everyday living and activities as well as for the associated values of beauty, recreation, society, spirituality and agriculture. The driving forces of landscape once used to lead to a unique coupling of socio-culture and ecology (Matthews and Selman 2006; Rishbeth 2004). The landscape approach regards the territory or space as a whole "combining physical, ecological, archaeological, historical, economic, and cultural perspective approaches to sustainable development" (Tengberg *et al.* 2012, 16). Therefore, the Socio-ecological Systems serve as an approach to these landscape dimensions by reconciling the complexities of scale and non-linear change (Wu 2013).

As revealed throughout this chapter, a landscape, whether it be the historical context or its present-day application in urban planning, geography, any analysis by means of Geographic Information Systems (GIS) and Remote Sensing, will demonstrate the applicability as "boundary objects and meeting points for different disciplines, theories, concepts, analytical tools, and scales" (Plieninger *et al.* 2014a, 5).

Consequently, landscape research allows for an integrative approach which is both complimentary as well as bi-directional between society and ecology, facilitating an inquiry into ecosystem and community change (Plieninger *et al.* 2015). The aspects of the current landscape research which ensure its conduciveness towards improving the understanding of multidimensional changes in SES have been described as follows (Plieninger *et al.* 2015):

- The link between people and environment to be analyzed at local levels.
- The landscape structure and land-use intensity are further understood through the capabilities of mapping and available GIS data. This enables us to understand land-use changes to a higher degree. Again, this focuses research on place-based analysis rather than a global scale, providing a possible "insight into the nested multi-scale dynamics of socio-ecological systems" (Plieninger *et al.* 2015, 5).
- The research includes a long-term landscape history, providing "chronologies of land-use practices and landscape features within the broader regional economic development and facilitate understanding of socio-ecological interactions between regions and across large distances, as well as the links between local landscapes and global economic systems in history" (Plieninger *et al.* 2015, 5).
- The methods to analyze the driving forces, processes and actors of landscape change allow for a better understanding of place and regional dynamics (Liu and Opdam 2014; Plieninger *et al.* 2015).
- As all people hold varied understandings of place, landscapes have values and meanings. This reinforces the importance of stakeholder analysis and the participation in research in order to understand the social complexities as well as contribute to spatial data.
- The landscape stewardship re-conceptualizes issues concerning sustainability in order to centralize human well-being within an improved management of resources and biodiversity rather than a singular focus on individualized ecosystems (Milder *et al.* 2013; Plieninger *et al.* 2015).

Landscape stewardship recognizes diverse perspectives and ways of knowing as well as the integration of traditional and local knowledge of resources and landscapes. As a continual process of human and environment interactions, (cultural) landscapes provide the current platform for the ever-entwined discourse of community, environment and heritage (Ianoş *et al.* 2013; Taylor and Lennon 2012a). In addition, this leads to respect for traditional ecological knowledge concerning landscape formation, recognizing the unique place of local communities and indigenous groups as stewards of the landscape. It is through their cultural and social practices that these landscapes continue to endure and support communities (Lennon 2006).

The above-mentioned aspects (a-f) of landscape research often overlap in focus, emphasizing once again the difficulty of extracting the anthropocentric or ecological elements from a landscape. Closely linking the physicality of the environment with the sociality of human interaction, landscapes accentuate the relationship of nature and society (Plieninger *et al.* 2015). Interactions in the Caribbean occurred long before any colonial contact, as Amerindian cultural and economic networks stretched across the region (Hofman and Hoogland 2011; Hofman *et al.* 2007; Hofman *et al.* 2014). Consequently, the present research issues require a framework capable of disentangling multiple dimensions, beyond what may be visible in a landscape.

As this dissertation considers land-change and community impacts, the analysis must evaluate societal and environmental dimensions in equal parts. Research in sustainable land-use has increasingly revealed that complex processes, both biophysical elements as well as economic and social interactions, are the underlying causes of land degradation or ecosystem destruction. Therefore, a multidisciplinary approach is required which is both integrative as well as holistic when analyzing socio-ecological interactions (Binder *et al.* 2013; Folke 2006; Folke *et al.* 2010).

2.2.1 Landscape and the community

The Caribbean historical context and present-day environmental and societal realities reveals the importance of dealing with landscape as a multi-nested scalar system of human and environment interaction. Without consideration of such multi-dimensions, the Caribbean landscape remains a European ideal of pristine beauty and exoticism, compartmentalizing society as well as the environment. In the Caribbean, the landscape has been drastically altered and degraded during the sugar monopolies and colonial expansion to the extent that the confrontation between reality and the imagined has created two spaces. One space comprised labor, discrimination and violence, and the other consisted of pristine nature to be enjoyed by the happy few and exported to the masses. In fact, it has been observed that the physical space between an estate and mountain grounds, or between an estate and villages, formed the boundaries between oppression and freedom (Richardson 1997).

The colonial experience has left behind immense modifications to the landscape caused by the drastic alterations to the spheres of population, economy and politics. These changes are easily discernable in the remnants of colonial architecture located at city centers and sugarcane fields, but not as visible when considering the significance of place to communities embedded in a post-colonialist context.

In certain instances, it may suffice to deal with heritage and natural resources separately. Within the Caribbean context however with its diverse history, colonization, local relationships and perspective on environment forces, these two domains have to be dealt with together. A violent, degrading past has been imparted on idyllic landscapes, forever shaping the way they are utilized and viewed by current Caribbean communities.

Indeed, the above introduction to the origins of landscape, colonial perceptions of the foreign environments, along with the beginnings of environmentalism, prove that the modern realities of climate change and environmental degradation enforce holistic action when addressing these current relationships encountered between community, environment and heritage. By considering the overarching political and economic forces at play within the context of land change and the impacts on the cultural ecosystem services, the present research aims at contributing to the dialogue on how these two aspects, nature and culture, enrich the communities' perceived well-being. Or, in other words, how assets are applied and translated by communities, in casu cultural ecosystem services, within certain contexts in order to create different livelihood strategies (Aggarwal 2006a; Aggarwal 2006b; Carney 1998; Hummel *et al.* 2013; Sherbinin *et al.* 2008) Returning to the main research question of assessing the impacts of land-change on cultural ecosystem services, or cultural meaning and value, the emphasis of this analysis begins with consideration of who is the community.

By first defining and understanding what the community comprises, the entangled aspects of history and land become crystalized, enabling an effective subsequent analysis. As the term "community" is frequently applied in participatory research, including this dissertation, it does raise questions of what is a community, when considering the role stakeholders, participants and collaborators play in these two case studies. Needless to say, the concept of a community also has a fluid definition, whether that includes geographic, religious, or cultural characteristics. Furthermore, it concerns most importantly a self-identification of those actively belonging to one and the same community (Aggarwal 2006a).

The Caribbean provides an interesting context to deal with the term "community" as local communities, or island communities, do not fit easily into bounded definitions because of historic forced migrations. In this research, a community is broadly defined as a geographically-based group of people with a shared overall history or identity. Further, the connection between community and culture is described by means of the definition referring to a "clusters of individual lives make-up communities, societies, and cultures" (Coles and Knowles 2001, 11). It is important to note here that a community does not imply any solidarity or a common perspective, rather that communities are dynamic in nature (Aggarwal 2006a). Hence, the term "community" is defined with little idealism concerning societal ties.

The present research bases its approach on the conclusion "that local populations have a greater interest in the sustainable use of resources than does the state or distant corporate managers, that local communities are more cognizant of the intricacies of local ecological processes and practices, and that communities are more able to effectively manage those resources through local or traditional forms of access" (Tsing *et al.* 2005, 1). However, despite community-based resource management leading often to more sustainable and long-term results, it is yet to be the norm. Land management still invokes the power of the "expert" to determine proper rule and regulation and the final advocation of protected places as separate spaces for people and nature. Borrini-Feyerabend and Tarnowski note the hypocrisy in that as we see that "on the side of practice, people worldwide are dealing with environmentally devastated areas as well as cradles of well-preserved biodiversity" (Borrini-Feyerabend and Tarnowski 2005, 76). Land will no doubt be continually shaped by societies. Therefore, the approach of this dissertation is built on participatory resource management or a community-based resource management, viewing the above-mentioned definition of the term "community" as integral to understanding the research.

2.3 Socio-ecological systems: the origins and definitions of terms

How then to integrate understanding of land-change, utilization, and community within the broader historical context of the Caribbean? As discussed in chapter 1, social and natural interactions are not only often complicated but also form dynamic relationships which evolve through time. Moreover, the majority of the impacts originating from ecological, economic and societal spheres create feedbacks, ultimately, transforming the environment as well as the community.

These systematic relationships between communities and landscapes can be conceptualized in a Socio-ecological System (SES). A SES consists of a geographical unit and its associated social actors and resources, including the adaptive spatial or functional boundaries which surround specific ecosystems. The interactions observed in such instances can "be understood as a result of a complex interplay between economic and political activities, environmental and climatic changes, and social and cultural transformations" (Oudenhoven *et al.* 2010, 11). Landscapes can be considered a socio-ecological system as it is once again the combination of human or societal realms with natural or ecological realms, thereby creating a tight nexus of interaction (Plieninger *et al.* 2014a). This framework considers both the ecological and the human context in each case study dealt with here as comprising a SES.

SES theory evolved from research published in an article by C.S Holling entitled, "Resilience and Stability of Ecological Systems" (1973) which deals with complex, adaptive systems. According to this theory, "there is no balance of nature, but non-equilibrium or multi-equilibrium conditions, unpredictable systems, subject to cycles of continuous change and renewal" (Berkes and Ross 2013a, 7). Moreover, it enables an understanding of how a system is both complex and multicomponent. When encountering any disturbances, a system modification will inherently ensue, leading to it either adapting or degrading. Much of its capability to adapt to such disturbances depends on the resilience of the system (Chapin *et al.* 2009a; Norberg and Cummings 2008).

In order to grasp the modifications within a system, or the dynamics between environment and society, any research is geographically situated, with an emphasis on place and culture (Berkes and Jolly 2001). A SES builds an important bridge between interdisciplinary studies as it recognizes "people and nature as interdependent systems" (Folke *et al.* 2010, 20). Therefore, through adoption of SES as an approach, the aspects of culture, economy, society, history, politics, and environment can be integrated in a holistic approach. This flexibility within SES allows for scales of interaction to be dissected, implying that communities become the basic element in the analysis of ecosystem and societal interactions (Brancalion *et al.* 2014; Oudenhoven *et al.* 2010). Whereas the field of socio-ecological systems research is vast, the present study will focus on the theory's emphasis of dynamism between past and present, as well as the entanglement of nature, culture, people, and place. Approaching the issues raised in this dissertation research within a SES framework not only allows for a micro- and a macro-scale conceptualization, but also social and environmental interactions while considering not only historical but also current eco-political contexts.

2.3.1 The resilience within SES and a community

To understand the dynamic processes between environment and society, the focus lies on change and resilience, not on preservation (Mace *et al.* 1998; Oudenhoven *et al.* 2010). Resilience analyzes "human-nature interactions in socio-ecological systems (SES) and explores how to deal successfully with climatic, economic, or social change" (Speranza *et al.* 2014, 109). Resilience within a SES is the "capacity of a system to absorb disturbance and re-organize while undergoing change so as to still retain essentially the same function, structure, identity and feedbacks" (Walker *et al.* 2004, 5). While not new, resilience or resilience thinking has developed to recognize the relationship between human and environment that remains in constant flux due to both direct and indirect connections (Dekens 2005; Folke *et al.* 2010).

This definition is further delineated by way of the following characteristics of resilience:
- the degree of system change while still maintaining function and structure.
- the system's capacity of self-organization.
- the system's ability for learning and adaption (Alliance 2010; Berkes and Jolly 2001).
- Consequently, resilience within a SES or the Socio-ecological Resilience (SER) emphasizes that the social and ecological elements cannot be dealt with separately, but should be regarded as interdependent, leading to a flexible epistemological approach in research (Deppisch and Hasibovic 2013; Folke 2006).

The three aspects of resiliency can be described as follows:
- persistence – resilience is the tendency of a SES subject to change in order to remain within a stability domain, continually changing and adapting yet remaining within critical thresholds.
- adaptability – part of resilience, capacity of a SES to adjust to its responses to changing external drivers and internal processes and thereby allowing for development within the current stability domain along the current trajectory.
- transformability – capacity to create new stability domains for development, a new stability landscape, and across thresholds into a new development trajectory (Folke *et al.* 2010, 20).

Stemming from the interdisciplinary nature of the methodology within an SES, resilience can also be understood from a variety of disciplines, including:
- ecosystems and environmental change (Berkes and Folke 1998; Carpenter *et al.* 2001; Cumming *et al.* 2013; Gunderson and Holling 2002).
- social, health, and psychology perspectives of communities and individuals (Buikstra *et al.* 2010; Heavyrunner and Marshall 2003; King 1995; Kulig *et al.* 2005; Maguire and Hagan 2007; Manyena 2006a, 2006b; Sapountzaki 2003).
- ecological economics (Perrings 1998; Perrings *et al.* 1995).
- environmental psychology (Lamson 1986).

This present research follows the literature of community resilience, a field that has evolved from the convergence of ecology, addressing the ecosystem resilience, (Chapin *et al.* 2009b; Holling 1973) and personal development, addressing health at an individual level (Berkes and Ross 2013b). While adhering to the biophysical sciences, community resilience remains grounded in the social sciences (Berkes and Folke 1998; Davoudi 2012; Wilson 2014). Community resilience may subsequently be defined as the "existence, development and engagement of community resources by community members to thrive in an environment characterized by change, uncertainty, unpredictability, and surprise" (Magis 2010, 402). Moreover, it represents an important indicator of well-being in the case of resource-dependent (e.g. rural, indigenous or place-based) communities (Berkes and Ross 2013a; Lu 2010; Maida 2007).

In many communities, local and traditional knowledge as well as experience represent important aspects of community resilience (Berkes and Folke 1998; Gunderson and Holling 2002). Because communities constantly change, their ability to adapt is paramount as they become active agents in their own SES and well-being (Magis 2010). Successfully resilient communities develop through learning to live with uncertainty through strategic planning or collective action, developing and engaging with diverse resources, and being active agents (Magis 2010).

According to K. Magis, too, the community resources can be broken into economic capital as well as into:
a. a natural capital consisting of resources and ecosystem services (Constanza *et al.* 1997; Goodman 2003).
b. a human capital comprising individuals' innate and acquired attributes, whether they are latent or manifest.
c. a cultural capital which "reflects communities' ways of knowing the world, their values, and their assumptions about how things fit together, represented by language, art, customs" (Flora and Flora 2004, 7).
d. a financial capital making financial resources available to be invested in the community for business development, civic, and social enterprise.
e. a political capital connecting community development with government resources and private investment (Magis 2010).
f. a social capital allowing community members to engage and participate.

As the above definition of community would imply, community resilience applies best to place-based communities (Maida 2007), and are less appropriate to those less connected to a geographical area (Ross and Berkes 2014). Therefore, the present study investigates the localized community level which is regarded as a lens through which to understand any change and any subsequent resilience. Whereas resilience at a higher level often attracts research, the local scale includes groups or individuals that can play important roles in a SES, as they are the learners from or the imparters of change (Berkes and Ross 2013a; Folke 2006; Goldstein and Brooks 2012; Wilson 2012). Furthermore, the development of resilience encourages the growth of other social characteristics, such as vision, leadership, trust, the development of social networks and information sharing across these networks, that influence whether a local group has the capacity to mitigate environmental feedback (Berkes and Turner 2006; Folke 2006; Folke and Hahn 2003; Lebel *et al.* 2006).

Community resilience evolves through modifications brought about by disturbances that occur inorganically or organically within the system. Resilience then invokes the notions of adaptive capacity i.e., the way a system responds to change by balancing between developing and sustaining their changes (Berkes and Ross 2013a; Folke *et al.* 2010; Olsson *et al.* 2004; Walker *et al.* 2006; Walker and Salt 2006). Adaption is not a homogeneous process, but is influenced by factors such as economic and technological development, social values, culture and class (Coulthard 2008). Whereas local communities are of course not in control of all the global conditions (e.g., trade policies, politics, climate change) which impact them, the ability to drastically shape the (immediate) landscape does exist.

The socio-ecological resilience approaches both the community and environment as interconnected systems with feedbacks which must be considered when in the analyzing of the drivers behind change. A SES framework is chosen because:

a. SES involves an understanding of multiple scales of socio-ecological interdependencies. Examples of friction between the global and local scales can be found due to the global, high interconnectivity and economic processes. In the Caribbean region, this phenomenon is reflected by means of its economic links within global markets followed by the impact felt locally when this process has come to an end. For example, the historic exploitation of resources during the sugar plantation era not only financed a large part of the industrialization in Europe, but also led to a local degradation of the soil and a stunted development. Accordingly, these global and local interactions result in positive as well as negative examples of socio-ecological interdependencies.

b. SES and its resiliency are emphasized because of the reality of the Caribbean context where development is clearly much desired. Approaching the environment from a purely conservationist perspective is shortsighted as it inhibits any local community interaction with its surroundings and even further segregates tourism from Caribbean daily life. Moreover, this detachment treats the islands as static landscapes. This is indeed entirely inadequate as it ignores the afore-mentioned global pressures and dependencies experienced by the island states as well as the accounted resource use, land-change and community needs.

c. SES theory focuses on participation with communities (Amudsen 2012; Christensen and Krogman 2012; Hegney *et al.* 2008a; Hegney *et al.* 2008b; Robinson and Berkes 2011).

In order to comprehend the interdependencies between environment and community, this research involves community in the form of input and workshops from the beginning phases of research planning. Such a process strengthens relationships between the community and the researcher, making research more effective. Moreover, community involvement leads to an efficient future sustainable management of the system or landscape as results are place-based and involve stakeholders (Berkes and Jolly 2001; Berkes and Ross 2013a).

To understand the connection between an SES and a landscape, Fig. 2 presents the components of a landscape/SES as they are modified by individuals and also by the key components of this landscapes/SES. Fig. 2 illustrates how parts of a landscape interact with how individuals use and modify their environments. This process, in turn, alters the relationship between people and their environments.

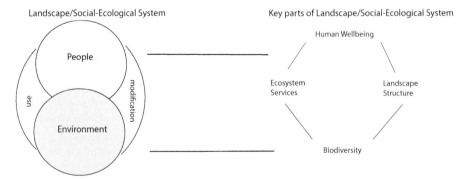

Fig. 2. Key components in a landscape and their connection to human use; adapted from Liu and Opdam (2014).

A landscape is composed of ecosystem services. As discussed in chapter 1, ecosystem services are essential for human life. These services (see Table 1) include provisioning (e.g., food, water, fibers), regulating (e.g., air and water purification, climate), supporting (e.g., soil formation, nutrient cycling) and finally, cultural (e.g., recreational, spiritual and social beneficiary) services provided by ecosystems (Boyd and Banzhaf 2007; Constanza *et al.* 1997; Daily 1997; Daily and Matson 2008; Fisher *et al.* 2009; Haines-Young and Postchin 2011; Kareiva *et al.* 2011; Karrascha *et al.* 2014; Sanchez-Azofeifa *et al.* 2007).

How these services are used does indeed influence human well-being as throughout these processes, direct and indirect factors impact these services within a landscape at a variety of scales. As time and use modify a landscape, the ability of that landscape to adapt and to maintain its resiliency is tested. From this broad framework, Fig. 3 presents the conceptualization of a landscape or SES through the scales (global to most local) of interaction (see below).

Products provided by ecosystems Energy Marine resources Fresh water Food Fiber	Benefits obtained from regulating ecosystem processes Flood prevention Climate regulation Erosion control Control of pests and pathogens	Cultural benefits obtained from ecosystems Educational Recreational Heritage Spiritual
Support required for the production of all other ecosystem services Nutrient cycling Soil formation Primary production		

Table 1. Ecosystem services; adapted from the Millennium Ecosystem Assessment (MEA)(2006).

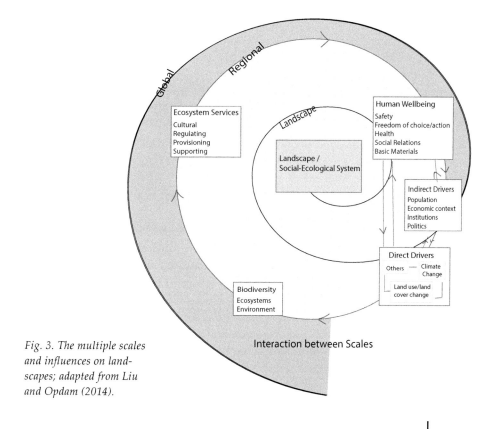

Fig. 3. The multiple scales and influences on landscapes; adapted from Liu and Opdam (2014).

2.3.2 Connecting to well-being: the Ecosystem Services and cultural values

From this theoretical introduction to landscapes/SES, it becomes obvious that land does not merely represent a physical space with environmental components, but rather a relationship comprising utilization, value and a history linked to a society. Such relationships are often felt much stronger in indigenous or rural communities (Wilson 2003). As a SES, or landscape, describes the overall level of connection with human society, the ecosystem services, then, deal with the specific parts of a landscape that create the meaning, value, attachment and utilization. As described above (see section 1.1), ecosystem services can be defined as "the benefits people obtain from ecosystems" (MEA 2005), further to be defined as provisioning, regulating, supporting and cultural services. Ecosystem services can be thought of as the building blocks within a SES, "founded on the principles of self-organization and regulation of ecological communities," (DeClerck *et al.* 2017, 93), that when in balance contribute to overall resilience (DeClerck *et al.* 2017; Ricketts 2004). Whereas all ecosystem services create an overall healthy ecosystem, the present research focuses on cultural ecosystem services in particular.

Cultural Ecosystem Services (CES) are defined as the non-material results of "human-environment interactions" (Pascua 2015). They integrate social and environmental considerations, bridge diverse academic disciplines and address real-world issues (Milcu *et al.* 2013, 44). CES have been described as the relationship resulting from the attachment of an individual to a certain place (Chan *et al.* 2012a) as well as a set of shared beliefs, a worldview or ideology derived either from indigenous identities or other perspectives relating to, or from the landscape (Winthrop 2014). CES have also been defined as inherent to well-being by providing a cultural context and interpretation (Baulcomb *et al.* 2015). This dissertation will define a CES as inherent to individuals, but especially to place-based communities that often are attached and value their landscape.

These values, or CES, are inherently as well as spatially linked to the landscape, constructed socially through time and place. However, CES remain subjective, providing a single landscape with multiple values, both personally and/or collectively. These values are Conceptualized by J. Stephenson (2008) into three components: forms, relationships and practices, Stephenson's cultural values model relates to the intrinsic subjectivity of value to a spatial entity, the landscape. For examples of this model which has been adapted to fit the context of the present two case studies, see Fig. 4.

The above components are considered to be dynamic and to interact continually within the landscape. Through time the relationships, processes and forms of cultural values will be modified according to context and society (Stephenson 2008). Despite the abstraction of the cultural-ecological services (CES), a separate aspect of ecosystem services (ES); it is no easy task to disentangle the application of a natural resource from its cultural value. Hence, each CES is complex and entangled within a landscape, but remains central to the understanding of SES (Wu 2013).

CES should not only be considered complimentary but also critically important in ecosystem research (Chan *et al.* 2011; Milcu *et al.* 2013). Yet, few studies include any CES and other or ES in decision making because of the fact they are

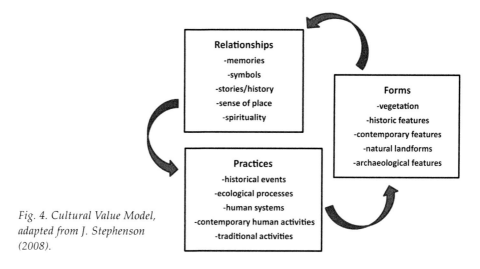

Fig. 4. Cultural Value Model, adapted from J. Stephenson (2008).

place-based, intangible, difficult to measure, and highly interconnected (Baulcomb *et al.* 2015; Chan *et al.* 2012a; Chan *et al.* 2012b; Daily and Matson 2008; Darvill and Lindo 2015).

Without a consensus on methodologies and definition, CES often do not have a place in landscape assessment or research. Despite this gap, researchers agree that CES are central to any ecosystem assessment as they provide the human context of natural resource management (Chan *et al.* 2011; Daniel *et al.* 2012; Liu and Opdam 2014; Pascua 2015). Despite the acknowledged link, the approach still remains limited. Oudenhoven *et al.* (2010) propose the application of socio-ecological indicators which are more inclusive of CES and the ES in order to comprehend the type of change occurring in the SES. Such indicators (e.g., cultural values or the multiple usage of land) provide us with reference points for understanding the breakdown of eventual cultural aspects related to ecological dimensions of a system. Whenever stress or degradation occurs within a SES, various aspects of society or environment experience modifications. Accordingly, the SES or landscape adjusts in response to these impacts. Such impacts, subsequently, lead to indirect or direct changes to both community and environment (Nabhan 2000). The loss of traditional knowledge can for instance cause changes, leading to a number of feedbacks, such as: "the disintegration of traditional socio-ecological systems, landscape degradation and loss of biodiversity, further eroding traditional knowledge in process" (Oudenhoven *et al.* 2010, 17). In fact, any landscape degradation in whatever form compromises the essential characteristics of culture which link society to the ecosystem (Brancalion *et al.* 2014; Groot *et al.* 2005), hereby affecting not only the ecological resiliency but also the cultural identity.

In these situations, "the health of the land and the health of the community are thought to be synonymous" (Richmond and Ross 2009). This health is cultivated through social, cultural, spiritual, economic, and physical connections (Brightman 1993; Richmond and Ross 2009). Landscape then provides "an essential component of community well-being and a common asset" (Council of Europe 2000, 14), creating a complex relationship between land, society and culture.

2.3.3 One concept of well-being

How then does this complex relationship between land and community and culture result in well-being? This section (2.3.3) will briefly review the term "well-being" in order to shed light on its fluidity and dynamism. The ensuing section reinforces the connection between well-being and land and community within framework of the present study.

Both approaches to understanding well-being are based on different perspectives. First, from a hedonic approach, an emphasis lies on the positive or negative emotions associated with life satisfaction (Diener 2000; Nisbet and Zelenski 2013). The second approach follows a humanistic perspective that terms well-being as a sense of purpose or meaning in life (Nisbet and Zelenski 2013; Ryff and Keyes 1995). Therefore the debate on well-being continues: is people's happiness "a human virtue, subjective feeling or an objective condition" (Ng and Fisher 2013, 308), or not?

Well-being remains an elusive, difficult notion to define – mainly due to the subjectivity, abstract nature and evolving definition of the term itself (Helliwell and Barrington-Leigh 2014; Ng and Fisher 2013; Summers *et al.* 2012). Within landscapes or SES, we have seen that ecosystem services are inherently built of natural and cultural dimensions (Holden and Bourke 2014). Consequently, the present research applies the Millennium Assessment (2005) definitions of well-being, conceptualized by five aspects of the basic material with which to build a prosperous life comprehending: security, health, good social relations, and freedom of choice and action (see Table 2).

The above survey provides us with a theoretical backing for the connection between land and well-being. While such determinants presented in table 2 probe the creation of personal well-being, the surrounding environment and public dimension, whether urban or rural, will either enhance or detract from one's own well-being (Dallimer *et al.* 2012). These linkages are proven through research into public health and environment (Fleuret and Atkinson 2007; Hegney *et al.* 2008a; Madge 1998; Raphaela *et al.* 2001; Wakefield and McMullan 2005; Wilson 2003). Within such a nexus of a landscape, ecosystem services (ES) play an integral part not only in creating but also in maintaining the multidimensional aspects

Security	Able to live in an environmentally clean and safe shelter
	Able to reduce the vulnerability to ecological stress and shock
Basic material for a prosperous life	Able to access resources to earn income and gain livelihood
Health	Able to be adequately nourished
	Able to be free from avoidable diseases
	Able to have adequate and clean drinking water
	Able to have clean air
	Able to have energy to keep warm and cool
Good social relation	Able to express cultural and spiritual values associated with ecosystems
	Able to observe, study and learn about ecosystems

Table 2. Determinant and constituents of well-being; adapted from the Millennium Ecosystem Assessment (MA 2005).

of well-being (Haines-Young and Potschin 2010). For example, the connection between ES and well-being is obvious when considering the material benefits (e.g., food, wood, water) or the regulating benefits such as air. When reflecting upon the anthropogenic impacts on ES, the human use of landscapes provides examples that can illuminate the connection of ES to human well-being (Daily 1997; MA 2003, 2005b). Human resource use can degrade land through an inequitable utilization of natural resources. This leads to visible modifications such as a decline in crop production, river decline, or deforestation. Often, in these situations, aspects of human well-being are unaccounted for, for instance, the ability to access resources. In other words, as ecosystem services diminish due to unsustainable use, the human capacity to maintain the five aspects of well-being also decreases. By understanding that a landscape inherently comprised of ecosystem services, the essentiality of their existence in well-being becomes evident (Haines-Young and Potschin 2010; Russell *et al.* 2013).

Last but not least, ecosystem services contribute to spiritual and cultural well-being through their interaction and attachment to nature (Carpenter *et al.* 2009; Haines-Young and Potschin 2010). Human use of a landscape also leads to embedded values. Through resource application, a synergetic relationship is formed between communities and their landscape by means of recreation, traditional knowledge, spirituality, memory or aestheticism (Atkinson 2013; Bieling *et al.* 2014; Engelbrecht 2009; King *et al.* 2014; Raudsepp-Hearne *et al.* 2010; Winterton *et al.* 2014; Wu 2013).

As demonstrated, ES, land and well-being are connected. As land-use will only continue to further land-change, grasping the interconnection between application and heritage remains key to achieving sustainability. Interestingly, despite the connection between land and well-being, little has been done to analyze the impacts of land-change and land degradation and the subsequent impacts on well-being (Raudsepp-Hearne *et al.* 2010). This framework for linking ecosystems services to human well-being is essential for understanding and developing rational policy responses to the many environmental challenges that confront developing societies. Ecosystem research that lacks an adequate consideration of the impact of human development on environment, as well as the reciprocal impact of environmental disruption on human development and well-being, will be without the central driver of change as encountered many societies and, ultimately, fail in promoting the sustainable utilization of environmental resources.

Therefore, land-change underpins societal transformations, shaping subsequent ecological and community consequences that result in a changing community well-being (Plieninger *et al.* 2015; Winterton *et al.* 2014). Despite this connection, it as yet remains difficult to define methodologies that probe the value of ecosystem services as to any contributions to human well-being (Chan *et al.* 2012a; Kumar and Kumar 2008; Norton and Noonan 2007; Scholte *et al.* 2015; Spangenberg and Settele 2010). However, progress in this respect can be noted (Arriagada *et al.* 2009; Gross-Camp *et al.* 2012; Scullion *et al.* 2011).

This progress further illuminates the need for locally based interventions in order to assess any land-change and associated impacts in today's world. Multi-scale (i.e., local to global scales) feedbacks do interact, leading to issues not only regarding the combination of ecosystem services that flow and are adopted in a landscape, but also the drivers of change, and how such modifications impact local flows of ecosystem services in other regions (Wu 2013). These challenges direct the focus of the present study on predominately rural communities, as the interaction between human use and land, leading to subsequent associated impact, is more visible. Furthermore, this research assesses impacts on CES because they not only contributes substantially to the overall community well-being (Wu 2013), but are also local-scale. Unlike other ecosystem services which may be applied by a variety of societies across regions, CES are innately tied to a specific location.

Specifically, this dissertation evaluates the land-change and subsequent impacts on cultural ecosystem services through an understanding of well-being. In addition, it focuses on the connection between environment, or landscape, and the creation of well-being. If we consider the meaning of well-being as linked to the personal attachment, a sense of belonging or purpose as well as feeling comfortable in his or her environment (Relph 1976; Rowles 1983; Seamon 1979; Williams 2002), it becomes clear why a landscape is so inextricably linked to people, cultures, environments and, finally, well-being.

2.4 Landscape, community and well-being

Through a landscape setting, the connected and entangled aspects of both culture and society are understood to be inherent to a social ecological resilience and well-being. As land is tied to place-based communities, comprehending a land-change leads to understanding local community patterns and process developments (Fox *et al.* 1995; Giannecchini *et al.* 2007). Focusing on the relationship between CES and the landscape, we can observe that:

a. an understanding of the effect of landscape change on CES exists. The present research will examine the trade-offs that occur whenever a change leads to the decline of other aspects, or degradation, which is not only related to resource use, but also to spirituality, aesthetic values, knowledge systems and recreation;

b. as values are connected to cultural identity and heritage, this study will also investigate the reason why land degradation is inherent to the degradation not only of ecological processes but also of heritage (Plieninger *et al.* 2015).

When dealing with community and land-use (i.e., landscape as a system or SES) this dissertation defines ecological and community degradation in the Caribbean region without being confined to historically burdened discourses. This proactive methodology and analysis seeks to understand the system as well as the stressors that induce change. From such a framework, the research conclusions purpose possible initiatives for future resilience in each case study, and for study of SES within the region as a whole.

3

Methodology

Part I. Macro factors of a system: society and ecology

Chapter 2 has explored the inherent dynamism of landscapes and intrinsic connection to ecosystem services. The interconnections of these services, provisioning, regulating, supporting and cultural, lead to a cycle of utilization and valuation by a community. While ecological and/or social processes prompt modification, landscape change results in a panoply of consequences. Landscape change leads to a variety of repercussions in both community and environment. Such impacts ultimately prove either harmful or beneficial to a landscape, depending on the related ensuing changes. However, when land change remains balanced, this process fosters well-being. Understanding landscape change, therefore, requires a holistic and multi-disciplinary analysis of blending methods and multiple lines of inquiry.

Several methodologies incorporate cultural values directly into an ecosystem assessment. Spatially explicit methods are often effective in linking value and service (Scholte *et al.* 2015; Tengberg *et al.* 2012; Wu 2013). However, a review of the literature in similar research contexts divulges a consensus that applying a mixed methods methodology, both qualitative and quantitative, provides for holistic analysis of land-use change (González-Puente *et al.* 2014). Such approaches combine social, cultural and ecological dimensions to create a complete analysis (Martin and Hall-Arber 2008; Plieninger *et al.* 2014a; Tengberg *et al.* 2012).

In order to analyze social and ecological elements together, the present research seeks to build an understanding of the landscape, or the Socio-ecological System (SES), by interweaving qualitative research with a geo-design whereby focusing on scale, community, and environment. Utilizing landscape as a spatial context for an analysis furthers the methodological query into context, sustainability, resilience, and well-being (Bourdeau-Lepage and Tovar 2013; Cumming *et al.* 2013; Fleuret and Atkinson 2007; MA 2003, 2005a, b; Winterton *et al.* 2014). By interrogating the impacts on cultural ecosystem services, this practice analyzes specific social and ecological changes present in local communities, thereby progressively contextualizing the local within a broader scale to comprehend ultimate changes in the overall well-being.

This chapter deals with the approach and methods followed in the research. Part I presents the overall methods applied in both case studies. The below section (3.1) describes the overall framework. Section 3.2 expands upon the definition of socio-ecological indicators applied in the subsequent analysis which initially relies on case-study interviews as a preliminary step in order to ground the subsequent research focus. The sub-section 3.2.1 contains a detailed explanation of the interview process and the ensuing analyses, including the software and visualization techniques applied. Section 3.3 presents the land-use/land-change analysis. Part II of chapter 3 discusses the specific methods with regard to each unique case study. Each case study (see 3.4 and 3.5) builds on methods introduced in Part I, but then diverges in specific methods. These methods respond directly to the type of land-change identified by the community that became the focus of each particular case study. Finally, section 3.6 presents several final thoughts and conclusions regarding the methodology.

3.1 Overall methods and approach

Modification to a landscape occurs when indirect and direct factors, often stimulated by human beings, interact across spatial, temporal and organization scales. Such interactions could be imagined as a complex web of tangled connections, forever binding human beings to their surroundings (Nelson *et al.* 2006). However, the result of a landscape change often includes land degradation, defined here as the "the reduction in the capacity of the land to perform ecosystem goods, functions and services that support society and development" (MEA 2005). Land degradation stems from extreme weather conditions, human activity and over usage (FAO 2016; WHO 2016). Land degradation results from direct causes, such as climate-change, nutrient absorption, and development. However, land degradation also results from indirect causes, such as demographic increases, economic instability, socio-political structures and cultural changes. Ultimately impacting the provision of ecosystem services as well as goods, land degradation not only influences soil, water, the biota and all aspects of man-made modifications to the landscape but also associated biophysical processes (Dalal-Clayton and Dent 2001; Nkonya *et al.* 2016; Symeonakis *et al.* 2016). A universal phenomenon, land degradation leads to severe consequences on overall quality of life (Okin *et al.* 2001).

As noted in chapter 1, rural or indigenous communities often rely on land resources in their proximity. Land-change and land degradation, consequently impacts their livelihoods first, revealing the importance of research such as this dissertation. Through a review of history and literature, it is obvious that land-use, resulting in land-change has occurred in both case studies. However, while land-change remains apparent, land degradation in the normative sense is not. As discussed in chapter 1 (see 1.3), community meetings identified examples of land change including the collapse of the sugar cultivation on St. Kitts and of the banana industry in the Kalinago Territory. These events will be explored further in chapters 4 and 5[15]. These land-changes do not inherently cause land degradation, as defined above. For example, the demise of an industrial agricultural

---

15 Field work also revealed other aspects of land change, related more directly to land degradation such as coastal erosion in St. Kitts and declining water resources in the Kalinago Territory. However, these examples only became apparent through extended fieldwork and community meetings. These examples and the methods pertaining to them are discussed in depth in section Part II of this chapter.

crop may lead to forest regrowth and an increased biodiversity (Grau *et al.* 2003). Nevertheless, any land-change, even if not culminating in degradation of natural ecosystems, can result in strong effects on the cultural significance of a landscape.

As discussed in the Introduction (see 1.1) chapter, the two selected case studies on the coastal villages of St. Kitts and on the Kalinago Territory respectively share similarities beyond their Caribbean location and common British colonizer. Both studies encapsulate coastal villages or communities which often uphold unique relationships with the surrounding marine ecosystems and which heavily rely on marine resources (Bridges and McClatchey 2009; Crowther *et al.* 2016; Jackson 1995). Furthermore, the subsequent landscape changes in both case studies result from global and local processes, creating both physical and societal transformations. However, it is also noted that these two case studies also present unique discrepancies, which concern to landscapes, land tenure issues and cultural identities, thereby creating a rich diversity when compared with each other. These differences, often compounded by local and global policies, also lead to varied ways in which communities access land.

To that end, the overall methodology adopted in both cases is the same: to analyze landscape use and cultural ecosystem services through an assessment of land-use/land-cover transformations and the ensuing impacts on community well-being within the landscape (Tengberg *et al.* 2012). In the investigation of each case study, the focus lies on integrating cultural ecosystem services through spatial methods in order to highlight any historic meaning, cultural relevance, and physical features (Reinar and Westerlind 2009; Tengberg *et al.* 2012) of a landscape change.

The goal of the methodology in both case studies merges the qualitative and quantitative data collected during research to create a single analytical enterprise in understanding the SES from a landscape approach. As stated before, the main research question in these case studies investigates the impacts of landscape change on Cultural Ecosystem Services (CES). At a macro scale, the overall methods analyze aspects of land change and CES through GIS/Remote Sensing, and socio-ecological indicators and interviews. In doing so, a multilayered analysis of spatial information and social phenomena becomes possible (Jong *et al.* 2011; Nkonya *et al.* 2016; Rindfuss and Stern 1998). This methodology takes inspiration from much of the recent research in ecology and society, and well-being. To link spatial and social dimensions on a macro scale, the research adapted the model presented in Tengberg *et al.* (2012), illustrated in Fig. 5.

First, an assessment of the system or landscape is established. This includes defining the boundaries and the focal point of the study and the type of landscape change. Through this evaluation, the stakeholders and natural resource users are identified, both directly and indirectly. During this stage it is assessed how social and ecological dimensions interact within a concentrated system or landscape. Second, disturbances or modifications with associated attributes are pinpointed which implies investigating any historic changes to ensure that past landscape changes can also adequately be accounted for in the analysis. Third, the threshold of the system is identified by applying socio-ecological indicators which determine the relationship between environment and society (UNU-IAS *et al.* 2014). This indicates that the social as well as the ecological dimensions of the present study

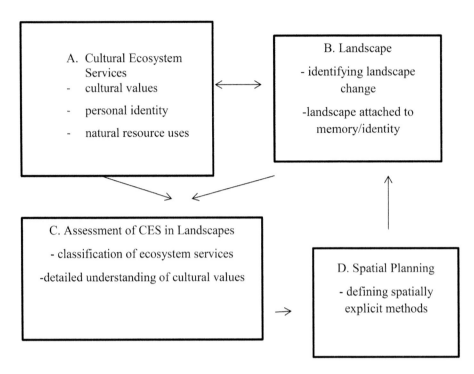

Fig. 5. Conceptual model of the linkages between the Cultural Ecosystem Services (CES) and cultural landscape approach; adapted from Tenberg et al (2012).

site are not only dynamic, but also related to each other. Fourth, the social networks encountered across a system are investigated. This is the most challenging research stage as coming to grips with the dynamics of societal interaction requires time. Often, for an outsider, a true understanding of the social networks proves impossible to accomplish.

Finally, the synthesis of results creates deliverables of possible future steps to take after assessing the current landscape changes. Ultimately, the aim is to understand the impact of culture and history on landscape as well as the reciprocal impact of landscape and ecological changes on culture, history and associated social values. Hereby an assessment methodology is applied which integrates a diverse array of data inputs into a coherent framework which is appropriate for each case study. Building upon the Tenberg *et al.*'s adapted model (Fig. 5), Fig. 6 reveals the entire methodological procedure, uniting the qualitative and quantitative means of investigation. The methods are further divided by macro factors and micro factors (see chapter 3, Part II). As a large number of methods have been introduced, Fig. 6 will be expanded upon in each specific case study section throughout this chapter (chapter 3, part II).

The main framework discussed above focuses on the main macro factors relevant to both case studies. Moreover, it provides an overall analysis sensitive to the drivers of the land-change through time. These macro factors purport the small island context, the overall historical background (including the introduction and collapse of the sugar and banana industries on St. Kitts and in the Kalinago Territory respectively), as well as the increasing environmental change in the Caribbean. This

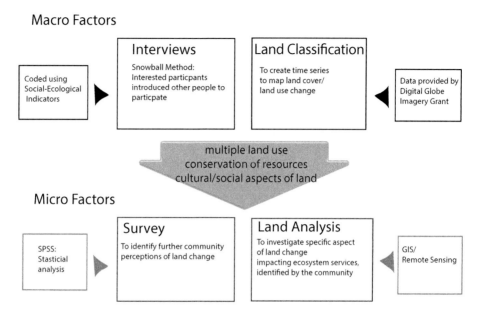

Fig. 6. The overview of the applied methodology in the case studies, merging qualitative and quantitative data.

process leads to analysis sensitive not only to landscape transformations entailing surface or physical changes, but also the embedded values of the landscape.

Land-cover change and its relationship to demographic or political ecology often dominate research in land use; and cover change (Arce-Nazario 2007a, b). Other studies on landscape change integrate oral histories into its methodology (Cross and Barker 1993; Fairhead and Leach 1996; Moore-Colyer and Scott 2005; Skaria 1999). In the present dissertation, the type of experienced land change being less obvious and the context of the Caribbean in each case study determined an all-encompassing methodology. To that end, the analysis is built on the integration of a land-cover change analysis, applying GIS/Remote Sensing, together with interview or qualitative data. However, quantitative and qualitative data are epistemologically at odds with each other. Spatial information, as defined by the scientific community, relies on great accuracy. Qualitative data acquired through local knowledge are powerful but concern a sparsely applied form of information within these kinds of spatial studies, caused by the incomparability with the type of spatial accuracy mentioned above. This research dilemma further resonates when we consider once again that the earliest scientific thought on the subject was inspired by European conquest and colonization in the New World, an element further highlighted by means of the theoretical framework presented in chapter 2.

The changing tides of landscape sustainability research has led to an emphasis on connecting these two dissimilar sets of data in casu cultural identity and natural resources. Ecological drivers of change in a landscape offer little information if not somehow assessed in relation to communities. Hence, local understanding of land-use change provides information that permits an analysis of non-linear, complex modifications in land dynamics driven by social and cultural processes (González-Puente *et al.* 2014). The methodology presented here inserts local perceptions directly into the analysis in order to provide more relevant and spatially explicit results (Dunn 2007; González-Puente *et al.* 2014; McLain *et al.* 2013; Ramirez-Gomez *et al.* 2013; Ramirez-Gomez *et al.* 2015). These two strands of research, quantitative and qualitative, augment each other by forwarding a community context as well as local environmental constraints.

Finally, when linking local knowledge and quantitative data in order to compose complementary data sets, the factors of scale imply that an analysis must be multifaceted as well as explicitly spatial to ensure a local context (Bethel *et al.* 2014; Moller *et al.* 2004). In both case studies, the analysis establishes this procedure through community partnerships. These collaborations shaped the direction of the present research, allowing an understanding of the specific case study at a local level. Based on this established community collaboration, the unique social, economic and environmental data mentioned in both case studies are analyzed in order to comprehend the drivers of landscape change in each respective case. Through this process of collaboration, one important outcome resulted in tangible deliverables, presented in the form of an environmental and societal database, and models. These deliverables enable community members as well as partners to continue a similar analysis of the landscape change, permitting a sustainable land and resource management. The specifics of these deliverables are discussed in the micro factors of each case study (see sections 3.4 and 3.5).

3.2 Research principles: the socio-ecological indicators

In order to establish the direction of research, the methodology takes its first step by establishing the position and surroundings of the case study. But how to do this within a context so complex at such a local scale? Again, returning to the metaphor of the web, this dissertation thought to understand how seemingly mundane changes in community livelihood, such as use of fewer recreational activities may actually be indicative of a much more tangled socio-ecological phenomenon. This research uses Socio-ecological indicators, as discussed in chapter 2 (Table 1) to disentangle these complexities. However this begins first with the collection of qualitative data, or community knowledge, accessed through interviews.

3.2.1 The interview process and protocol

Following a period of familiarization with each case study location (including the various villages and hamlets, points of interest and communal areas) interviews were conducted with willing community members. The interviewee selection began with establishing informal personal connections with inhabitants of the villages in each case study. To broaden each case study's social network, these individuals identified those fellow residents considered most familiar with the past land-use changes and those most willing to share any relevant information. The process of snowball sampling ensued, which requires the researcher judgment and the community feedback regarding who may be the most knowledgeable in terms of interviewees, creating a non-random selection (Biernacki and Waldorf 1981; Cohen-Shacham *et al.* 2015; Faugier and Sargeant 1997; Vogt 1999). Snowballing relies on meeting community members who then suggest other suitable candidates. This procedure ensured that the overall selection of participants was based on the community identification of knowledge and expertise rather than on random selection or the researcher's own preferences.

Throughout each case study, interviews followed a protocol, ensuring the adhesion to a strict code of ethics. In order to follow guidelines and ethical standards, a preliminary meeting was always held in which the research purpose, questions, and intended outcomes were clarified. To those interested in participating, a brief explanation of the interview format was provided along with the researcher's contact details. Interviews proceeded shortly thereafter either at the homes of the interviewees or at an agreed upon location. All interviews are recorded after an informed verbal consent was forwarded by each individual. Participants were made aware of their control over the interview, including the opportunity to terminate it at any given moment. If they decide not to share information within a research context, their contributions would be deleted. The data gathered remains confidential, unless an interviewee expressed the desire to utilize his or her name in connection with his or her knowledge.

As the research questions were formulated in collaboration with community members and in accordance with the outcome of the preliminary field work, it was considered best to maintain an open structural approach towards the qualitative research and the ability to adapt, while modifying the theoretical implications of the findings. The questions were determined beforehand in order to ensure that each interview followed a similar format whereby the main questions were asked in the same order. Moreover, they were arranged according to theme (*e.g.*, community and environmental changes, use of environmental resources, economy, historical context, places of importance, associated memories) and sought to establish any connections between themes rather than to view each theme as separate. As the questions were open-ended, the responses varied. The interviewees own experience sometimes dictated the direction of the interview. However, answer comparison across interviews remains possible as the same questions are posed throughout. The interview continued without interruption by the researcher. Each semi-structured interview was personal, in-depth and continued for between 30 and 60 minutes, hereby providing information on how individuals as well as their families related to the perceived village and environmental changes. The interviews provided an understanding of (a) the possible friction encountered between the local and the majority of global scales and (b) how these interactions affect an individual's well-being within his or her community. For a survey of all interview questions for both case studies and those specific to each case study, see Appendix A, Table 34. Ultimately, interview revealed details concerning the history of each case study area as well as provided a setting in which to establish a relationship with community members. The recorded interviews were then transcribed and coded following the methodology described below (see 3.2.2).

All in all, thirty interviews took place on St. Kitts with two or more residents of each village located within the case study area. In Dominica, sixty interviews were conducted, all with inhabitants of the Kalinago Territory. Members of local governmental agencies were also interviewed in order to gain a broader understanding of the regional and national implications, and their effects on society and the environment (Creswell 2007, 2009; Saldana 2013; Spradley 1979, 1980). On St. Kitts, members of the Ministry of Environment. Ministry of Culture, Ministry of Gender Affairs and the National Trust were involved. In the Kalinago Territory, members of the Department of Planning, the Forestry Department, the Ministry of Kalinago Affairs and the Kalinago Territory Council participated.

3.2.2 Interview analysis using socio-ecological Indicators: coding and the discourse network analysis

Before discussing the application of the socio-ecological indicators in interview data, a brief background on the coding protocol and procedure follows. In order to analyze the interview data, the research draws inspiration from Qualitative Content Analysis or QCA (Krippendorff 1980; Kyngas and Vanhanen 1999; Mayring 2014). This method of interview analysis aims not only at being systemic and objective in creating usable inferences about interview data that is often be subjective and difficult to manage. Furthermore, it allows final interpretations to be original and provide new insights stemming from the interview data (Elo and Kyngäs 2008). A QCA consists of a variety of techniques with which textual data can be analyzed and is extremely useful when dealing with interviews (Mayring 2000).

First and foremost, all the recorded interviews, including the questions, were transcribed. The analytical process of a QCA follows three phases in order to remain as systematic as possible by means of determining standards applied throughout the research process. The preparation phase states the research question, next the unit of analysis is defined, and then, the entirety of the data is examined. In this case, the unit of analysis comprises a selection of words that is subsequently coded. This code is defined by a main theme, or socio-ecological indicator and a sub theme, or a specific description of socio-ecological indicator (see Table 3). For more information on how interviews were linked with these socio-ecological indicators, see Appendix A.1, Table 35 and Appendix A.2, Table 36.

Coding is a method of categorizing or abstracting main points from relevant citations within an interview (Mayring 2000, 2014). In this phase, the research follows procedures which combine deductive with inductive reasoning. A loose reading of the transcribed interview text took place in order to grasp the main directions and themes through open-coding. This reading serves to familiarize oneself with the transcribed interview. Descriptive codes are chosen which describe the basic topics present in a specific part of the interview data.

This brief introduction to coding provides the rationale for the application of socio-ecological indicators as codes in interview analysis. In doing so, the socio-ecological indicators reveal community perceived any changes within the Socio-ecological System (SES) or landscape. These indicators reflect upon the social, cultural, natural, and economic aspects of each SES. For example, losing traditional knowledge whenever native plant species disappear can lead to transformations in rural livelihoods and ecosystems (Nabhan 2000; Oudenhoven *et al.* 2012; Oudenhoven *et al.* 2010). Adapted from van Oudenhoven *et al.* (2010) and UNU-IAS (2014) to fit the specific context of each case study, these indicators direct the subsequent course in this dissertation (see Table 3).

Main theme	Sub theme (Description)
Retention and acquisition of indigenous knowledge	Widespread use of knowledge Transmission of knowledge across generations Geographical diffusion of knowledge Documentation of knowledge or acquisition of knowledge: innovation and experimentation Acquisition of knowledge: innovation and experimentation
Use of indigenous and local languages	Number of speakers Existence of education in the indigenous and local languages Existence of community media Percent of children learning the indigenous and local languages
Demographics	Level of emigration from traditional territories Number of generations interaction with the landscape
Cultural values	Folklore associated with cultivated and wild plants and animals Cultural practices: ceremonies, dances, prayers, songs, and other cultural traditions Persistence and respect of sacred sites
Integration of social institutions	Existence/continuation of traditional land tenure systems, indigenous governance, customary laws and the degree to which they are applied to the management of resources Acceptance of social institutions across generations Use of traditional exchange and reciprocity systems (seed exchange, barter)
Food sovereignty and self-sufficiency	Availability of safe, nutritious and culturally appropriate food in sufficient quality and quantity The abundance and use of traditional foods, seeds and medicines in the local production system Intensity of fertilizer, insecticide and/or herbicide use on agricultural land Contribution of traditional subsistence activities to indigenous communities' economy
Multiple uses of land and plants	Multiple uses of a species (food, material, soil nutrient enrichment, shade) Diversity of cultivated crops and varieties: grains, fruits, legumes, vegetables, tubers Diversity of food sources gathered from the wild: roots, berries, mushrooms, fish meat Number of traditional cultivars or species preferred for distinct uses The use of traditional medicine Diverse agricultural systems: intercropping, agroforestry, silvo-pastoral integrated farming and cultivation systems
Complexity and intensity of interactions with the ecosystem	Diversity of components in the landscape used and maintained by communities: forest, riparian forest, fishing grounds, pasturelands, home gardens, cultivated fields, orchards
Conservation of resources	Rates of landscape degradation Degree to which depletion of use of water, soils, forest, pastures is prevented Monitoring of resource abundance and ecosystem changes Conservation of agricultural and wild biodiversity Mechanisms for the total or partial protection of species and habitats; harvest restrictions
Degree of autonomy; indigenous rights	Access to indigenous lands, territories, natural resources, sacred sites and ceremonial areas Recognition of indigenous institutions by both external entities and community members Existence of legal frameworks for indigenous veto over the use of indigenous lands Levels of threat from *e.g.* illegal encroachment privatization, government, expropriation, forced resettlement Practice of free, prior and informed consent in development activities Recognition and respect of sacred sites by local communities, governments, and development industries

Table 3. Socio-ecological Indicators; adapted from van Oudenhouven et al. (2010) and UNU-IAS (2014).

Interviews provided valuable information regarding perceived land-change. By applying these SES indicators as codes to interviews conducted on St. Kitts and in the Kalinago Territory, the method established a coherent manner in which to analyze interview data as well as a direction for subsequent methods in the research. Each interview transcript was systematically coded according to the afore-mentioned socio-ecological indicators.

In this research, coding was applied using Discourse Network Analysis (DNA)[16], and defined socio-ecological indicators (see Table 3), specific to each case study. Indicators represent main themes which are then connected to descriptions or sub themes. Each selected interview statement fits a specific main theme which is then further broken down into a specific sub theme. The relationship between the main theme and sub theme is either positive or negative. The relationship is positive if the interviewee, when discussing the main theme, agrees that the sub theme is still followed, or that certain practices still continue. If, in fact, the interviewee disagrees that such subthemes are still followed or practiced, the relationship between the main theme and the sub-theme is considered negative. This allows for an organized, methodical approach to coding interviews. Whereas the transcription and the coding of the interviews was executed as systematically as possible, resources did not permit any application of certain quality-control methods followed in larger studies, such as the coding of the same text by other individuals in order to find any discrepancies or coder biases. However, the codes, or the applied main and sub themes, applied to each transcription were reviewed by a number of researchers in the Nexus1492 project to ensure a general agreement of the selected codes before the final codes were determined. For the percentages of the main codes and sub codes for both case studies, see Appendix A., Figs. 57 and 58, Appendix A. 1.1, Fig. 60 and Appendix A 2.1, Fig. 61.

Next, the coded results were visualized in order to determine the main focus of each case study which was subsequently discussed and agreed upon collaboratively with the community partners. The coded interviews were next exported as Geography Markup Language (GML)[17] files into Visone[18], visual network analysis software. In order to further this analysis, affiliation networks were built by linking the main themes and sub themes through the positive or negative relationships extracted from the interview coding. An affiliation network consists of a two-mode network defined by two non-overlapping sets of entities (Wasserman and Faust 1994). Usually these entities are qualitatively very distinct from each other. For instance, one mode can comprise a set of actors and the second mode a set of events the actors participated in. Here we define themes and sub themes as the two modes and, the positive and negative mutual relations as connections between them (Leifeld 2012). For example, if an interviewee discusses the continuation of certain cultural practices, such as important days, songs, or myths, the main theme of "Cultural Values" would forward a positive edge to the sub-theme of "Folklore,

---

16   Discourse Network Analysis, http://www.philipleifeld.de/software/discourse-network-analyzer/discourse-network-analyzer-dna.html.
17   GML- defined as "an XML grammar for expressing geographical features. GML serves as a modeling language for geographic systems" (Consortium 2016).
18   Visone software, http://visone.info/.

songs and rituals that live on through cultural practices". This visual representation presents us with a better understanding of complex relationship among themes and sub-themes (see Appendix A 1.2, Fig. 59, Appendix A 2.2, Fig. 62). From this graphical representation of socio-ecological indicators, revealing the general agreement between main themes and sub themes by community members, an overall insight into the community concerns regarding their landscape arises. Interviews provide key information not only on any landscape changes but also on the way it impacts the socio ecological aspects of life. Therefore, utilizing interview data within a visual web, the perceived breaks or discords by community members within their landscape or SES becomes apparent. Through such a process, socio-ecological indicators and interview data establish the groundwork on which to commence subsequent research focus and methods. In Part II of this chapter, the focus of each case study approach builds its methods around the key breaks revealed by means of this procedure.

3.3 Analysis of the land-use and the land-change

Because of the historical context, the long-term land-use and land-cover change has formed an important part of the analysis executed in both case studies. Their island landscapes were drastically shaped and modified through industrial agriculture, leaving traces in the ground as well as social interactions. St. Kitts has witnessed more than 300 years of sugar cane cultivation, whereas Dominica has experienced the rise of the "Green Gold", a reference to the hugely profitable export of bananas during the 1980s. Coming to grips with the modified landscape and linking it to ethnographic data forms an important dimension of each case study. Both issues will be further dealt with in chapters 4 and 5. Section 3.3 of this dissertation will cover the overall methods followed in both case studies to deal with the changing landscape experienced in St. Kitts and the Kalinago Territory, Dominica.

As discussed in chapter 2, the present research acknowledges the unique and complex relationships between human and environment interaction. It is further noted in chapter 2 that land-use is linked to CES. Consequently, any modifications in land-use or land-cover may lead to repercussions on the associated meanings of the landscape, cultural identity and ultimately community well-being. Prior to introducing the specific methodology adhered to, certain terms pertaining to the GIS/Remote Sensing techniques followed will be defined in order to ensure cross-disciplinary understanding.

Land-cover and land-use are two frequently confused terms. Land-cover is defined by the actual physical state of the land, either urban, forested, savannah, grassland, that is created on the basis of a classification system. Any changes in land-cover can be interpreted either as a change in the classification system, scale or aggregation, or as a change in actual threshold values which define a specific land-cover class. Land-use is defined by its relation to being utilized by individuals, such as in settlement, agriculture, or pasture. Land-use modifications do not always lead to an ensuing land-cover change. For example, forest plantations and primal forests both represent the same land-cover (*i.e.*, forested), but are quite dissimilar types of land-use. Additionally, land-use is often defined as a single application by humankind, but the term "land" often serves multiple purposes simultaneously.

While satellite imagery, GIS and remote sensing has led to advances in the field of land classification, the drivers behind land-use and land-cover changes are often confusing as well as difficult to discern as a human activity. Environmental and atmospheric modifications impact the classification of satellite imagery. Furthermore, the results of such classifications describe land-cover changes, the actual land type, or classification, rather than the way it is being, or will be, utilized. Consequently, the GIS, or satellite data, pertaining to land-cover are seldom sufficient. Such methods can detect a change in land-cover, but do not reveal the applications or purposes behind any land-cover transformation (Dale and Kline 2013). No matter the scale of the satellite imagery, it will never detect the differences between fallow land, speculatively-held land for development, and a recently planted crop (Dale and Kline 2013). Therefore, an attempt to analyze any changes in land-cover by means of the GIS/Remote Sensing over time, without simultaneously examining land-use changes, can lead to a variety of confounding results (Dale and Kline 2013; Lenz and Peters 2006). Since change implies a deviation from a baseline, analyzing any changes in land-cover, land-use and/or land management requires considering what the baseline for any change entails. Again, this raises another issue because the historic variability of a landscape is inherent, resulting in broad definitions of what a baseline may be (Dale and Kline 2013). Finally, a landscape will inherently have on-going (*e.g.*, climate change) versus event-based land-use changes (*e.g.*, floods), impacting land-change analysis studies. These two influencers of land-change may present us with extremely dissimilar implications within the results, but rarely can they be assessed separately. Hence, outcomes in land classification research may include possible misinterpretation of landscape indicators.

To overcome the challenges presented above, the GIS/Remote Sensing analysis focus is first defined by the above socio-ecological indicator analysis. Furthermore, the GIS/remote sensing analysis used in this dissertation merges with qualitative data (Jones *et al.* 2007). This procedure not only grounds the community perspectives within a spatial context, but also incorporates any knowledge provided by community stakeholders concerning any land-use changes directly into the research. Integrating social and cultural factors into land-use changes within the GIS has been noted as an important step in creating a better understanding of the local context.

The present research aims at providing an accurate environmental analysis of any land-use change embedded in relevant societal information extracted from interviews and surveys arranged in a GIS format. This goal can be reached by applying the Local Ecological Mapping (LEM) and Sense Of Place Mapping (SOPM) techniques which both integrate local ecosystem services and local belief systems into the physicality of place. In that case, this study combines these methods of acquiring local information on ecosystems and natural resources as well as the significance of locations (Althausen *et al.* 2003; Feagan 2007; Fox 2011; Plieninger *et al.* 2013; Powell 2010; Raymond *et al.* 2009; Ruiter 2012; Ryden 1993; Soini 2001; Trincsi *et al.* 2014).

3.3.1 The historical land-change and community perceptions

It is important to note that the mapping methods adopted in this dissertation have specific historical connotations in the Caribbean: early mapping tools served to appropriate plots of land located within the region, whereas the current application of the modern mapping tool contributes to community autonomy in land-use and the access to land. As maps or geographic data such as GIS/remote sensing are embedded with societal and cultural meanings, they endure as a powerful vehicle for shaping the public perceptions of the location (Colchester 2005; Duncan 2006; Featherstone 2003; Fox 2011; Fox *et al.* 2005; García-Nieto *et al.* 2015; Gardner-Youden *et al.* 2013; Gilmore and Young 2013; González-Puente *et al.* 2014; Jackson 1989; Kosiba and Bauer 2012; Lopéz *et al.* 2012; McLain *et al.* 2013; Powell 2010; Rocheleau 2005; Rundstrom 1990; Smith *et al.* 2012; Wood 1992). As mapping is essentially Cartesian in nature, GIS and the other satellite imaging tools do not reflect the intuitive ways in which local communities interact with and view their local environment. This is another reason why qualitative data grounded in community collaboration form a key element in the present research. Including community stakeholders within the established direction of the research and the mapping/GIS data analysis and process, the data remains balanced, combining so-called expert and local knowledge. By combining the GIS and mapping tools within a holistic and collaborative approach, communities are placed at the very heart of landscape change and degradation.

3.3.2 The land classification

In order to understand environmental and human interactions through time, any related landscape changes and drivers had to be analyzed. This first required identifying parcels of land-cover within a specified time series. As this means of identification did not exist for either case study, a time series of land classification maps had to be created. This preliminary step was completed utilizing the same methodology for each case study in order to comprehend the changes behind the land-cover/land-use variation. The subsequently acquired information was extremely helpful as an addition to the present research, and also served the many community partners involved, as this type of data is by and large not available to the Caribbean. For comparability, the landscape change to measure land-use/land-cover change was kept the same whenever possible with regard to both case studies.

Creating an accurate and functional land classification scheme for the proposed time series (which ran between 1980 and 2015) requires flexibility as well as adaptability in any research situation. In land classification, the large number of possible methods implies that the most appropriate analysis must best interpret the available data, or imagery. However, the Caribbean region proved especially challenging. As these imagery data were limited, the preferred method was based whenever possible on literature which included comparable research issues as well as freely available resources comprising software and imagery (Anderson 1976; Fox *et al.* 1995; Giannecchini *et al.* 2007; Sumarauw and Ohgushi 2012). Such a protocol enabled the transmission of data and methods effectively to community partners at the completion of the study. After reviewing the literature and available data, the classification of the two case studies was composed applying the Maximum Likelihood Supervised Classification and ISO unsupervised classification with ArcGIS and Erdas Imagine[19]. A first attempt was made by utiliz-

---

19   Erdas Imagine: image processing software, http://www.hexagongeospatial.com/products/power-portfolio/erdas-imagine.

Date and location	Satellite sensor	Image ID	Cloud cover	Spatial resolution
St. Kitts 3/3/2006	Quickbird	1010010004D81900	8%	2.4 m.
St. Kitts 3/3/2015	WWV3	1040010009B56600	5%	1.84 m.
Dominica 2/18/2005	Quickbird	1010010004E1F00	6%	2.4 m.
Dominica 12/16/2014	WWV2	102001003BCEC000	3%	1.84 m.

Table 4. Selected imagery applied in the land-use/land-cover analysis.

ing freely available Landsat data. However, the 30-meter resolution of the cell size proved too large to provide the necessary details. Subsequently the Digital Globe[20] Foundation Imagery Grant provided the required imagery.

The intended aim of the land classification analysis was to establish a classified time series (which ran between 1980 and 2015) of both islands and in particular with regard to each case study area. Sadly, this proved almost impossible. Merely insufficient high-resolution and cloud-free imagery proved to be available during most of the above-mentioned time span. For these reasons, any imagery was limited to a selection of two dates for both islands. For the selected imagery used throughout the duration of the research, see Table 4.

On St. Kitts, the sugar cane industry finally came to an end in 2006. On Dominica, the banana industry collapsed in 2005. These two dramatic moments in the history of each island's landscape were not only identified during interviews but also by means of the above-mentioned visualization process applying socio-ecological indicators. The accuracy of each classification was completed thanks to aerial imagery forwarded by the GIS Dept. of the Ministry of Environment (St. Kitts) and the GIS Dept. of the Ministry of Planning (Dominica).

3.3.3 The preprocessing of data

Preprocessing the data included orthorectifying[21] and geometric corrections[22]. The data obtained from the Digital Globe Foundation Imagery Grant had already been radiometrically corrected. It was thus not necessary to repeat this procedure in the analysis. The received data were also orthorectified, but here large overlay issues between the two dates for St. Kitts and Dominica were noted. Hence, the data were orthorectified again by means of Digital Elevation Models kindly provid-

---

20   Digital Globe: https://www.digitalglobe.com/.
21   Orthorectification concerns "… the process of removing the effects of image perspective (tilt) and relief (terrain) effects for the purpose of creating a planimetrically correct image. The resultant orthorectified image has a constant scale wherein features are represented in their 'true' positions" (OSSIM 2014).
22   A Geometric Correction concerns "The correction of errors in remotely sensed data, such as those caused by satellites or aircraft not staying at a constant altitude or by sensors deviating from the primary focus plane. Images are often compared to ground control points on accurate basemaps and resampled, so that exact locations and appropriate pixel values can be calculated" (Esri 2017).

ed by the Ministry of the Environment (St. Kitts) and the Ministry of Planning (Dominica). However, the imagery for both islands still did not line up pixel to pixel. Accordingly, the images were georeferenced to each other, resulting in an error margin of a few meters at most (as opposed to the 10 – 30m error in the original datasets). The Root-Mean-Square Error (RMSE)[23] for both sets of georeferenced data was kept below 10%.

Following georectification, the data were resampled to ensure that the images acquired the same pixel size in each case study. In St. Kitts, the data for 2006 were provided with a resolution of 2.4 m. and the data for 2015 a resolution of 1.84 m. The 2015 data were resampled to a cell size measuring 2.4 m., while snapping the raster resolution of the 2006 data. In Dominica, the 2005 raster also obtained a cell size of 2.4 m and the 2015 raster a cell size measuring 1.84 m. To maintain compatibility, the 2014 raster was resampled to 2.4 m.

Cloud coverage was removed prior to any classification. This procedure was executed by drawing polygons around the cloud coverage in the GIS data. These shape files were then converted into a mask extracted from the satellite imagery, thereby creating cloud free imagery. However, this also limits land classification in certain areas, notably in the Kalinago Territory.

3.3.4 Supervised and unsupervised classification

After data processing, the land classification of Dominica and St. Kitts was carried out by means of the ISO Unsupervised and the Maximum Likelihood Supervised Classification methods in order to compare the accuracy of both results. This classification is based on user-defined training areas which generate a signature file which in turn then serves to classify the entire image. Moreover it, this classification clusters similar pixels into a set number of categories. Next the user identifies the land-cover classes by applying information stemming from secondary land data. The categories of land classes on St. Kitts were defined as "Urban", "Cropland", "Forest", "Bare", "Grass", and "Water", and on Dominica as "Urban", "Low Vegetation", "Forest", "Bare", and "Water". Despite the high resolution imagery provided, it was difficult to discern the pure cropland from low vegetated areas on Dominica due to dense vegetation.

In the Maximum Likelihood Supervised Classification methods, training data were produced for each case study. Thirty areas of interest were chosen to represent each of the afore-mentioned land classes for both St. Kitts and Dominica. This selection was executed by referencing the aerial imagery provided by community partners and Google Earth, delivering a higher level of accuracy. In the ISO Unsupervised classification, forty unsupervised categories were chosen. Utilizing aerial imagery, Google Earth[24], and high resolution satellite data forwarded by the Digital Globe Foundation, the pixels were manually modified in order to fit the selected five categories. This allowed for a compari-

---

23 The RMSE measures the differences between the actual result and the predicted result that is predicted by a mode and the values actually observed, or how much error is predicted between two datasets (2016a).
24 https://www.google.com/earth/.

St. Kitts Land Class	2006	2015	Dominica Land Class	2005	2014
Urban	1	10	Urban	1	10
Cropland	2	20	Low Vegetation	2	20
Forest	3	30	Forest	3	30
Bare	4	40	Bare	4	40
Grass	5	50	Water	5	50

Table 5. Land-cover reclassification, St. Kitts and Dominica.

son as well as for the refining of categories until the desired classes for each case study were met by means of clustering and reclassification. For the results of the Iso Unsupervised Classification of the coastal villages' case study in St. Kitts, see Appendix B 1. Figs. 63 – 65, and Tables 37 and 38. For the results hereof of the Iso Unsupervised Classification of the Kalinago Territory, see Appendix B 2. Figs. 66 – 68, and Tables 39 and 39). In order to analyze the changes occurring in the time series for both islands, the classified satellite imagery was reclassified to represent each land class code as described in Table 5.

Following a reclassification, a Raster Math tool served not only to add the values of the earlier date to the most recent data but also to produce a land-use change raster. This procedure provides each pixel with a value describing the original land class with regard to the earlier date of the satellite imagery and what the pixel had become in the most recently executed the satellite imagery.

3.3.5 Accuracy assessment

In order to analyze the accuracy of the results, an error matrix was set up for each date and classification by first creating 200 random points with the Create Random Points tool. The following step was to apply the Extract Values to Points tool on each of the land-use classifications and dates. This procedure adds the raster value as an incoming attribute to the point's layer. Utilizing secondary sources comprising highly detailed satellite imagery provided by Google Earth, aerial photographs, and a Digital Globe Foundation imagery grant, the values of the extracted pixels, or land classes, were confirmed as either being correctly or incorrectly categorized. Next, a final check applying ground field observations based on extensive fieldwork determined further accuracy in the two case study areas (CAMFER ; Ismail and Jusoff 2008). The Frequency tool calculates the frequency of each combination of truth and prediction value which can be applied with the Pivot Table tool. The Frequency toolset also defines the predictions as rows, the truth values as the pivot field, and the frequency as the value field.

Finally, a cross tabulation matrix was created in order to compare the user's accuracy with the producer's accuracy. Table 6 presents the accuracy assessment (Cleve *et al.* 2008; Hengl and Rossiter 2002; Hughes *et al.* 2006; Rozenstein and Karnieli 2011) for each year, arranged as both an ISO Unsupervised Classification and a Maximum Likelihood Supervised Classification for St. Kitts as well as for Dominica.

From these results, Maximum Likelihood Supervised Classification proved to be the most relevant to adopt in the analysis of land-cover/land-use change for

The Iso Unsupervised Classification 2016, St. Kitts

		Actual							
		Forest	Urban	Water	Crop	Bare	Grass	Total (predicted)	User's accuracy (%)
Predicted	Forest	35	0	0	0	2	6	43	0.814
	Urban	0	3	0	0	0	1	4	0.75
	Water	0	0	107	0	0	0	107	1
	Crop	0	0	0	3	1	5	9	0.6
	Bare	0	1	1	0	2	0	4	0.5
	Grass	3	0	0	19	0	18	40	0.45
	Total (actual)	38	4	108	22	5	30		
	Producers accuracy (%)	0.921	0.75	0.991	0.136	0.4	0.6	Overall accuracy	81.2%

The Maximum Likelihood Supervised Classification 2006, St. Kitts

		Actual							
		Forest	Urban	Water	Crop	Bare	Grass	Total (predicted)	User's accuracy (%)
Predicted	Forest	33	0	0	0	0	6	39	0.846
	Urban	0	2	1	0	0	0	3	0.667
	Water	0	0	107	0	0	0	107	1
	Crop	4	1	0	9	2	12	28	0.75
	Bare	0	1	0	1	3	0	5	0.6
	Grass	1	0	0	12	0	10	23	0.435
	Total (actual)	38	4	108	22	5	28		
	Producer's accuracy (%)	0.868	0.5	0.991	0.409	0.6	0.357	Overall accuracy	80%

The ISO Unsupervised Classification 2015, St. Kitts

		Actual							
		Forest	Urban	Water	Crop	Bare	Grass	Total (predicted)	User's accuracy (%)
Predicted	Forest	30	0	0	2	1	1	34	0.882
	Urban	0	2	0	0	0	0	2	1
	Water	0	0	111	0	0	0	111	1
	Crop	0	1	0	12	1	9	23	1.3
	Bare	1	3	0	0	6	1	15	0.667
	Grass	3	0	0	6	1	5	15	0.33
	Total (actual)	34	6	111	20	13	16		
	Producer's accuracy (%)	0.882	0.33	1	0.6	0.769	0.313	Overall accuracy	85%

Table 6. Accuracy assessment St. Kitts and the Kalinago Territory. Continued on next page.

both Dominica and St. Kitts[25]. First, the topography of Dominica varies drastically. In classification, these undulations between elevations create shadows or darker pixels, resulting in forested areas often misclassified as water in the ISO unsupervised classification. Second, in the case of St. Kitts, the categories "Grass" and

---

25 The final land classifications of both case studies focused on the study site, rather than the entirety of each island to preserve spectral integrity of land class types.

The Maximum Likelihood Supervised Classification 2015, St. Kitts

		Actual						Total (predicted)	User's accuracy (%)
		Forest	Urban	Water	Crop	Bare	Grass		
Predicted	Forest	27	0	0	1	1	0	29	0.931
	Urban	0	6	0	0	3	1	10	0.6
	Water	0	0	111	0	0	0	111	1
	Crop	3	0	0	6	3	8	20	0.75
	Bare	1	0	0	0	6	1	8	0.75
	Grass	3	0	0	13	0	6	22	0.273
	Total (actual)	34	6	111	20	13	16		
	Producer's accuracy (%)	0.794	1	1	0.3	0.462	0.375	Overall accuracy	81%

The ISO Unsupervised Classification 2005, the Kalinago Territory

		Actual				Total (predicted)	User's accuracy(%)
		Cloud	Low Vegetation	Forest	Urban		
Predicted	Cloud	59	0	0	0	59	1
	Low Vegetation	0	11	3	0	14	0.79
	Forest	0	8	117	0	125	0.94
	Bare	0	1	0	0	1	1
	Total (actual)	0	0	0	1	1	1
	Producer's accuracy (%)	59	20	120	1	Overall Accuracy	94%

The Maximum Likelihood Supervised Classification 2015, the Kalinago Territory

		Actual				Total (predicted)	User's accuracy (%)
		Cloud	Low Vegetation	Forest	Bare		
Predicted	Cloud	56	0	1	0	56	100
	Low Vegetation	0	15	5	0	20	0.75
	Forest	0	3	114	0	117	0.974
	Urban	2	2	1	1	6	0.167
	Total (actual)	58	20	121	100		
	Producer's accuracy (%)	0.97	0.75	0.96	1	Overall accuracy	93%

The Maximum Likelihood Supervised Classification 2014, the Kalinago Territory

		Actual				Total (predicted)	User's accuracy (%)
		Cloud	Low Vegetation	Forest	Bare		
Predicted	Cloud	33	0	0	0	33	1
	Low Vegetation	0	8	3	0	11	0.727
	Forest	0	6	132	0	138	0.966
	Bare	0	0	14	1	15	0.071
	Total (actual)	33	12	149	1	Overall accuracy	87%

Table 6 continued. Accuracy assessment St. Kitts and the Kalinago Territory. Continued on next page.

The Maximum Likelihood Supervised Classification 2014, the Kalinago Territory

		Actual				Total (predicted)	User's accuracy
		Cloud	Low Vegetation	Forest	Urban		
Predicted	Cloud	33	0	0	0	33	1
	Low Vegetation	0	9	10	0	11	0.474
	Forest	0	5	138	0	138	0.965
	Urban	0	0	1	1	15	0.5
	Total (actual)	33	14	139	1		
	Producer's accuracy (%)	1	0.643	0.993	1	Overall accuracy	90.5%

Table 6 continued.

Landscape Change	Stakeholders (inside and outside of the local context)	Associated resource use
Industrial agriculture		
St. Kitts Sugar plantation system	Laborers, plantation owners, villagers	Sugar, mountain areas, soil, water, cultural associations
Dominica Banana exportation	Farmers, banana industry export markets, transportation services	Water, banana crops, associated agricultural crops, soil, cultural associations
Environmental Degradation		
St. Kitts Coastal erosion	Local communities, tourists	Fish, beaches, coastal vegetation, cultural associations
Dominica Limited water resources		Rivers, streams, vegetation resources, fish, cultural associations

Table 7. Socio-ecological system assessment and the main focus.

"Crops" are very similar, making it difficult for the ISO unsupervised classification to differentiate between these two features of the Kittitian landscape. As the focus of this analysis sought to investigate the changes to the rural landscape, as most communities in the case study of St. Kitts are based in rural area, again, it was decided to utilize the results of the Maximum Likelihood Supervised Classification. The subsequent GIS analyses in the micro factor methods of each case study used and built upon the outcomes of land classification of this section.

Part II. Micro factors of the local landscape context

The present section addresses the micro factors used in the methods of each case study. Community collaboration, interview data analyzed through socio-ecological indicators, and land change analysis of the macro factors determined the appropriate land-use/change analysis and the subsequent ethnographic methods to fit the context of each case study. For a breakdown of each case study's overall focus, see Table 7.

The below sections discuss the specific methods followed in each case study: the coastal villages of St. Kitts (section 3.4) and the Kalinago Territory (section 3.5).

3.4 The coastal villages of St. Kitts: the study area and background

With the Atlantic Ocean positioned off its eastern coast and the Caribbean Sea off its western coast, the island of St. Kitts (37 km x 8 km) is part of the northern Leeward Islands of the Lesser Antilles. To its South, separated by a 13 km. wide strait, lies the sister island of Nevis. With a population of c. 45, 000, together these two islands form the Federation of St. Kitts and Nevis (Agostini *et al.* 2015; Association 1990; Carter 2010b; Edwards and Jacque 2007; Lawrence 2014; Roebuck *et al.* 2004).

Dominated by a dormant volcano, Mount Liamuiga (h. 11,156 m); the landscape of St. Kitts consists of sloping fields of volcanic fields, segregated by deep ghauts or gulleys (Association 1990). The capital, Basseterre, is the largest town on the island. To its west the second largest town, Sandy Point, is located. One main road encircles the island, intersecting most villages along the way. The present case study area is situated west of Basseterre, made up of eleven villages interspersed between former estates, stretching from the village of Challengers to Fig Tree (see Fig. 7).

Defined together with local partners, the research questions, or the ultimate case study focus, determined that main issues are:

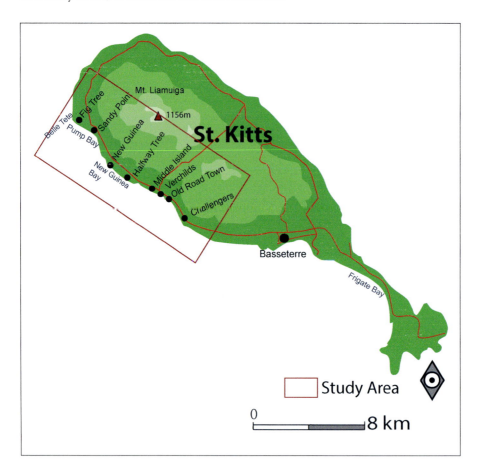

Fig. 7. Case study settlement locations on St. Kitts.

- What is the current environmental state of the coastline located within the study area?
- What do the current communities think of the environmental state of this coastline?
- Which environmental or social changes have these communities experienced?

The case study area, situated between Challengers and Fig Tree (see Fig. 8), was identified as relevant for a variety of reasons. In formulating the research together, the community stakeholders, local partners and interested members of the public defined the case study area an important location needing attention. Such community partners included members of the Department of Physical Planning and Environment, Ministry of Sustainable Development (DPPE), and in particular Graeme Brown, the Physical Planning Assistant/GIS Officer. Community stakeholders explained that this particular area has experienced extraordinarily far-reaching environmental degradation and land-use changes. In fact, many described the road leading from Challengers to Fig Tree as falling into the sea (CAA 1990). As most villages sit along this main road, the erosion into the sea impacts the nearby villages. Since 2005, the Kittitian government has considered options to reroute the main island road or to force a community resettlement. Furthermore, the study area boasts a long history of human interaction and houses important cultural heritage sites. Discovered in the vicinity of Challengers and Old Road village, Amerindian settlements and petroglyphs at Carib Rock and Bloody River remain as some of the last evidence of the rich Amerindian presence on the island. The early colonization by the French and British settlers in this part of the island shaped the historical landscape. Finally, the environmental history of the sugar cane plantations and the British colonization captures the issues of the access to land, exclusion and associated values to remain of significance even to the present day. For these reasons of complex heritage, and the altering livelihoods of the present communities due to environmental change, require further study with special attention to the historical (*i.e.*, sugar plantations) and current land-use to understand its effects on local communities with regard to economic, social and cultural changes.

As discussed in section 3.2, interviews revealed the focus of the research through coding using socio-ecological indicators. This preliminary method informed subsequent steps taken in the research focus particular to the St. Kitts case study (see Figs. 8 and 9). The results of the coded interviews have led to a focus on the following three socio-ecological indicators:
- the "Multiple Uses of Land" with an emphasis on the lack of access to mountain grounds or agricultural plots of land located in the case study area.
- the "Resource Conservation" centering on land degradation, in particular on coastal erosion occurring along the coastline of the case study area.
- the "Cultural/Social aspects" of land-change experienced or perceived by the communities;

The specific methods applied to explore these three indicators comprise two sub-sections in which: (a) the GIS/Remote Sensing methods identify how the land and coastline have changed and (b) the survey data procedures serve to link physical transformation with community perceptions. For a definition of the methodology followed specifically in the case study on the coastal villages of St. Kitts, see Fig. 8.

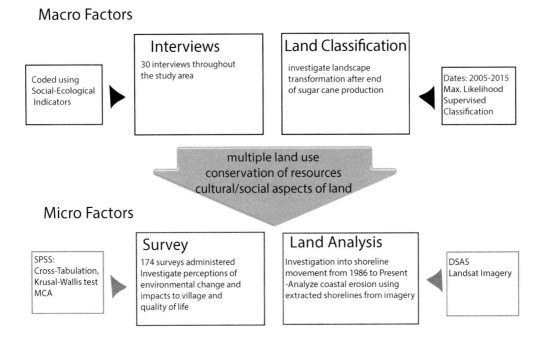

Fig. 8. Macro and micro factors relevant to the coastal villages of St. Kitts case study.

3.4.1 Integrating the ecological and community knowledge in land-change analysis: coastal erosion

To understand the coastal changes discussed in the survey and interview data, coastal erosion and the impacts on the coastline are analyzed with the Digital Shoreline Analysis System (DSAS) (Thieler *et al.* 2008), a freely available ArcGIS plugin provided by the United States Geological Survey (USGS). DSAS assesses any shoreline movement, specifically to comprehend the coastline evolution in the case study area as described by interviewees. The DSAS plugin produces a variety of statistics based on the intersection of multiple shorelines by transects cast from a user-defined baseline. Utilizing this procedure, multiple shorelines extracted from various types of imagery can be applied and analyzed to produce a glimpse of modifications in shorelines through time. Possibly reducing the accuracy of the results, a variety of errors can occur during this analysis, mainly caused by using multiple types of imagery. For this reason, this analysis utilized only the Landsat imagery to account for the possibility of error when combining the various imagery sources (Ruggiero *et al.* 2013). For more information on the type of error and meter error, see Table 8.

Using LANDSAT MSS, TM, ETM, OLI-TIRS imagery, acquired for the years 1986, 1989, 1999, 2003, 2006, 2013, and 2015, served as a long term georectified

Type of Error	Aerial photos (1950s-1960s)	Satellite imagery (1990s- present)
High water-line uncertainty	14.8 m	--
Digitizing	1 m	--
Aerial photos	.3 m	--
Position uncertainty	--	4.1 m

Table 8. Associated error types linked to the various types of imagery.

Date	Landsat Scene ID	Landsat	Time
12/12/2015	LC80020482015010LGN00	Landsat 8, OLI_TIRS	14:32:11
8/16/2013	LC80020482013116LGN01	Landsat 8, OLI_TIRS	14:33:49
1/25/ 2006	LE70020482006025EDC00	Landsat 7, ETM	14:22:02
3/2/2003	LE70020482003129EDC00	Landsat 7, ETM	14:20:49
12/8/1999	LE70020481999342EDC00	Landsat 7, ETM	14:24:59
10/17/1989	LT50020481989274XXX09	Landsat 5, TM	13:57:46
3/15/1986	LM50020481986074AAA03	Landsat 5, MSS	13:58:10

Table 9. Selected shoreline data, St. Kitts.

dataset to extract historic shoreline vectors (see Table 9). Due to the high number of images with cloud coverage, determining a dataset with regular time intervals proved impossible. Table 9 shows the imagery used.

These shoreline dates remain significant, however, as they investigate the coastal impacts of Hurricane George, which hit St. Kitts in 1998, and the construction of Port Zante, a new 27-acre cruise-ship marina located at Basseterre, in 1996. Furthermore, as the sugar cane industry came to an end in 2005, any subsequent changes of the seascape could also be explored. Whereas the results cannot confirm any correlations between these aspects and the experienced erosion, it is still helpful when evaluating any increase in erosion from 2006 to date. The year 2015 was selected as it was the most recent and most cloud-free satellite image available at the time of study.

To affirm an accurate comparison across shorelines, georeferencing ensured a proper overlay of the imagery. Next, the shorelines were extracted. Defining the actual shoreline presents issues because it can often relate to tides and wave break. This phenomenon is noted as a relevant issue of shoreline extraction methods, needing attention when comparing multiple dates (Himmelstoss 2009). As the study area is located on the Caribbean Sea/western coast of St Kitts, there is little wave undulation. Accordingly, the difference between wave breaks is usually minimal. In the shoreline vector extraction, one conventionally applies the high-water line, *i.e.* base of the berm (Maloney and Ausness 1974; Pajak and Leatherman 2002) in order to mark the landward extent of any wave action (Woodroffe 2003, 277) so that it can serve as the boundary between sea and land, because the high-water line is fixed. However, the present study area consists of large stretches of shoreline cliffs. For this reason, utilizing the actual waterline to extract the shoreline

Fig. 9. St. Kitts Coast Guard carrying out a shoreline survey (photo by author).

vectors proved impossible. Additionally, the low resolution of the Landsat data limited all identification of wave breaks and berms. However, any errors are expected to be small because of the vertical nature of most parts of the shoreline, and the micro tidal range of the Caribbean Sea, typically measuring between 10 and 20 cm (Kjerfve 1981).

The Normalized Difference Vegetation Index (NDVI) of each image was calculated to separate water pixels from land pixels. This procedure provided a more distinct shoreline, enabling proper shoreline extraction for each image date (Boak and Turner 2005). The shorelines of each date were then digitized manually. For this research, the shoreline was defined as the first non-water pixel. Finally, a baseline, from which the subsequent transects are cast, was created by generating a 200-meter buffer of the 2015 shoreline.

3.4.2 Linking physical changes with community perceptions

As the St. Kitts case study area stretched along a 12 km coastline, any satisfactory results and conclusions could not be drawn from only thirty interviews. Consequently, a paper-based questionnaire, or survey, was developed to account for the limited time frame and the lack of unequal spatial distribution of interview respondents in the study area. Designed in a two-stage process with a first draft being shared with local partners, this survey contained both open-ended as well as multiple-choice questions to ensure that the language, flow and contents were accessible. While the interviews revealed the main opinions, the semi-structured surveys inquired into the deeper relationships between land-use change, the community perceptions of change, and the impacts upon well-being. Because of the existing collaboration with partners from the Ministry of Environment of St. Kitts, the semi-structured surveys were also designed to be not only easily transferable but also helpful for future governmental planning initiatives. For this reason, the subjects of the questions as well as the included demographic data were jointly created. Finally, the semi-structured surveys also served as a key component of the linkage between the spatial data and the socio-cultural contexts.

The final survey consists of three main sections comprising twenty-seven questions. Section One collects information on the respondent's age, occupation, village and domestic situation. Section Two probes his or her views on coastal threats, coastal change, flooding, environmental changes, and incoming developments. In Section Two, an agreement scale was applied to answers ranging from 1-5: (1) completely agreeing, (4) completely disagreeing and (5) having no knowledge of the variable. For the questionnaire, see Appendix C and Table 41.

The survey process was conducted throughout the second and third stage of the field work. Its implementation involved both a person-to-person as well as an online method. In the case of the person-to-person implementation, surveys were executed in each village throughout the study area whereby an attempt was made to do so either in the evenings or on Saturday mornings when most people would be at home.

Graeme Brown, the GIS officer attached to the Dept. of Physical Planning and Environment (DPPE), the Ministry of Sustainable Development (St. Kitts), acted as an important community liaison, introducing the survey and the interviewer to each participating household. Each respondent was selected independently from the household members rather than by means of the researcher's personal input. Such a process proved extremely helpful as it quickly established community links. The villages concerned are quite small, making such connections extremely important. All answers were filled in on the paper-based survey form by the interviewer in order to see to it each survey resembled a conversation and not an implemented exam. Discussions and important topics mentioned during the 15-30 min. interviews were annotated on the survey form. In order to reach more households, several other members of the Nexus 1492 research team contributed by means of administering questionnaires.

Additional community involvement occurred thanks to collaboration with the Verchilds High School, facilitated by Marcela Berkley, a teacher at this school. The survey was administrated in two Social Studies/History classes as a coursework activity. Finally, an online version of the survey was created in order to not only enlarge the volume of the interviewees but also expand the geographic extent of its reach. This survey was posted on the Department of Culture's Facebook page, which has significant online traffic thanks to a strong social media presence thereby enabling the acquisition of information to serve as a means of comparison from individuals not residing in the study area. 174 households were interviewed, representing 13% of the total households in the study area (Department of Statistics & Economic Planning 2001). Within this sample population, gender was almost evenly divided, with 51% female. The majority (15.5%) work as merchants or in tourism related employment (13.2%). Finally, 73.6% live with extended family in one household. For more information concerning the data distribution, refer to Appendix D.2).

3.5 The Kalinago Territory, Dominica: study area and background

Dominica is part of the Windward Islands located in the Lesser Antilles. Its 750 km2 can be described as extremely rugged. Its highest peak named Morne Diablotins reaches 1,447 m. The island's luscious rainforests experience heavy rainfall, especially in its mountainous heartlands. With 72,003 inhabitants, Dominica remains

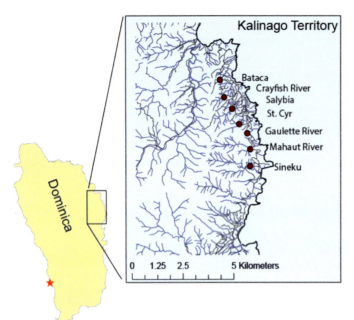

Fig. 10. The Kalinago Territory, Dominica.

predominantly rural with the exception of the urban areas, such as the capital Rousseau and the northern town of Portsmouth (Carter 2010a).

Similar to many other Caribbean islands, the economy of Dominica depends upon tourism and agriculture. Currently, the tourism market, while growing rapidly, is comparatively small when compared to neighboring isles (Cherrett 2011; Turner 2015). The Kalinago Territory can be found on the island's eastern coast. (See Fig. 10).

Collaborating with community members, the focus and questions of the Kalinago Territory case study dealt with:
- Has the local physical landscape changed in recent years?
- How has the cultural landscape, understood as the interaction between the community and the landscape, transformed?
- How have these changes impacted the local socio-ecological system?

Once a partnership between the researcher and the community had been established, in particular with Cozier Fredrick, the Development Officer at the Department of Development and Gender Affairs at the Ministry of Kalinago Affairs and co-founder of the Salybia Heritage and Restoration Project (SHARP) as well as with Kimani John (SHARP), collaborations further expanded in order to include members of the National Employment Program (NEP), Dilianie Darroux (Officer of Land Registry), Jason Jones (Agricultural Extension for Department of Agriculture), and Danne Auguiste (IT specialist). This community involvement also included members of the Department of Agriculture, Marcus Philip and Asher Burton. These partnerships facilitated the research in the study area.

Community members already noticed a changing landscape (*e.g.*, declining agriculture, soil erosion, land slippage) in recent years. These environmental aspects have also led to noticeable changes in community dynamics throughout the Kalinago Territory. The SHARP was developed in 2015 as a community NGO in Salybia, the historic center of the Kalinago Territory, in response to these community and environmental

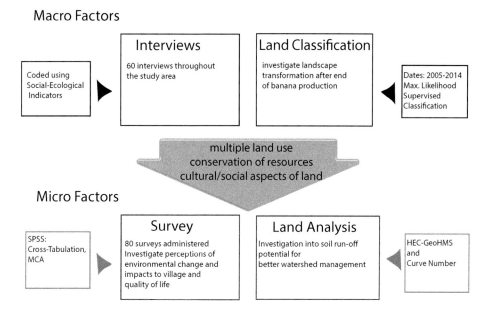

Fig. 11. Macro and micro factors relevant to the Kalinago Territory case study.

modifications. The purpose of the SHARP is to monitor/counter those changes by means of a land-use analysis and restoration works, involving local community members. Salybia was one of the first hamlets to be established in the Kalinago Territory and is considered the epicenter of activities and Kalinago life (Campbell 2001; Layng 1983). This collaboration presented an ideal opportunity to (a) work alongside the community, (b) conduct research of mutual benefit to both parties and (c) contribute to concerted efforts of any future land management practices.

As discussed in chapter 3, the Kalinago Territory case study research was determined through community collaboration as well as socio-ecological indicators based on interview analysis. Through this method of using socio-ecological indicators, the focus of the particular research in the Kalinago Territory included;

- The "Multiple Uses of the Land" as revealed through land- change and the impact on agriculture and fishing as both a cultural and resource service.
- The "Resource Conservation" or the decline in water resources of the Kalinago Territory and the associated impacts on resource services.
- The "Socio-Cultural Aspects" of a community change and their association with land-change.

The subsequent methods discussed in this chapter fit the specific investigation of this case study to answer the research questions. For the overall, specific methodology of macro and micro factors followed in the Kalinago Territory case study, see Fig. 12.

3.5.1 Integrating ecological and community knowledge in land-change analysis: community mapping and river degradation

At the Ministry of Planning and the Ministry of Lands and Surveys, little GIS data existed for the Kalinago Territory to complete more complex analysis required in the case study. For this reason, the preliminary research step in this case study entailed collecting the missing data. Community collaborative efforts involving a variety of geospatial and community mapping events took place throughout the Kalinago Territory. The community mapping components followed methodologies proposed in examples of similar research into land planning and socio-ecological systems within small rural communities (Cambraia 2013; Fox 2011; Fox *et al.* 2005; Gardner-Youden *et al.* 2013; Gilmore and Young 2013; Kosiba and Bauer 2012; Plieninger *et al.* 2013; Powell 2010; Ramirez-Gomez *et al.* 2013; Ramirez-Gomez *et al.* 2015; Smith *et al.* 2012; Soini 2001). The mapping methodology aimed at mobilizing community participation in defining and delineating important boundaries, locations, natural resources, and community value. In doing so, communities identify areas that may be at risk or degraded, and may not only require more protection or development, but are nonetheless of interest to the community.

The community mapping components are divided as follows: (a) a collaborative Geographic Information System based on community-sourced data, (b) community mapping workshops, and (c) a land survey of agricultural land throughout the Kalinago Territory. The resulting information was merged with national data in order to create an overarching database which is stored with the Kalinago Council, the Ministry of Kalinago Affairs and the Department of Lands and Surveys and Planning. Therefore, the acquired knowledge can be utilized with regard to a better land and resource management in future years. Moreover, the summation of the mapping activities allowed for collaboration and exchange with community members.

Thanks to the collaboration with Dilianie Darroux, Jason Jones, Kimani John, Danne Auguiste, Marcus Philip and Asher Burton of the Department of Agriculture, along with other community members, a GIS database was created. Hereto the interested local stakeholders conducted a GPS and field surveys jointly throughout the entire territory. Here GPS points as well as tracks were recorded for roads, streams, frequented trails, important sites and other geographic locations, to be found at Atkinson in the north down to Castle Bruce in the south. In total, 112 (natural) sites were assessed.

Three community mapping workshops were conducted in the town of Salybia. They took place during the SHARP meetings and followed methodologies proposed in similar research concerning any land planning and socio-ecological systems within small rural communities (Cambraia 2013; Gilmore and Young 2013; Plieninger *et al.* 2013). As the Kalinago Territory is isolated from much of the rest of Dominica, any governmental land planning occurred without the actual participation of those residing in the territory. The above workshops can mediate information between local governmental agencies, the Kalinago Council and community members of Salybia. Materials created for these workshops included a 3D aerial model of the Salybia area produced with the help of community members utilizing a drone (June 2015) as well as satellite images depicting Salybia which the Department of Lands and Surveys provided. During these workshops, this 3D

Fig. 12. Cozier Frederick leading a community mapping workshop in Salybia.

model was displayed in order to allow the residents of Salybia to establish a more informed opinion on the evolving transformations.

Further, the model and imagery led to subsequent discussions on community assets in Salybia as well as on the kind of development the community required. This resulted in the creation of a variety of community-planned maps for improving areas mentioned in the discussions. As the community members were invited to add locations to the map, while designating areas or exact locations considered important or modifiable. The created maps served as part of the land planning for future SHARP activities and development. This approach presents one of the few ways to integrate the information within other spatially explicit domains. Moreover, it reveals a major issue in the combining of spatially joined information with community perspectives. Neither of these two elements is more important than the other and merely represents two types of knowledge systems which require complementing rather than mutual elimination.

After GPS and GIS training workshops had been held in Salybia in June 2015, a clear interest arose in using and adopting the technology to map individual land boundaries[26]. The creation of the Kalinago Territory GIS database prompted a discussion on instituting a land survey throughout the entire territory. As no such survey had been conducted since 1901, the Kalinago Council or the Department of Agriculture could only provide little information concerning the planning and management of plots of land located in the Kalinago Territory where hardly any current specifications concerning the total acreage of cultivated land are available. This fact limits any possible investments or agricultural subsidies being provided by the government. Moreover, only a small number of farmers know the exact acreage of the land they cultivate, making the purchase of seed as well as inputs (*e.g.* fertilizer, pesticides) complicated.

---

26 While the Kalinago Territory is defined by its communal land title, individuals living there still have individual plots of land that they use and cultivate. While variations exist, land can be obtained by purchasing a particular parcel from someone if it is already being used and cultivated, cultivating land that is not being used, cultivated, or that no one has claimed, and finally, claiming land passed through through generations. Of course, variations exist on all.

Fig. 13. Marcus Philips and Asher Burton collecting GPS points during a land survey (photo by author).

To respond to the communities' concerns regarding land, a survey hereof took place in June-July 2015 and in January-February 2016 with the assistance of Dilanie Darroux (Ministry of Kalinago Affairs) and Marcus Phillip, Asher Burton and Jason Jones (Department of Agriculture). First, fliers describing this process were distributed throughout each hamlet at commonly frequented locations. The goal was not only to reach as many farmers registered with the Department of Agriculture as possible, but also other interested individuals. After an initial meeting with the Kalinago Council comprising local government members and Dilianie Darroux, a scheduled date was determined to return and map the land acreage. Utilizing a GPS, one would walk the border lines of their plots of land together with a Kalinago Council Member to ensure that measurements of these boundaries were not exaggerated. The GPS provided an immediate estimation of land acreage and forwarded it directly. This information was saved and later added to the GIS database along with the land owner's name. By storing these data in this database, they can be updated, applied in land disputes, and serve as a visual representation for stakeholders. All in all, thirty farms were surveyed and mapped.

3.5.2 Watershed management in the Kalinago Territory

A watershed is defined as a geographic area in which water flows across or under land, through a river, stream, lake, aquifer or ocean. A watershed boundary follows the highest point around stream channels and ends at the lowest point where the water leaves the watershed. Most of the water within a watershed comprises a combination of rainfall, storm water runoff and a water source, such as a river. The quality and quantity of storm water depends on the type of land modification (*e.g.*, related to agriculture, mining, roadways, urban areas) occurring in the watershed. Consequently, all activities (*e.g.*, related to agricultural, developmental, and domestic matters) will impact the health standards of water resources within the watershed. All the surface water features and storm water runoff within a watershed will ultimately drain into other bodies of water (Bruijnzeel 1990; Protection 2015).

Watershed management is extremely challenging because it involves multiple sources of degradation such as air, land and water (Adham *et al.* 2014; CATHALAC 2007; 2003; Wani *et al.* 2007; Wani *et al.* 2008). A complicating factor of this form of management is, that despite its definition, a watershed is never simply a hydrologic unit but also the "socio-political-ecological entity which plays a crucial role in determining food, social, and economical security and provides life support services to rural people" (Wani and Garg 2009, 3). Addressing the issues linked to watershed management often leads to an effective growth in agriculture, development and the social and institutional infrastructure. This outcome can result in societal improvement, for example, "food production, improving livelihoods, protecting environment, addressing gender and equity issues along with biodiversity concerns" (Wani and Garg 2009, 1). The complexities of watershed management and the lack of available data needed for the Kalinago Territory presented little flexibility in terms of providing a possible solution. Therefore, as hydrology tools were not available, this research relied on a GIS methodology. This limits the depth possible in the research, but it does allow for continual management and updating as the subsequent data produced is stored at the Ministry of Kalinago Affairs.

Managing a watershed involves attention to land use and changing land cover. In agricultural landscape, this includes specifically, crop diversification, as well as inputs, such as fertilizers or pesticides. Water and soil conservation are the primary steps of watershed management which are divided into in situ or ex situ management. In situ management includes terracing fields. Such practices are upheld in order to ensure the health of the soil, allowing the ground water to refill, and to protect land from degradation. Ex situ management includes the building of dams, gullies or stream channels in order to reduce any peak discharge. In the Kalinago Territory, the water and soil are currently managed by means of in situ techniques (Joshi *et al.* 2008; Sheng 1990; Tomer 2004; Wani *et al.* 2007; Wani *et al.* 2008; Wortmann *et al.* 2008). Here, too, watershed management remains a relevant issue, especially in rural areas with growing populations still dependent on agriculture. Furthermore, it is an area of high elevation, implying that a run off into stream areas is likely. As preliminary interviews suggest, understanding the possible threats to water resources in the Kalinago Territory is an issue of interest to the community.

Tomer (2004) executes watershed management by the following three steps of identification: (a) acquiring the environmental data (acquired in this case for all of Dominica from the Department of Planning) (b) surveying streams within the study area and, (c) conducting interviews with residents. The second step comprises identifying the problems within the watershed. This includes: (a) physical problems *e.g.*, steep slopes, slide-prone soils or intense rain falls, (b) resource problems, *e.g.*, shifting cultivation, forest destruction, over grazing, and c(c) end problems, *e.g.*, soil erosion, landslides or heavy sedimentation. The third step entails possible land and resource management alternatives which would have to be enacted by the Ministry of Kalinago Affairs or the Kalinago Council. Consequently, analysis produced deliverables that were then shared with the local government and ministries to aid in the land management process. Analyses were executed by means of the ArcGIS plugin, Hydrologic Modeling System (HEC-HMS)[27]. The plugin, created by the United States Army Corp of Engineers, provides a set of procedures, tools and utilities with which to process geospatial data in ArcGIS: a toolkit for engineers and hydrologists through which to visualize spatial information, document the watershed characteristics, perform a spatial analysis, delineate sub-basins, streams and construct basins.

Utilizing national data acquired from Dominica's Department of Planning, including soil type, soil group, elevation and topography, the preprocessing analysis included a depression-less DEM, flow, flow direction, flow accumulation, stream definition, stream segmentation and catchment grid delineation. For these results, see Appendix F, Figs. 80-82. From these preliminary datasets, the HEC-HMS plugin produces the Curve Number for the study region. The curve number indicates the amount of runoff (*i.e.*, the quantity of soil that leaks into river areas from the surrounding land- cover during a rain event) potential. Curve Numbers are calculated based on the soil and ground cover properties to next determine the high or low risk of a runoff in a certain area. Soil properties are based on the hydrologic soil classification of Groups A, B, C, and D with more sands in Group A and more clay in Group D. In addition, Group A soil would have the least runoff and Group D the most.

The filtration of water through the soil is based on the soil's hydrologic group, making this element an important component of the CN calculation. This coefficient alters the total precipitation to the runoff potential after taking into account the losses of evaporation, absorption, transpiration, surface storage. A higher CN value gives a higher the runoff potential (Adham *et al.* 2014; Soulis and Valiantzas 2012; Sumarauw and Ohgushi 2012).

To create a CN Grid for the study area, a merged polygon of land-use and soil types was generated to define the percentage of the soil types, A, B, C, D and the land-use types. This polygon is then entered into the HEC-HMS model. This procedure was executed using the imagery dates of 2005 and 2014. Similar to the land change/land use analysis, these two dates act to compare the changes in runoff potential caused from the transformed land-cover through time. This analysis creates a time series comparison of run-off potential for the study area, enabling the examination of the changing curve numbers through time. To then assess the difference between two afore-mentioned years, the images were reclassified in order to subtract the most recent from the earliest to establish where the largest mutations in curve number (CN) values occurred between the two above years. To examine the change through time, each CN related to the time series was also compared by creating a cross-tabulation matrix. For the results hereof, see section 5.3.

---

27 http://www.hec.usace.army.mil/software/hec-geohms/

3.5.3 Linking physical changes with interviews and surveys

Following the interview process and socio-ecological analysis, a variety of topics often appeared in discussions with community members. Land-change, the demise of the banana production and of agriculture, as well as a community involvement proved to be factors not only in a transforming landscape surrounding Salybia but also in the territory as a whole. For this reason, in collaboration with Dilianie Darroux, a survey was developed in order to investigate the main elements of any landscape change as revealed through field work as well as the topics dealt with in the afore-mentioned interviews. This survey sought information relevant to a variety of landscape changes, including significant territory, hamlet and land changes. Special attention was paid to topics regarding agriculture, water resources, and community activities (*e.g.*, economic, education and political changes). Finally, demographic information was also collected (*e.g.*, on age, gender, hamlet location). Implemented in the Kalinago Territory over a 4-week period (in casu mid-January 2016 – to mid-February 2016), this survey (which would usually take between 15 and 20 min. to complete) was administered in person, whereby the interviewer wrote down the spoken answers of the respondent. All in all, seventy-one households, covering c.11% hereof, were surveyed (Central Statistical Office and Finance 2011).

This survey included an additional land mapping component whereby interested individuals could map their land boundaries with a handheld GPS unit in order to determine their acreage. As the Kalinago Territory is communal land, no one holds an individual land title. However, individuals do cultivate or build their own houses on designated plots. For this reason, knowing an exact acreage would be useful for understanding how land in the Kalinago Territory is being used. Furthermore, as this research was developed with community partners at the Extension Office of the Department of Agriculture of Dominica, these mapped lands would also lead to valuable information to how land is being cultivated in the Kalinago Territory. Knowledge concerning the exact acreage, the correct amount of pesticides or fertilizers, often provided by the Department of Agriculture, would now be available. Finally, this procedure enabled the acquired spatial data (*i.e.*, on the land-cover and acreage of each participant's land) to be connected with each participant's personal perceptions of landscape change. For the complete survey, see Appendix D, Table 48.

Similar to the database analysis conducted for the case study on St. Kitts, basic statistics first assessed the data collected in the implemented survey in the Kalinago. This involved descriptive and inferential statistics, including measures (*e.g.*, frequency, median, mean) to get to grips with the overall dataset.

The majority 43 out of 71 (60.6%) of the respondents was male, a normal outcome as the Kalinago Territory is a rural society, implying that mainly men walking on a road are encountered. In addition, 42.3% of the respondents consisted of 20-30 year olds. This majority can be explained as this territory has a relatively young population overall (Central Statistical Office and Finance 2011) whereas 48.3% of the respondents originated from the Salybia/Point hamlet area. Furthermore, as the researcher was based here, more interaction occurred in this hamlet where the Kalinago Council and the SHARP reside too. For all the demographic distributions, see Appendix D, Tables 48-51.

The land-change overall, land-change within hamlet, land-change within the Kalinago Territory
Agriculture production, soil fertility, crop yield, input amount
Water resources
Community change, community activities, education possibilities, political changes, business opportunities, ease to start a business
Desired Future: For the Kalinago Territory to stay the same, to have more nature, to have more development, to have more agriculture

Table 10. Explored relationships applying the MCA.

To ensure that the data could be analyzed effectively, relevant aggregations had to be established within the database. As subsequent data analysis relied on a Multiple Correspondence Analysis (MCA)[28], the dataset had to account for any possible influences, as MCA is sensitive to the frequency distribution of the categories of the analyzed variables in the sense that it attributes more weight to the categories with lower frequencies. Hence, original variables were recoded, while aggregating the categories related to the negative and the positive perception of changes. First, variables considering the perceived modifications to land and territory are analyzed together, including land-changes, territory changes and hamlet changes. The values range from between 1 and 5, whereby 1 = very negative, 2 = negative, 3 = positive, 4 = very positive, 5 = not affected. This aggregation was modified to: 1 = very negative, 2 = negative, 3 = positive or not affected. Variables concerning agricultural production and community changes were aggregated in the same way in order to ensure an accurate representation of results. For the original distribution of the data prior to the aggregation of values together with the newly aggregated variables and their frequency distribution, see Appendix D, Figs. 54-56. In order to analyze the data properly using MCA, a number of dimensions have to be chosen. Numerous ways exist to determine the dimension number, however, this research determined dimension number by following the rule of thumb that the total inertia explained by dimensions chosen be greater than 0.8. Depending on the variable relationships explored, either two or three dimensions explained 85% of the total inertia in each analysis. Accordingly, the number of dimensions used in the analyses varies in subsequent chapter 5, section 4.2 and 4.4 (VanPool and Leonard 2011). The resulting database analyzed the variable relationships found in Table 10.

3.6 Final thoughts: challenges and partnerships

The present chapter has dealt with the underlying methodological design. Before addressing the results of each case study (see chapters 4 and 5), the methodological challenges, including possible biases resulting from qualitative data and GIS errors, remain important to discuss. Needless to say, researcher biases occur inevitably in

---

28 A Multiple Correspondence Analysis comprises an extension of correspondence analysis (CA) which allows one to analyze the pattern of relationships of several categorical dependent variables. As such, it can also be seen as a generalization of principal component analysis when the variables to be analyzed are categorical instead of quantitative (Abdi and Valentin 2007).

any kind of study involving multiple datasets. Deliberating on these possible limitations from the start of the research ensures a methodological design that alleviates a number of these concerns. From the very onset, community collaboration establishes the research direction. This approach guarantees the intended direction of the research as relevant to local communities discussed in each case study. Moreover, these methods are varied and flexible, acknowledging the multidisciplinary nature of the data as well as the complexity of the research questions. Accordingly, it is important to be aware hereof before embarking upon any research. A variety of control measures were implemented in order to limit these partialities.

As this study evolved from collaboration and exchange with local partners, the researcher's presence in the community was accepted, establishing trust with stakeholders, and, ultimately, data reliability. The research questions and methodology evolved from community collaboration, ensuring that possible researcher biases remained limited. Ethical standards including anonymity, disclosure of research purpose and interviewee's full control over their data, certified that participation was based only on the interviewee's desire and interest. Each interviewee on St. Kitts and in the Kalinago Territory was given the opportunity to acquire the audio recording and transcription of their interview.

To limit interview biases, the present research applied rigorous quantitative methods (*e.g.*, coding, network analysis, surveys) and standardized qualitative data collection (*e.g.*, field work observations, interviews) to answer research questions pertaining to community perceptions and values of the landscape (Oomen and Aroyo 2011). However, these interviews do not represent the only sources of data, as they serve to inform other subsequent methods such as spatial analysis and statistical methods derived from survey data.

Spatial data presents methodological considerations. Considering the defined or precise results obtained in spatial analysis, the method highlights the possible differences between perceived change and the described analyzed change. Scale always remains an issue as, as the GIS and the spatial analysis work at a specific scale, whereas the analyzing of landscape change occurs across scalar boundaries.

As mentioned above, available spatial imagery often insufficiently covers the Caribbean region. However, due to a generous grant from the Digital Globe Foundation, the satellite data in this study is some of the best available data for the region. Whereas an analysis remains contingent on the availability of imagery and other relevant data, an additional and more advanced analysis may not be possible due to the lack of data and software licenses. These limitations all point to the main issue: a GIS analysis is a representation of reality, and never the actual reality itself. A spatial model can never contain the nuances and subtleties of a landscape.

When it was possible, all software used was open source. Furthermore, all methods and analyses (regarding GIS/Remote Sensing, the survey database) were not only explained but also shared with community partners, the Ministry of Environment and Planning (St. Kitts), and the Department of Planning (Dominica) in order to not only ensure the continued application but also transfer of knowledge. Interview data are more sensitive than methods and analyses. Consequently, the transcriptions and audio recordings are placed in long term storage at the Data Archiving and Network Services (DANS). As with all research, the issue concerning the long-term storage of both qualitative and quantitative data comes into play (McLain *et al.* 2013). In order to overcome this and other concerns, the present study builds its methods in close cooperation with local stakeholders. All community partners have access to their particular interviews if desired. Moreover, collaboration with local governmental agencies enabled appropriate storage methods to be followed, implying that these agencies and the key community members have received copies of all the data and results.

Finally, this dissertation would not have been possible without the trust and support of the communities' active within the study area. Throughout the research process, methods and interactions with community members always followed a personal code of respect as well as the Nexus Ethics Code and the code of conduct at Leiden University. Despite sincere efforts to establish an open dialogue and collaborative research base, this dissertation clearly represents only a specific perspective of each case study. In pursuing ethical research, this dissertation will never describe absoluteness. However, the four years of time devoted to the entirety of this research project does offer an insight into the reality of authentic and complex relationship between community and land.

4

The coastal villages of St. Kitts
The bitterness of sugar

Heading west from the busy bus station of Basseterre, St. Kitts' capital, the road winds along the coast, weaving through hamlets and vistas of wide Caribbean bays. The apex of Mount Liamuiga rises in the distance surrounded by rolling green fields that eventually descend to meet villages that line the shore. The empty fields offer a beautiful yet stark contrast to the crowded shores dotted with houses. Leading west from Basseterre, near the village of Challengers, the road passes through a forested area and crosses the Bloody River. A short walk up the ghaut[29] from this river leads to a spectacular view presenting petroglyphs lining the high walls of the gully. The first settlers of St. Kitts, Amerindians moved northward from South America to settle on the island. During the 17th century, members of this Amerindian group were massacred at Bloody River when, according to historical sources, the French and English troops stationed on the island betrayed the trust of the Kalinago, trapping them inside this ghaut. Popular legend accounts that this river ran red with blood for days, hence the names Bloody River and Bloody Point which refer to the promontory on the coast. The surviving Amerindians fled further south to the islands of Dominica, St. Lucia and St. Vincent. The pre-European presence of the Amerindians on St. Kitts left traces, such as the Stone Fort petroglyphs near the village of Challengers and scatters of pottery sherds recovered from archaeological sites situated all over the island (Armstrong 1978; Dyde 2005; Goodwin 1978; Goodwin 1979; Hoffman 1973; de Ruiter 2012).

Traveling past Challengers, the village of Old Road Town (commonly referred to as Old Road) is reached. Here Sir Thomas Warner landed in 1624, marking the start of the English presence on St. Kitts. The fertile and lush landscape presented him with a welcome change from the swampy lands he had experienced in Guiana (Dyde 2005). The road from Old Road Town leads through the village of Halfway Tree, so named after its location at the half way point between Basseterre and Sandy Point Town (commonly referred to as

---

29   Ghauts, ghauts, or gulleys, are deep ravines leading from higher elevations down towards the coast.

Sandy Point). Winding past an impressive colonial fortress, the largest in the Eastern Caribbean and known as Brimstone Hill, the road eventually leads to Sandy Point Town which is larger than the other villages located in the case study area, as it was once the British administrative center and the island's first town with a flourishing port. That legacy is evident thanks to the local road and street names, many of which copy those of well-known English streets, such as Downing Street.

At Downing Street the road forks. Following the road down towards the sea, the village of Fig Tree appears, a small and isolated fishing village. When the French arrived here in 1625, a year after the British, the colonists divided the island into a French and British section, separated by means of a boundary line. Fig Tree marked the endpoint not only of that line but also of the region examined in this case study.

Today, the main island road winds through the 11 villages of the study area. The Caribbean coast often right near the edge of the road. On the other side, vast, overgrown fields of defunct sugar fields border the towns. Most towns have access to the sea coast, with Old Road, Sandy Point and Fig Tree being traditional fishing villages, though no data exists on the amount of fish catches from this area. There are 2 secondary schools and 2 primary schools in the study area. There are 8 churches of various Christian denominations in the study area. As community partners contributed and collaborated throughout the research process, all the acquired data was stored at the St. Kitts Department of Physical Planning and Environment, making it available for any future land management plans.

This chapter presents the results of field work conducted along the Caribbean coast of St. Kitts. Drawing on the collaboratively developed research focus, this case study explores the changing landscape and subsequent impacts on socio-ecological indicators (as defined in chapter 3.4) i.e., the multiple uses of lands, resource conservation and socio-cultural aspects. Discussed in section 3.4, these aspects are further investigated by means of stakeholder surveys and the GIS mapping of key physical indicators to assess the impact of landscape change on cultural ecosystem services. Part I (see below) offers a brief physical overview of the region, connecting the landscape to the historical forces that shaped it. In particular, this section deals with (a) the shaping of the physical and cultural landscape of this small region by exploring the transformative impact of historical forces while centering on the outcome of the early growth, lengthy dominance, and (b) the recent collapse of the sugar cane industry, and its effect on the society, politics, public space and environment. Part II (see below) draws on both GIS and interview/survey data in order to examine the impact of these forces on the land-use/land-cover and coastal erosion, and on the socio-ecological indicators discussed in chapter 3. Part III (see below) presents the preliminary conclusions of the case study.

Part I. A recent history of the Kittitian landscape

4.1 St. Kitts under British colonization

The story of sugar was not all sweetness. Sugar and slavery developed hand in hand in the English islands

Dunn 1973, 189.

The historic accounts recorded by Peter Lindström, a Swedish engineer, who visited St. Kitts in 1654, reveal his amazement when he describes "a very fertile island, there grows oranges, lemons, sweet oranges, potatoes, bananas, sugar, tobacco, nutmegs, walnuts, chestnuts, grapes, red, blue, white and brown pepper and ginger and innumerable quantity of all kinds of valuable and rare fruit" (Dyde 2005; Lindeström 1925, 75). This observation would sadly stand in stark contrast to the island's future landscape.

With the signing of the Treaty of Utrecht in 1717 (Crist 1949), St. Kitts came entirely under British control. It was to be administered jointly with Anguilla, Nevis and the British Virgin Islands. As the island of Barbados had already been ecologically depleted due to producing sugar cane from 1640 on, the island of St. Kitts provided fertile soils, suitable for the planting and cultivation of sugar cane (Richardson 1983, 10). During the 17th century, this isle was quickly divided into large plantations, leading to the demise of small land owners and agricultural diversity. Extensive tracts of land were planted with cash crops such as indigo, tobacco, coffee, and finally sugar cane (Charles 2007; Dyde 2005; Mahler 1981). Little was done during the early stages of the colonial rule to encourage any social development on St. Kitts. Rather, attention and resources focused on expanding the production of monocrops (Rouse-Jones 1977). Whereas it was indeed rightfully called a "social failure" (Rouse-Jones 1977, 221), St. Kitts did become one of the best examples of the British sugar empire, as it proved to be an ideal location for mono agriculture thanks to its fertile soils and relatively flat landscape. British landowners reaped the benefits of these geographical features as St. Kitts became the "single richest colony in the British empire" (Nisbett 2008, 963) based on its size and population, exporting more than 9000 tons of sugar per annum during the heyday of the sugar industry (Dyde 2005, 84). With sugar production, a new era of plantation culture began, shaping Kittitian life, with lasting impacts till today (Charles 2007).

4.1.1 The impact of the sugar industry on historical land-use and society

Three centuries dominated by the cultivation and processing of sugar cane present the most tangible examples of historic dependency and exploitation on St. Kitts. Indeed, one would be hard-pressed to understand the local pattern of land-use/land-change or the interconnections of culture and nature, as well as the current relationships to this landscape without taking account of the impact of sugar on the Kittitian landscape and society (Fleming 1987; Richardson 1983).

The legacies of sugar and plantation society live on in the current land degradation and societal divisions. First, the extreme shift in land-use and land-cover required the transformation of turning St. Kitts into a sugar exporting powerhouse and had a major impact from the very onset of the planting cycle. Intensive agriculture, especially of sugar cane, degrades the soil immensely. The natural geomorphology of the island compounds this issue, with its sloping fields and porous soils located on the mountain sides separated by deep ghauts. In the event of heavy rains, these denuded soils wash away quickly either into the ghauts or the sea (Crist 1949). Furthermore, the overexploitation of land has created infertile soils, which have ultimately led to the importation of expensive fertilizers. Forests were cut down in order to make way for sugar cane fields. As trees are key actors in climatic and water cycles, this deforestation has eventually caused a lower water supply (Crist 1949). While such intensive agricultural regimes occur in other examples, it is important to note that the entirety of the arable land on St. Kitts "was destabilized, modified, and depleted by centuries of colonial control" (Richardson 1983, 8).

One of the most socially influential and exploitative aspects of the plantation economy comprises the dependency on the institution of slavery. The arduous, dangerous and labor-intensive process of sugar production required a huge work force. Over 115,000 enslaved Africans were transported to St. Kitts (Rouse-Jones 1977). At the height of the sugar plantations, the enslaved African population outnumbered Europeans by 8 to 1 (Rouse-Jones 1977, 100). In fact, Angola Town was named after the large number of newcomers with Central African roots (Nisbett 2008).

By the 18th century, 90% of the land on St. Kitts – and virtually all the fertile soil – was utilized for growing sugar cane for exportation, leaving little space to build settlements on. In fact, many present-day villages are still historically located at a fringe, or in areas where growing sugar cane was impossible, and not at a location which benefits the population. These villages grew crowded, leaving little land for any community planting. Landowners were obliged to provide "one acre for every ten Negroes, exclusive of plots or gardens which the slaves cultivated on their own account" (Crist 1949, 139). Land for the enslaved and eventual day laborers was never made available for any farming near villages. Instead, sugar laborers would have to ascend Mount Liamuiga, where small plots of crops were cultivated and livestock raised. This tradition passed from generation to generation (Pulsipher 1994). Providing food and provisions, these small plots became indispensable for village communities in order to keep starvation at bay (Crist 1949; Greening 2014; Richardson 1983).

As profit was essential, any wealth acquired from producing sugar was rarely invested back into St. Kitts towards stimulating the development or the infrastructure in order to create any livelihood diversification for its inhabitants. The consequences of slavery deeply affected the social hierarchy of the colony because a small group of affluent white landowners found themselves co-residing on a small island with a large population consisting of skilled, enslaved peoples. The former group lived in constant fear of the latter, resulting in strict rules which not only influenced the sociality of slave villages, but also the subsequent land relationships of those enslaved (Crist 1949). Colonial authorities never envisaged St. Kitts to evolve into a productive society including community and land. It was more "the place where England finds it convenient to carry on the production of sugar, coffee, and a few tropical commodities" (Mill 1885, 693).

4.1.2 Land after slavery

The Latifundia perdidere the Antilles, as they did Italy of old. The vicious system brought its own Nemesis

Crist 1949, 144.

The Emancipation Act of 1833 (Sheridan 1961) slowly began the process of formally ending slavery, declaring that all children born as slaves and under the age of 6 would be set free on August 1, 1834 (Dyde 2005, 153). The remaining enslaved population was declared Apprentices, or indentured servants, to their former owners. This ruling involved being paid 40.5 hours a week for working for their previous owners over a period of 6 years. This measure was justified as a stage of adjustment in the Commonwealth, because many rich plantation owners did not wish to lose the possibility of profiting from free labor (Richardson 1998, 275). Rightly so, this system of apprenticeship led to great discontent among the enslaved as it was not an envisioned or deserved freedom. However, as there was little available land, the majority of the previously enslaved had few options, effectively forcing them to continue working on the sugar plantations.

Even after the abolishment of slavery in 1834 (Parliaments 1833), little actually changed within the social hierarchy, leading to a continual division of community and land on St. Kitts. The sugar industry remained as the only type of employment, reinforcing century old marginalization. The lives of now indentured laborers resembled far too closely the lives of those previously enslaved, as both livelihood flexibility and land continued to be unobtainable for villagers (Crist 1949; Dyde 2005; Fleming 1987; Greening 2014; Richardson 1983).

Conflicting ideas on freedom and possibilities resulted in protests and sugar cane arson on St. Kitts (Richards 1988). A large number of indentured laborers also fled to the central mountain range, including Marcus, "King of the Woods". He was renowned for his courage and had escaped the plantation on which he worked, seeking refuge in the woods located behind a village named Challengers. The founding of "free villages" proved to be one of the first attempts to create any livelihood diversity. Challengers was the first of these villages. Founded in 1840, it was named after John Challenger, a black customs officer who had started to sell and lease land in small plots, arousing great fear of such independence among the neighboring plantation owners. Eventually, the presence of idle land resulting from former sugar estates (e.g., Sadlers, St. Pauls's, and Tabernacle) led to the founding of other free villages on the island (Dyde 2005).

Although the sugar estates were supposed to provide land to workers under a gentlemen's agreement of sorts, any implementation of this understanding proved quite insufficient. Finally, in 1942, legislation was passed to rectify this situation. This law forced plantation owners to reserve a mandatory 20% of their land for food crops (Crist 1949). As expected, this new law was vehemently opposed by sugar estate owners. It is noted that the land situation remained unaltered as "there are few independent farmers; the best land is for the most part used for the big cash crops" (Crist 1949, 141). Rented by laborers from the sugar estates, small agricultural plots for personal use continued to exist high up in the mountains. Such a continuation of sugar land relations only further exacerbated the land degradation and land scarcity, as many residents and laborers on St. Kitts have since faced a future of either unemployment or migration.

4.1.3 Shaping the landscape: independence and land

In 1976, the Government of St. Kitts ultimately nationalized the sugar industry, which covered "roughly 80% or over 32,000 acres (129.50 km2) of land" (Greening 2014, 65). The Labor Movement, and in particular Robert Bradshaw,[30] orchestrated this key turning point in the island's own path towards independence, which eventually materialized in 1983, and its relationship to land (Hubbard 2002). The power of the ruling class comprising planters had now been broken, terminating the extreme colonial-implemented and socio-economic divisions on the island.

Unfortunately, even as St. Kitts moved through the process of independence and as sugar became less and less profitable, the newly independent Kittitian government did little to increase any local land access or to diversify into other agricultural products. For example, we see evidence of a similar situation when reading that "perhaps more than any other Caribbean nation, the Kittitian economy is dependent on the fluctuating prices and markets of sugar. St. Kitts is virtually the only Caribbean island where sugar still maintains its historic stronghold" (Fleming 1987, 9-10). This fact is visible in the land tenure of the island at that time.

In 1975, just prior to the nationalization of the sugar industry, there were 2,466 highland farms, or mountain grounds, on St. Kitts. As many as 1,968 farms covered less than 1 acre (0.004 km2) (Richardson 1998). Twelve years later, the 1987 census would indicate an increase of 3000 small farms throughout the island which by and large yet again merely measured less than 3 acres (0.012 km2) (Association 1990, 141). Throughout the 1990s, sugar would remain the economic mainstay of this island. The island's 176 km2 was divided into only sixty-six unique estates, as all land remained covered with sugar plantations (Association 1990). These land tenure statistics suggest how little was done to create any land access for individuals on St. Kitts, preserving its land-related economic and societal divisions.

Such little progress in land tenure could be understood hypothetically if sugar was indeed still an economically profitable product. However, it is reported that despite the sugar industry continuing, "its future prospects hardly look as bright as in decades in the past" (Association 1990, 9). In fact, such concerns over land access and shifting away from growing sugar cane had been discussed as early as the late 1940s (Crist 1949). During the independence movement, the new government leaders not only discussed alternatives to sugar cane but also a push for agricultural products (Edwards and Jacque 2007; Fleming 1987). Nevertheless, no planned and prepared transformation in land-use occurred. This lack of action resulted in a similar post-independence landscape as had existed during the colonial landscape. According to the 1990 CAA document, the government did not intend to sell the

---

30 Robert Bradshaw (1916 – 1978) supported the Labor Movement and was sympathetic to the sugar workers plight for better working conditions and wages. He became an influential politician in the Kittitian independence movement, instrumenting talks on self-rule with the British colonial power but. sadly passed away before St. Kitts gained independence. See Fleming 1987; Hubbard 2002.

land, making it the sole owner of 90% of the land on St. Kitts (Association 1990). This situation has led to unclear tenure agreements, the outcome of which was: small land owners were not only less likely to try to obtain more land, but also less likely to improve the land. The social structure of the plantocracy/slavocracy which had existed for 300 years was still locked into place, "with the government now acting in the position of the planters" (Hubbard 2002, 152), affecting the economy, politics and, most importantly, any relationship to the land.

4.1.4 The collapse of the sugar industry in 2006

> *Sugar cane, to which everything else had been sacrificed, proved sometimes, indeed, a valuable servant: but too often a tyrannous and capricious Master*
>
> Crist 1949, 145.

Sugar production on St. Kitts declined, largely as a result of external market forces, but it took a powerful exogenous shock to force a large-scale transformation in the pattern of land. This upheaval took the shape of international trade rule measures that removed the preferential tariff and quota treatment for the sugar imported from St. Kitts sugar to the UK, resulting in the collapse of this Caribbean isle's sugar industry in 2005 (Ahmed 2001; UN and CEPAL 2005).

During the mid-2000s, all preferential access to the EU markets terminated for the Caribbean islands, consequently resulting in the demise of the cash-crop industries and of the rural employment ((OECS) 2005). As the sugar cane agriculture came to an exhaustive end in 2006, alternatives were regarded as imperative to "replace the empty 4,500 hectares (45 km2) of land" (Greening 2014, 65). Following the shutdown of the sugar industry, the associated nationalized land was earmarked for a variety of applications in accordance with the St. Christopher National Physical Development Plan (Board *et al.* 2006). The 15-year plan earmarked 6.5% of the land for agriculture (Development Control and Planning Board. 2006). Yet, strangely, few changes have been made on St. Kitts. Sadly, despite all the talk of undertaking a planned diversification of land-use and adopting technological advancements in agriculture, no long-term land-use project seems to be enacted.

However, instead of a landscape evolution, the land-use has remained relatively static due to the following related factors:

- Any land access is still impossible for the majority of the residents of St. Kitts. The process of actually obtaining land from the government is both lengthy and arduous. A large part of the land may appear to be fallow (i.e., at the stage of crop rotation in which the land is deliberately not used to raise a crop) while it is in the process of being redistributed (A19 2016). Land ownership continues to be out of reach for many Kittitians (Greening 2014). A 2015 study reveals that despite the fact that 78% of Kittitians own their homes, whereas only 35% possess the land surrounding it (Lowitt *et al.* 2015, 1371). Of the farmers interviewed, only 8% possess their farm. However, the results of the present research would refute the claim: Kittitians are not interested in their land and especially not in small land holdings located in the mountains.

- The colonial intervention of the landscape only emphasizes the importance of mountain grounds to Kittitians, as it was one of the few uncontrolled spaces accessible to them. As many indigenous ethnic groups were eliminated as a result of European control in the Caribbean, the importation of enslaved Africans led to completely new interactions with a foreign landscape, which were "invariably mediated and determined by a white planter class" (Richardson 1983, 7). It has been noted that many believe "that highland agriculture on the island is a throwback to plantation days when mountain plots were allocated for slave farming" (Richardson 1983, 40). These mountain grounds became extremely important aspects of daily life (Clark 2013; Goveia 1965). Similar to the situation encountered for instance on the isle of St. John, any leftover land was given to slaves, presenting families with the possibility to complement their limited rations. This left-over land remains an important beacon in post-sugar landscapes. As has been explained in research carried out on St. John, the reaction of creating a mountain ground envisioned that "people have staked out a life situated within changing fields of global relations" (Olwig 1999, 440).
- On a local scale, the creation of family land, such as mountain grounds, was an act of resistance to slavery. Therefore, the significance of these grounds should be noted, as its cultural and historic background envelops more than a simple Caribbean land-use system (Besson 1987, 1995; Olwig 1995). Many have cited the legacy of the oppressive plantation life as the reason why the younger generations in the Caribbean of today refuse to work in agriculture. However, this simple abstraction of the historical context and the present-day land scarcity can be refuted by much evidence encountered in the Caribbean (Fleming 1987; Greening 2014; Olwig 1980, 1999; Richardson 1983). Owning land signifies "pride, prestige and a sense of rootedness" (Richardson 1998). Examples hereof can be found throughout colonization and concern the importance of land to maroon communities, runaway slaves and revolts during the 1800s (Richardson 1983).
- As land redistribution has still not occurred at a quick enough pace, these mountain grounds represent part of the only available land to many Kittitians. Nonetheless, even this mountain land has become inaccessible in the past decades (2000s). As the lower elevation sugar land was not redistributed, it has remained virtually untouched after sugar production. Whereas the undisturbed land has supported biodiversity and forest regrowth, these environmental changes have further influenced any land access and subsequent successful farming. Due to this regrowth, the mountain grounds are inaccessible as land, and roads leading up to the small agricultural plots remain unmanaged and overgrown. As much as 73% of surveyed farmers identify pests, in particular the Grivet African Green Monkey (Chlorocebus aethiops), as one of the most challenging aspects of producing a successful crop (Lowitt *et al.* 2015, 1372). Historical evidence suggests these monkeys first arrived on St. Kitts during the 18th century, when French colonists introduced them as pets from West Africa (Rodrigues 1984).

- St. Kitts has replaced one monoculture with another or the economic machine of tourism (Greening 2014, 74). Tourism began to develop during the 1980s, but major capital was required for initial investments, making the transition difficult and unsteady. The current similarities, as the dependency on monoculture and tourism are undeniable; they continue to lead to little land access for local villages. Tourism is an unreliable and unpredictable market, often results in the concentration of economic return in the hands of few with a minimal trickle down into local villages.

Additionally, the government started the "Citizenship-by-Investment" program in 1984, on which is commented that it "allows foreign nationals to purchase land at a certain cost in exchange for Kittitian citizenship and the added perks of access and travel to certain European countries" (Greening 2014, 65). This policy again reduces land access to local communities. Tourism has been historically concentrated in the southeastern peninsula of St. Kitts. By confining this socio-economic phenomenon to a specific part of the island, little economic development or investment into local markets has occurred elsewhere (Greening 2014; Samuel 2011), leading again to isolation of these communities. Although a certain push has been observed to encourage eco-tourism on St. Kitts, this has only further separated Kittitians from their land as "resources through new forms of labor focused on individual and direct interaction with foreign visitors, rather than collective, group work directly with the land" (Greening 2014, 74). Land on St. Kitts continues to be the island's main "bounty" (Clark 2013, 42), as the economy has never developed past a "monopolized system dependent on a main foreign exchange earner which happened to be land based" (Clark 2013, 42). Land access for local populations continues to be limited as the current situation has pitted agriculture, tourism and local communities against each other (Clark 2013).

Finally, as the sugar industry was never allowed to terminate gradually in the aftermath of economic downturns occurring throughout the 19th and 20th centuries, no independent middle class evolved on St. Kitts. On other Caribbean isles, however, we see a shift from sugar or other monocrops to a diversity of crops either during the Independence Era (1960 -1970) depending on the location, or shortly thereafter, offering innovative ways for local communities to gain access to land. For example, the plantation system terminated much more naturally and earlier on Nevis, the sister island of St. Kitts. Here land-use was not entrenched with sugar cane cultivation mainly because of a more mountainous topography. It has been reported that "Land-use contrasts between the two islands are therefore reflected by cultural differences between Kittitians and Nevisians" (Richardson 1998, 375). Unfortunately, this phenomenon has not been recorded on St. Kitts.

Whereas the sugar industry was the most profitable, "Kittitian workers became some of the most impoverished" (Fleming 1987, 309), as the colonial past left an inheritance of deprived rural communities and environments (Richardson 1983). This context has led to the continuation of historically impoverished rural settlements as well as to an increasing reliance on food imports – indeed an incomprehensible dilemma when considering the quantity of fertile land on St. Kitts (Fleming 1987; Greening 2014). Colonial exploitation has created a system of being "precariously dependent upon imported food, fuel, clothing and building materials", a system that has continued to the present day (Richardson 1983, 377). In fact, it has been asserted that the vulnerability of St. Kitts stems from the fact it has entirely depended on sugar ever since colonial times (Clark 2013, 12).

Accordingly, we can observe a continuation of the ecological deterioration of the land that "can be explained not so much by the fact that people and land have been historically combined, but that they have been separated" (Richardson 1983, 172). The historic context of sugar production in combination with subsequent land degradation and push towards tourism has led to the depletion of natural and agricultural diversity as well as to the impeding of the development of an established working middle class (Fleming 1987). Unfortunately, this event is not uncommon in the history of colonization as many European countries have exploited resources in distant landscapes. Such examples can be found globally but widespread in the Caribbean region, leaving behind new relationships between land and community.

Part II. Landscape: use, modification and value

I used to do a lot of planting when I was young. Used to go up in the mountain, I used to do that a lot, but [not] *today.*

A27 2014.

4.2 Multiple use of lands: analyzing the land-cover change

The dominance and prolonged cultivation of sugar cane on St. Kitts is unique to the Caribbean. Not only has the spatial hegemony of land access remained relatively similar as vast fields now lie fallow after the collapse of the sugar industry, but the social hierarchy continues and perpetuates the normalcy of land-use, as land owners are few. Even with the conclusion of the Sugar Era, the Kittitian landscape continues to reproduce symbols of oppression, vast wealth, or heritage. As the discussion in Part I illustrates, land availability and fertility was not the problem. The issue lies in the social structures which not only created but were also left encrusted in the evolving landscape. If much of the land now lies fallow or is diverted towards the development of tourism, it replicates historic land-use patterns, providing goods and services which remain unavailable to local Kittitians as were sugar and sugar revenues in the past (Clark 2013; Found and Berbés-Blázquez 2012).

This section will explore the changing landscape of St. Kitts by merging the results of land- change/land-cover satellite analysis with interview perceptions and survey data. As a starting point, the land-use/land-cover change was analyzed in order to investigate the impact of the collapse of sugar cane cultivation on the case study landscape. As mentioned in Part I, the sugar cane agriculture had occupied the larger part of the island's surface, including the case study area, for over 300 years until this industry came to an end in 2006. As discussed in chapter 3, in order to analyze any landscape changes, and in this case, the modifications ensuing from the termination of the sugar cane agriculture, satellite imagery dating to between 2006 and 2015 served to create a time series of land-changes. Combining the 2006 imagery data with the comparable data for the same landscape in 2015,

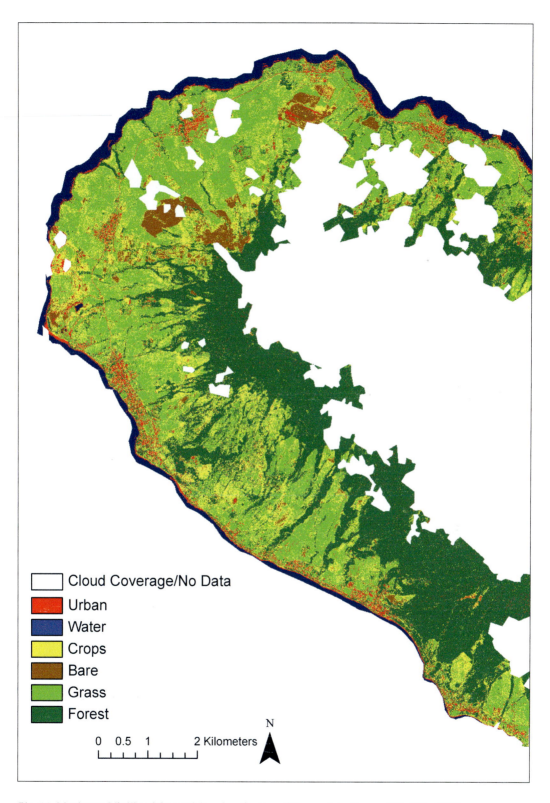

Fig. 14. Maximum Likelihood Supervision classification of the coastal villages of St. Kitts, 2006.

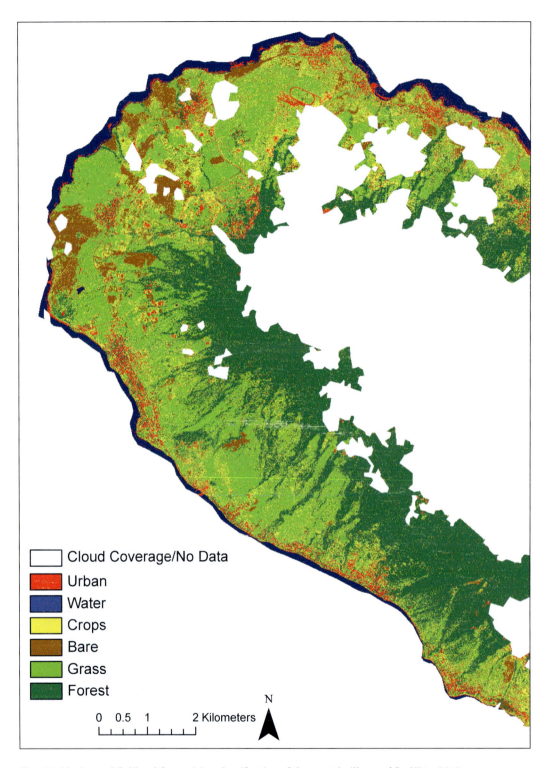

Fig. 15. Maximum Likelihood Supervision classification of the coastal villages of St. Kitts, 2015.

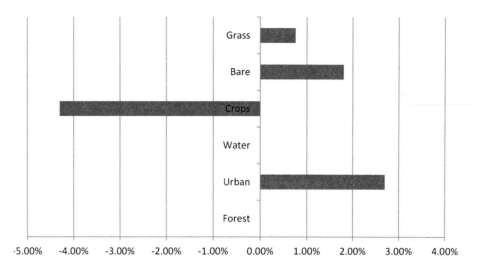

Fig. 16. Total percentage of each land class regarding the gains and losses (2006-2015), the coastal villages of St. Kitts.

the land-use/land-cover changes were revealed. This satellite imagery was classified by means of ArcGIS Maximum Likelihood Supervised Classification. For the results of the classified 2006 and 2015 images, see Figs. 14 and 15.

The results presented in Figs. 14 and 15 illustrate a modification of a decline of forest and increase in grasslands and urban areas located within the study area on St. Kitts. These results are broken down further (see Fig. 16) and indicate an overall decline in crop (-4.30%), and forest (-0.01%) covered areas. No change in water is observed. For this reason, changes in water will not be considered in the subsequent analysis, because of the imagery used for classification of the coastal villages of St. Kitts; the surrounding Caribbean Sea was classified as well, implying that water pixels occupy a large amount of total overall pixels. We can observe an overall increase in the urban (2.70%), bare (1.80%) and grass (0.76%) sectors. While these percentages may seem small, only 9 years has passed, revealing a rapidly changing landscape of an area covering less than 100 km2. These results also provide a preliminary indication of the type of occurring land-change.

To further understand these calculations, specifically where a land-change takes place, the two classified images of 2006 and 2015 serve to create an image that identifies where land-cover shift towards the new types of land class. The specific modifications are presented in Appendix E, Figs. 70-74. For the landscape transformations occurring between 2006 and 2015, see Fig. 17.

These preliminary results reveal a changing landscape within the coastal study area of St. Kitts. Not surprisingly this study area is increasingly urban (2.70%) with other increases in bare (1.80%) and grasses (0.70%). Crops drastically declined (-4.30) in comparison with the rest of the land cover classes. Interestingly, forest declined only slightly (-0.01). Such a slight decline might appear unexpected in an increasingly urbanized area; however, the forested areas represent part of the natural reserve that makes up Mount Liamuiga. The next step of the present research investigates the transitions between land class types as either gains, or loses, at the expense of another type of land class.

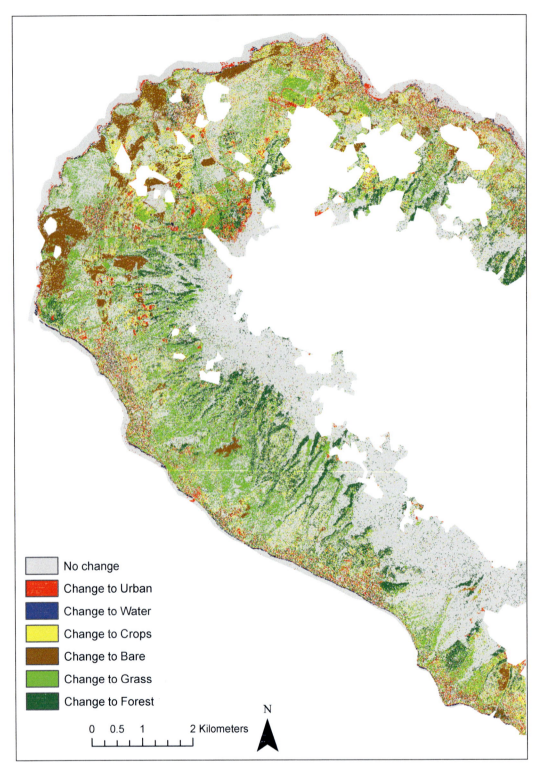

Fig. 17. Overall land class changes of the coastal villages of St. Kitts, indicating land cover modifications between and 2006 to 2015.

Land Class Type	2006 Area	2006 Coverage	2015 Area	2015 Coverage
Urban	34556.49 ha.	4.0%	57687.48 ha.	6.7%

Table 11. Total acreage changes of land class Urban

Land Class Type	2006 Area	2006 Coverage	2015 Area	2015 Coverage
Bare	35488.8 ha.	4.1%	50604.48 ha.	5.9%

Table 12. Total acreage changes of land class Bare.

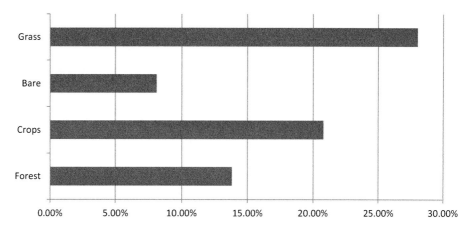

Fig. 18. Urban gains: contributions from other land classes, 2006-2015.

First, we consider the changes to the "Urban" land class which have increased significantly (+2.6%) during the nine-year period. For the exact acreage increase of the total land cover, see Table 11.

Fig. 18 presents the transitions from other land classes to the gains observed in the "Urban" land class.

The "Urban" land class type has gained the most from "Grass" (28.66%), and "Crops" (20.88%) land class types. These transitions can be explained by the demise of the sugar-cane cultivation and other agricultural-related activities in the study area. Grasses can indicate land that remains grass or overgrowth throughout the time, and most likely as well, land that remains fallow but will be planted.

As the case study area becomes more and more urbanized, any land-changes will of course result in underdeveloped land converting into urban areas, explaining the contributions from "Bare" and "Forest". As mentioned before, the forest remains mainly intact in St. Kitts due to its status as a natural reserve.

Second, we may consider the changes to the land class "Bare" in Table 12.

The type of modification leading to changes within the land class type "Bare" is explored in Fig. 19. The latter land class type has gained 51.50% from the "Grass" and 26.47% from the "Crops" land class type. This may suggest that numerous previously planted fields are now either fallow or no longer utilized. This assumption would support the described modifications of sugar land to bush land, or overgrown areas, throughout the study area.

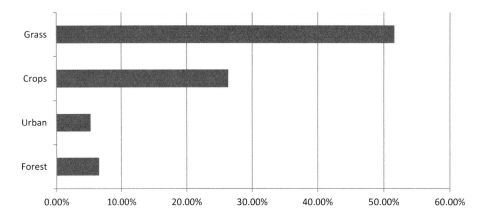

Fig. 19. Bare gains: contributions from other land classes, 2006-2015.

Land Class Type	2006 Area	2006 Coverage	2015 Area	2015 Coverage
Crops	163677.9 ha.	19.1%	127217.79 ha.	15%

Table 13. Total acreage changes of the land class Crops.

Land Class Type	2006 Area	2006 Coverage	2015 Area	2015 Coverage
Grass	273394.26 ha.	32%	279864.63 ha.	33%

Table 14. Total acreage changes of land class Grass.

Third, we consider the changes occurring in the land class type "Crops." For the overall decline in the acreage of "Crops" see Table 13. This phenomenon can be explained by the fact that the sugar cane cultivation has terminated in the study area, resulting in the end of industrial agriculture on St. Kitts.

Fig. 20 deals with the type of gains acquired from other land classes attributed to the new land-cover comprising the land type of "Crops". 46.00% of any crop land swapped from the land class of grasses. As a reminder, this does not mean that crops gained in total acreage. In fact, "Crops" declined more than 4%. This statistic, instead, reveals that despite the significant drop in total acreage of crops in the study area, grasses contributed to its total acreage in 2015. This coinciding gain and loss of land class types reveals even more a changing agricultural landscape.

Next, we consider the changes taking place of the "Grass" land type. For the increase of grasses within the study area, see Table 14. Despite this being only one percentage, the study area still is small in size. An increase of one percent of grasses translates to an increase of one percent of unused, under-cultivated and undistributed land.

Fig. 21 indicates the land class type "Grass" has gained significantly from "Crops" (27.00%) and "Forest" (17.30%). This outcome would indeed be consistent with the type of land-change occurring as sugar cane cultivation leads to an increase in fallow, or overgrown, fields.

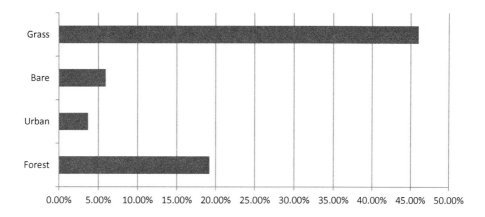

Fig. 20. Crop gains: contributions from other land classes, 2006-2015.

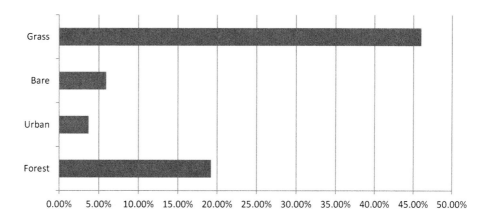

Fig. 21. Grass gains: contributions from other land classes, 2006-2015.

The findings not only suggest that crops have become overgrown but also that agriculture has not continued in traditional areas, such as on mountain grounds. However, when comparing the results regarding land classes of "Grass" and "Crops", it seems to be counterintuitive that both appear to be mutually gaining and losing. This assessment may be an outcome of the difficulty of applying satellite imagery in order to distinguish any reliability between crops and grassland, leading to the misclassification of the "Crops" and "Grass" land type classes. This would result in more pixels being classified as "Crops," when in actual fact; they are "Grass" pixels. Alternatively, it also reconfirms the decline in agriculture because infertile soils located closer to villages and towns within the study area are the result of many years of sugar cane cultivation, leading to a conversion of new land types and an ultimate planting of crops at a further distance.

Finally, we explore the changes taking place in the land class type "Forest." For all the changes observed in this class between 2005 and 2015, see Table 15. Again, while the change is only 1 percent, it is significant considering that most of the forest in the study area is in a natural reserve.

Land Class Type	2006 Area	2006 Coverage	2015 Area	2015 Coverage
Forest	300623.94 ha.	35.2%	292646.07 ha.	34%

Table 15. Total acreage changes of land class Forest.

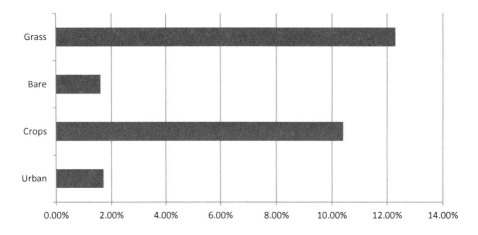

Fig. 22. Forest gains: contributions from other land classes 2006-2015.

For the outcome as further explored by means of the gains acquired from other land classes to the "Forest" land class type, see Fig. 22. The types of gains presented reveal that forest areas, if any shift has occurred, gains from "Grasses" (12.30%) and "Crops (10.40%). However, it is significant to note that these percentages are quite low. Indeed the actual forest cover dating from 2005 more or less occurs at the same location. Moreover, it has lost more rather than obtained any acreage.

All these results, consequently, reflect the lack of any land distribution after the sugar land was nationalized and the industry closed down (see Part I). This outcome is reflected in the changing land-cover types converting to mainly grass land. As the study area lies within a rural part of St. Kitts, there is no great increase in urban development except for a small number of housing developments. While these are representative of a specific model, the land-cover classification data presented here throughout in the Figures and Tables reveal that significant landscape changes have taken place on St. Kitts between 2006 and 2015.

Land-use, agriculture and mountain plots were often points of discussion during interviews. For example, one respondent says, "Well, I have to think of the mountain area – where the people in the areas were amazing. They were farmers, farming, house, and the non-sugar productive areas, more to the forests. What is now the Kittitian Hill (hotel and resort), nearby here, is an area that used to be used for farming and comprises about 400 acres (1.62 km2)" (A9 2014). Farming on the mountain grounds occurred regularly, providing food security for many communities. Agriculture here was not only more than an aspect of food security, or a necessity, but also a recreational activity. When discussing the access to these grounds, where her family used to spend time, one interviewee described a different picture: "There is change a lot. Because the

Fig. 23. Empty sugar cane fields present an odd but beautiful landscape (photo by author).

lands that we had, we don't have no more" (A1 2014). As another respondent explains, "Matter fact, we used to go into the hills and maybe pick vegetables, you get water, you brought salt from back home. We used to spend the whole day up there" (A2 2014). Interviewees discussed the regular tending to crops in the mountains, forwarding provisions to their families and towns, and spending the entire day up in the mountain to relax. In sum, mountain grounds represented an important dimension of Kittitian life as it not only provided food security, but also recreational, social and familial effects.

When the sugar production finally terminated in 2006, there was no agricultural crop to replace it. Without any maintenance of the area, the fields have now become overgrown, blocking the roads leading up to mountain grounds (Clark 2013, 52). As is apparent through the interview data, the inaccessibility to farming land and traditional family plots has created a negative situation for communities. Roads are "being blocked. You can't go into the hills freely. Mark you, there are older heads who know where the roads are, you know, cut them out into the hills and so on" (A2 2014). Subsequently, the community members residing in the study area "feel bitter because there is not enough traffic towards the hills" (A2 2014). The little agricultural production which does occur in this study area is impacted by means of the island's monkey infestation. One interviewee explains that these feral animals set off towards the villages and "come down here to seek food because there is none up there (mountain grounds)" (A2 2014). As other participants explain, the abandonment of land from the closing of sugar factories allowed the monkey population to increase.

Fig. 24. This chimney, a remnant of the sugar cane industry, still stands in the overgrown fields located at the foot of Mount Liamuiga (photo by author).

The problem of inaccessible land and overgrown fields can be attributed not only to the collapse of the sugar industry but also to a failure of the government to redistribute land. This signifies a larger issue within the political economy of St. Kitts. Here politics and the government played a much larger role in interviews than expected. While survey questions, did not specifically concern the role of government, it would be naïve to assume that the subject would not be broached. Land, its use, and heritage remain highly politicized and contested issue no matter where, but even more so in previously colonized landscapes (Vidal 2003). During both surveys and interviews, respondents frequently expressed their disillusionment with the political system regarding land redistribution. As one informant explained, the government gives "permission to people who give them money. It's very simple. It's a totally corrupt system" (A10 2014). People often were quite negative about the government's lack of a clear policy regarding the land which can be observed from the following description of land sales: "So that is why it is so upsetting to see the new government who took the land in the first place, giving the land, not even leasing, but selling it to outsiders and playing politics with it. Instead of putting it up to a vote, a referendum. It's the people's land" (A11 2014). Another interviewee also discussed how the land is being sold for development but not to local farmers: "I guess some of the lands was sold for development, which hasn't come off, so then the farmers they hadn't anywhere to plant" (A3 2014).

The survey also explored other modifications in agriculture policy and landscape use which have influenced the quality of life of the survey respondents. The answers were unsolicited as individuals could forward their opinion on a modification they felt most strongly about, and on the impact on their quality of life. Without prompting any kind of question about agriculture, 23 out of 174 respondents replied that changes in the landscape related to agriculture as well as environmental degradation have created negative impacts on their quality of life. This outcome, combined with the interview data and the physical land changes observed in the results obtained through the GIS/Remote Sensing discussed above, reveals a complex picture of land-use/land-change on St. Kitts which highlights the links between land degradation, community and culture.

Fig. 25. Clearing the heavy overgrowth to create a path through now discarded sugar cane fields (photo by author).

During the Sugar Era (18th to 21st century) on St. Kitts, land was utilized principally for commercial exploitation and export. The growing of sugar cane was an all-encompassing, brutal agricultural process, which oppressed the people and depleted the land. The roads up the mountain slopes beyond the cane fields led to small hillside plots on which many people frequently grew their own crops, providing traditional means of nutrition and recreation. These mountain grounds represent a historic vestige dating from a time when providing for families was possible. Less than twenty years ago, going up to the mountain grounds was a social event, too, as entire groups set off for a cookout or to harvest the small fields.

Now, without the maintenance of roads on which access mountain plots, without any sugar cane industry in which to work and, without any effective government program to redistribute the former sugar cane fields to the local residents so that this land could be converted to other agricultural uses, these roads remain blocked. Subsequently, many fields lie fallow and communities no longer have any access to a vital part of their former socio-ecological freedoms. Regionally speaking, land redistribution throughout the Caribbean remains an issue to this day, as colonial land practices and monoculture economies were commonplace throughout the islands (Mycoo 2017; Weis 2007). The result is unemployment, growing dependence on imported foods and a breakdown in traditional community relationships and values. Clearly, this land-use and land-change has led to impacts on food security, cultural values and ultimately the community well-being.

4.3 Resource conservation: the impacts of coastal erosion, rising sea levels and beach access restrictions

The preceding section (4.2) on land-use/land-cover change has examined both the extent and the impact hereof on St. Kitts. However, as an island, it would be impossible not to consider the relationship between Kittitians and the Caribbean Sea or the Atlantic Ocean. The sea, beach and coastal activities form an important aspect of everyday life in the study area. This section explores the impact of coastal changes and, in particular, will draw on a combination of interviews, survey data and the GIS/Remote Sensing results. First, numerous community stakeholders revealed a deep concern regarding the perceived rapid rate of coastal erosion. Second, subsequent interviews and survey data provided a larger dataset to explore the coastal issues which communities within the study area experience. Finally, such concerns are further investigated by applying the GIS analysis in the study area. St. Kitts continues to face many coastal problems that have been documented pre-independence. Such coastal issues, including overfishing, coastal erosion (exacerbated by sand mining) as well as damaged ecosystems linked to coral reefs and mangroves, and an inadequate waste disposal systems have been documented since the early 1990s (CAA 1990). Mining sand, despite being illegal, remains a problem as it is required when carrying out development construction. A 1988 report suggests that such mining should be carried out exclusively at Belle Tete, north of Fig Tree (Association 1990, 122). Sand mining continues legally and sometimes, illegally to this day, leading to further coastal erosion, ultimately reflected in the fewer number of boat landing sites on the beaches of Fig Tree and Sandy point.

In 1988, fish landing areas were observed along the entire coastline of St. Kitts (Association 1990, 120), but now only exist in Basseterre and Old Road Town. Coastal management and natural resources have been a topic of discussion on St. Kitts for years. In fact, a planning unit was created in 1987 to deal with environmental and developmental issues encountered along the coast by means of a 4-year plan. Unfortunately this proposal was delayed and no further action was undertaken (Association 1990). It had included recommendations for sewage and waste management treatment in coastal areas, sand mining, pollution control, fishery recommendations, and a coastal setback of up to 50 to 100 m from the sea (CCA 1990). However, regrettably, more than 25 years have since passed in the course of which little has been done to account for such coastal issues. Plans for an integrated full marine zoning project were researched in 2015 (Agostini *et al.* 2015), but the researchers noted it was difficult to keep the process going in order to complete the final enactment of the program. Moreover, it appears that coastal area sectors (e.g. fishing, tourism) are valued for their contribution to the profitability of a handful of resort operators, providing only a limited perspective on the wide array of values attached to the coastal ecosystem.

The importance of the sea often arose both throughout the interviews and the survey implementation. It was stated: "Well the sea has always been important for the people of St. Kitts" (A12 2014). Individuals frequently mentioned the changing shoreline, frequently attributing this to the growing number of hurricanes. For example, it is commented on the conservation of the shoreline at Sandy Point, "We have had a problem over the years. The hurricanes usually come from the southeast

Fig. 26. Village houses located very close to the water's edge (photo by author).

and then we get it particularly this side. So we have had a lot of erosion along the coast going right down to Fig Tree. I suffer that a lot back here" (A13 2014).

To date this transforming coast of St. Kitts has led to:

> *impacts on community activities and recreation. Perry Peats, a resident of Challengers, often mentioned the disheartening fact that the eroded coastline prevented any customary swimming and fishing in the sea by the village, referring to the inhabitants of his village as, "Seafarers, so because the coastline, the coastline is being straightened out, there is no longer a bay, no sand accumulates there anymore"* (A14 2014).

A change in fishing techniques to be observed at the traditional village of Fig Tree which is described thus, "Well at one time, they had nine net boats, fishing boats, they would catch the ballyhoo, the jacks, and what not. Now they only have one. One and you can't even find them because men have other jobs. Because they not relying on the fishing for their living anymore" (A4 2014). Many fishermen stated that eroding shorelines have forced them to fish further away from the beaches, as the sea grass beds become degraded due to the increased sediment, destroying the fish breeding areas. Economic aspects are also important to consider with regard to the decline of fishing, as its modern methods have become more expensive and the markets more competitive. However, it is clear that, due to economic reasons and degraded shorelines, a decline in this livelihood has occurred, as is explained as follows: "Me, myself as a fisherman. So that's a tradition that is gone now for something like four generations" (A12 2014; A23 2014).

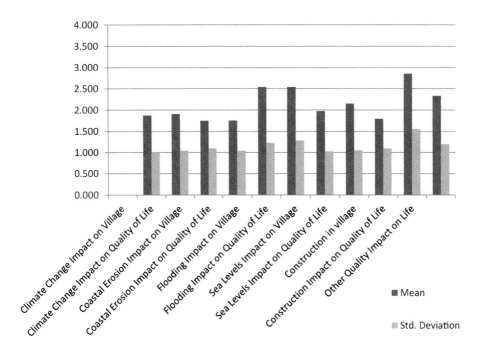

Fig. 27. Mean and standard deviations of the variables of coastal changes whereby 1 represents the negative and 4 the positive changes.

These environmental factors which limit any sea and beach access are compounded by land management policies influenced by economics. Whereas tourism brings economic development, it often leads to limited beach access for local communities. One interviewee stated: "The beach is supposed to have a public access. I mean, if you have a development that takes up every square inch, then how do you get to the beach? It's not officially disallowing it" (A15 2014). These perspectives of a transforming and in fact degrading coastline are explored further by means of the subsequently administered survey in order to understand how environmental variables, including the coastline, impacted not only the daily life but also quality of life as experienced the villages of St. Kitts.

As described in chapter 4, the administered survey in the case study area explored the relationships of coastal change with both demographic and location variables. Coastal change variables include the impact of sea-level fluctuations, flooding, and coastal erosion inflicted on each village and the quality of life. Demographic variables include gender, occupation and age. Specific variables explore specific village locations or village groups. The overall results will be presented first and, important demographic differences explored next.

In Fig. 27, the mean and standard deviation of community perceptions to each relevant coastal change variable are presented. The scale on the Y-axis is representative of very negative (1) to very positive (5). Hence, the results reveal an overall negative perception of all coastal change variables mentioned by survey respondents. The majority of the negative variables are related to coastal erosion and the climate change impacts on the variable ""Village" as well as on "Quality of life". These

		Very Negative	Negative	Positive	Very Positive	Measure	Approximate Signficance
Gender	♂	33	21	14	16	Pearson's Chi	0.164
	♀	40	31	15	4	Kendall's Tau-c	0.077

Table 16. Perceptions of changes in sea-level fluctuations at the coastal villages of St. Kitts based on gender.

results are indicative of a changing shoreline, which is severely affected by coastal erosion, climate change, and to a lesser degree by sea level (rise) and flooding.

This preliminary analysis reflects an overall negative perception of coastal changes within the study area. The results hereof can be broken down further by means of demographic variables in order to comprehend the perceptions of coastal changes in greater detail. Only the significant relationships will be discussed here. For a complete exploration of the variables, see Appendix E. 2, Tables 52-59.

The relationship between gender and the impact of sea level (changes) on the village is revealed to be moderately significant. This outcome is obvious when considering the significant Pearson Chi-Square test result of the Gender and Sea-level fluctuations of .164 and a Kendal-Tau-C result of .077 (see Table 16). However, Table 16 also presents a number of individuals, both men and women, who perceive sea level fluctuations as positive. This may relate to the understanding of sea-level fluctuations in terms of ebbs and flow, as in the natural tides, rather than to changes in higher sea levels due to sea rise.

To investigate this correlation further, the occupations of the men who answered either 1 or 2, (i.e., either in a very negative or somewhat negative manner) regarding any sea-level fluctuations were reviewed. Of the eighty-four men who answered with 1 or 2, only fifteen noted their occupation to be farmer or a fisherman. Not one of the latter groups noted a positive change concerning the sea. It may be added here that the male survey respondents working as farmers or fishermen all hail from the villages of Old Road Town or Fig Tree. These historic fishing villages cause the interaction with the coast to be even more marked when compared to the other coastal villages located in the study area. As few women who contributed to the survey have found employment in the agriculture and none have done so in the fishing sector, this situation would influence their personal specific perspective on any sea-level fluctuations.

Interestingly, despite the significant relationship of sea level change on village locations and gender, there is no significance related to gender and the effects of sea-level fluctuations on the quality of life. The resulting interpretation is: the sea level still affects the quality of life for all survey respondents no matter the gender. These results disclose that, although gender has some effect on how any modifications in the landscape (e.g., climate change, coastal erosion) are perceived, there is no difference between the genders regarding their perception of the subsequent effects on their quality of life. Apparently, individuals working closer with the land or sea perceive greater modifications in sea levels. In this case, this opinion is divided by gender because more men are fisherman or work the land. A significant

		Very Negative	Negative	Positive	Very Positive		
Age Group	15-20	42	7	4	4		
	21-30	10	4	0	2		
	31-40	16	9	0	9		
	41-50	11	7	0	4	Measure	Approximate Significance
	51-60	17	7	0	8	Pearson's Chi	0.024
	61 and above	8	3	2	0	Kendall's Tau-C	0.034

Table 17. Perceptions of the coastal erosion at the coastal villages of St. Kitts based on age groups.

		Very Negative	Negative	Positive	Very Positive		
Age Group	15-20	40	9	5	3		
	21-30	9	5	0	2		
	31-40	19	6	3	6		
	41-50	7	12	0	3	Measure	Approximate Significance
	51-60	18	5	2	7	Pearson's Chi	0.029
	61 and above	6	4	2	1	Kendall's Tau-c	0.016

Table 18. Perceptions of the coastal erosion and the impact on quality of life on St. Kitts based on age groups.

relationship also exists between the demographic variable of age and the perception of coastal erosion impacts on a village. Results show a Pearson's Chi Square of .024 and of a Kendall Tau-C of .034 (see Table 17).

An overwhelming number of younger people from Age Group 1 (15-20 years old) considered the coastal erosion effects to be the most negative (42 out of 57 respondents). The Age Group 5 (51-60 years old) also rated the changes of coastal erosion effects on village as most negative (17 out of 32 respondents). This resembles the relationship of age and of the coastal erosion effects on the quality of life (see Table 18), with a Pearson Chi-Square Test of .029 and a Kendall's Tau-C of .016.

Again, Age Groups 1 and 5 responded highly negatively with the respondent sample sizes of 40 out of 57 (Age Group 1) and 18 out of 32 (Age Group 5) respondents. Age Group 3 (31-40 years old) also reflected highly negatively with 19 out of 34 respondents. Therefore, any coastal erosion with respect to the impact on villages and the quality of life would be generally speaking seem to be viewed negatively by most age groups. However, this opinion also echoes that the younger and older generations have similar perspectives, indeed by and large negative ones, on the coastal erosion effects influencing the villages and the quality of life. This view may be caused by the exposure of such topics while attending school, thereby providing younger generations with a quicker grasp on environmental changes.

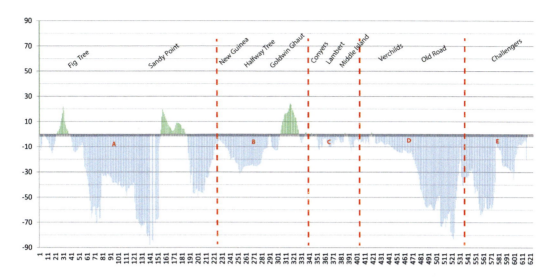

Fig. 28. Net Shoreline Movement (2006-2015) of the coastal villages, St. Kitts. Figure created with the aid of Julijan Vermeer.

Elder generations may notice a difference as they have witnessed or experienced such changes through time.

The results presented here, revealed through overall perceptions of coastal changes and subsequent explorations into demographic variables as well as the perception of coastal changes, expose a vulnerable coastline. The present section explores locational differences regarding the perception of coastal changes. This includes an analysis of the coastal erosion trends which have been examined by means of the GIS/Remote Sensing. The outcome hereof will be investigated first, supported by data based on survey results as well as interviews.

Again, it is important to note that a wide variety of coastal changes can be observed, as disclosed by the preceding survey results. The specific resource conservation issue of coastal erosion was selected because of its relevance to community stakeholders. Furthermore, as reflected in the overall perceptions of coastal changes results (see Tables 21 and 22), any coastal erosion and impacts on villages and the quality of life are perceived as the most negative. Applying the plugin Digital Shoreline Analysis System from the USGS (Thieler *et al.* 2008), the changing shoreline, including its accretion and erosion, are first explored. For the extracted Landsat shorelines dating from 1986, 1989, 1999, 2003, 2006, 2013, and 2015, and a baseline from which transects were cast, see Appendix E., Fig. 75.

The Net Shoreline Movement (NSM) and End Point Rate (EPR) were calculated. For the NSM of the present case study, see Fig. 28. The NSM determines the overall movement as either accretion or erosion. To analyze the shoreline data more effectively, thirteen villages were grouped, based on their geographic proximity, and parish or district. Moreover, their group numbers served to interconnect the survey data. In Fig. 29, the numbers indicated on the X-axis represent the shoreline in particular for those village groups. Accordingly, we deduce overall erosion occurring in all village groups, except with regard to the first transects of Village

Calculation	Result
Mean rate	-1.25218m
Standard deviation	0.459869m
Highest accretion	0.66m
Highest erosion	-3.03m

Table 19. Total End Point Rate of the study area, 1986-2015.

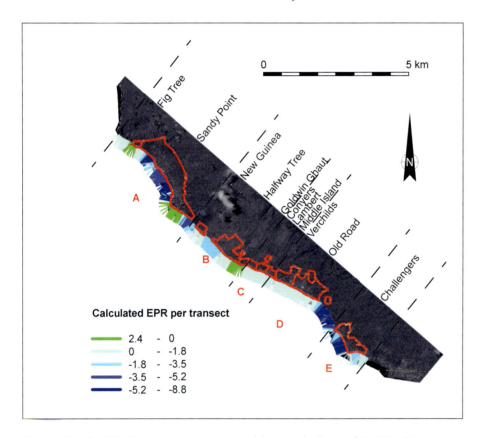

Fig. 29. Visualized End Point Rate (2006-2015) of the coastal villages of St. Kitts. Figure created with the aid fo Julijan Vermeer.

Group A (11.26 m.). This phenomenon may be related to the location where the south side of St. Kitts meets the west side. The three highest NSM for the afore-mentioned 29-year period was found to be in Village Group A (-75.13 m.), Village Group D (-89.55 m.) and Village Group E (-65.94 m.).

Table 20 identifies the mean rate, standard deviation, highest erosion and highest accretion for the EPR for the entire study area. The results of negative mean rates of EPR prove that coastal erosion is an omnipresent phenomenon in the case study area.

The EPR for each transect is displayed graphically (see Fig. 29). The scale ranges from dark blue to light blue to green, whereby dark blue indicates the most negative rates of erosion and green the positive rates of accretion. Fig. 30 indicates the erosion throughout the village groups, concentrated in Village Groups A, B and D as is indicated by means of high negative EPR values. Accretion is encountered in Village Group A, indicated by the positive values of the EPR.

Group	A	B	C	D	E
Villages	Sandy Point Town, Fig Tree	Halfway Tree, New Guinea, Goldwin Ghaut	Lamberts, Middle Island Conyers	Old Road Town, Verchilds,	Boyd's Village, Challengers, Stone Fort
No. of Transects	227	110	57	144	68
Mean Rate	-1.08863	-1.29532	-1.17621	-1.47662	-1.31304
Standard Deviation	0.454882	0.410642	0.273892	0.503444	0.354228
Highest Accretion	0.66	-0.1	-0.65	-0.62	-0.27
Highest Erosion	-2.53	-2.21	-2.01	-3.03	-2.22

Table 20. End Point Rate by village group of the coastal villages of St. Kitts.

Village Group	Very Negative	Negative	Positive	Very Positive	Measure	Approx. Significance
A. Sandy Point, Fig Tree	26	15	2	3		
B. Goodwin Ghaut, Halfway Tree, New Guinea	10	6	2	2		
C. Conyers, Lamberts, Middle Island	3	7	3	3		
D. Old Road, Verchild	24	17	11	4	Pearson's Chi	0.013
E. Boyd's Village, Challengers, Stone Fort	7	6	6	3	Kendall's Tau-C	0.546

Table 21. Perceptions of survey respondents of the sea-level fluctuations, based on village groups.

To analyze the variability dealt with in Fig. 29, the results were broken down according to village group numbers, which is the implemented geographic division applied in the administered survey. Breaking down the results for each geographic Village Group (see Table 20) the significant result reveals that the erosion appears to be occurring at a much more extreme rate in the villages of Fig Tree and Sandy Point Town (Village Group A) as well as in Old Road Town (Village Group D) and Challengers (Village Group E).

These results prove that coastal erosion occurs physically in the shoreline trends dating to between 1986 and 2015. However, in order to understand these erosion trends in relationship with community perceptions, the Village Groups (A-D) are linked to survey data results. First, we explore the relationship between any sea-level fluctuations and the perceptions of these fluctuations associated with each different Village Group. The outcome delivers a Pearson's Chi Square value of .013 and a Kendall's Tau C value of .546. Respondents from Village Group D (Old Road Town and Verchilds) and Village Group A (Sandy Point and Fig Tree) deliver the highest number of negative answers, 24 and 26 respectively, for the value of 1, i.e., the most negative (see Table 21).

This result is similar to the relationship between a village group and sea-level impact on the quality of life with a Pearson's Chi-Square value of .032 and a Kendall's Tau-C value of .348. Village Groups D and A answered negatively with 22 and 20 respondents respectively for the value of 1. Whereas higher sea levels are not always indicative of coastal erosion, perceptions of a higher sea presented by survey respondents are in fact related to an eroding coastline, causing the sea to appear higher (see Table 22).

Village Group	Very Negative	Negative	Positive	Very Positive		
A. Sandy Point, Fig Tree	20	13	10	3		
B. Goodwin Ghaut, Halfway Tree, New Guinea	10	5	4	1		
C. Conyers, Lamberts, Middle Island	1	9	4	2	Measure	Approx. Significance
D. Old Road, Verchild	22	15	13	6	Pearson's Chi	0.032
E. Boyd's Village, Challengers, Stone Fort	5	4	6	7	Kendall's Tau-C	0.348

Table 22. Perceptions of survey respondents of the sea-level fluctuations on the quality of life, based on village groups.

Village Group	Very Negative	Negative	Positive	Very Positive		
A. Sandy Point, Fig Tree	37	4	1	4		
B. Goodwin Ghaut, Halfway Tree, New Guinea	14	3	1	2		
C. Conyers, Lamberts, Middle Island	7	6	0	3	Measure	Approx. Significance
D. Old Road, Verchild	29	15	2	10	Pearson's Chi	0.215
E. Boyd's Village, Challengers, Stone Fort	9	7	1	5	Kendall's Tau-c	0.005

Table 23. Perceptions of survey respondents of coastal erosion, based on village groups.

Exploring the relationship of location and coastal erosion, this investigation also analyzed the relationship between village group and perceived impact of coastal erosion on both villages and quality of life. There apparently appears to be a slight correlation between a village group and the coastal erosion impacts on a village with a Pearson's Chi-Square value of .215 and Kendall's Tau C value of .005 (see Table 23). Evidently, Village Group A (represented by 37 individuals) and Village Group D (represented by 29 individuals) perceive coastal erosion impacts on villages as very negative.

Moreover, we see here that Village Group A (Sandy Point and Fig Tree) comprising 34 individuals and Village Group D (Old Road and Verchilds) comprising 28 individuals rate the coastal erosion impacts on quality of life as very negative. Table 24 reveals a Pearson's Chi-Square value test of .215 and a Kendall's Tau-C value of .003. From Tables 22-23, investigating the impact of sea-level fluctuations on village locations and Tables 23 and 24, examining the consequences of the coastal erosion on village locations, it is clear that the changing coastline of the study area negatively impacts the case study villages. However, the results also reveal that these perceptions are felt stronger in casu more negatively in Village Groups A and D. As observed in Fig. 30 and Table 21, these village groups are experiencing some of the worst coastal erosion as disclosed by the DSAS results.

Finally, variables of sea level and coastal erosion change and a village group are combined in a Krusal-Wallis test in order to understand the correlation of this pairing of variables. This approach served to emphasize whether the sea level is in-

Village Group	Very Negative	Negative	Positive	Very Positive	Measure	Approx. Significance
A. Sandy Point, Fig Tree	34	7	1	4		
B. Goodwin's Ghaut, Halfway Tree, New Guinea	12	6	2	0		
C. Conyers, Lamberts, Middle Island	7	3	1	5	Measure	Approx. Significance
D. Old Road, Verchild	28	15	6	7	Pearson's Chi	0.215
E. Boyd's Village, Challengers, Stone Fort	9	7	1	5	Kendall's Tau-C	0.003

Table 24. Perceptions of survey respondents of coastal erosion on the quality of life, based on village groups.

Village group	Coastal erosion effect	Coastal erosion effect on the quality of life
Significance	.020	.042
Village Group	**Sea-level fluctuations**	**Sea-level effects on the quality of life**
Significance	.002	.085

Table 25. Krusal-Wallis test, relationship between village group and combined environmental changes of coastal erosion and sea-level fluctuations impacts on village group and quality of life.

dependent of any coastal erosion changes in the Village Groups. Table 25 indicates a significant relationship between these combined variables of sea level and coastal erosion and their relationship to village group. From these results, it not only appears that villager environmental do changes but that impacts on the quality of life are indeed very much geographically based.

These geographic differences in perception are supported by the results obtained by means of the DSAS plugin. As indicated in Figs. 29 and 30, the Village Groups A and D have the highest observed coastal erosion in this study area. This result combined with the survey data discussed here reveal that perceptions of coastal erosion as well as the coastal changes are stronger at geographic locations where coastal erosion takes place at a faster pace. Based on the results considering the EPR and NSM combined results of the Village Group, and environmental variables, the village location is apparently an important variable not only as to the perception of the environmental variables but also to the quality of life.

A changing shoreline may be caused by not only coastal erosion, but also by a variety of environmental influences, such as sea-level fluctuations. These aspects of sea-level and coastal erosion affect not only changes in the village groups but also the quality of life. It is important to note that the sample size for the survey analysis was not as balanced as desired. Village Groups D and B also comprise the highest number of respondents, with 56 people and 46 people, respectively, answering the survey. Furthermore, the villages of Old Road Town and Fig Tree are traditional fishing villages. Of the 19 respondents with agriculture or fishing as a livelihood, only 4 do not reside Village Groups D and A. Subsequently, the experiences of any coastal change will be perceived stronger in these village groups.

The combined data analysis of interviews, surveys and GIS analysis provide an in-depth interpretation of landscape change and associated impacts on cultural ecosystem services. Further, as these modifications continue to influence livelihoods, there is also a link to the quality of life. The survey data suggest a changing landscape. Today, coastal erosion leads to repercussions of both environmental and social characteristics in local communities. Ecosystem services, such as natural resources (e.g. sea grass beds, fish), have declined due to environmental changes. Moreover, social activities (e.g., bathing, village continuity) are all affected. This erosion can be linked to natural causes, (e.g., hurricanes, sea patterns), but also to development and neglect. "Where the sea water. They all in the sea. Shore then take my land. Me have nothing now. So we lost some meters of beach here" (A4 2014), one respondent stated with regard to the sea encroaching on his land which used to be meant for planting and was located at the villages of Fig Tree and Sandy Point.

The environmental changes influence the quality of life of the community by reducing fishing areas, degrading the beaches and affecting the development and houses along the sea shore. These aspects all contribute to a declining community well-being as individuals can no longer take part in previous and important recreational and economic activities which defined community life in St. Kitts.

4.4 Shifting community: socio-cultural aspects of landscape change

The preceding sections on modifying land-use patterns and degrading coastal resources have revealed the pathways through which land use and socio-political factors interact in order to produce cultural as well as social impacts. In section 4.2, for example, recently restricted access to mountain grounds effects access to local food production, recreational activities and customary practices. Coastal erosion leads to limited fishing and beach access, which are relevant to both community livelihoods and associated traditions. The consequences of these natural modifications on social and cultural life remain equally as important as a natural resource of degradation. This phenomenon may appear unrelated to the more environmentally associated processes described above. However, as the landscape has changed, so too has the relationship between land and individual, ultimately leading to profound changes in society and culture. As discussed, these aspects of environment utilization for cultural purposes comprise cultural ecosystem services. How individuals in the coastal villages of St. Kitts react to such changes in their landscapes, or how they position themselves within a changing landscape will be explored in this subsequent section.

The historical section (see 4.1) clearly indicates the capacity of politics and of the economy to produce visible landscape modifications which affect each form of community well-being. In addition, they have shaped the use as well as the value which individuals attach to their surrounding land and community. A number of such transformations have been positive. For instance, since the 1950s, the number of roads and houses has significantly increased. Community development (e.g. increased possibilities in education and housing) have presented more opportunities to many individuals residing within the study area. It is reported that, "Well when I was a child, a little girl, Sandy Point didn't have any roads, dirt roads, no lights, this was in darkness" (A1 2014). Or, as another interviewee firmly states, "Well, St. Kitts has come a long way. A long way. Like when I was young, we had to walk it to Basseterre to town" (A5 2014). Accordingly, community development has introduced positive aspects to the rural areas of St. Kitts, mirrored in the administered survey conducted in the study area. Urban development is most frequently cited as a positive change. Of the 174 household surveys, eleven freely mentioned (urban) development as a response of positive change.

Modernization and development usually involves shifts in community character. Interviewees discussed a current lack of interaction between age groups. This issue was described as follows: "… is very hard to talk to young kids coming up today, it's very difficult. You try to tell them to right, and they feel like they minding their business or trying to disturb them" (A7 2014). This opinion is echoed by an interviewee from Fig Tree, "You don't have the people, like myself, in the evening, go to places and sit down, just like you are in my house and have a conversation. You don't have that anymore, you only have rubbish" (A4 2014). Disappointment regarding a lack of interest of community members to set off on nature hikes with him is expressed thus: "People don't like to go there, just to wilderness" (A20 2014).

The interview data results could be suggestive of a bias caused by the senior age of the interview participants. However, a sentiment of dissatisfaction of community changes re-occurs in the survey data. For example, on St. Kitts, individuals often mentioned an altering of social interactions between residents of the various villages interviewed in the course of the present study. One respondent from Old Road, St. Kitts, reported: "To me, the community ain't no help to me" (A27 2014). Though generational, the lack of any economic opportunities combined with a social isolation within the rural study area does appear to influence the interaction between groups. For example, one interviewee candidly commented: "Some of these fellas take laziness. Gone into the bush and plant laziness. Quicker money, quicker money in the bush, quicker dead. But if you decide to work, you work in the sea. You couldn't work anymore. The easiest way, the easiest way now, the younger ones, they go into the woods and plant [marijuana]. But quicker dead" (A17 2014).

This dissatisfaction with the socio-economic situation by residents in the study area again is reflected in survey data. When answering the question of regarding any type of change and the subsequent impact of those modifications on the quality of life, 34 out of 174 households cited, crime, gangs, lack of any community involvement, and poverty to be negative elements impacting the study area. Accordingly, the overall economic stagnation leads to societal problems in the rural landscape of St. Kitts. This opinion is reflected again in the overly negative response to environmental changes with an impact on the quality of life. It is further echoed in the survey response to the question: have any other modifications strongly affected village life. Only 11.5% (20/174) answered independently that either the society or the people were the root cause of these negative influences on village life, indeed a significant statistic to consider when answers were open response. Needless to say, this development becomes even more unfortunate when considered in conjunction with the idle, empty landscape. These aspects of community life are again linked to the political divisions concerning land access and land redistribution. Several individuals expressed distrust and suspicion of the government's actions and economic ventures.

It lies beyond the scope of the present research to draw any conclusions regarding the politico- and economic influences or incentives in St. Kitts, but it is relevant to mention them as an influential factor within the landscape of this case study. This research would argue that as individuals are forced to situate themselves within an atmosphere of uncertainty, involving politics and economic stagnation, we see not only the visible results on the landscape, but also the involvement within the community, as wellbeing declines.

Part III: The significance of fallow land: case study observations

> *Plantation sugar-cane landscape has been the most distinctive cultural landscape in a number of Caribbean islands since colonization, surviving in its basic form for over 500 years.*

Found and Berbés-Blázquez 2012, 164

The rich history and heritage of St. Kitts comes alive through the present in-depth study which has focused on an illustrative 12 km long coastline extending from the village of Challengers to the village of Fig Tree. The results reveal physical changes in land and coastal areas, leading to a variety of cultural and societal impacts, ultimately resulting in declining community well-being. By applying data collected through a variety of sources, including historical research, interviews, surveys and GIS/Remote Sensing, it is possible to trace the links between history, land, shoreline, culture and community. Interdisciplinary methods such as these listed above indicate not only that land and coastal degradation is taking place. The main findings dealt with in this research reveal these connections brought about by land-use and land availability, environmental degradation (including coastal erosion) and impacts on cultural space.

First, the cultivation of sugar cane dominated the economy, the landscape and the community life of St. Kitts for over 300 years, until c.2006. Here, sugar monoculture, on a massive scale, has continued to shape the landscape. Severe soil degradation as well as engrained societal hierarchies influences the access to land even to this day. Mountain grounds and agricultural plots, sites representing facets of the important local heritage and history, are now difficult to reach due to overgrown, idle sugar fields. Coupled with an invasive infestation caused by the African Green Monkey, this overgrowth has impeded the traditional local agriculture, limited the food security hereby eroding a way of life with its associated cultural values, while leaving the islanders heavily (and needlessly) dependent on imported food.

This subsistence agriculture on mountain grounds has not only nourished community ties but has also become a rich part of the cultural heritage. While results reveal subtle human and/or natural degradation in the case study, the present situation illuminates how even the most minute land change impacts cultural values throughout the study area. Ironically, the lack of land management or lack of human intervention has led to a cessation of access to the mountain grounds which comes with an overgrowth and a monkey infestation. This land-change has resulted in limited food security as well as degraded community values, and finally, restricted access to important heritage sites, such as the mountain grounds.

Second, coastal erosion has created an extreme and visible threat to land access as the shoreline continues to erode. Such a result and subsequent impacts on fishing, has limited food security, viability of fishing as economic livelihoods, and the cultural values associated with the beach and fishing. The consequences of coastal erosion are immediate due to the high vulnerability resulting from hurricanes and/or other natural disasters.

Third, community values related to land access, agriculture, and coastal erosion reveal that these land and sea modifications influence society, ultimately impacting the community well-being. Cultural values are tied to land access, whether that be shoreline or mountain grounds. This connection can be observed throughout the plantation system period, from the 18th century up to the present. These aspects concerning land, sea and culture cannot be regarded as separate but rather as components of a sphere of interactions encountered at the community level, but impacted by means of regional politics, global economics, and climate change.

Similar to many other island nations, this case study has witnessed a fast-paced sense of change concerning many aspects of life. Community life takes them in its stride, as the results of this research disclose both supportive and disenchanted perspectives of the current situation. Referring to the definition of well-being (see chapter 2) (see 2.4) (MA 2003, 2005a, b), the present case study reveals how land change ultimately impacts wellbeing in terms of one's use of the land and one's social relationships. For example, the increase in crime has also influenced the security aspect of well-being. In addition, environmental changes have proven to effect ecosystem services, ultimately leading to modifications in community dynamics and well-being. Moreover, the community well-being is affected because local industries, local heritage sites and livelihoods are impacted too.

5

The Kalinago Territory
Land for survival, land as a burden

The rocky, windswept Atlantic coast of the island of Dominica winds from bay to bay through villages and fertile fields. Beyond Pagua Bay, the road breaks into a steep incline, weaving past blue ocean vistas. On clear days, the French island of Marie-Galante, at a distance of c. 60 km., is visible across the Caribbean Sea. Continuing up a steep mountain incline, the road meanders past small villages. Hidden between rocky cliffs and densely forested mountains, the Kalinago Territory consists of a 15 km2 tract of land located in the central-northeastern part of Dominica. Here, historically isolated and rural, a single main road connects the eight villages, or hamlets, named Bataca, Crayfish River, Point, Salybia, St. Cyr, Gaulette River, Mauhaut River and Sineku. On one side of this road, lush vegetation and fields lead up to an eventual high mountain ridge. On the other side, a steep slope drops towards to the Atlantic Ocean. North of the Kalinago Territory, the villages of Atkinson and the fishing port of Marigot are situated. Continuing south from this territory, the road runs past the village of Castle Bruce, ultimately leading west across the mountain ridge towards Roseau, the island's capital. In the Caribbean region, where most traces of the previous Amerindian inhabitants have been wiped from popular memory,[31] the inhabitants of the Kalinago Territory are the only indigenous group on Dominica to have special status and a communal land title (dating back to the 1900s), which preserves this territory and physically ties its community to the land (Strecker, 2016; Hofman and Hoogland forthcoming).

The 8 villages of the study area that make up the Kalinago Territory include 2 primary schools and no secondary schools. The Chief and council's office is located in the Kalinago Territory as well as police station, a variety of small merchants, 7 churches of various Christian denominations and 2 health centers. While the main road sits high from the Caribbean Sea's edge, the rocky coast was home to many fishermen. Because of the calmer bays in Salybia, this village was a popular landing spot for fisherman.

---

31 This does not include the overwhelming archaeological evidence and petroglyphs in the region as well as the number of contemporary indigenous communities such as the Santa Rosa First Peoples Community in Arima, Trinidad and the Garifuna communities still living in the northeast of St. Vincent and in Central America. For more information on contemporary indigenous communities on the insular Caribbean islands, see Forte 2006.

This chapter deals with the results of a collaborative landscape research completed in the Kalinago Territory. As discussed in chapter 3, the research focus was determined in conjunction with local partners. The present chapter is divided into Parts I, II and III (see below). First, a historical context presents the key moments in Kalinago history, tracing the past land-use to the current landscape. As source remain limited for the Kalinago Territory and it's specific relations to land, this section bridges relevant historic information to understand the current relationship of land and community in the Kalinago Territory. Second, to understand the impacts of landscape changes on cultural ecosystem services (CES), a narrative weaves through the socio-ecological indicators of the "Multiple Use of Lands", "Resource Conservation" and "Cultural/Social aspects". Finally, overall observations regarding the case study are presented. Part III draws general insight about the case study and the impacts of land change on CES and wellbeing.

Part I. A recent history of the Kalinago landscape

5.1 The Kalinago Territory and its historical background

Simply put, the Kalinago Territory endures because of its history and geography. The island's topography influenced its place in the history of Caribbean colonization. Whereas St. Kitts with its rolling plains became one of the first colonies of the British Empire, the tall, steep mountains of Dominica protected the island from any early colonization and later interest of a possible site for plantation economy (Honychurch 1995). This historic narrative serves to create a context for the ensuing processes that shaped the Kalinago Territory landscape.

As information on Kalinago and Amerindian life in the Caribbean originates primarily from European accounts, documents and reports forwarded by various official colonial governments (Gregoire *et al.* 1996; Hulme 1986), a lack of unbiased knowledge of their history exists. The writings of two French missionaries, Raymond Breton (1609-1679) and Jean-Baptiste Labat (1663-1738), though biased, describe the Carib people inhabiting the Lesser Antilles during the mid- to late 17th century (Breton 1999; Labat 1970). Labeling them with an arbitrary and haphazard life style, Labat was nevertheless an important defender against the popular claim that cannibalism occurred in the Kalinago community (Honychurch 1995, 33). Despite this, numerous Kalinago colonial stereotypes perpetuate in modern Caribbean history and education (Gregoire *et al.* 1996, 107).

Kalinago presence can be noted in treaties, official documents dating from the 17th to the 20th century, and the reports forwarded by anthropologists such as Taylor (1938), Rouse (1948), Vérin (1961) and Layng (1976). However, in the Caribbean region, the common perception remained that Amerindian communities either disappeared entirely, or became fully assimilated into national societies. Such a perpetuated myth has caused an absence of attention on the continued presence of actual indigenous communities in the region (Boomert 2002; Boucher 1992; Hofman and Hoogland 2012; Hofman *et al.* 2015; Hulme 1986; Hulme 2001; Hulme and Whitehead 1992).

5.1.1 The early European contact and the British occupation

Historically, the Lesser Antilles remained relatively untouched by the Spanish during the early contact period (Gregoire *et al.* 1996; Hofman *et al.* forthcoming). Without any sources of gold, the islands were called "Islas Inútiles" (Kossek 1994; Mans forthcoming; Porter 1984, 80). As the Colonial Era continued into the 17th and 18th centuries, the British and the French Empires sought to assert their domination. The Lesser Antilles became a "playground" for these European nations, leading to evolving confrontations with the indigenous populations (Laffoon *et al.* 2017). European proclamations of power over the Lesser Antilles came only after fierce resistance. As colonial powers controlled more and more of the Lesser Antilles, indigenous populations fled to the islands of St. Vincent, St. Lucia and Dominica (Boucher 1992; Crispin and Kanem 1989; Kossek 1994). Dominica itself was left untouched by the European colonizers until relatively late in the 17th century (Patterson and Rodriguez 2004). Mountainous and rugged, the island's terrain was too difficult to settle on or to be made suitable for any cash crop plantations, maintaining the Kalinago persistence and resistance to the European colonization of Dominica.

These combined factors led to a certain colonial gentlemen's agreement: the English and the French declared Dominica neutral throughout the 17th century (Boucher 1992; Honychurch 1995). However, this declaration had little to do with any respect for the indigenous populations, but existed rather as a political move to keep specific islands neutral in the game of exploitation and conquest. Furthermore, a duplicitous manner of dealing with Caribbean ethnic groups emerged throughout the Colonial Era, both acknowledging their inherent right to land, and claiming this same land. For example, the British colonial government advised its officials to encourage Amerindian populations to join its side (Boucher 1992). At this same time, these officials were not allowed to settle on Dominica. Furthermore, the British colonial government maintained its claim of sovereignty over this isle, negating the Kalinago presence, claiming it as "unoccupied" (See Article Two of its Charter in Moreau de Saint-Méry, Loix and Constitutions, 1:30) (Boromé 1967). In contrast to this supposed island "inoccupation", the 1666 Guadeloupe treaty between the French and English acknowledged the presence of the Kalinago people and their territorial rights to the islands of Dominica and St. Vincent. The signing of the treaty was in fact attended by fifteen Kalinago representatives from both these isles (DuTetre 1667; Kossek 1994). However, as the 17th century progressed into the 18th century, Dominica became increasingly caught between French and English attempts at conquest.

With sugar production exhausted on the islands on St. Kitts and Barbados by 1750, the British were eager to claim Dominica. They took over Dominica completely in 1764 in accordance with the Treaty of Paris signed after the Seven Year's War between France and Britain (Boucher 1992; Gregoire *et al.* 1996; Hulme 1986; Taylor 2012). This treaty made no mention at all of the Kalinago living on Dominica, despite their known existence and past presence at other treaty signings (Boucher 1992, 107). Once the British colonial power had acquired control over the island, the Kalinago presence was further ignored when the dividing and selling of land, in surveyed lots. At that time, the indigenous population was disseminated all over Dominica. However, as more and more British colonists arrived to settle on the island during the 18th century, the Kalinago were forced to move and to be subsequently restricted to the areas located in the direct vicinity of the hamlet of Salybia (Atwood 1791; Bell 1902; Gregoire *et al.* 1996; Layng 1976; Luke 1950). Leaving the 232 acres of land to the Kalinago should not be seen as an act of good faith on the part of the British. Rather, this land surrounding Salybia was considered the most inferior parts on the island characterized by a severe topography and an undulating landscape, making the cultivation of plants extremely difficult. The British administrator Sir Henry Hesketh Bell[32] proposed to expand the territory to 3,700 acres in 1903. Accepted in the subsequent 1903 Official Gazette, an issued "Government Notice" (Government Printing 1903) describes the "Carib Reserve,"[33] according to Bell's report dated July 29, 1902 as follows (Strecker 2016):

> *It appeared to me very desirable that the limits of the Reserve should be properly and finally delimited, and I commissioned Mr. A. Skeat, a licensed surveyor, to survey the land held by them and to make a plan. He was instructed to follow the recognized boundaries of the Reserve and to adopt, wherever possible, streams, cliffs, and other natural landmarks.*

At this time, little contact existed between the Kalinago Territory and the rest of Dominica. According to Layng (1983), the territory remained recognized more by its customs, land-use and a lack of concern, rather than on the basis of respect. This disdain ensured that the territory continued relatively isolated from colonial settlers. Little development took place as it remained difficult to access, continuing subsistence agriculture provided the main livelihood.

However, such isolation did not keep adjacent colonial conflicts and trading from impacting the Kalinago Territory. Canoeing continued to be the fastest means of travel. Many Kalinago traders journeyed to the islands of Guadeloupe and Marie-Galante on canoes in order to barter with the French, rather than trekking through the mountains and forests to reach the capital of Roseau located in the southwest of Dominica. Eventually, this trading relationship led to the 1930 Carib War (Hulme 2001), when British attempted to seize the so-called contraband or traded goods imported from the neighboring French islands into the Kalinago Territory. This event led to the death of five Dominican policemen and two Kalinago men.

After the trial and acquittal of the Kalinago and Chief Jolly John for their involvement in the 1930 Carib War, a Royal Commission was set up in 1931 to investigate the possible causes behind the related disturbances. This Royal Commission decided that not only should the Kalinago not possess a common land title, and also that no power should reside in the position of chief. The deciding argument was: the Kalinago had lost their "indigeneity", or cultural and physi-

---

32 Administrator Bell to Mr. Chamberlain, Report on the Caribs of Dominica, 29th July 1902. Accessed at the British National Archives, ref: CO 152/425/1, para.38 on p. 77.
33 The Kalinago Territory was known officially as the Carib Reserve until February 2015, when an official name change took place. At the first meeting of the first session of the Ninth Parliament, the Carib Territory Amendment Act was passed to this end.

cal specificity (Kossek 1994). To maintain control over the Kalinago Territory, the British Commission Report of 1932 (1932, 32) stated:

> *No power, authority, or jurisdiction whatever should be given to the chief, whose functions would be purely advisory. It is obvious that to grant any jurisdiction or power to the chief would imply the necessity of supplying him with the force necessary to implement his decisions, a course not only difficult but most undesirable.*

The aftermath of the skirmish led to the dismantling of the chiefdom in the Kalinago Territory. The original 1903 survey of this territory was stolen during the skirmish, ultimately reducing its actual demarcations to 232 acres rather than the 3,700 acres set aside by the 1903 survey completed by Administrator Bell (Hulme 2001). Keeping the territory intact, land tenure remained as the only right vested to the Kalinago people. While the afore-mentioned 1903 land survey sought to define the hazy boundaries of the Kalinago Territory, in reality, it did little to create any lasting clarity regarding its boundaries, independence, or autonomy. The original 1903 survey includes landmarks not indicated on any current map, such as the Ballata Ravine and Raymond River (Layng 1976), continuing the enigmatic nature of this territory and its boundaries. It was not until 1978 that the British government allocated a more precise position to the boundary, defining it as the Madjini River, or what was considered the Raymond River. However, once again many considered this as a strategic move to take power away from the Kalinago. As stated by Chief Fredrick, "Why then is the line going from 'Raymond River northward? This is not a rhetorical question. Good acres of land on which Carib children can be fed wiped out by a single stroke of the pen!" (Frederick 1981, 12).

5.1.2 The Kalinago Territory: land, power and politics

In 1953, after continual lobbying from the Kaliango, the Chief's office was finally reinstated. The length of the chief's office term was reduced from a lifelong time span to 3 years. Furthermore, a Kalinago Council was created. However, no budget or judicial authority was granted to the Chief or the Council, merely the right to provide assistance in land disputes (Kossek 1994; Owen 1974). Similar to the 1932 Commission Report, the Council continues to maintain only the land held in a collective tenure. This measure has historic importance as it represents, in recent memory, the Kalinago assertion for independence being hindered by a colonizer or foreign government, in this case the British.

Even though the relative isolation throughout the Colonial era created a strong sense of Kalinago loyalty to the territory land (Crispin and Kanem 1989), the colonial government as well as the subsequently independent Dominican government has continually attempted to put an end to any form of Kalinago power. First, in 1966, a policy proposed replacing the Chief and council with a village council, aimed at assimilating the Kalinago people into the greater Dominica. The Kalinago rejected this initiative. Second, throughout the 20th century, certain political parties and various religious institutions appear to divide rather than unite the community (Kossek 1994). Third, the Dominican government has attempted to convince the Kalinago to apply for singular land titles, whereby the communal land title as well as the power of the Chief would be destroyed (Kossek 1994; Owen 1974).

With Dominican independence in 1978, the Kalinago sought more representation within the new government. With the "Carib Reserve Act" of 1978, they finally re-obtained the communal land title taken from them by the invading British marines during the so-called Carib War of the 1930s (Gregoire *et al.* 1996; Kossek 1994). This "Carib Reserve Act" "granted collective title to the residents of the Kalinago Territory and legally instituted the position of the Kalinago Chief and Council, to be elected every 5 years by the territory's residents" (Strecker 2016, 171) (see Carib Reserve Act 1978 for more information).[34]

Despite this legal representation, politics and contention surrounding the communal land title, land tenure, and the land itself remain deeply embedded not only in recent history but also in any future continuation of the Kalinago Territory. According to Mullaney (2009, 71), the Kalinago "have yet to secure full legal title to the land and continue to contest on behalf of the entire population both terms of governance and their citizenship status with the central Dominican Government." This implies that in spite of having a communal land title, the Kalinago Territory is limited in its actual autonomy and independence when compared with the rest of Dominica. This is perhaps best exemplified by the relationship between the Ministry of Kalinago Affairs and the Chief and Council. This ministry was established in 2000 by the Dominican government and first headed by a Parliamentary Secretary. In this sense, the Ministry represents the needs of the Kalinago people as an acting governmental body. However, with wording stating that the Chief and Council "shall have sole custody, management and control of the Reserve, for and on the behalf of the residents of the Reserve" (Carib Reserve Act 1978, 25), there remains a lack of clarity to the division of any decision-making powers between the Kalinago Chief and Council on the one hand, and the Ministry of Kalinago Affairs on the other (Strecker 2016).

The question of individual land tittles continues to be a subject of discussion among the territory's inhabitants. A communal land title preserves the integrity of the Kalinago Territory from any outside encroachment, enabling it to continue to exist in the most physical sense. However, this issue remains complex as individual land titles would provide loans and bank credit, enabling possible personal advancement in the Kalinago Territory. The community as a whole remains divided on the issue of communal land. For example, the Carib Council minutes of March 1990 reveal that individuals residing at the hamlet of Bataca wanted private titles whereas the inhabitants of Sineku did not. Additionally, a 1990 Carib Territory survey discloses that a majority of the Kalinago wanted private titles (Kossek 1994). While unsuccessful, other attempts to create some form of credit line to increase development in the territory have been made by both the Kalinago Territory local government and the Dominican government (Gregoire *et al.* 1996).

---

34 Carib Reserve Act 1978, Chapter 25:90, available at: http://www.dominica.gov.dm/laws/chapters/chap25-90.pdf.

Remaining as a communally titled land holding, the Kalinago Territory not only continues to be economically isolated, but also endures as a physical space of cultural identity. No wonder the issue of communal land title and land more generally lies at the heart of matters, deeply embedded within economic, cultural and social structures of the community. For better or for worse, land remains an integral part of Kalinago identity.

5.1.3 Shaping the current Kalinago Territory landscape

As sugar profits dwindled in the Caribbean, the urgent search for alternative export goods to fill the void began. Previously grown only for local consumption, (Fridell 2010, 287), "Green Gold" or bananas offered this new cash crop, quickly defining the economies of many islands in the Lesser Antilles (Clegg 2002; Fridell 2010; Wiley 1998, 2008). The total banana export burgeoned here from 100,000 tons in 1963 to 275,000 tons in 1992 (Fridell 2010, 288). Dominica relied on bananas to such an extent that this fruit provided "50 to 70 percent of all export earnings and over one-third of all employment" (Fridell 2010, 288). In fact, British government officials stated that at the time Dominica and the other Windward Islands had become "more dependent on their banana exports than any other state in the world" (Myers 2004, 34).

The banana trade even reached the isolated Kalinago Territory. Disconnected from the rest of Dominica, due to steep and muddy roads, little economic development could be noted until the early 1980s (Gregoire *et al.* 1996). This situation changed dramatically with the introduction of the banana export market during the early 1980s. In the Kalinago Territory, unlike the rest of Dominica, large land tracts were available thanks to its special communal land title status, facilitating the establishing of banana plantations (Gregoire *et al.* 1996; Hulme and Whitehead 1992). The global banana market now shifted the land-use from small plots of agroforestry systems (Mullaney 2009) to banana plantations throughout the territory.

The banana export and its consequences drastically altered numerous aspects of life in the Kalinago Territory. First, a main paved road provided connectivity through the territory as it linked the towns of Castle Bruce to the south and Marigot to the north (Gregoire *et al.* 1996; Kossek 1994; Layng 1983). Second, the economic prospects for numerous Kalinago transformed, as it brought about an unknown wealth with non-seasonal and reliable (Gregoire *et al.* 1996; Layng 1983). One could now rely on the stability of a weekly income, enabling many families to improve their living conditions thanks to innovations and education opportunities. Third, the above-mentioned newly built road resulted in first-time visitors entering the territory, creating a traditional handicraft market. Such an economic opportunity implied that cash was now readily available, causing credit not as much required for personal economic development as had been the case beforehand.

However, as we have seen in chapter 4, regarding the subject of sugar and St. Kitts, cash crops are never sustainable in the long run. Built on preferential trading between the United Kingdom and the governments of the Lesser Antilles, the banana export market, similar to other cash crops, created a close-knit relationship between all the main stakeholders involved in exporting Caribbean bananas, except for the farmers themselves. Between 1955 and 1995, the banana export company named Geest "enjoyed virtual monopoly as the sole transporter and marketer of bananas shipped from Dominica" (Wiley 2008, 80). The Banana Act of 1959 obligated banana farmers to sell all exportable fruit to the Banana Growers Association (BGA) which had a contract with Geest and in turn provided bananas for up to 60% of the British market. This trading practice was dismantled in the course of the 1990s by the World Trade Organization, backed by the United States (Fridell 2010). This measure, along with Black Sigatoka disease[35], put a momentous end to the banana export market throughout the Lesser Antilles.

Unfortunately, the market break-up did little to consider the after-effects on small rural farmers involved. Nothing since has come close to replacing the economic stability, or in other terms dependency, of the banana trade, a fact impacting the Kalinago Territory to this day. There are no other agricultural markets feasible, as any other grown crop in this territory depends upon a purchase by tourists or hucksters who rarely make the trip up into the territory. Since the demise of the banana industry, weekly or bi-weekly paid jobs in the Kalingo Territory have become rare. Even tourism here has declined as the Kalinago handicraft items make their way to the capital of Roseau, keeping profits far from the Kalinago Territory borders (Mullaney 2009). This large economic vacuum leaves a visible reminder throughout the landscape as banana plantations have now converted to the small agroforestry plots of years before. In sum, the historical background on the Kalinago Territory provides a context for how land-change, linked to independence and isolation as well economic opportunities and development, leads to subsequent impacts on CES.

Part II. Landscape: use, modification and value

5.2 Multiple uses of the land: an analysis of the land-cover changes

Because the Carib Territory has land and its land is fertile.

Francois Barrie, 14/7/2015, Salybia

On Horseback Ridge Road lies a bluff from which one can look down upon the expanse of the entire Kalinago Territory (see Fig. 30-31). Small agricultural plots are interspersed with houses built on rolling hills, leading eventually towards the choppy Atlantic Ocean. When taking in this impressive vista, it is striking to realize that only a decade ago this area was entirely filled with banana plantations. As discussed above (see section 5.1.4), the Kalinago Territory has gone through extreme changes, trans-

---

35 Black Sigatoka Disease or Black Leaf Streak is a leaf spot disease responsible for 50% or more yield losses of banana crops and premature ripening. It is found in a wide range of banana varieties, including plantains, cooking and dessert bananas. The expense (15-20% of the final retail price) of treating the disease makes growing bananas almost impossible for small farmers today. Along with Grenada, the Grenadines, St. Lucia, St. Vincent and Guyana, Dominica is one of the most effected countries by Black Sigatoka (Organization 2013).

Fig. 30. View from Horseback Ridge Road en route to the Kalinago Territory (photo by author).

Fig. 31. The Kalinago Territory expanse as observed from Horseback Ridge Road (photo by author).

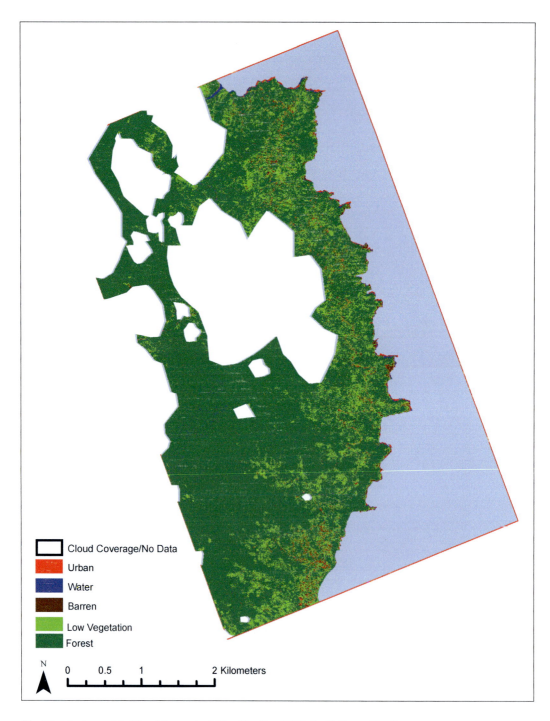

Fig. 32. Maximum Likelihood Supervised Classification 2005, the Kalinago Territory.

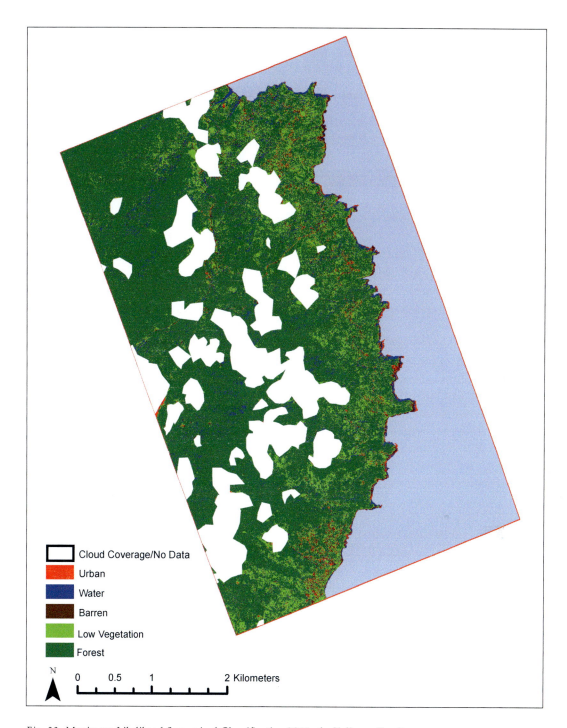

Fig. 33. Maximum Likelihood Supervised Classification 2014, the Kalinago Territory.

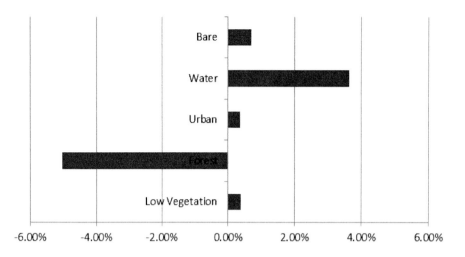

Fig. 34. Percentages of the total land class type changes between 2005 and 2014, the Kalinago Territory.

forming in less than 50 years from subsistence agriculture into industrial banana plantations, and subsequently into the current, new form of subsistence agriculture. As local agricultural practices have modified considerably because the combination of accompanying innovative developments and connectivity not only with the rest of Dominica but also further afield, the physical landscape of the Kalinago Territory, and by extension the relationship of its residents with this landscape, have also altered. In order to explore the impacts on CES in the Kalinago Territory, the present research will consider any landscape modifications based on the GIS/Remote Sensing results as well as on community perspectives.

As discussed in chapter 3, these physical land changes, or land-use/land-cover changes, have been explored by means of the Maximum Likelihood Supervised Classification and ISO Unsupervised Classification for the two significant years in casu 2005 and 2014. (See Appendix B. 2). The banana industry ended just prior to 2005. The year 2014 was selected because, when the present research was carried out, the date provided the most recent high resolution image with the least amount of cloud coverage. Therefore, 2005 and 2014 deliver us with a glimpse into the modifications which evolved during the ensuing years. Figs. 32 and 33 deal with the land-cover classification for these two in order to establish a comparison. It may be noted here that the white patches have been omitted as they represent cloud coverage.

From a visual inspection, the Kalinago Territory has clearly remained in a relatively rural and forested condition between the years 2005-2014 (due to the overall green color of Figs. 32-33). However, Fig. 33 does illustrate increases in low vegetation and urban areas as the forested areas appear less intact. For the percentage change of the land class type, see Fig. 34. Apparently, "Forest" has transformed the most, with a decline of -5.04%. Increases have occurred in the classifications "Urban" (0.35%), "Barren" (0.68%) and "Low Vegetation" (0.37%). It is important to mention here that the increase in the land class type "Water" is most likely caused by a misclassification, and not by any factual water increases. As mentioned

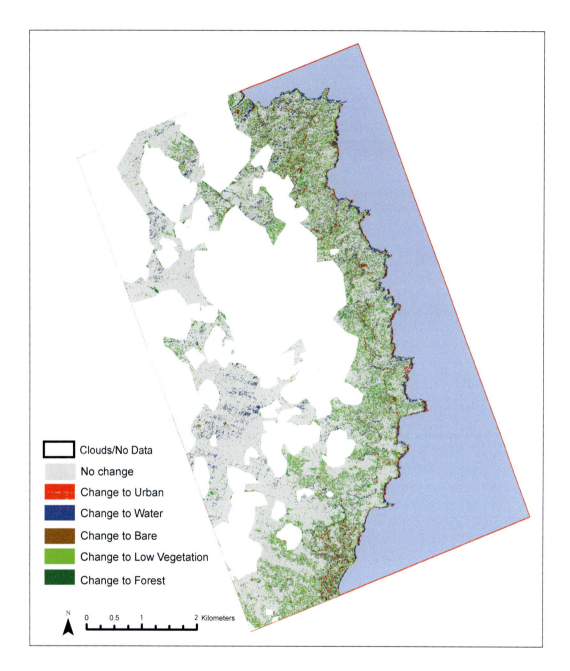

Fig. 35. Overall land class changes in the Kalinago Territory, indicating the modification of the land-cover changes between 2006 and 2015.

in chapter 3, cloudless satellite imagery of the Kalinago Territory was difficult to obtain, impacting certain results. For this reason, "Water" will not be considered a significant land-change and will not be further discussed. For the results of the "Water" land change, see Appendix B. 2, Table 41 and Fig. 69.

Modifications are further explained (see Fig. 35), by the resulting land change raster of the time span 2005-2014. As can be interpreted on the basis of the image,

Land class type	2005 Area	2005 Coverage	2014 Area	2014 Coverage
Urban	180.80 ha.	1.5%	223.46 ha.	1.8%

Table 26. Total acreage changes of land class: Urban.

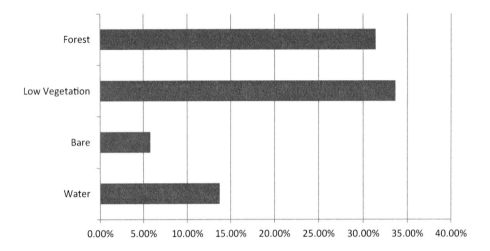

Fig. 36. Urban gains: contributions from other land classes, 2005-2014.

we see an increase in "Urban" areas throughout the Kalinago Territory. However, it is important to note that the red areas, indicating a transformation from other land classes to the "Urban" land class, and positioned along the shoreline, are most likely misclassified. They are in fact either rocky or bare grounds. The increase in urban areas is most prominent in the southern part of the Kalinago Territory. The rise in the number of "Water" pixels observed in the grey areas is most likely misclassified, too. Based on their location, these pixels can more justifiably be classified as "Forest". Such misclassifications are the outcome of the local mountainous and varied elevation (see chapter 3). In the north-eastern areas we note an increase in areas colored bright green, referring to a "Low Vegetation" land-cover. In fact, a modification towards "Low Vegetation" is often found in combination with brown or "Bare" land class types as encountered throughout the Kalinago Territory. Such a land pattern occurs regularly along the main road.

The Figs. 32-35 reveal changes in all land classes for the time span 2005-2014, but most notable in the ""Forest" and ""Low Vegetation" land classes, with urban and bare areas still being relevant but of a less drastic nature. However, these results do not reveal the type of transformation. More specifically, it is important to realize how, for example, the land class covers have resulted in gains when compared with other land classes. To explore this, the specific increase or decline in land class types and the subsequent contributions to these landscape dynamics are revealed below. For the imagery of each specific land class change, or the gains to each land class extracted from another, see Appendix F. 1, Figs. 76-78.

First, the land class type "Urban" is explored. The total area (ha.) of the "Urban" land class has increased between 2005 and 2014, as indicated in Table 26.

Land class type	2005 Area	2005 Coverage	2014 Area	2014 Coverage
Bare	208.86 ha.	1.7%	292.05 ha.	2.4%

Table 27. Total acreage changes of land class: Bare.

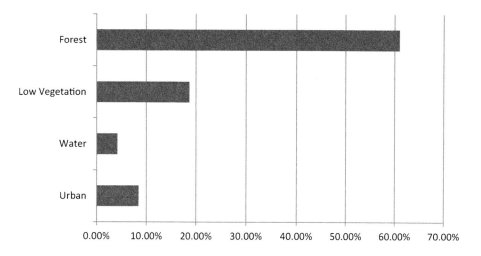

Fig. 37. Bare gains: contributions from other land classes, 2005-2014.

To understand Table 26 further, the breakdown of losses from other land classes to the gains of "Urban" land class is found in Fig. 36. Apparently, the "Urban" land class has gained mainly from "Low Vegetation" (33.64%) or "Forest" (31.40%). These dynamics reveal an urbanizing Kalinago Territory at the expense of natural vegetation.

Second, the land class type "Bare" reveals an increase of almost 84 ha. between the time span 2005-2014 (see Table 27).

According to Fig. 37, the increase in the land class "Bare" has occurred due to losses of "Forest" (60.98%) and "Low Vegetation" (18.69%). This indicates again that the Kalinago Territory is shifting quickly towards a more urbanized landscape. One inference signifies that a clear cutting of land had occurred, often resulting in land being abandoned. Or have certain environmental factors perhaps led to the soil being less productive when compared with previous planting seasons?

Third, "Low Vegetation" has interestingly increased 45 ha. through time, making up 17% of the entire Kalinago Territory (see Table 28).

Fig. 38 reveals further information on the type of land changes experienced in the "Low Vegetation" land class category. "Forest" (59.85%) has contributed almost exclusively to the growth of the "Low Vegetation" land class. The Kalinago Territory has evolved from mainly forested landscape to more urbanized one.

In Table 30, it is indicated that the land class type "Forest" makes up 74% of the total Kalinago Territory, and that it has decreased with 617 ha. between 2005 and 2014.

The type of gains to the "Forest" land class is explored in Fig. 39. Considering Fig. 39 and Table 29, the change between "Low Vegetation" and "Forest" is highly dynamic: "Low Vegetation" has contributed 11.36% to the "Forest" gains.

Land class type	2005 Area	2005 Coverage	2014 Area	2014 Coverage
Low Vegetation	2041.93 ha.	16.7%	2086.93 ha.	17.0%

Table 28. Total acreage change of the land class: Low Vegetation.

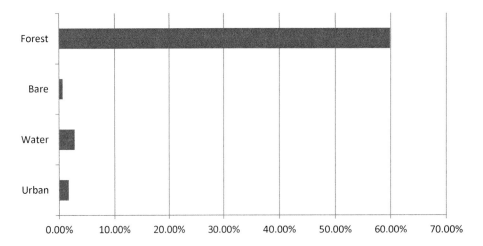

Fig. 38. Low Vegetation gains contributions from other land classes, 2005-2014.

However, as this percentage remains quite low, this outcome indicates that, in spite of being a modifying landscape, the Kalinago Territory remains forested and rural. This would indicate that by and large this part of Dominica has been relatively covered in forest through time.

Fig. 39 proves that the "Forest" land class type has declined over time, because of a growth of urbanization, clear cutting, and the return to small agriculture plots. Even though the forested areas remain large throughout the Kalinago Territory, this modification may be indicative of a local economic shift.

Based on these GIS/Remote Sensing results, the landscape dynamics not only reveal a relatively forested Kalinago Territory but also a rapid transformation. Any land-cover change is evidently being impacted, as the "Low Vegetation," "Bare," and "Urban" land class types increase. These classified land cover data were also utilized in subsequent land analyses (see 5.3), such as the Curve Number Analysis presented in the Resource Conservation. From the historical context discussed above, these landscape changes towards an increasing low vegetation could be extrapolated to a global economic shift, notably evolving from the demise of banana exportation and the Black Sigatoka disease, which maintained a relatively forested landscape. In turn, these global processes lead to visible local land changes.

The phenomenon land-cover is clearly changing. However, without any understanding of how individuals perceive these modifications in the Kalinago Territory, the results presented here would remain purely pixel-based. Nevertheless, they can only be interpreted within the context of community perceptions investigated

Land Class Type	2005 Area	2005 Coverage	2014 Area	2014 Coverage
Forest	9678.07 ha.	79.1%	9061.12 ha.	74%

Table 29. Total acreage changes of land class: Forest.

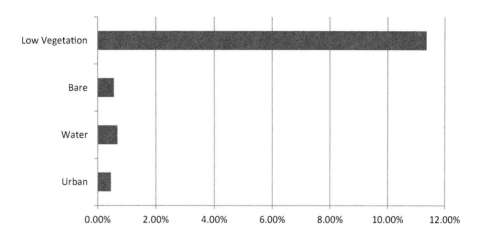

Fig. 39. Forest gains contributions from other land classes, 2005-2014.

through surveys and interview results. In order to explore this further, the community survey[36] provides a context and deeper understanding.

First, the overall mean perceptions of land, territory and hamlet transformations are illustrated (see Fig. 40). The scale ranges from 1 to 3, whereby 1 is perceived as negative and 3 as positive. The outcome reveals that overall modifications in the landscape are considered neither very positive nor negative. Nevertheless, land-changes appear to be viewed slightly more negative than any hamlet and territory changes.

Second, these variables were then explored by means of a Multiple Correspondence Analysis (MCA) in order to reveal the community perceptions of overall land-change on the one hand and land-change within each hamlet on the other hand. As a reminder, during each relationship of variables explored, the number of dimensions changes depending on whether or not the value of the total inertia was greater than 0.8 when using two or three dimensions in the analysis. Table 31 concerns how the variables, "Territory", "Hamlet", and "Land", are related, or how perceptions of change in one variable may be related to perceptions of change in another variables. From Table 31, the variables of "Territory" and "Hamlet" are related, meaning that any perception of change, negative or positive felt by survey respondents concerning on of these variables will often be the same type of perception for the second variable. However, any changes of perception regarding the variable of "Land" are not linked to these other two the variables "Hamlet" or "Territory".

---

36 See section 3.5 for more information on the survey carried out in the Kalinago Territory.

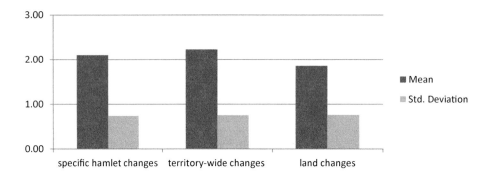

Fig. 40. Perception of any hamlet, territory, land and changes as expressed by the respondents of the survey residing in the Kalinago Territory whereby 1 represents the negative and 3 the positive changes.

	Dimension		Mean
	1	2	
Land changes	.266	.180	.223
Territory changes	.830	.700	.765
Hamlet changes	.877	.740	.808
Active Total	1.972	1.619	1.796

Table 30. Discrimination measures of variables: Land, Territory, and Hamlet. The filled-in cells denote the significant relationships.

These results are further explored in Fig. 41 which represents the categories of the variables considered in the analysis as points in the dimensional space generated by the MCA. The variables are determined by way of a number and color. Numbered diamonds refer to the category (1 = negative changes/perceptions, 2 = no change, 3 = positive changes/perceptions). Colored diamonds pinpoint the categories (blue = hamlet changes, light brown = territory changes, green = land changes). Points closely positioned indicate that the categories tend to occur together.

For this specific analysis, two dimensions were selected as they explain the 88.6% of the total variation encountered among the variables. It is also important to further pay attention to where these variables are located in space (see Fig. 41).

All in all, individuals respond similarly with regard to changes involving both "Hamlet" and "Territory" as is suggested by the fact that the categories of these two variables are positioned closer to each other. When considering each category or variable, however, the "Hamlet Changes" (blue diamonds) and "Territory Changes" (grey diamonds) are located closer to each other, generally speaking. Interviewees tended to answer differently about land-change. Accordingly, the "Land-change" (green diamonds) is distanced from the other variables. The numerals 1, 2, and 3 denote any perceived modification as negative (1) to positive (3). By and large, we observe an association between the variables, as suggested by the clustering of categories ("Hamlet", "Territory", "Land") with perceived changes (1, 2, 3) indicated in Fig. 43. It can be ascertained that the perceived changes with Value 1, 2 and 3 tend to cluster in the scatter plots, suggesting an overall agreement between the respondents' answers. Dimension 1 discriminates

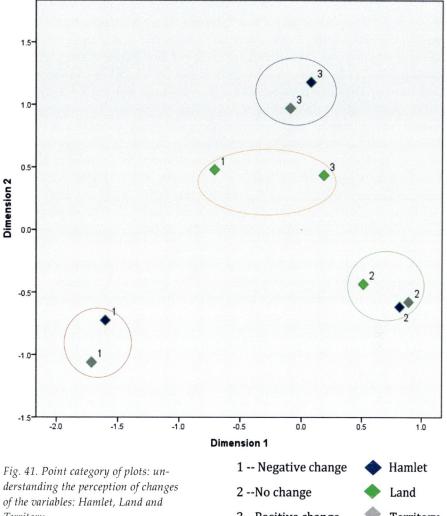

Fig. 41. Point category of plots: understanding the perception of changes of the variables: Hamlet, Land and Territory.

1 -- Negative change ◆ Hamlet
2 -- No change ◆ Land
3 -- Positive change ◆ Territory

between the negative categories of all the variables from the other categories. Interviewees feel similarly negative (Value of 1) about any territory and hamlet changes. Individuals who opine that the territory has changed negatively will add that their particular hamlet has changed negatively, as the red circle encompassing these variables indicate. Those who answer positively (Value of 3) about any territory changes will also reply positively about hamlet changes, suggesting again a clear clustering, as the blue circle (see Fig. 41) denotes Individuals who hold the view there has been no change will feel the same across all variables, territory, hamlet and land, as the green circle illustrates. However, the category "Land" is more difficult to understand. A number of respondents express positive opinions on land-changes, presenting it with the Value of 3. Others find perceived changes to land to negative, giving it Value 1 as is suggested by means of the orange circle (see Fig. 43).

The final conclusion based on the above information leads to the following observations. While any "Hamlet" and "Territory" changes are perceived as neither negative nor positive, this does not necessarily imply that land changes will be perceived as negative, too. A strict correspondence of any "Hamlet" and "Territory" modifications can be determined, but this is not the case when considering any land changes. Hence, it is understood that individuals will feel similarly, negative or positive, about these "Hamlet" and "Territory" issues. This assumption is probable as the "Hamlet" and "Territory" categories imply not only land but also socio-economic developments in general everyday life in the Kalinago Territory. However, land remains a contested issue as respondents do not seem to agree on whether land changes have been positive or negative overall. Taking these results into consideration by means of Fig. 43, it appears that while one often thinks that changes (either positive or negative) may be take place throughout the this territory as well as in their own hamlet, one often does not think that any positive transformations will unfold with regard to the land.

The outcome of the above MCA (as presented in Fig. 41) is further investigated applying demographic variables in order to explore any possible differences in how individuals perceived land-change based on location (hamlet), gender, or the age of the respondent. First, no clear clustering appeared when considering the relationship between land, territory and hamlet variables and location (hamlet). This suggests that, generally speaking, individuals residing at the same hamlet of the

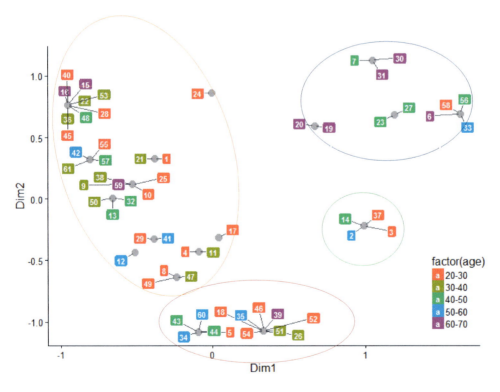

Fig. 42. Point category of plots: understanding the relationships between the perception of changes regarding the variables, Land, Territory and Hamlet, and the demographic factor of age.

Kalinago Territory feel similarly negative about "Territory" and "Hamlet" changes. To explore this further, Fig. 42 delves into the demographic relationship of Age and any perceived changes to the subjects of "Territory", "Hamlet" or "Land. Often earlier generations may respond negatively on the changing landscape because the present landscape may differ dramatically from what they remember. However, there is no clear clustering regarding age (see Fig. 43). To interpret Fig. 43, the red circle denotes individuals who have extremely negative perspectives regarding "Hamlet" and "Territory" changes. The green circle indicates those who do not think a transformation has taken place regarding the variable "Land". The blue circle indicates those who speak positively of changes regarding "Territory" and "Hamlet"" issues. Finally, the orange circle designates those who feel either extremely negative or extremely positive about land-changes. The color of each box indicates the age group to which the numbered individual belongs. We see that the age groups vary in each cluster of opinions.

As discussed in Part I (see above) the historical context section, the rural subsistence agriculture common to the Kalinago Territory shifted to industrial banana plantations during only the past 30 years. This modification occurred throughout the entire territory, drastically shaping the entire expansion and marketing of agriculture. These survey results of the perceptions of land, territory and hamlet shifts (see Figs. 41 and 42) echoed the results also found in numerous interview data. Pointing at the surrounding fields next to his house, one respondent remarked: "I had bananas, I had dasheen,[37] and all this area was bananas" (B8 2015). Or, as another interviewee stated while also pointing at the surrounding landscape "All that was figue[38] . Right, Figue was big" (B58 2015). Furthermore, interviewees mentioned that forest areas had been cut down, firstly in order to grow mixed crops and secondly to expand the urban areas. Subsequently, the low vegetation increases and urban areas are built. In addition, the coverage of the land-use type "Urban" increases as the number of inhabitants of the Kalinago Territory grows which in turn leads to further development.

If the results of the interviews, surveys and the GIS/Remote sensing concerning the evolving landscape are combined, the Kalinago Territory appears to be changing rapidly, pointing to evidence of modernization as well as less land utilization. The landscape shifts as seen in the GIS/Remote sensing analysis of declining forests and increasing low vegetation as well as bare areas represent a visible transformation, experienced by community members of the Kalinago Territory. Such landscape perceptions, combined with GIS/Remote Sensing, begin to reveal a landscape in transition. Landscape transformations clearly reflect both positive and negative impacts on the Kalinago Territory. On one hand, accompanying modernization leads to Territory development. On the other, the land declines in productivity and use.

As seen above, the altering landscape has led to a decline in land use. In the Kalinago Territory, agriculture often delivers more than just a livelihood: it also

---

[37] Dasheen is a root vegetable, anda common staple in the Caribbean, especially in the Kalinago Territory.
[38] Figue is a colloquial term applied when referring to a banana.

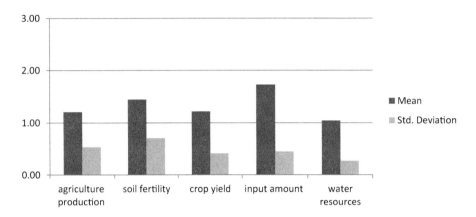

Fig. 43. Overall perceptions expressed by the survey respondents regarding modifications to agricultural variables, whereby 1 represents the negative and 3 the positive changes.

	Dimensions			Mean
	1	2	3	
Agriculture Production	.612	.198	.428	.413
Soil Fertility	.445	.752	.004	.400
Crop Yield	.544	.674	.012	.410
Input Amount	.072	.110	.545	.242
Water Resources	.567	.121	.371	.353
Total	2.240	1.854	1.359	1.818

Table 31. Discrimination measures of variables: Agriculture, Soil Fertility, Crop, Input Amount, and Water. The filled-in cells denote the significant relationships.

serves as the cultural backbone for the community. Throughout the interviews, this importance of agriculture was obvious. In the past, agriculture was defined by self-sufficiency, or as one interviewee explained, "People planted their own food, they reared their own animals" (B30 2015). He then added that agriculture "just took a downward trend, people don't farm like they used" (B30 2015).

To further analyze the landscape changes in the Kalinago Territory, specifically those regarding agricultural cultivation, the administered survey sought to quantify the perceived modifications in order to yield, production, water resources, and amount of inputs (i.e. fertilizer or pesticides) with regard to agriculture. Figure 43 presents the overall perceptions of changes in agricultural variables. The scale ranges from 1 to 3, with 3 being the most positive. An important note is that, in reference to any input amounts, a higher score suggests more inputs are required, rather than a higher score suggesting that input amounts are perceived as positive. Moreover, this result indicates that water resources are on the decline in the Kalinago Territory because they are perceived as very negative. Soil fertility is one of the higher variables, but the input amount is also quite high, indicating that respondents believe that significantly more fertilizers and pesticides are needed to keep the soil fertile.

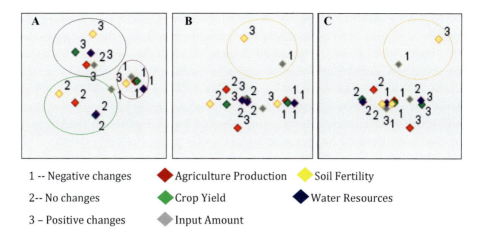

Fig. 44. Joint category of plots: understanding the relationships between the perceptions of changes of the variables: Agriculture Production, Soil Fertility, Crop, Input Amount, and Water Resources.

A Multiple Correspondence Analysis (MCA) was performed in order to explore the type of relationships between agricultural variables. This analysis applied three dimensions, hereby explaining 82% of the variation, which is sufficient. Table 31 reveals the discriminative measures of the three dimensions utilized to understand the relationships of the variables. We can see that the first dimension discriminates between the variables known as "Agricultural Production", "Crop Yield" and "Water Resources", whereas the second dimension discriminates between "Soil Fertility" and "Crop Yield", and the third dimension leaves us with the final variable: "Input Amount". An intuitive relationship appears from these results. It stands to reason that any agriculture production would be related to water, or the amount of water needed to moisten those crops, influencing the final crop yield. Furthermore, it makes sense that soil fertility also impacts the final "Crop Yield." Needless to say, the Input Amounts relate to the personal choice of the farmer involving the use of pesticides and fertilizers. Because inputs, fertilizers or pesticides are less available due to the costs, the lack of a relationship with this variable to others may also be explained.

Fig. 44 represents these results graphically, with all the correspondences placed between variables. As with the preceding MCA (see Figs. 43 and 44), the numbers of each diamond defines the perceived modification (1 = negative perception/changes, 2 = no change, 3 = positive perception/changes), whereas the colored diamonds define the variables (agricultural production, crop yield, water resources, input amount). If diamonds are closely positioned (on the graph) this indicates that the categories tend to occur together. In general, we can observe an association between the variables, as the clustering of categories (Values 1, 2, 3) in Fig. 46 suggests Having established that the Values of 1, 2 and 3 of the respective variables tend to cluster in the scatter plots, an agreement between the respondents' answers can be proposed.

Beginning with Box A (see Fig. 44), we can observe a discrepancy between the negative categories of all the variables when compared with the other categories. In fact, the variable of negative perceived changes (1) of all the agricultural variables are associated with higher values as presented in Box A and denoted by means of the red circles. The variables "Soil Fertility", "Water Resources", and "Crop Yield" are all perceived as negative with a value of 1. This would imply that they are perceived as negative together. The values of 2 and 3 placed in the left part of Box A are denoted by means of a black and a green circle respectively. The value of 2 (green circle), illustrates no change, and is related to the variables: "Soil Fertility", "Agriculture Production" and "Water Resources". The value of 3 (black circle) relates to all the variables. These results highlight the correlations between the variables of the agricultural production, crop yield, and water resources as well as the correlation between the variables of the soil fertility and crop yield. This outcome suggests that individuals feel negative about the transformations taking place within the agricultural cultivation, when considering these variables as a whole.

However, interpreting the relationship of the variables positioned in Boxes B and C is more difficult. Denoted by the orange circle, these variables relate to "Input Amounts" or fertilizers and pesticides, and "Soil Fertility"(1). The values of 1 and 3 of these variables apparently correspond. The corresponding points are always placed slightly outside the main clustering cloud of variables as is illustrated by means of the orange circles. Survey and interview answers concerning the "Input Amounts" were heterogeneous among the respondents of which several relied upon organic pesticides or fertilizers, and others on commercial products. Farmers applying organic pesticides would not note an increase in farming costs. However, those using commercial products would note an increase in such costs. During the banana cultivation period, all inputs were provided by the banana export company. Hence, agriculturists in the Kalinago Territory never had to purchase either pesticides or fertilizers for their crops themselves. This benefit kept costs low but also created a dependency. Nonetheless, it was often reported that applying more inputs caused a notable increase in farming costs.

When considering the variables as a whole, the survey discerned an overall decline in agriculture production, crop yield and water resources. Furthermore, interviewees who answered negatively with regard to the changes to the crop yield also perceived declines in soil fertility. However, depending on the farmer's own use of pesticides and fertilizers, the perception of input amount varies which, for this reason, as yet is not correlated to any other agriculture-related variable.

If agriculture has historically been the backbone of the Kalinago Territory, the banana industry maintained its continuation, keeping the economy of this part of Dominica in a constant motion. The banana, or figue, industry brought in regular incomes, providing economic stability for many families. One interviewee explained it thus: "It is for my family that is how I maintain my family […]. All my children go to school on figue money" (B58 2015). As already stated, the profitability of the banana sector created a reliance that came to a dramatic conclusion during the early 2000s. This event has negatively impacted agriculture throughout the Kalinago Territory, as described as: "And was it hard when the bananas stopped being bought. Yes, it was hard but, in the 1990s I had plenty [sic] bananas, the

Sigatoka took over, I abandoned most of my field" (B48 2015). According to another respondent, "Everyone has become poor since bananas" (B8 2015).

During the banana boom, fertilizer and pesticides as well as market access and shipping, were all provided by the overseeing banana company. Without this support, the expenses next led to a decline in farming as newly incoming costs as well as unreliable markets created a possible risk for the Kalinago people, not a profit. Ultimately, the banana industry required constant fertilizers and pesticides, which has led to the current soils being degraded. Among the interviewees who noted this fact, one respondent commented: "Well, the land has become less healthy, because at one time in the 60s or 70s, we used pesticide, ramizone, insecticide, and this has ruined the environment" (B8 2015). Consequently, the land requires more inputs which, because they are too expensive, create an even further decline in agriculture. Without any governmental push for agricultural diversification or a dependable foreign market, working in agriculture has become too expensive and instable as a livelihood. As one interviewee explains, "People just don't plant as many as they did, because they are so expensive and you can't get the material, the inputs that you need, so, people have tried and they have diversified, but it's not as booming as bananas used to be" (B40 2015).

However, the style of banana monocrop agriculture not only encouraged but also ensured that little agricultural diversity, except for personal consumption, remained during the final stages of the banana boom. An interviewee describes the fate of this agriculturally dependent relationship as follows: "The Kalinago people just farm, ship their produce to England, then it would better. Now the Reserve, is a struggle. It's a struggle" (B7 2015). With the demise of the banana trade, there was no push into other crops nor could the government install measures in order to establish any diversification. As one interviewee explains, "Right now, we are less in agriculture, because the government is saying there is a market here, but when they come, they don't get the market for you. So you just lose confidence" (B8 2015). People rely on outside actors such as hoaxters[39], yet again an irregular source of income, in order to buy their crops and bring them to the market. This phenomenon creates a very unstable relationship, as residents of the Kalinago Territory need the "hoaxters so you can get some income, pay their bills" (B21 2015).

Furthermore, the survey investigated the perceptions of agriculture and their relationships to demographic variables (in casu age and hamlet location). Results hereof reveal that these variables do not significantly impact the perceptions of agriculture in the Kalingo Territory where the agriculture perceptions are indeed entirely negative. Despite this lack of indication in the survey data, the interview data disclose that many believe that a generational divide causes the agricultural decline: "People don't want to go into agriculture, especially young people, because agriculture is what you work, you have to have your dirty clothes, turned clothes, and then agriculture in Dominica is very primitive, no tractors or what have you" (B30 2015). Elder generations often discussed that the physical effort or labor required by agriculture has created a lack of interest amongst the younger gen-

---

39 Hoaxters are private vendors who drive through Dominica buying agricultural products to sell to national and international markets.

Fig. 45. Mapping a field in the course of the Kalinago Territory land survey (photo by author).

Fig. 46. These undulating fields encountered in the course of the Kalinago Territory land survey reveal the variability of use and fallow (photo by author).

eration concerning the continuation of farming. Younger community members, such as one interviewee, also noted this decline in farming, explaining that "young men who have family land who don't farm, but would rather go into security in Portsmouth or Rousseau" (B16 2015), for reasons relating to a regular income rather than a lack of will to carry out any physical labor. The lack of financial security offered by agriculture evidently leads to its ultimate decline when observing members of the younger generations who continue such a livelihood.

To summarize, as observed in the land-cover analysis presented above, an increased urbanization as well as deforestation has occurred in the Kalinago Territory since 2005. These physical modifications are visible in the land-change analysis completed for the years 2005 and 2014 (see Figs. 32-35). These landscape modifications are revealed not only in satellite imagery but also in the perception of the landscape by individuals, disclosed through both interview and survey data. Considering the Kalinago Territory, its hamlets and landscapes, individuals hold pessimistic views on the current lack of solid land-use. Such views only augment when considering agriculture and cultivation in the Kalinago Territory, as individuals express negative opinions on the decline in agriculture and crop yield. Despite being a relatively rural and isolated area, this territory has also experienced a rapid, dramatic modification in land-cover, witnessing a transformation from bananas fields into overgrown or fallow fields, all within a single decade. Furthermore, as most households depended on the banana production in one form or another, the type of landscape modification not only impacted the landscape. Indeed, the entire community, "did change" (B28 2015). While land remains plentiful and accessible in the Kalinago Territory thanks to the continuation of the communal land title, nevertheless, little effort or development is related to the land.

5.3 Resource Conservation: Water Resources

"People don't go to the rivers anymore so they have left them, so they've become abandoned.

B40 2015

The Kalinago Territory is fortunate to be transected by not only ocean-bound, clear rivers and streams flowing from the surrounding mountains. This water resource has remained an important element in the Kalinago Territory. In the past, the Kalinago people were dependent on river water for daily washing, cooking, drinking, and agricultural irrigation. While many houses have pipe-born water, river water continues to be utilized in many agricultural activities, even more so as the availability of rain water is no longer predictable. As one respondent explains, "Because of climate change, during the rainy season, you expect rain, but the rain still does not fall. If you check the ground, it is pretty dry" (B47 2015).

Fortunately, despite the changing environment, many inhabitants of the Kalinago Territory have been able to depend on these riverine water resources for irrigation as well as other needs. The importance of running water is proven by results of the CN Grid of 2005 and the CN Grid of 2014, see Figs. 48 and 49. From this comparison, we see a relatively uniform grid value attributed to Fig. 48 for the year 2005, indicating relatively uniform CN values throughout the Kalinago Territory. This is in comparison to the patchiness, or areas with higher CN values (indicating higher potential for run-off potential) observed in 2014 (see Fig. 49). This patchiness again reflects the results of a changing land-cover as seen in the results

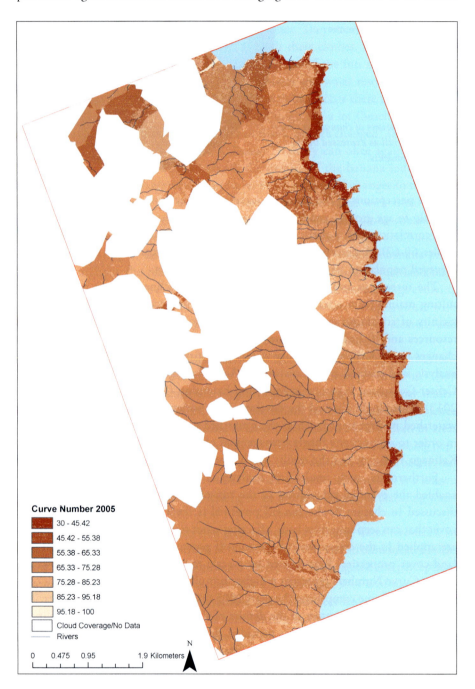

Fig. 48. Curve Numbers of 2005, the Kalinago Territory.

presented in 5.2 (see Figs. 33-37). Unlike forested areas, bare and urban land-covers are less capable of retaining water during run-off events. Landscape modifications resulting in a shift to bare or urban land cover in the course of the past decade, subsequently, leads to a higher run-off because of the land cover properties.

Based on this annual comparison, we can observe that modifications have taken place throughout the Kalinago Territory. However, it remains important to

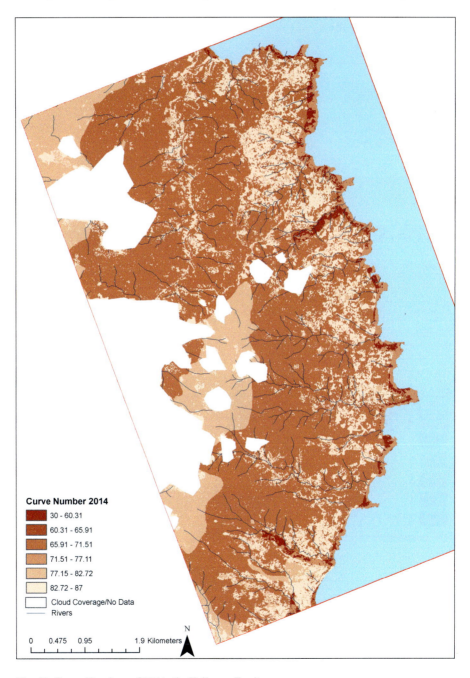

Fig. 49. Curve Numbers of 2014, the Kalinago Territory.

investigate where the largest changes of the CN values occur within the defined time period. For example, where the CN value has shifted from a low value of 30 to a higher value of 70. These types of jumps between the CN values would indicate an alarming transformation in the landscape, as a run-off is much more likely. Fig. 50 presents the CN shifts between 2005 and 2014. To interpret Fig. 50, the category "No Change" refers to the fact no changes of the CN value occurred within the location and the time period. Value 1 represents an increase of a single value in the CN. Value 2 represents an increase of two values in the

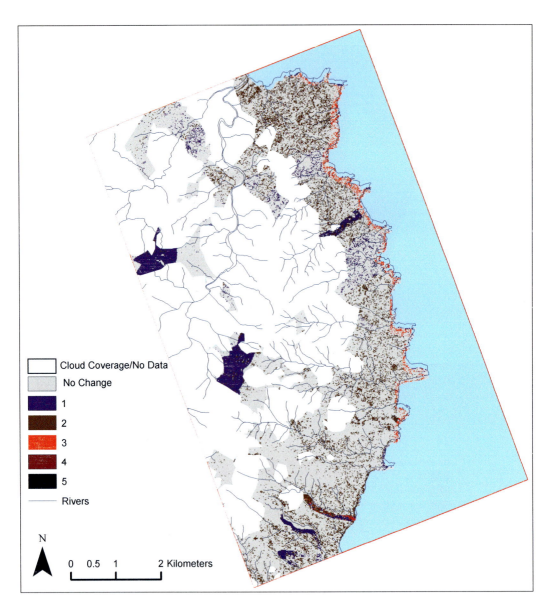

Fig. 50. Shifts in CN values as recorded between 2005 and 2014 in the Kalinago Territory whereby the numbers indicate a larger modification from the original low CN value (2005) to a higher CN value (2014).

CN. Value 3 represents an increase of three values in the CN. The relatively large amount of grey throughout the Kalinago Territory proves that by and large the CN values have remained relatively the same and that it has experienced a relatively stable run-off through time.

However, as the present research considers the impacts of any land-change on the water resources, including both the associated natural and cultural properties, this outcome also indicates possible linkages to the observed decline in water resources perceived by the Kalinago people. Considering Fig. 50 again, the higher values of the CN reflect a similar pattern to that of the patterns of land-change discussed in section 5.2. Higher CN values are found in similar positions where land any cover-change has shifted to "Bare" and "Urban" (see 5.2, Fig. 36 and 37). Furthermore, these results disclose an increase in the CN values within the direct vicinity of streams, rivers and hamlets. Fig. 50 reveals the higher CN values aligning with that of streams and rivers of the Kalinago Territory, as their higher values highlight them against the rest of this territory. A concentration of the changing, higher CN values along riverbeds represents the fact that these river areas may experience either an increased run-off, or the increase of soil and sediment flowing into the river during storm events, through time. The results support the perceptions regarding the declining water resources expressed by the survey respondents residing in the Kalinago Territory. With changing land patterns, a rise in the CN values are now found increasingly at the river areas, leading to a decline in water resources, as deforestation along the river beds increases a run-off into these important resources.

This environmental issue of declining water resources in river areas due to deforestation is not only perceived by Kalinago community members, but also appears in the satellite imagery analysis as presented in both the land change data (Fig. 32-35) and the CN value change (Fig. 48-50). Using land use/land cover data, this link between forested areas and declining water resources versus bare or urbanized areas and declining water resources has been explored already in the island of Puerto Rico (Scalley and López-Marrero 2014). However, the overwhelming perception of a decline of water resources by individuals living in the Kalinago Territory reveals further the impact. In the interview and survey data of this case study, the decline in water resources results in changing behavior, with less use and recreation in and around rivers or stream environs.

Considering sections 5.2 and 5.3 together, we grasp the cause and effect of any land-use/land-cover change on other natural resources. First, landscape shift, though subtle, lead to a decline in forested areas, and increases in low vegetation and urban areas (see Fig. 37). However, without management, such land shifts can result in other unforeseen subsequent impacts, or in this case, declining water resources. As revealed here, the clearing of land near rivers and streams has led to an increased run-off, adding more soil and sediment to these watersheds, thereby limiting important water resources. However, such landscape modifications can never be considered the outcome of natural processes alone but must be viewed within the context of the multi-scalar influences of politics, economics and society. With an increasing population, declining stable employment in the Kalinago Territory, and a reduced reliance on managed agriculture, the landscape is no longer the same.

5.4 Shifting community: the socio-cultural aspects of landscape change

How does such a modified landscape impact the society and culture we encounter in the Kalinago Territory? As we have seen, the declining agriculture and water resources can be traced directly and indirectly to the end of the banana export system in the Kalinago Territory. As a rural and agriculturally-dependent community up until very recently, the experienced social and cultural changes in the Kalinago Territory would evoke strong reactions, as individuals must negotiate their position on a daily basis.

The introduction and ultimate collapse of the banana industry as well as the accompanying urbanization and development in the Kalinago Territory have led to an altered landscape. Because of the booming banana export combined width the push into the global market, the Kalinago territory witnessed rapid community development including amenities (e.g. pipe-born water, electricity, paved roads, and increased education and employment opportunities). Such facilities and services, accompanied by the construction of schools, improved health services, and an increased access to other parts of Dominica, are clearly regarded as positive aspects, warmly welcomed by the community.

Notwithstanding these positive changes[40], coinciding with the demise of the banana industry and the introduction of development and modernization, certain negative perceptions of land resources concerning land-use, agricultural decline and water resources reveal yet another aspect of these modernizations. As discussed in chapters 2 and 3, a changing landscape impacts natural resource as well as associated cultural aspects. In agricultural landscapes these impacts, therefore, are perceived even stronger, as community members must readjust cultural associations to adapt to an evolving landscape. These aspects have been touched upon (see 5.2). For example, surveys and interview results reveal that many Kalinago perceive the changes in their landscape, and declining water resources in a negative manner. Underlying these landscape changes, one interviewee explains: "the loss of agriculture is also affecting the passing down of heritage" (B60 2015).

While heritage is subjective and difficult to define, one clear example hereof as a living practice, handed down from past generations to the future is termed "Koudmen[41]." Koudmen is a community practice, which has long been associated with rural agriculture in the Caribbean, and was especially prevalent in the Kalinago Territory. This tradition relies on reciprocity as well as the exchange of labor (e.g., collectively clearing agricultural fields, pulling in boats, building houses) and occurred throughout this part of Dominica. One interviewee says, "Koudmen was a very critical part of the community" (B26 2015). Another respondent notes, "The Koudmen thing is like a cooperation, people come together, we build a house, I'll help you tomorrow and each of us have our house" (B28 2015), while a third reports, "Before you used to call that Koudmen, and they

---

40 It is important to note that the present research does not indicate that the infrastructure and the increased opportunities are perceived negatively by the inhabitants of the Kalinago Territory.
41 The term "Koudmen" is spelled here in accordance with the *Dictionary of Caribbean English Usage* (Allsopp 1996).

would help you in your garden" (B34 2015). Yet another interviewee mentions, "If I was going to make a garden, the whole people would come help. Or you'd ask one and everybody would come" (B1 2015).

The importance of Koudmen as a link between community members remains clear. However, despite its social significance, this practice has been described as declining or even having completely disappeared in recent years. A variety of reasons seem to lie behind this wane. First, as illustrated in section 5.2, we see an overall decrease in agriculture across the Kalinago Territory. Presented in survey and interview data, fewer farms and less cultivation lead to less agricultural work, ultimately decreasing the occurrence of Koudmen. Second, while related to the decline in agriculture, the increasing urbanization and development within the Kalinago Territory has led to a monetized society. The practice of Koudmen has become increasingly unnecessary as it does not provide a monetary exchange so necessary for families living in the territory. As one interviewee explained, the demise of the banana trade did more than just influence the economy, it affected "the whole community, because when banana was growing, everybody would have a portion, everybody would get something, and then they would have more money, so they would buy more, buy from the fisherman, fisherman would get from them. So it was a cycle" (B22 2015). Third, a decrease in social cohesion in the Kalinago Territory has led to a decline in any community interaction. Throughout the interviews, a clear community shift became apparent. For example, one respondent mentions, "everybody is more about themselves" (B36 2015). This situation has impacted not only how people socialize but also their interpersonal relationships. Individual interviewees often spoke of the lack of a positive interaction between the hamlets. For instance, one respondent said, "Because sometimes people don't really communicate" (B7 2015). Overall, one interviewee stated that the "the community is less connected" (B51 2015).

While this phenomenon could be often attributed to a generational divide, as older generations often feel disenchanted with a changing society, this opinion on a disengaged community is shared by younger generations as well. For example, an interviewee in her early twenties stated: "growing up, we had a lot more socialization" (B8 2015). It is important to note that Koudmen, or "cooperative workgroups", were no longer an important activity because of economic and technological changes in the Kalinago Territory (Layng 1983, 14). This would suggest that the number of activities, such as Koudmen, were already waning during the early 1980s. However, in the interviews, this decline did not appear to be the case, as individuals considered the decline of Koudmen a relatively recent phenomenon, dating to the past 15 to 20 years. Hence, the decline of the Koudmen tradition represents not only a changing landscape, with a decline in agriculture and cultivation, but also a loss of social cohesion, and community engagement.

A Koudmen enabled not only reciprocity in agriculture, but also fishing in the Kalinago Territory. As a labor-intensive task, fishing relied on the community coming together to pull in the boats and nets. All participants would be paid with fish from the catch. The importance of fishing is not only tied to food security, but also deeply connected to the Kalinago identity. As one respondent stated: "Culture, fishing was a part of it, but then the fishing, we have no more"

Fig. 51. A canoe, being hollowed out and carved by hand from Gommier tree (Dacryodes excelsa) which was later sold outside the Kalinago Territory (photo by author).

(B7 2015). Referring to the entire territory, one interviewee describes the fact that "all these little hamlets used to be little fishing areas" (B24 2015). In the villages of Aywasi and Salybia Bay, individuals noted the presence of at least six to ten canoes in the recent past. Canoe building, bringing in fish to the shores and fishing as an activity, all required the assistance by and the cooperation of many. Again, these individuals refer to a recent decline in fishing, rather than a decline observed generations ago.

Once again, the practice of fishing has indeed waned. One interviewee explains that albeit relevant to the Kalinago Territory; people no longer go down to the bay and fish: "Now, people don't really fish again" (B20 2015). Financially, traditional canoe fishing has become less viable due to the competition from a nearby new fishery complex located at Marigot. One interviewee described that "boat fishing has faded away, again as I say, I am not sure, maybe financially, all the other areas have better boats than us, better fascinators and things" (B8 2015). While the decline of fishery may be seen as unrelated to any land-use changes, the disappearance of traditional subsistence activities, point again to the shifting landscape of

Fig. 52. Drying reeds of the auro (u)man (Ischnosiphon arouma) plant to produce baskets (photo by author).

the Kalinago Territory. The broader impacts of the land changes on society have led to a decrease in important cultural practices, such as Koudmen and fishing.

The data above reveal an overall negative perception of social changes, as individuals cite less social cohesion and activities, which ultimately cause the decline of communal heritage. As time-honored, cultural traditions(e.g., Koudmen, fishing) are often the foundations of community life and of the livelihoods in small isolated communities, the disappearance of such activities not only reveal a real transformation, they also speak to the broader global processes occurring alongside the everyday life of the members of such communities.

As we have seen in the decline of Koudmen, land and society transform simultaneously. However, the connections between landscape change and these types of social change are less obvious. The administered survey investigated the relationship between landscape shifts and the loss of heritage in the broader realm of community life, exploring perceptions of the community change (e.g. community activities and involvement herein, political influences, economic and education possibilities, the desired future direction of the Kalinago Territory). While such an investigation into the perceptions of community, education, politics, and economics may appear unrelated to the larger context of any landscape changes dealt with in the present case study, one must consider how land or landscapes entail the human and place relationships. Moreover, referring back to the communal land title of the Kalinago Territory, the land remains essential to the continuation of the identity and culture of its inhabitants.

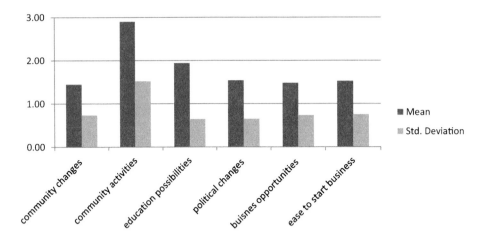

Fig. 53. Overall perceived community changes in the Kalinago Territory, whereby 1 represents the negative and 3 the positive changes.

Fig. 53 charts the overall perceptions of survey respondents regarding the direction of the trends discussed in these social variables. The scale again ranges from 1 and 3, the latter representing the most positive perceived community change. A score of 1.5 corresponds to a "neutral" perception. Fig. 53 discloses a clear negative perception related to trends in business opportunities and the ease with which one can start a business. This can be also understood as an economic opportunity made available the Kalinago Territory. Further, political changes are also seen as negative. In spite of a positive perception of community activities, their overall community changes are viewed as slightly negative. Finally, education possibilities are perceived as having improved slightly.

To observe the correlations between these variables, Table 32 explores the Discrimination Measures: Community, Education, Business, hereby comparing how people perceive these related variables. It is relevant to note here that business opportunities reflect the variable of economic opportunity in the Kalinago Territory. Dimension 1 discriminates between the categories of political changes, business opportunities and the ease with which to start a business, whereas Dimension 2 discriminates between the categories of business opportunities and community activities. Finally, Dimension 3 discriminates between the categories of community and political changes. This assessment discloses that respondents hold similar views on the changes in politics as they do on changes observed in available business opportunities. The same logic continues in Dimensions 2 and 3. For example, Dimension 2 reveals that one has similar thoughts on community activities and business opportunities. Dimension 3 reveals shared ideas concerning community as well as political changes. From this initial result, it is interesting to discover that the prevalence of politics is a factor related to other parts of community life.

The results (see Table 32) are visualized in Fig. 54. Once again, the latter Figure represents the categories of the variables considered in the analysis as points

	Dimension			Mean
	1	2	3	
Community changes	.290	.199	.733	.407
Community activities	.334	.349	.022	.235
Education possibilities	.363	.111	.057	.177
Political changes	.672	.123	.449	.414
Business opportunities	.675	.613	.061	.450
Start a business	.637	.273	.034	.315
Active Total	**2.971**	**1.669**	**1.355**	**1.999**

Table 32. *Discrimination measures of variables: Community, Education, Politics, and Business. The filled-in cells denote significant relationships.*

in the dimensional space generated by MCA[42] analysis. The numbers define the categories or values whereby 1 = negative perceptions/changes, 2 = no change, 3 = positive perceptions/changes, whereas the colored diamonds define the variables: Community changes, Community activities, Education possibilities, Political changes, Business opportunities, Start a business. The diamonds placed whenever at a close distance indicate that the categories tend to occur together.

Fig. 54 again reflects the correlations among specific community life variables presenting an apparently positive/stable perception of community changes and education opportunities, whereas business opportunities and politics are perceived as correlated and negative. These results reveal a complex impression of the Kalinago Territory, often echoed in interviews and field work. As suggested by the clustering observed in the blue circle of Box A, individuals who feel positive about one variable will commonly feel positive about subsequent variables. The red circle in Boxes A and B suggests that individuals will commonly perceive the variables referred to as Community change, Community Activity, Ease to start a business and Political changes, to be negative. Finally the orange circle in Boxes B and C reveals an outlier, because the variable "Community changes" with a value of no change appears by itself. Such a result suggests that a number of individuals believe the Kalinago Territory to be stagnant, with little development or change taking place. Increasing connections with the communities outside this territory have led to a rapidly modernizing community, resulting in more education opportunities as well as a certain increase of community development, creating positive overall perceptions for several survey respondents with regard to the Kalinago Territory. On the other hand, economic stagnation and political developments have not brought on any positive changes. Accordingly, it becomes apparent that any developments in the political arena when negatively perceived are often related to negative changes in business matters which are usually related to community activities. Finally, negative political events affect community changes as well.

Subsequently, these correlations were analyzed by means of demographic variables referred to as "Hamlet" and "Age". The results hereof, however, suggest no clear clustering, indicating that the correlations among any community change

---

42 See section 3.5 for further information on the Multiple Correspondence Analysis (MCA).

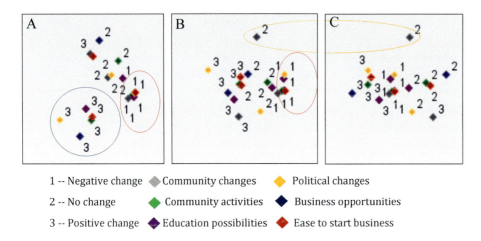

Fig. 54. Joint category of plots: understanding the relationship between perception of the changes concerning the variables of Community, Education, Politics and Business.

variables were valid throughout the Kalinago Territory, rather than relating to perceptions of those positioned in a specific hamlet or age group.

This outcome of the survey results regarding the community, land and politics (see Figs. 53, 54 and Table 32) reflect the opinions and perspectives verbalized and discussed in the interview data which reveal the extent to which such processes of community division have occurred. First, the role of politics in the Kalinago Territory has led to further division rather than political engagement. Supporting the wrong party lines seemed to have repercussions for an individual's daily life. Politics were forwarded as the reason behind (not) being employed or (not) acquiring building materials. As one interviewee said, "Politics, changed everything around" (B3 2015). Dominica has established a two-party system, with strong personalities and national attention. Further, as described in the historical context (see chapter 3, Part I), the Kalinago Territory has a Council and Chief as well as Ministry of Kalinago Affairs. This situation has often brought about a misinterpretation of powers by this Council and Chief as well as this Ministry, which one interviewee describes as follows:

> *It keeps it a political shady, it brings political controversy, it could bring unity, on both ends, in other words, both extremes is bad. If you have a chief who is a line to the current government, he may initiate policies that are not good for the people. Whereas, if the chief is not in unison with the Ministry, there will be fighting and conflict and nothing will get done. So, what I'm saying, while the Ministry is good, it should not be engulfing the Council, it should be supplementing, it should be clear lines of their jurisdiction (B28 2015).*

By and large, this division of political power has caused sparse developments or economic activities in the Kalinago Territory, which have recently lead to general discontent, "Everybody is sick of it now. The government, they are red or blue, it's a problem" says one interviewee (B15 2015). Things remain this way until elections come around. A history of favors for votes exists for the building of houses or the supplying of materials, thereby creating a culture of dependency. "People are more reliant on the state for their income, and there is only so much that the government can do" (B29 2015). Governmental parties gain support through promises and quick fix solutions rather than lasting public policy to benefit the entirety of the community (B26 2015). Returning to the survey data results concerning the perceptions of land (see section 5.2), this dissatisfaction expressed by interviewees regarding the lack of any development and change in the Kalinago Territory supports these results (see Figs. 40-43), as the survey respondents perceive the static state of "Hamlet" and "Territory" in a negative manner.

Second, religion has divided rather than united people. As one interviewee remarks, "It remains to this day a very divisive part of our community. There are multiple Christian organizations trying to, those things are so foreign to our culture and our ancestry, the political system remains divisive. As another interviewee concludes, "I think the territory needs to mature" (B26 2015). The afore-mentioned attempt has created divisions within a small and close-knit community, as one respondent mentions, "The whole thing, when politics or religion got a regional stronghold, lifestyle changed" (B8 2015). Interestingly, almost all community members believe that "All of us are divided by politician and religion. That is what separated, divided us" (B31 2015).

Clearly influencing both the personal and communal identity of those residing in the Kalinago Territory, the act of uniting around one religion or one political party has fractured their society. Such divisions impact social cohesion, resulting in little momentum towards community independence, self-reliance and community development. These divisions have only hardened with the economic vacuum created by the demise of productive agriculture because individuals no longer have a viable income or livelihood for their families.

Finally, the present survey investigated the desired future directions of the Kalinago Territory as expressed by its inhabitants. An overwhelming desire for change is revealed (see Fig. 55), as we see results suggesting that individuals are not satisfied with the current state of this territory. Results reveal they wish more development, agriculture, and nature conservation. In Fig. 55 (in which 1 represents a low and 3 a high desire for change), we can observe (a) how low the standard deviation is for all three variables, suggesting very little difference among responses, and (b) a clear balance between the three variable of development, agriculture and conservation, suggesting a desire for a balanced landscape which presents us with an interesting aspect as these three elements are often at odds with each other.

This outcome reveals, which in spite of the type of landscape changes (e.g. agriculture decline), residents of the Kalinago Territory aspire to return to an agricultural landscape, providing more opportunities or development possibilities as well as increased nature conservation. In the above sections 5.2 and 5.3, a changing landscape is revealed which has resulted in modified natural resources as well as indirectly in the impacts on subsequent cultural practices. Here, in section 5.4, the impacts of these transformations on the cultural aspects of the society have been explored. When considering the desired future directions of the Kalinago people together with the data collected concerning the community, economic, and the political changes, the present research demonstrates that local landscape transformations lead to repercussions in multidimensional aspects, including social and environmental.

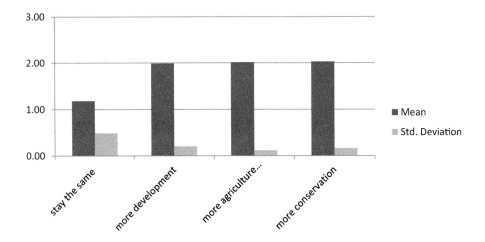

Fig. 55. Desired changes as defined by survey respondents, the Kalinago Territory.

Part III: The Kalinago Territory at a crossroads

Whereas the land-changes and associated societal shifts dealt with in this chapter are not uncommon in many rural communities of today, the speed of the ensuing results remains dramatic. The modifications in the Kalinago Territory has precipitated a decline in (a) the traditional agriculture and the reliance upon local produce, (b) the economic viability of agriculture and (c) the concerns regarding the health of natural ecosystems, such as local watersheds, and (d) the community practices that maintain cultural as well as societal connections.

Agriculture in the Kalinago Territory provided self-reliance and cultural preservation. These characteristics continued during the boom of the banana industry, as agriculture still remained the most common livelihood in the Territory. However when the banana trade proved no longer profitable, an altered landscape with less cultivation and management of land took root. Such land change results ultimately impacted other aspects, leading to declining water resources and negative perceptions of the landscape. Economic uncertainty in this region only serves to reinforce such negative community perceptions of the changing landscape, and by extension, society. As individuals shifted their livelihoods away from agriculture, a decline also occurred in the continuation of numerous traditional processes in agriculture and associated cultural practices. We see a clear breakdown of tradition in casu the Koudmen phenomenon. In rivers and streams, we see a decrease in recreational activities, such as bathing or swimming with friends and family.

Such accompanying economic changes have further impacted societal relationships, as individuals position themselves to cope with the landscape modifications. The present research would argue that landscape changes, resulting from economic and political causes have resulted from an economic vacuum which in turn has led to not only social isolation within the community but also to the rise of community divisions augmented through dependency relationships created by political as well as religious factions.

However, despite such community divisions and negative perceptions regarding any land-change in the Kalinago Territory, it remains relevant to consider the local land status. As discussed throughout this chapter, the communal land title held by the Kalinago people reflects both possibility and disillusionment. On one hand, the communal land title offers the preservation of land, which potentially could be developed or cultivated by Kalinago. Such possibilities illustrate the unique status of the Kalinago Territory within the Caribbean, where land access for many communities continues to be evasive. On the other hand, a communal land title reveals the complexities of rural communities when thrust into a globalized world. Nevertheless, the larger global processes and the political leadership as played out in the Kalinago Territory still hold back any positive community development.

In sections 5.2 and 5.3, the results provide a detailed account of the impact of land-use and land-change on each cultural ecosystem service (CES). As demonstrated above, the methods employed were multidisciplinary, a necessity to fully understand the shifts both in society and environment. If we consider the definition of well-being as presented in the Millennium Assessment (MA 2005a, b; MEA 2005) (see section 2.4), individuals in the Kalinago Territory describe a loss in material goods and resources as well as a decline of social relationships. Based on the totality of the results, the landscape change, or the changing nature of agriculture and its relationships have impacted the land cover, water resources and every associated CES resulting in a genuine effect on community well-being.

6

Discussion and Conclusions

As a geographic region, the Caribbean is perhaps more aptly characterized by its differences rather than by its similarities. With heterogeneous societies, multiple histories, and a rich biodiversity, the landscapes of the Caribbean archipelago represent a unique interaction between human and environment, shaped by centuries of modification and exploitation. As such, exploring local level landscape changes in the Caribbean would deliver an expected, diverse array of results. However, as we have seen, while presenting unique examples of landscape change, the results of the two case studies in St. Kitts and the Kalinago Territory both reveal the fundamental link between land and community.

This study has taken an interdisciplinary approach incorporating perspectives from political ecology, environmental humanities and ecological sciences to investigate the relationship between local scale land use and community wellbeing in two case studies on the islands of St. Kitts and Dominica. As described in chapter 2 (see 2.3), landscapes, or socio-ecological systems (SES), represent the place of human and environment interaction. Landscapes provide key services to communities, rendering them essential for the protection of human well-being. In agricultural or rural systems, this relationship between services and well-being is even stronger, particularly as regards the production and usage of natural resources for livelihoods (Reid *et al.* 2006). The unique position of agrarian landscapes, observed in the present case studies, highlights the symbiosis of nature and culture, which is often overlooked.

This chapter departs from the specifics of each case study in order to draw some overall conclusions on the findings. First , it begins with a discussion of the two case studies, presenting specific results, along with those comparable in both cases. It then moves on to discuss the comparability or uniqueness of the results within the region and the larger context of the research. The outcome of each case study emerged only by following the applied theory and methods. Accordingly, this chapter also draws some observations on the formulation, practice and execution of the framework and methodology applied in the research, specifically the novelty of its application. The final section of this chapter links the results and methods to the broader context of global environmental, development and climate change discourse, again disclosing the implications of the findings for today's landscapes and rural communities. Coming full circle, the study concludes with a number of considerations regarding the current position of rural landscapes.

6.1 Discussion on the case study findings

The islands of St. Kitts and Dominica share a geographical region and a common colonizer, but also have diverse histories and geographies, which have in turn affected the current populations in different ways. The diversity observed on these two islands and investigated in the course of the case studies reveals the importance of localized examples of landscape-change and subsequent effects. Whereas the differences in the specific historical contexts and landscapes remain substantial, a range of subtle similarities involving land change do support broader conclusions of the position of the cultural ecosystems (CES) within the SES of these two case studies.

6.1.1 Landscape change and community well-being

First, landscape change has occurred in both case studies since independence, ultimately impacting on well-being through a range of direct as well as indirect effects. However, a significant factor in the findings is that this type of landscape change does not imply landscape degradation in the normative sense. To date, most scholarly research has explored degrading land practices leading to negative impacts on both natural and cultural resources (Blaikie and Brookfield 1987; Plieninger *et al.* 2014b; Willow 2014). When referencing only the land-change data or land-cover/land-use modification of these two case studies (see 4.2 and 5.2), the results present no severe landscape degradation, nor any drastic decline in natural species or resources[43]. Both case studies have, however, witnessed slight increases in urbanization, as well as decreases in the degree of forestation, and increases in low vegetation, grass or bare areas. More significant change was only observed in the coastal villages of St. Kitts, where the altering shoreline has led to severe coastal erosion.

However, even if overall physical landscape change is not drastic, the immaterial changes that have taken place since independence appear to be far-reaching. In these two case studies, landscape change cannot be discernable as a direct result of any climate or environmental change. Most landscape modifications that have had a negative impact on these communities have resulted from a combination of factors, stemming from broader global economic policies as well. Even slight landscape transformations bring on a variety of interconnected effects on community that can be observed in two prominent ways in each case study.

Each case study reveals that landscape or environmental degradation – signifying not only the tangible but also, and perhaps more importantly, the intangible changes – is brought about by a variety of interconnected causes, impacting not only natural resources but also community livelihoods. First, in the coastal villages of St. Kitts, we see that the altering shoreline has led to severe coastal erosion. However, community members view this erosion as the result not only of increased storm frequency caused by climate change, but also shoreline development. Coastal erosion has strongly influenced the cultural values of the communities involved. For example, communities no longer use the shore for recreational purposes. Swimming, fishing and spending time by the sea are pastimes that make up a part of the community cultural memory.

---

43 This result considers the land use/land change analysis of both case studies. The severe coastal erosion in St. Kitts and the declining water resources in the Kalinago Territory, while related, are not considered in this discussion of land change.

In addition, we can observe that the changing landscape has resulted in limited land access to important community mountain grounds. Without any access to these areas, the community has not only witnessed a decline in agriculture but also in associated practices of recreation and sociability. However, the situation remains complex as the previously cultivated sugarcane fields still remain undistributed. Overgrown and unused, these fields lay as a fallow backdrop to the surrounding villages.

Second, in the Kalinago Territory, the connection between landscape change and the impacts on cultural values appears to be even stronger. The declining land use and land degradation have resulted from a variety of causes in the Kalinago Territory. Deforestation, resulting from increased development and changing economies of this territory (in particular, the demise of banana production, brought about by the end of preferential trading with the UK) and perhaps too by the fact that climate change induces drier periods, has led to a decreasing number of water resources located along river beds. This phenomenon has indeed influenced many cultural activities. Inhabitants of the Kalinago Territory no longer utilize the rivers for recreation or fishing. With the collapse of banana cultivation, engaging in agriculture has become a financial risk. This in turn has caused a dwindling of traditional community activities such as Koudmen, the reciprocal labor tradition. Revealing the butterfly effect (i.e., minute causes can have larger effects) of larger global processes, combined with internal factors (e.g., small landscape shifts) has ultimately influenced other, seemingly unrelated, aspects of daily life.

6.1.2 Synergies and antagonisms in access to land

When considering these changes, we must remember that the land patterns in both case studies did not develop naturally, but were imposed by foreign interests. While the term "agriculturist" may be applied broadly in both case studies. The reason for this is that many individuals may not be engaged in agriculture all year round, or on a large scale, while they do plant a variety of crops near their homes or in backyard gardens. However, such cultivation remains in stark contrast to the monocrop intensive agriculture implemented in each case study, leaving behind dependencies and deflated economies. While exploitative and degrading to both the community and the soil, sugarcane on St. Kitts is not comparable to the relative wealth that banana exportation brought to the Kalinago Territory. Both systems ultimately favored foreign markets. The nd of sugarcane and banana cultivation in both case studies have revealed tangible results of an exploitative system, but the roots of the system remain. As both the banana and sugar industry have come to an end, a viable agricultural industry in both case study areas has yet to develop. Furthermore, rural communities of St. Kitts and the Kalinago Territory have become increasingly engaged and dependent on the global economy. This increasing connectivity within the globalized world, albeit positive in numerous aspects, has nevertheless led to a ecrease in the number of former livelihoods (e.g., farming practices, recreational activities along the riverbeds) as well as a decline of cultural ecosystem services (CES). When reflecting upon these shifts in community life and the overall dissatisfaction expressed by community members, it is important to remember the historic and economic contexts leading to indirect impacts on each case study landscape.

On St. Kitts (Chapter 4), the brutality and oppression of slavery, forced labor, and the ensuing continuation of sugarcane cultivation with paid workers active on most of the island's arable land, has shaped the interaction with the landscape to the present day, as sugarcane agriculture ended only 10 years ago. The drastic change from sugarcane to overgrown fields has not led to community benefits. Whereas the backbreaking, exploitative work is fortunately now a thing of the past, the former sugar-producing plots of land have not been redistributed. During the Sugar Era, it was possible to access mountain grounds which included marginal plots of land and which were not only important for food security, but also for cultural values and practices. Within the current context of increasing connectivity with the rest of the world, these issues of land access create more vulnerabilities, as rural communities in St. Kitts once again compete against foreign markets for land located on their own island. As tourism becomes engrained in the economic backbone of St. Kitts, one needs to consider the actual benefits of tourism and the availability hereto when considering rural communities such as those encountered in the St. Kitts case study.

As discussed in chapter 5, the introduction of bananas into the Kalinago Territory brought stable incomes as never witnessed before. The economic activity spurred a new found affluence and the continuation of agriculture also saw to it that certain social and cultural traditions were preserved. As banana production ended in the early 2000s, so too did the wealth and monocrop dominated landscape. Reliance and dependency was built into the entire banana production system, providing farmers in the Kalinago Territory with little choice regarding the chain of events because decisions were made on a global level. With no other exportable crop or access to markets, agriculture was no longer a viable option for most people. The demise of banana production in this territory has imposed an economic vacuum, as few find work here. Whereas land is plentiful, opportunity is not.

The results of both case studies question whether small farm agriculture continues as a possible livelihood in a world consisting of industrial agriculture. However, such forms of agriculture serving local consumption contrast starkly with the industrial agriculture with which much of the Caribbean archipelago had been familiar since the dawn of European colonialism.

Perhaps the most significant distinction between these two case studies concerns the communities' access to land. On St. Kitts, the inhabitants of the case study area rarely owned any land due to historic land use. As discussed in chapter four, individuals overcame this by growing and maintaining agricultural plots in the mountains. However, the government has not re-distributed the previously cultivated sugarcane lands, making Kittitians landless while residing in a fallow landscape. Repercussions of this include direct effects of declining local agricultural production. However, with less available land and growing populations, indirect effects related to social change lead to cramped villages, insecure living situations, increased crime, and an increased threat from coastal erosion. The eleven coastal villages of St. Kitts have little bargaining or political power. The villagers remain isolated from each other, meaning little mobilization occurs.

The Kalinago Territory, on the other hand, remains protected legally as a territory thanks to the communal land title recognized by the Dominican national government. The land and any associated resources, consequently, remain available to residents of this territory. With available land, the Kalinago have the flexibility in many ways that Kittitians do not. Setting aside the issues of credit and available economic opportunity and development in the Kalinago Territory, an inherent security exists in knowing that one's home and land will always be there. Despite the lack of national or international market for agricultural crops, farmers in the Kalinago Territory take pride growing their own vegetables and fruit, even if it is only for their families and neighbors. Land also provides another important factor in Kalinago wellbeing, that of unity. As discussed in chapter five, the Kalinago Territory's unique communal land title preserves a common cultural identity as much as it prevents economic development. However, in many ways, the Kalinago as a people persist as unified in their attachment to their land, and by extension, remain mobilized in defense of their rights. Today's prevailing discourse leading to increased respect for indigenous land rights plays to the Kalinago advantage in exceptional ways. The Kalinago people, once ignored, are now heard. One example is the establishment of the Office of the Ministry of Kalinago Affairs as part of the Dominican government. By defining themselves through their indigenous background, the Kalinago people now harness a power not available to the coastal villages of St. Kitts.

Indigenous communities have frequently been described as some of the most vulnerable populations due to reliance on natural resources and the impacts of climate change, and more importantly, the historic marginalization that continues today in the form of political and economic disadvantages (Bollig and Schulte 1999; Couzin 2007; Laidler 2006; Smith and Rhiney 2016). While this is true, the present research would argue that Caribbean rural communities, whether indigenous or not, experience a similar marginalization resulting from the historic, and now repeating, patterns of social, political, economic and environmental exclusion not merely on a local but also on a global scale. The communities of both St. Kitts and Dominica, including those located in the Kalinago Territory, continue to experience similar historic vulnerabilities and disadvantages.

This observation stands not as a critique of indigenous rights in the Caribbean or globally. Rather, this research suggests that the unique situation of the Caribbean requires a different perspective when analyzing the marginalization that can occur. Here, the uniqueness of the Caribbean results in historic marginalization, due to the forced labor of various ethnic people, notably enslaved Africans. If we consider the 500 years of dominance perpetuated in the Caribbean by European colonizers, the North American influence, the multinational powers and the continued marginalization, repetition continues of the well-known, but unanswered for, exploitative past. Therefore, when considering the relationship between indigenous and non-indigenous in the Caribbean, there exist subtleties not present in other indigenous versus colonizer situations. This research would argue that such nuances in the Caribbean permit and even foster dynamic identities.

6.1.3 Agricultural production and the effects of mono-cropping

As witnessed throughout this research, the landscape remains sustainable or resilient whenever the utilization of the land and resource regeneration is balanced. However, external forces (e.g., the introduction of industrial agriculture, agriculture mono-cropping, agricultural intensification) result in landscape simplification. Instead of creating biodiversity and heterogeneity within a landscape, a single crop simplifies the use of the land, leading to a decline in ecosystem services. The argument could be made that monocrops represent productive use of the land, as intensive wealth and yield is possible. However, this research would argue against such notions as the two case studies provide clear example of the negative aftermath of mono-cropping on community and environment. In both case studies, the end of monocrop style agriculture has led to a different type of simplified landscape, one that could also be defined as detrimental to land use. Overgrowth has taken over the landscapes of previous sugarcane fields in St. Kitts and banana plantations in the Kalinago Territory. In one way, the natural diversity of plants has returned. However, it would be a stretch to call this overgrowth beneficial to the biodiversity of the landscape, as it is mainly weeds or grasses, often overtaking the remaining trees or other vegetation. Farming has become further limited in both case studies.

Furthermore, the cyclical nature of overgrowth, and slash and burn techniques in the Kalinago Territory has also led to declining water resources. Consequently, in both scenarios of land use, monocrop or post-monocrop regrowth, the change from a productive landscape to limited use results in repercussions that include impacts on natural resources, and cultural values. The difference between a productive and simplified landscape requires greater attention as two case studies reveal the needed balance between use, destruction, and regrowth.

Despite limits on land access and the history of monocrop plantations, agriculture remains an important element in small Caribbean communities. We see this fact, not only in the study presented here, but also in a variety of research conducted in this region (Beckford and Rhiney 2016; Lowitt *et al.* 2015; Rhiney 2015; Smith and Rhiney 2016). However, the historic processes of colonization, monocrop agriculture and land access continue to hamper any local agricultural development. While often explained away by the apparent vulnerability of small farmers, digging deeper into the issue of declining Caribbean agriculture reveals "the systemic way these individuals and their livelihoods have been marginalized over the years as their degree of exposure to climate-induced hazards. Rising input costs, changing levels of government support, uneven access to markets, and the unequal distribution of natural resources such as land, all create differentiated sensitivity to both climate variability and change" (Rhiney 2015, 110). Certain evidence points towards modifications, leading to more equitable land relationships within local communities. Lowitt states that: "Caribbean agriculture is undergoing substantial restructuring as it shifts from one system centrally organized around export production to one increasingly focused on domestic markets" (Lowitt *et al.* 2015, 1367). If true, this would imply that one is finally able to cater to local markets and producers rather than the often fickle foreign markets (Lowitt *et al.* 2015; Ville *et al.* 2015; Weis 2007).

Through this understanding of the role of agriculture and land in the Caribbean context, the decline of agriculture and the associated landscape change reveals multilayered impacts. As agriculture provides a space for community engagement which fosters mutual exchange, this interaction within important community areas (e.g., mountain grounds, coastal areas, river beds, agricultural fields) has also dwindled since the demise of industrial agriculture. As the present research results prove, small-scale farming still represents an important backbone of rural communities on the two islands. However, both case studies also reveal that agriculture still falls below the levels witnessed in the past, especially within the Kalinago Territory. It is important to note that in both case studies, this decline includes not only the end of industrial agriculture but also of small-scale family agriculture. The two case studies illustrate that, whereas individuals would like to engage in more farming, there is not enough market access in order to sell crops, limiting any production thereof and ultimately restricting entry into domestic markets. The connection between the land use-change and the subsequent community and societal changes in both case studies reveals a finding perhaps most relevant for the continued study of Ecosystem Services (ES). The results illustrate that community members do not separate nature from culture. This finding resonates with many other studies that also reveal the absence of a boundary between the cultural and natural domains often only prescribed by external knowledge (Diaz *et al.* 2015; Gfeller 2015; Gratani *et al.* 2014). This fact is further reflected by the all-encompassing term "land" of which individuals in both case studies spoke of in order to describe all natural and cultural processes. In these two case studies, "land" represents more than its pure physical and earthly sense, but rather spirituality, a connection to the past and present, and a defining attribute of someone's identity. The phenomenon of connecting land and culture is, of course, present throughout the world (Barrena *et al.* 2014; Fletcher *et al.* 2007; Hofman and Hoogland 2015; Nettley *et al.* 2014; Tarraguel *et al.* 2012). As land transforms, so too do the human relationship or attachment to that land. The connections between these two domains reveal their inextricable overlap. As discussed in Chapter 2 (see 2.4), the intrinsic linkage of use and value in a landscape reaffirms the link with the landscape, land-use and community well-being (Fleuret and Atkinson 2007; Holden and Bourke 2014; Laird *et al.* 2014; Larson *et al.* 2015; Winterton *et al.* 2014).

6.1.4 The (re) positioning of individuals and community in a changing landscape

As the results clearly reveal that landscape changes and the subsequent impacts have occurred in both case studies, it then becomes important to consider the way in which communities perceive and adapt to these developments. In both case studies, discussions on landscape changes have manifested a remarkable local knowledge. This fact addresses the importance as well as the continuation of local knowledge concerning natural resources, climatic patterns, planting seasons and, in sum, a substantial familiarity with interacting with the surrounding environment. On small islands, local knowledge is a common and often under-valorized aspect of rural livelihoods (Beckford and Barker 2007; Danielsen *et al.* 2014; Gadgil *et al.* 2003). Understanding this knowledge also proves an overall community awareness of the landscape modifications, as was encountered in the course of these two case studies. It was obvious, through interviews and surveys, that communities spoken to in both case studies expressed a full awareness of the complex factors which directly and indirectly influenced land use-changes.

Furthermore, both case studies prove that perceptions of environmental change or climate change are often linked to demographic factors, such as one's occupation. For example, on St. Kitts, fisherman viewed the impacts of coastal erosion and the sea-level changes to be more negative than those who did not work within an environmental context with the sea on a day-to-day basis. In the Kalinago Territory, most respondents rate the decline of fishing, while not related to an environmental impact per se, as negative. Here, individuals whose livelihoods deal directly with the environment on a day-to-day basis showed a more marked concern for any associated environmental effects. Such results speak to the linkages between the island livelihoods and dependence on natural resources and specifically on oceanic resources (Bauma *et al.* 2016; Hau'ofa 1994; Keegan *et al.* 2008; Turner *et al.* 2007). This outcome further implies that the cultural space that exists beyond the land boundaries of an island remains paramount for understanding the islander identities and their perceptions of environmental changes. The significance of coasts and seas for small island populations is noted throughout their past as well as their current communities (Bridges and McClatchey 2009; Crowther *et al.* 2016; Jackson 1995).

From these ranging influences of land change on CES, we see overall that well-being remains intrinsic to the outcome of how individuals feel connected both mentally and physically to a specific location, comprising environment as well as society, through the utilization of landscape services, including the regulating, provisioning and supporting of cultural components. The overall dissatisfaction of community life expressed by individuals illustrates a change in well-being. Respondents in both case studies have experienced declines in social cohesion as well as in the freedom of choice or opportunity (MA 2003). Considering the entirety of the landscape of each case study, we acknowledge the interaction of scales, direct and indirect influences as well as the dualism of nature and culture that ultimately impacts well-being.

These two case studies, while different in terms of island histories, reveal that land degradation alone does not account for all effects on CES. Rather, a series of indirect and direct factors, in this instance related to globalization and the opening of markets, collide on a local scale, resulting in a broad array of impacts. That is not to say that any modernization or development represent a hindrance to community life. On the contrary, these developments have also brought modern infrastructure, access to education, and technological advancement as well as connectivity for many inhabitants of St. Kitts and Dominica. Individuals have become more increasingly linked via the internet and/or telephone than ever before, creating innovative frames of reference for younger generations. In both case studies, individuals have mentioned the educational opportunities now facilitated by means of recent forms of connectivity and technology, which link them with the rest of the world, leading to possible new opportunities. We also then see how such aspects of modernization lead to a variety of landscape modifications, first witnessed in the demise of the monocrop culture and now currently in the transforming landscape. These results, consequently, reveal a deeper question of whether community life and engagement must come at a cost to modernization. Can both traditional aspects of life and modern connectivity co-exist within a single community?

We can observe the effects of landscape modification on well-being when further disclosing the evidence of any community changes taking place in both case studies. While well-being is complex and multilayered (Engelbrecht 2009; King *et al.* 2014; Willox *et al.* 2013; Yang *et al.* 2013), the results of both case studies concretize the fact that well-being remains an inherent part of continued practices within a landscape. Examples thereof extracted from both studies include: (a) the fishing areas and mountain grounds of St. Kitts, (b) the rivers and agricultural practices of the Kalinago Territory, which provide food, resources, while regulating natural processes, and (c) cultural attachment.

Whereas the results sketch a negative picture of daily life, it must be emphasized that both case studies reflect communities that play an active role in the daily lives of their members, and not of any vulnerable or passive islanders. Both case studies provide unique abilities to transform the paradigm of landscape changes. First, local stakeholders shaped the direction of the investigation through collaboration, flipping the usual power relations within research. Community collaborators took advantage of the presented opportunities in order to better their own communities. As such, the final outcome is of significance to communities and can be used by them going forward, especially the community mapping component. Second, the continuation of local knowledge concerning the environment and natural resources in both case studies disclose an endurance of alternative methods to approaching environmental and climate changes. These two aspects also reveal that one can take control while the inevitable landscape transformations continue to occur, not only in these two case studies, but globally, whenever a certain degree of local control can be taken.

6.2 Innovation and implications of the methodology

While theory and methods are limitless in research, this research found its relevance in integrated methodology, allowing simultaneous analysis of questions pertaining to land and community. As both case studies illustrate, dealing with natural resources without discussing culture and society frequently proves to be insufficient. The current practice in heritage management as well as in natural resource management encourages the establishment of relationships between the community and resources (Antczak *et al.* 2013; Caspersen 2009; Clark 2009; Lilley 2009; Logan 2012; Pwiti 1996). Nevertheless, despite a similar language and desired goals, the above disciplines comprising heritage and natural resource management do not often cross-pollinate, which often leads to a disconnect between the holistic reality and the discrete policies. In certain instances, dealing with heritage and natural resources separately may suffice. However, the results of both case studies indicate the need for a combination of both approaches.

As stated in chapter 2, this research takes much inspiration from landscape theories. Socio-ecological Systems (SES), and Ecosystem Services (ES) serves as the ultimate framework for methods and case studies. Representing a landscape as SES enables us to dissect the embedded parts whereby they do not become separated from the entire system. The present research has expanded from the more conservationist context in order to encompass a more systematized approach towards elements of community, heritage and environment encountered in the specific settings of the Caribbean.

The merging of nature and culture within a landscape, or SES, depends on flexible and analytical analyses. Currently, we have no single, agreed-upon method in order to dissect the impacts of land-change on CES within the SES. This allows for a variety of methods to be considered. In a large part of the literature on the ecosystem service and on the integrated land management, we find support for any multidisciplinary methods which grapple with environmental and/or social issues (Albert *et al.* 2016; Baulcomb *et al.* 2015; Bethel *et al.* 2014; Brancalion *et al.* 2014; Chan *et al.* 2012a; Chan *et al.* 2012b; Constanza *et al.* 1997; Darvill and Lindo 2015; Folke and Hahn 2003; Hart *et al.* 2015; Soini 2001; Wylie 2008).

Expanding upon the afore-mentioned literature, Socio-ecological (SES) framework favors a deeper analysis through an interdisciplinary approach. In both case studies, a range of methods produced diverse data, including community mapping, cultural mapping, GIS/Remote Sensing, and network visualization (Malpas 2008; Young and Gilmore 2013). Other comparable methods include more ethnographically focused examples of interviews, focus groups and surveys (Darvill and Lindo 2015; Lane *et al.* 2005). While varied, methods served to complement each other, combining different knowledge systems in order to produce holistic results. For example, all data gathered quantitatively (i.e., by means of GIS/Remote Sensing, statistical measures, coding) provided a counterpart consisting of data gathered qualitatively (i.e., by means of visualization techniques, community mapping, interviews, surveys). This procedure ensured that any relying upon one type of data above the other never occurred.

Similar multidisciplinary research projects recorded the problems associated with the data compatibility between the analyses of socio- environmental factors (Garbach 2012; McLain *et al.* 2013). The present research faced comparable issues, but sought to overcome any subsequent impediments by creating a systematic tool kit to innovatively merge qualitative and quantitative methods, while valorizing localized and placed-based research. The overall concept began with community involvement, departing from the definition of the research problem. This ensured that the research not only focused on issues relevant to the communities, but also supported the implementation of the necessary fieldwork and improved the sustainability of the research results.

The toolkit approached each case study at both the macro level and micro level, thereby blending the varied data to arrive at rounded conclusions. Preliminary GIS and remote sensing served as macro factors to understand the entirety of the landscape in each case study. This included analyzing patterns of land use/land change through time. Preliminary interviews are an example of macro factors, or analysis applied in both case studies regardless of the context. In fact, each case study began by means of preliminary interviews that directed further the subsequent analysis.

For example, in these preliminary interviews, individuals discussed aspects of the changing shoreline, mountains or agriculture and watershed. Thanks to collaboration with community members, governmental agencies and NGOs in each case study, methods appropriately identified environmental and socio-economic issues behind the symptomatic changes in the landscape (e.g., land degradation, declining water resources and agriculture)(Borrini-Feyeraband *et al.* 2004). Combining the GIS results of land change with the discussed topics in interviews provided a means forward to micro factors of analysis.

To understand the micro factors in each case study, modified socio-ecological indicators (Oudenhoven *et al.* 2012; Oudenhoven *et al.* 2010) determined the next steps. Interestingly, the socio-ecological indicators identified (i.e., Multiple Uses of Land/Plants, Conservation of Resources, Culture/Society shift) were identical in both case studies. These broad indicators were applied in the overall land-use/land-change, and developed through a spatial analysis in order to define the unique focus of each case study. This procedure included (a) an investigation into the land-change through a spatial analysis for both case studies, (b) a coastal erosion analysis, (c) a community perceptions survey for St. Kitts and the GIS database and, (d) a land mapping and run-off potential for the Kalinago Territory. Using such an approach combing landscape and SES, we can begin to grapple with the question of how communities can overcome overarching global structures that undoubted lead to local natural resource inequalities (Aiken and Leigh 2011).

Such a methodology, then enabled the production of tangible deliverables. In both case studies, all data collected and analyzed is accessible to community members. All GIS analyses are stored in governmental ministries, community organizations or local government. In collaboration with the Ministry of Environment of St. Kitts and Nevis, a coastal prediction model was built specifically for the coastal villages case study (Stancioff *et al.* 2017)[44], revealing the future impact of continued erosion on environment and community in the area. Furthermore, to address the multivocal community heritage that was revealed throughout the research in St. Kitts, together with the Ministry of Culture, an interactive crowdsourcing website, www.culturesnaps.kn, was also created[45]. In the Kalinago Territory, the research ultimately led to the development of an entire GIS database for the Kalinago Territory. Such data are stored at the Department of Planning and Ministry of Kalinago Affairs, in Roseau, as well as at the Kalinago Council office, in the Kalinago Territory. Furthermore, in collaboration with the Kalinago Council and the Ministry of Kalinago Affairs, a land boundary mapping survey began during the research to collect the boundaries of individual's farms throughout the Kalinago Territory. A first of its kind, this survey gave farmers exact acreage of their farm, creating a database of the cultivated land in the Territory. Finally, deliverables included a watershed management plan

---

44 This collaboration was possible because of efforts bu Julijan Vermeer (Nexus 1492, the Netherlands), dr. Anirban Mukhopadhyay (IIRS, India), Graeme Brown (Ministry of St. Kitts, St. Kitts) Samantha de Ruiter (Nexus 1492, the Netherlands), dr. Prof. Corinne Hofman (Nexus 1492, the Netherlands).
45 Culturesnaps.kn was created also in collaboration with dr. Habiba (Nexus1492, Germany) and Marlene Philips (Ministry of Culture, St. Kitts).

to address the declining water resources in the Kalinago Territory[46]. In doing so, research results serve the community in future land management and planning.

Implementing an overall method at the initial phase of the methodological approach proved impossible. However, upon reflection of the completed investigation, it became clear that a single method was not necessary, or in fact, helpful. This research supports the conclusion that transparent methods must be developed in order to further examine the connection between ecosystem services and well-being. With the entirety of the research now finished, the success comes from community collaboration remaining fundamental. In this manner, the research produced new findings as well as tangible products that can be used and maintained by community members for years to come.

6.3 Final conclusions

The results from this research have broader implications that merit further reflection. As the emphasis of this research lay on localized, small-scale examples of land-use and landscape change, this penultimate section will address how the acquired information fits into a broader global context.

Despite the nd of formal colonial occupation, exploitative systems continue to exist. In fact, today's rural Caribbean agriculturists are unable to sustain themselves within the current economic system due to global trade laws, inaccessible markets, food imports and the overall devaluation of agriculture (Shah and Dulal 2015) (see chapter 2). Such external market forces demand dependency on foreign markets to fuel Caribbean economies. Although monocrop agriculture (e.g., sugarcane and banana cultivation) has come to an end, comparable exploitative patterns reoccur.

It is no stretch of the imagination to extrapolate the economic dependencies created by a local monoculture agriculture as similar to the current dependence on tourism markets, at present the most profitable economic machine in the region. Regarded as one of the most tourist dependent parts of the world (Carrigan 2011; Gossling 2003), the Caribbean isles have become even more impacted by means of dips or highs, dominated by a "mass-based corporate tourism" (Pattullo 1996, 105), and ultimately resulting in the redefinition of "its physical landscapes" (Pattullo 1996, 105). Unfortunately as land continues to be modified by means of foreign investment and foreign utilization, tourism- influenced land-use patterns are comparative to former colonial land patterns. Therefore, clashes between the local and the global, with dominant political or economic global forces, lead to real, tangible local changes. Land becomes central in the negotiation between external pressures, direct and indirect influences, and the community. Whenever such relationships play out, the local human-environment relationships modify in innovative manners, shaping culture, land-use and well-being (Agnoletti 2014; Guttmann-Bond 2014). (Liverman 1990; Rhiney 2015).

Though the term vulnerability is often used when discussing the eventual impacts of climate change on the Caribbean islands, and more broadly, islands in general, vulnerability does not present us with any reasonable solutions or options. It serves

---

[46] The efforts of Kimani Lapps, Cozier Frederick, Dilianie Darroux, Asher Burton, Marcus Philip, Danne Auguiste and Peter Sinnott enabled the successful completion of these projects.

as a catchall, actually misrepresenting islands (Bertram and Poirine 2007). A large part of today's research on climate change and small islands has focused on the vulnerabilities of a specific region, rather than on the active response of their communities (Adger *et al.* 2007; Barker *et al.* 2009; Barnett *et al.* 2008; Barnett and Waters 2016; Blaikie *et al.* 1994; Boruff and Cutter 2007; Cameron 2012; Cardona 2011; Chambers 1998; Cooper 2012; Ford *et al.* 2006; Stancioff and Hofman 2017). Here, an issue arises when considering the fact that small islands represent great diversity in geography, topography, environment, demography and culture. Subsequently, the reactions to environmental impacts will vary in each island community case (Lyth *et al.* 2016; Nunn 2009; Stojanov *et al.* 2016; Tompkins 2005).

Beyond the geographical diversity of islands presenting varying responses to climate and environmental change, local perceptions to these landscape changes also dictate how any future action is taken with regard to each island culture (Farbotkoa and Lazrus 2012; Granderson 2017; Nunn *et al.* 2016; Wolf and Moser 2011). Based on the examples of St. Kitts and Dominica, landscape change can never be linked to climate change only. All events included in any landscape transformations occur through a cycle of indirect and direct factors, relating not only to the climate but also to global economy and politics.

The focus of the global community on predicting any climate change impacts on small islands actually discloses once again that, at the most basic level, the political power structures remain the same. This concentration on vulnerability or adaptability to climate change deflects away from the actual reasons that cause rural communities and Caribbean islands to experience any environmental change, as it is easier to blame nature for unfair destruction than economic exclusion for unequal footing in the global marketplace. Continuing to be at the forefront of global discussions (King 2004), the discourse on climate change and related environmental management acts to "depoliticize" the systemic root of development problems in small islands or rural communities (Kelman 2014). Such academic debates on global climate change present us with only a partial understanding of reality. By accepting islanders as vulnerable, as researchers and the global community do, we acknowledge that a discourse reaches beyond global or regional scales to interact through scientific knowledge in order to either exclude or impose power on a very local level. It is through understanding the narratives of peoples or regions, without overlooking the actual local reality or local agency (Arnall *et al.* 2014; Furedi 2007), that we can begin to understand the profound effects of climate change..

This research reveals that rather than mitigating climate change or environmental change solely within a regional or global approach, emphasis must include the local experience. Such a finding remains true for all geographies. However, as this dissertation has focused on islands, the importance of this finding must be placed within the context of a global misrepresentation of islands as small and, therefore, as vulnerable. If we shift perspectives, the isolated or separation caused by water becomes a causeway, connecting the Caribbean islands into a much larger system (Benítez-Rojo 1992; DeLoughrey *et al.* 2005; DeLoughrey and Handley 2011). Environmental changes come with a range of associated effects that will modify island life. However, small island responses to climate change reveal flexibility and adaptability, even in combatting the ensuing environmental destruction that they themselves had little responsibility in creating. The island experience varies greatly in challenges associated with climate change. Nevertheless, islanders themselves remain active when dealing with such modifications, leading to possible insights benefitting the global community (Barnett and Campbell 2010; Berkes 2009; Green *et al.* 2010; Leonard *et al.* 2013; Mercer *et al.* 2007; Mercer *et al.* 2012).

How do we break from such patterns of repetition? First, the implementation of methods that put sustainable landscapes or social-ecological systems at the forefront must become a given. Countless other examples of research reveal that such conclusions are not mere coincidence. Accordingly, any land management must include strategies sensitive to the context of rural communities that incorporates an integrated research framework. Additionally, such research initiatives require implementation at the local level. This outcome is supported by other studies that have increasingly indicated the relevance of including local knowledge into land management planning (Beckford and Barker 2007; Briggs 1995; Campbell *et al.* 2011). This fact will not only maintain and protect any local knowledge but also add value consisting of local expertise and culture (Roncoli *et al.* 2002). Furthermore, the integration of local knowledge into land management and climate change planning remains instrumental for the effective, sustainable planning.. Examples of local implementation include not only sustainable land practices, but also encouraging economic policies that make it possible for local communities to endure, such as promoting local agriculture and inclusive local value chains. Such processes would promote inclusivity and development.

These two case studies reflect that vulnerabilities are a matter of reimagining constraints. In the time of Amerindian settlements, the Caribbean Sea served as a connective body of water, creating regional alliances and fostering trade. The Caribbean islands today have a wealth of knowledge, expertise and resources. However, after centuries of forced alienation, these local ties need to be recreated, exploring local cooperatives or inter-island alliances. Building regional alliances depends further on a restructuring of global relationships. Aside from such climatic processes, the historic political power structures and current core/periphery relationships continue to influence the direction which small island states take (Arnall *et al.* 2014; Kelman, Gaillard, *et al.* 2015).

If climate vulnerability exists in the Caribbean, they stem from historic marginalization, exploitation and dependencies (Campbell *et al.* 2011; Gamble *et al.* 2010; McGregor *et al.* 2009). Addressing this matter demands a reassessment of the global economic system in order to create a theoretical shift towards a fairer trade and investment agreements fostering added value to not only the continuation of rural agriculture systems but also to the diverse responses to change (Campbell *et al.* 2011; Chambers 1998; Scoones and Thompson 1994). While this is a very macro-level aspiration, one concrete way in which to shift power relations would be to change who is in control of research. Today, connectivity and access exists at a new unknown level. Transfer of knowledge allows for new possibilities in training and capacity building. As a researcher in a European funded project, I would call upon any new funding opportunities to stipulate for increased representation of islanders or rural communities in the project. There must be increased transparency, democratization of knowledge and focus on training of local professionals within global agencies and research institutions.

The two case studies dealt with here provide us with first-hand evidence of community effects without relying on methods which may over-extrapolate or mismatch in scale. The global research framework perhaps should not only reassess its need for completely infallible definitions but also acknowledge the inherent subjectivity of culture, nature and well-being as encountered in the domains of land management and ecosystem service research. The collected results based on these research methods further supports individuals, communities and governments which have traditionally adapted to environmental change throughout time (Mimura *et al.* 2007; Rhiney 2015). Without such an implementation and reinforcement of this traditional, historic adaptability, there is little sustainability in adaptation and mitigation plans (Gamble *et al.* 2010; Roncoli *et al.* 2002). This includes any future action and should pay particular attention to (a) refining or downscaling data to local levels, (b) more in-depth community experiences, and (c) a better understanding of the impact on the environment of interaction between global policies, society and economies (Gamble *et al.* 2010).

These consequences are witnessed not only in these two case studies, but globally. Rural communities are continually forced to adapt to fluctuations in international markets, environmental changes, community migration and abandonment. The patterns of landscape change and the emerging impact of cultural values could then indeed be considered to be inevitable in today's world with its continuous modifications and modernization. Marginalized communities, such as those located in the rural landscapes of St. Kitts and the Kalinago Territory, are often disregarded by global policy makers, but nevertheless experience rapid changes in community and land-use. The well-being of these communities, therefore, is similarly impacted when compared to the welfare of many other rural worldwide communities. When considering the significance of agrarian landscapes in providing key ecosystem services, their destruction ultimately impacts human well-being.

The case studies reveal that the everyday life on these island communities is not one of vulnerability. Instead, individuals express a clear dynamism and flexibility when they value their landscape and recognize its changing nature. Moving forward, a paradigm shift is required that recognizes the vitality of these communities, rather than ascribing them a silent, passive fate. Such a direction provides the opportunity to dismantle the pre-existing marginalization small islands continue to face. By directly investigating the experienced transformation which individuals perceive in their surroundings, a land management or ecosystem service assessment can depart from focusing on how local communities fit into global phenomena of land-change, to rather center on how communities can assert their diversity within this global process.

Epilogue

After Hurricane Maria devastated Dominica, it was over a month before I heard from anyone that I had worked with in the Kalinago Territory or in St. Kitts.

In St. Kitts, more of Old Road Town washed into the sea, taking the famous Sprat Net and fisheries complex with it.

The destruction experienced in the Caribbean in 2017 reveals the sheer power of nature. Addressing the General Assembly of the United Nations after Hurricane Maria, Prime Minster Skerritt of Dominica said "To deny climate change, is to procrastinate while earth sinks, it is to deny a truth that we have just lived"[47]. He, like many others, has revealed once again the sad reality of who actually pays for climate change. Far away from the people I worked with in Dominica and St. Kitts, it feels futile to put into words my own feelings about their experience, as I know full well that I am fortunate to have never experienced such total destruction.

Even though this storm lends weight to the vulnerability narrative, I still believe that only viewing small island states in this way misses the point and eschews the fundamental link between global policies and local impacts. First, climate change is not a 'natural' construct, devoid of human responsibility. Second, the communities in the islands affected display an extraordinary amount of resilience and defiance, as evidence by the statement above. Although it lies beyond the scope of this dissertation, the issue of climate justice, it seems, is inextricably related. But looking back at the four years of research and the destruction possible in just one night, it would be a disservice and insult to not seek innovation in the wake of devastation.

What can we offer as a global community besides the inevitability of climate change?

---

[47] Roosevelt Skerrit, "UN Assembly address" (speech, New York23/09/2017), UN Web TV, http://webtv.un.org/watch/player/5584856254001.

References

1978. Carib Reserve Act. In Laws of Dominica ed, TheGovernment Printing Office. Dominica.

2016a. "Root Mean Square Error RMSE in GIS", accessed 12/04/2016. http://gis-geography.com/root-mean-square-error-rmse-gis/.

2016b. "Supervised and Unsupervised Classification in ArcGIS", last Modified 30/07/2016, accessed 4/08/ 2016.

Adams, W.M., and J. Hutton. 2007. "People, parks and poverty: Political ecology and biodiversity conservation", Conservation and Society 5 (2):147-183.

Adger, W.N., Jon Barnett, K. Brown, N. Marshall, and K. O'Brien. 2013. "Cultural dimensions of climate change impacts and adaptation", Nature Climate Change (3):112-117.

Adger, W.N., S. Agrawala, M.M.Q. Mirza, C. Conde, K. O'Brien, J. Pulhin, R. Pulwarty, B. Smit, and K. Takahashi. 2007. "Assessment of adaptation practices, options, constraints and capacity", in Climate Change 2007: Impacts, Adaptation and Vulnerability – Contribution of Working Group II to the Fourth Assessment Report of the Intergovernmental Panel on Climate Change, edited by M.L. Parry, O.F. Canziani, J.P. Palutikof, P.J. van der Linden and C.E. Hanson, 717-743. Cambridge, UK: Cambridge University Press.

Adham, M. I., S. M. Shirazi, F. Othman, S. Rahman, Z. Yusop, and. Z. Ismail. 2014. "Runoff Potentiality of a Watershed through SCS and Functional Data Analysis Technique", Scientific World Journal.

Agarwal, A., S. Narain, and A. Sharma, eds. 1999. Green Politics: Global Environmental Negotiations. New Delhi, India: Center for Science and Environment.

Aggarwal, P. 2006. "Understanding the Community" in Participatory Lifelong Learning and Information and Communication Technologies. New Delhi: Jawaharlal Nehru University.

Aggarwal, R.M. 2006. "Globalization, local ecosystems, and the rural poor", World Development 34 (8):1405-1418.

Agnoletti, M. 2014. "Rural landscape, nature conservation and culture: Some notes on research trends and management approaches from a (southern) European perspective", Landscape and Urban Planning (126):66-73.

Agostini, V.N., S.W. Margles, J.K. Knowles, S.R. Schill, R.J. Bovino, and R.J. Blyther. 2015. "Marine zoning in St. Kitts and Nevis: a design for sustainable management in the Caribbean", Ocean and Coastal Management 104:1-10.

Ahmed, B. 2001. "The Impact of Globalization on the Caribbean Sugar and Banana Industries", The Society for Caribbean Studies Annual Conference, Nottingham, UK.

Aiken, S.R., and C.H. Leigh. 2011. "In the way of development: indigenous land-rights issues in Malaysia", The Geographical Journal 101:471-496.

Albert, C., C. Galler, J. Hermes, F. Neuendorf, C. von Haaren, and A. Lovett. 2016. "Applying ecosystem services indicators in landscape planning and management: The ES-in-Planning framework", Ecological Indicators (61):100-113.

Aldemaro, R., and S.E. West, eds. 2006. Environmental Issues in Latin America and the Caribbean. Dordrecht: Springer.

Alliance, Resilience. 2010. "Assessing resilience in socio-ecological systems: Workbook for practitioners." http://www.resiliencealliance.org/3871.php.

Allsopp, R. 1996. "Koudmen", in Dictionary of Caribbean English Usage. Oxford: Oxford University Press.

Alpin, G. 2007. "World Heritage Cultural landscapes", International Journal of Heritage Studies 13 (6):427-446.

Althausen, J.D., C.G.S.T.C. Kendall, V. Laksmi, A.S. Alsharan, and G.L. Whittle. 2003. "Using satellite imagery and GIS in the mapping of coastal landscapes in an arid Environment", in Desertification in the Third Millennium, edited by A.S. Alsharhan, W.W. Wood, A.S. Goudie, A. Fowler and E.M. Abdellatif. Rotterdam: A.A. Balkema/ Swets and Zeitlinger.

Amudsen, H. 2012. "Illusions of resilience? An analysis of community responses to change in northern Norway", Ecology and Society 17 (4):46.

Anderson, J.R. 1976. A Land Use and Land Cover Classification System for Use with Remote Sensor Data. US Government Printing Office.

Anderson, W. 2002. Caribbean Environmental Law Development and Application: Environmental Legislative and Judicial Developments in English-Speaking Countries in the Context of Compliance with Agenda 21 and the Rio Agreements. Mexico: UNEP Regional Office for Latin America and the Caribbean.

Angelstam, P., M. Grodzynskyi, K. Andersson, R. Axelsson, M. Elbakidze, A. Khoroshev, I. Kruhlov, and V. Naumov. 2013. "Measurement, collaborative learning and research for sustainable use of ecosystem services: Landscape concepts and Europe as laboratory", Ambio 42 (2):129-145.

Antczak, A., M.M. Antczak, G.G. Hurtado, and K.A. Antczak. 2013. "Community Archaeology in Los Roques Archipelago National Park, Venezuela", Sociocultural Identity 2 (24):201-232.

Antrop, M. 2005. "Why landscapes of the past are important for the future", Landscape and Urban Planning 70 (1-2):21-34.

Antrop, M. 2006. "Sustainable landscapes: contradiction, fiction or utopia?", Landscape and Sustainability 75 (3-4):187-197.

Anyon, R., T.J. Ferguson, and C. Colwell-Chanthaphonh. 2005. "Natural Setting as Cultural Landscapes: The Power of Place and Tradition", USDA Forest Service Proceedings.

Arce-Nazario, J. A. 2007a. "Human landscapes have complex trajectories: reconstructing Peruvian Amazon landscape history from 1948-2005", Landscape Ecology (22):89-101.

Arce-Nazario, J. A. 2007b. "Landscape Images in Amazonian Narrative: The Role of Oral History in Environmental Research", Conservation and Society 5 (1):115-133.

Armstrong, D.V. 1978. "Archaic shellfish gatherers of St. Kitts, Leeward Islands: a case study in subsistence and settlement patterns." Master's Thesis, Department of Anthropology, UCLA.

Arnall, A., U. Kothari, and I. Kelman. 2014. "Introduction to politics of climate change: discourses of policy and practice in developing countries", The Geographical Journal 180 (2):98-101.

Arriagada, R.A., E.O. Sills, S.K. Pattanayak, and P.J. Ferraro. 2009. "Combining qualitative and quantitative methods to evaluate participation in Costa Rica's of payments for environmental services", Journal of Sustainable Forestry (28):343-367.

Atiles-Osoria, José M. 2014. "Environmental Colonialism, Criminalization and Resistance: Puerto Rican Mobilizations for Environmental Justice in the 21st Century." RCCS Annual Review (6)

Atkinson, S. 2013. "Beyond components of wellbeing: The effects of relational and situated assemblage", Topoi (32):137-144.

Atwood, T. 1791. The History of the Island of Dominica. London: Frank Cass.

Bahre, C.J. 2016. A Legacy of Change: Historic Human Impact on Vegetation in the Arizona Borderlands. Phoenix: University of Arizona Press.

Baker, A. 1992. "Introduction", in Ideology and landscape in historical perspective: essays on the meaning of some places in the past, edited by A. Baker and G. Biger. Cambridge: Cambridge University Press.

Bankoff, G. 2001. "Rendering the world unsafe: 'vulnerability' as a western discourse", Disasters (25):19-35.

Barker, D., D. Dodman, and D. McGregor. 2009. "Caribbean Vulnerability and Global Change: Contemporary Perspectives", in Global Change and Caribbean Vulnerability: Environment, Economy and Society at Risk, edited by D. McGregor, D. Dodman and D. Barker. Mona: University of the West Indies Press.

Barnett, J., and J. Campbell. 2010. Climate Change and Small Island States: Power, Knowledge, and the South Pacific. London/Washington DC: Earthscan.

Barnett, J., S. Lambert, and I. Fry. 2008. "The Hazards of Indicators: Insights From the Environmental Vulnerability Index", Annals of the Association of American Geographers 98 (1):102-119.

Barnett, J., and E. Waters. 2016. "Rethinking the Vulnerability of Small Island States: Climate Change and Development in the Pacific Islands", in The Palgrave Handbook of International Development, edited by J. Grugel and D. Hammett, 731-748. London, UK: Palgrave Macmillan UK.

Barrena, J., L. Nahuelhual, A. Baez, I. Schiappacasse, and C. Cerda. 2014. "Valuing cultural ecosystem services: agricultural heritage in Chiloé Island, southern Chile", Ecosystem Services (7):66-75.

Baulcomb, C., R. Fletcher, A. Lewis, E. Akoglu, L. Robinson, A. von Almen, S. Hussain, and K. Glenk. 2015. "A pathway to identifying and valuing cultural ecosystem services: an application to marine food webs", Ecosystem Services (11):128-139.

Baum, G., I. Kusumanti, A. Breckwoldt, S.C.A. Ferse, M. Glaser, A. Kunzmann, L. Adrianto, Dwiyitno, S. van der Wulp. 2016. "Under pressure: investigating marine resource-based livelihoods in Jakarta Bay and the Thousand Islands", Marine Pollution Bulletin 110 (2):778-789.

Bauman, Z. 2001. Community: Seeking Safety in an Insecure World. Cambridge: Polity Press.

Baver, S. L., and B. Deutsch Lynch. 2006. "The Political Ecology of Paradise Caribbean Environmentalisms", in Beyond sun and sand: Caribbean environmentalisms, edited by S.L. Baver and B.D. Lynch, 3-16. New Brunswick: Rutgers University Press.

Beckford, C., and D. Barker. 2007. "The role and value of local knowledge in Jamaican agriculture adaptation and change in small-scale farming", The Geographical Journal (173):118-128.

Beckford, C.L., and K. Rhiney. 2016. "Geographies of Globalization, Climate Change and Food and Agriculture in the Caribbean: Climate Change, Gender and Geography", in Globalization, Agriculture and Food in the Caribbean: Climate Change, Gender and Geography, edited by C.L. Beckford and K. Rhiney, 3-22. London: Palgrave Macmillan.

Bell, H. H., 1902. Report on the Caribs of Dominica. London: H.M.S.O.

Bender, B. 1993. "Landscape – Meaning and Action" in Landscape: Politics and Perspectives, edited by B. Bender, 1-17. Providence, RI: Berg.

Benítez-Rojo, A. 1992. The Repeating Island: The Caribbean and the Postmodern Perspective. Translated by J.E. Maraniss. Durham, NC/London: Duke University Press.

Bergamini, N., R. Blasiak, P. Eyzaguirre, K. Ichikawa, D. Mijatovic, F. Nakao, and S.M. Subramanian. 2013. Indicators of Resilience in Socio-ecological Production Landscapes (SEPLs). In UNU-IAS Policy Report. Nishi-ku, Japan: United Nations University.

Berkes, F. 2009. "Indigenous ways of knowing and the study of environmental change", Journal of the Royal Society of New Zealand 39 (4):151-156.

Berkes, F., and C. Folke. 1998. "Linking social and ecological systems for resilience and sustainability", in Linking social and ecological system: management practices and social mechanisms for building resilience, edited by F. Berkes, C. Folke and J. Colding. Cambridge: Cambridge University Press.

Berkes, F., and D. Jolly. 2001. "Adapting to climate change: Socio-ecological resilience in a Canadian western Artic Community", Conservation Ecology 5 (2):18.

Berkes, F., and H. Ross. 2013. "Community Resilience: Toward an Integrated Approach", Society and Natural Resources 26:5-20.

Berkes, F., and N.J. Turner. 2006. "Knowledge, learning and the evolution of conservation practice for socio-ecological system resilience", Human Ecology 34 (4):479-494.

Berrang-Ford, L., J.D. Ford, and J. Paterson. 2011. "Are we adapting to climate change?", Global Environmental Change (21):25-33.

Bertram, G., and B. Poirine. 2007. "Island Political Economy." In A World of Islands, edited by Godfrey Baldacchino, 323-378. Malta: Institute of Island Studies, Miller House Agenda.

Besson, J. 1987. "A paradox in Caribbean attitudes to land" in Land and Development in the Caribbean, edited by J. Besson and J. Momsen, 13-45. London: Macmillan Caribbean.

Besson, J. 1995. "Land, Kinship, and Community in the Post-Emancipation Caribbean: A regional View of the Leewards", in Small Islands, Large Questions: Society, Culture and Resistance in the Post-Emancipation Caribbean, edited by K.F. Olwig, 73-99. London: Frank Class.

Bethel, M.B., L.F. Brien, M.M. Esposito, C.T. Miller, H.S. Buras, S.B. Laska, R. Philippe, K.J. Peterson, and C. Parsons Richards. 2014. "Sci-TEK: A GIS-Based Multidisciplinary Method for Incorporating Traditional Ecological Knowledge into Louisiana's Coastal Restoration Decision-Making Processes", Journal of Coastal Research 30 (5):1081-1099.

Bettini, G. 2013. "Climate Barbarians at the Gate? A critique of apocalyptic narratives on 'climate refugees'", Geoforum (45):63-72.

Bieling, C., T. Plieninger, H. Pirker, and C.R. Vogl. 2014. "Linkages between landscapes and human well-being: An empirical exploration with short interviews", Ecological Economics (105):19-20.

Biernacki, P., and D. Waldorf. 1981. "Snowball sampling: problems and techniques of chain referral sampling", Sociological Methods and Research 10 (2):141-163.

Binder, C.R., J. Hinkel, P.W.G. Bots, and C. Pahl-Wostl. 2013. "Comparison of Frameworks for Analyzing Socio-ecological Systems", Ecology and Society 18 (4):26.

Blaikie, P., and H. Brookfield, eds. 1987. Land Degradation and Society. New York: Routledge.

Blaikie, P., T. Cannon, I. Davis, and B. Wisner. 1994. At Risk: natural hazards, people's vulnerability, and disasters. London: Routledge.

Blowers, A., and P. Leroy. 1994. "Power, politics and environmental inequality: A theoretical and empirical analysis of the process of 'peripheralisation'", Environmental Politics 3 (2):197-228.

Boak, E. H., and I.L. Turner. 2005. "Shoreline Definition and Detection: A Review", Journal of Coastal Research 21 (4):688-703.

Bodenhamer, D.J. 2007. "Creating a Landscape of Memory: The Potential of Humanities GIS", International Journal of Humanities and Arts Computing 1 (2):97-110.

Bollig, M., and A. Schulte. 1999. "Environmental change and pastoral perceptions: Degradation and Indigenous knowledge in two African pastoral communities", Human Ecology 27 (3):493-514.

Boomert, A. 2002. "Amerindian – European Encounters on and around Tobago (1498-ca. 1810)", Antropológica 97 (98):71-207.

Boomert, A. 2016. The indigenous peoples of Trinidad and Tobago from the first settlers until today. Leiden: Sidestone Press.

Boromé, J.A. 1967. "The French and Dominica, 1699-1763", The Jamaican Historical Review (7):9-39.

Borrini-Feyeraband, G.M., G.M. Pimbert, M.T. Farvar, A. Kothari, and Y. Renard. 2004. "Sharing Power: Learning by Doing in Co-Management on Natural Resources throughout the World". International Institute for Environment and Development and World Conservation Union (IUCN)/CESSP/CMWG, CENESTA, Iran.

Borrini-Feyerabend, G., and C.B. Tarnowski. 2005. "Participatory Democracy in Natural Resource Management: A 'Columbus's Egg'?", in Communities and Conservation Histories and Politics of Community-Based Natural Resource Management, edited by J.P. Brosius, A. Lowenhaupt Tsing and C. Zing, 69-90. Walnut Creek: AltaMira Press.

Boruff, B.J., and S.L. Cutter. 2007. "The Environmental Vulnerability of Caribbean Island Nations", American Geographical Society 97 (1):24-45.

Boucher, P.P. 1992. Cannibal Encounters: Europeans and Island Caribs, 1492-1763. Baltimore/London: Johns Hopkins University Press.

Bourdeau-Lepage, L., and E. Tovar. 2013. Well-being disparities within the Paris region: a capitalist spatialized outlook. Université de Paris Ouest Naneterre.

Boyd, J., and S. Banzhaf. 2007. "What are ecosystem services? The need for standardized environmental accounting unites", Ecological Economics 63 (2-3):616-626.

Brancalion, P.H.S., I. Villarroel Cardozo, A. Camatta, J. Aronson, and R.R. Rodrigues. 2014. "Cultural Ecosystem Services and Popular Perceptions of the Benefits of an Ecological Restoration Project in the Brazilian Atlantic Forest", Restoration Ecology: The Journal of the Society for Ecological Restoration 22 (1):65-71.

Brandes, U.. and Wagner, D. 2011. Visone, University of Konstanz and Karlsruhe Institute of Technology Visone, University of Konstanz and the Karlsruhe Institute of Technology.

Braziel, J.E. 2005. "'Caribbean Genesis': Language, Gardens, Worlds (Jamaica Kincaid, Derek Walcott, Edouard Glissant)", in Caribbean Literature and the Environment, edited by E.M. DeLoughrey, R.K. Gosson and G.B. Handley, 110-127. Virginia: University of Virginia Press.

Breton, R.. 1999. Dictionnaire caraïbe-francais, edited by M. Besada Paisa, J. Bernabé, S. de Pury, R. Relouzat, O. Renault-Lescure, M. Thouvenot and D. Troiani. Paris: Karthala.

Bridges, K.W., and W.C. McClatchey. 2009. "Living on the margin: Ethnoecological insights from Marshall Islanders at Rongelap atoll", Global Environmental Change 19 (2):140-146.

Briggs, J. 1995. "The use of indigenous knowledge in development: problems and challenges", Progress in Development Studies (5):99-114.

Brightman, R. 1993. Grateful Prey: Rock Cree Human-Animal Relationships. Berkley: University of California Press.

Buck, L.E., J.C. Milder, T.A. Gavin, and I. Mukherjee. 2006. Understanding Ecoagriculture: a Framework for Measuring Landscape Performance. Ecoagriculture Partners, Department of Natural Resources at Cornell University.

Buell, L. 1996. The Environmental Imagination: Thoreau, Nature Writing, and the Formation of American Culture. Cambridge, MA: Harvard University Press.

Buell, L. 2001. Writing for an Endangered World: Literature, Culture, and Environment in the U.S. and Beyond. Cambridge, MA/London, England: The Belknap Press of Harvard University Press.

Buikstra, E., H. Ross, C.A. King, P.G. Baker, D. Hegney, K. McLachlan, and C. Rogers-Clark. 2010. "The components of resilience – Perceptions of an Australian rural community", Journal of Community Psychology 38 (8):975-991.

Cambraia, L. 2013. "Using Concept Mapping in Community-Based Participatory Research: A Mixed Methods Approach", Journal of Mixed Methods Research 7 (3):274-293.

Cameron, E.S. 2012. "Securing Indigenous politics: a critique of the vulnerability and adaptation approach to the human dimensions of climate change in the Canadian Arctic", Global Environmental Change 22 (1):103-114.

CAMFER. "7.3 Conventional Multispectral Classification Methods", University of California at Berkeley, accessed 24/02/2017.

Campbell, D., D. Barker, and D. McGregor. 2011. "Dealing with drought: small farmers and environmental hazards in southern St. Elizabeth, Jamaica", Applied Geography (31): 146-158.

Campbell, S., 2001. "Defending Aboriginal Sovereignty: The 1930 'Carib War' in Waitukubuli (Dominica)". Dominica Country Conference, Dominica.

Cardona, O.D. 2011. "Disaster risk and vulnerability: notions and measurement of human and environmental insecurity", in Coping with global environmental change, disasters and security: threats, challenges, vulnerabilities and risks, edited by H.G. Brauch, U.O. Spring, C. Mesjasz, J. Grin, P. Kameri-Mbote, B. Chourou, P. Dunay and J. Birkmann, 42-67. Berlin: Springer.

Carney, D., ed. 1998. Sustainable rural livelihoods. What contribution can we make? London: Department for International Development (DFID).

Carpenter, S.R., B.H. Walker, J.M. Anderies, and N. Abel. 2001. "From metaphor to measurement: resilience of what to what?", Ecosytems 4:765-781.

Carpenter, S.R., H.A. Mooney, J. Agard, D. Capistranod, R.S. DeFriese, S. Díaz, T. Dietz, A.K. Duraiappah, A. Oteng-Yeboah, H.M. Pereira, C. Perrings, W.V. Reid, J. Sarukhan, R.J. Scholes, and A. Whyte. 2009. "Science for managing ecosystem services: Beyond the Millennium Ecosystem Assessment", Proceedings of the National Academy of the Sciences 106 (5):1305-1312.

Caribbean Conservation Association. 1990. St. Kitts and Nevis Country Environmental Profile.

Caribbean Landscape Conservation Cooperative. 2013. Governance and Operational Charter.

Carrier, J.G. 2003. "Mind, Gaze and Engagement", Journal of Material Culture 8 (1):5-23.

Carrigan, A. 2011. Postcolonial Tourism Literature, Culture and Environment. New York: Routledge.

Carson, R. 2002. Silent Spring. Boston, MA: Houghton Mifflin Harcourt. Original edition, 1962.

Carter, S. 2010a. National Environmental Summary Commonwealth of Dominica, edited by the United Nations Environment Program.

Carter, S. 2010b. National Environmental Summary Federation of St. Kitts and Nevis. St Kitts and Nevis: United Nations Environmental Program.

Caspersen, O. H. 2009. "Public participation in strengthening cultural heritage: the role of landscape character assessment in Denmark", Geografisk Tidsskrift- Danish Journal of Geography 109 (1):33-45.

CATHALAC. 2007. Integrating Watershed and Coastal Areas Management in the Caribbean Small Island Developing States [IWCAM. Capacity Assessment of Geographic Information Systems Capabilities of the Caribbean: Regional Assessment Report. The Water Center for the Humid Tropics of Latin America and the Caribbean (CATHALAC).

Central Statistical Office and Ministry of Finance. 2011. 2011 Population and Housing Census, edited by the Commonwealth of Dominica. Rosseau, Dominica.

Centre, Caribbean Community Climate Change. 2011. Implementation Plan to guide the Delivery of the Regional Framework to Achieving Development Resilient to Climate Change. Caribbean Community Climate Change Centre.

CEPF. 2010. Caribbean Islands Biodiversity Hotspot Ecosystem Profile Summary. Critical Ecosystem Partnership Fund.

Césaire, A. 1939. Cahier dún retour au pays natal. Paris: Présence africaine. Original edition, 1939. Reprint, 2014.

Césaire, A. 1972. "Discourse on Colonialism." Monthly Review Press:1-10.

Chambers, R. 1998. "Editorial Introduction: Vulnerability, Coping and Policy", IDS Bulletin 20 (2):1-7.

Chan, K.M.A., A.D. Guerry, P. Balvanera, S. Klain, T. Satterfield, X. Basurto, A. Bostrom, R. Chuenpagee, R. Gould, B.S. Halpern, N. Hannahs, J. Levine, B. Norton, M. Ruckleshaus, R. Russell, J. Tam, and U. Woodside. 2012. "Where are cultural and social in ecosystem services? A framework for constructive engagement", BioScience (62):744-756.

Chan, K.M.A., T. Satterfield, and J. Goldstein. 2012. "Rethinking ecosystem services to better address and navigate cultural values", Ecological Economics (74):8-18.

Chan, K. M.A., J. Goldstein, T. Satterfield, N. Hannahs, K. Kikiloi, R. Naidoo, N. Vadenboncoeur, and U. Woodside. 2011. "Cultural services and non-use values", in Natural Capital: Theory and Practice of Mapping Ecosystem Services: Theory and Practice of Mapping Ecosystem Services, edited by P. Kareiva, H. Tallis, T. H. Ricketts, G. C. Daily and S. Polasky. Oxford: Oxford University Press.

Chapin, F.S., G.P. Kofinas, and C. Folke, eds. 2009. Principles of ecosystem stewardship: resilience-based natural resource management in a changing world. New York, NY: Springer.

Charles, B.L. 2007. Beyond the Legacy of Slavery: From St. Kitts to Sierra Leone. U.S. Virgin Islands: Christiansted.

Cherrett, N. 2011. Innovation in the tourism sector: a case study from the Commonwealth of Dominica In Studies and Perspectives. Port of Spain: ECLAC Subregional Headquarters for the Caribbean

Christensen, L., and N. Krogman. 2012. "Social thresholds and their translation into socio-ecological management practices", Ecology and Society 17 (1):5.

Clark, J. 2013. "Land and Livelihood in St. Kitts: Global Change and Local Vulnerability". PhD, University of the West Indies.

Clark, K., 2009. "From regulation to participation cultural heritage, sustainable development and citizenship", in Forward Planning: the Function of Cultural Heritage in a Changing Europe, edited by R. Weber, 103-112. Strasbourg: Council of Europe.

Clegg, P. 2002. The Caribbean Banana Trade: From Colonialism to Globalization. International Political Economy Series. London: Palgrave Macmillan.

Cleve, C., M. Kelly, F.R. Kearns, and M. Moritz. 2008. "Classification of the wildland-urban interface: A comparison of pixel- and object-based classifications using high resolution aerial photography", Computers, Environment and Urban Systems 32 (4): 317-326.

Cohen-Shacham, E., T. Dayan, R. de Groot, C. Beltrame, F. Guillet, and E. Feitelson. 2015. "Using the ecosystem services concept to analyze stakeholder involvement in wetland management", Wetlands Ecological Management (23):241-256.

Colchester, M. 2005. "Maps, Power, and the Defense of Territory: The Upper Marzruni Land Claim in Guyana", in Communities and Conservation Histories and Politics of Community-Based Natural Resource Management, edited by J.P. Brosius, A. Lowenhaupt Tsing and C. Zerner, 271-303. Walnut Creek: AltaMira Press.

Coles, A.D., and J.G. Knowles, eds. 2001. Lives in Context: The Art of Life History Research.Walnut Creek, CA: AltaMira Press.

Commission Report. 1932. Conditions in the Carib Reserve and the Disturbance of the 19th of September 1930. London: Her Majesty's Service Over Seas.

Committee, World Heritage. 1992. Convention concerning the Protection of the World Cultural and Natural Heritage. UNESCO.

Consortium, Open Geospatial. 2016. "Geography Markup Language" Open Geospatial Consortium, accessed 06/12/2016. http://www.opengeospatial.org/standards/gml.

Constanza, R., R. d'Arge, R. de Groot, S. Farber, M. Grasso, B. Hannon, and M. van den Belt. 1997. "The value of the world's ecosystem services and natural capital", Ecological Economics 25 (1):3-15.

Conway, D.. 1998. "Misguided Directions, Mismanaged Models, or Missed Paths?", in Globalization and Neoliberalism: The Caribbean Context, edited by T. Klak, 29-49. Lanham, MD: Rowman and Littlefield Publishing Group.

Cooper, J. 2012. "Fail to Prepare, Then Prepare to Fail: Rethinking Threat, Vulnerability, and Mitigation in the Precolumbian Caribbean", in Surviving Sudden Environmental Change Answers from Archaeology, edited by J. Cooper and P. Sheets. Boulder: University Press of Colorado.

Cosgrove, D.E. 1985. "Prospect, perspective and the evolution of the landscape idea", Transactions of the Institute of British Geographers 10 (1):45-62.

Coulthard, S. 2008. "Adapting to environmental change in artisanal fisheries – insights from a South Indian Lagoon", Global Environmental Change 18 (3):479-489.

Couzin, J. 2007. "Opening doors to native knowledge", Science (315):1518-1519.

Creswell, J.W. 2007. Qualitative inquiry and research design: choosing among five approaches. London: Sage.

Creswell, J.W. 2009. Research design: qualitative, quantitative, and mixed methods approaches. London: Sage.

Crispin, G., and N. Kanem. 1989. "The Caribs of Dominica: Land Rights and Ethnic Consciousness", Central America and the Caribbean 13 (3).

Crist, R.E. 1949. "Static and Emerging Cultural Landscapes on the Islands of St. Kitts and Nevis, B.W.I.", Economic Geography 25 (2):134-145.

Crosby, A. W. 1986. Ecological Imperialism: The Biological Expansion of Europe, 900-1900. Cambridge: Cambridge University Press.

Crosby, A.W. 2003. The Columbian Exchange Biological and Cultural Consequences of 1492, 30th Anniversary ed. Westport. London: Praeger.

Cross, N., and R. Barker. 1993. At the Desert's Edge: Oral Histories from the Sahel. London, UK: Panos Publications.

Crowther, A., P. Faulkner, M.E. Prendergast, E. M. Quintana Morales, M. Horton, E. Wilmsen, A.M. Kotarba-Morley, A. Christie, N. Petek, R. Tibesasa, K. Douka, L. Picornell-Gelabert, and X.C.N. Boivin. 2016. "Coastal Subsistence, Maritime Trade, and the Colonization of Small Offshore Islands in Eastern African Prehistory", The Journal of Island and Coastal Archaeology (11):211-237.

Cumming, G.S., P. Olsson, F.S. Chapin III, and C.S. Holling. 2013. "Resilience, experimentation, and scale mismatches in socio-ecological landscapes", Landscape Ecology (28).

Cumper, G. 1954. "Labor Demand and Supply in the Jamaican Sugar Industry." Social and Economic Studies 2 (4).

d'Hauteserre, A. M. 2006. "Landscapes of the Tropics: Tourism and the new cultural economy in the third world", in Landscapes of a New Cultural Economy of Space, edited by T.S. Terkenli and A.M. d'Hauteserre, 149-169. Netherlands: Springer.

Daily, G.C. 1997. Nature's Services: Societal Dependence on natural Ecosystem. Washington DC: Island Press.

Daily, G.C., and P.A. Matson. 2008. "Ecosystem Services: From theory to implementation", Proceedings of the National Academy of Sciences 105 (28):9455-9456.

Dalal-Clayton, B.D., and D.L. Dent. 2001. Knowledge of the Land, Land Resources Information and Its Use in Rural Development. Oxford, UK: Oxford University Press.

Dale, V.H., and K.L. Kline. 2013. "Issues in using landscape indicators to assess land changes", Ecological Indicators (28):91-99.

Dallimer, M., K.N. Irvine, A.M.J. Skinner, Z.G. Davies, J.R. Rouquette, L.L. Maltby, P. H. Warren, P.R. Armsworth, and K.J. Gaston. 2012. "Biodiversity and the Feel-Good Factor: Understanding Associations between Self-Reported Human Well-being and Species Richness", Bioscience (62):47-55.

Daniel, T.C., A. Muhar, A. Arnberger, O. Aznar, J.W. Boyd, K.M.A. Chan, R. Costanza, T. Elmqvist, R.G. Ribe, T. Schauppenlehner, T. Sikor, I. Soloviy, M. Spierenburg, K. Taczanowska, J. Tam, and A. von der Dunk. 2012. "Contributions of cultural services to the ecosystem services agenda", Proceedings of the National Academy of Sciences 109 (23).

Danielsen, F., P.M. Jensen, N.D. Burgess, I. Coronado, S. Holt, M.K. Poulsen, R.M. Rueda, T. Skielboe, M. Enghoff, L.H. Hemmingsen, M. Sorensen, and K. Prihofer-Walzl. 2014. "Testing Focus Groups as a Tool for Connecting Indigenous and Local Knowledge on Abundance of Natural resources with Science-Based Land Management Systems", Conservation Letters 7 (4):380-389.

Darvill, R., and Z. Lindo. 2015. "Quantifying and mapping ecosystem service use across stakeholder groups: Implications for conservation with priorities for cultural values", Ecosystem Services (13):153-161.

Dash, J.M. 1998. The Other America: Caribbean Literature in a New World Context. New World Series. Charlottesville: University of Virginia Press.

Davidson-Hunt, I.J., and F. Berkes. 2003. "Nature and society through the lens of resilience: toward a human-in-ecosystem perspective", in Navigating Socio-ecological Systems: Building Resilience for Complexity and Change, edited by F. Berkes, J. Colding and C. Folke. 53-82. Cambridge: Cambridge University Press.

Davoudi, S. 2012. "Resilience: a bridging concept or a dead end?", Planning Theory and Practice 13 (2):299-307.

de Las Casas, B., and G. Sanderlin. 1971. Bartolomé de Las Casas: a selection of his writings, edited by G. Sanderlin. New York: Alfred A. Knopf, Inc. Original edition, 1542.

DeClerck, F.A.J., S.K. Jones, S. Attwood, D. Bossio, E. Girvetz, B. Chaplin-Kramer, E. Enfors, A.K. Fremier, L.J. Gordon, F. Kizito, I. Lopez Noriega, N. Matthews, M. McCartney, M. Meacham, A. Noble, M. Quintero, R. Remans, R. Soppe, L. Willemen, S.L.R. Wood, and W. Zhang. 2017. "Agricultural ecosystems and their services: the vanguard of sustainability?", Current Opinion in Environmental Sustainability (23): 92-99.

Dekens, J. 2005. "Livelihood Change and Resilience Building: A Village Study from the Darjeeling Hills, Eastern Himalaya, India". Master's Dissertation, University of Manitoba.

Deloughrey, E.M. 2001. "'The litany of islands, the rosary of archipelagos': Caribbean and Pacific Archipelagraphy", ARIEL: A Review of International English Literature 32 (1), 21-51.

DeLoughrey, E., J. Didur, and A. Carrigan. 2015. "Introduction: A Postcolonial Environmental Humanities", in Global Ecologies and the Environmental Humanities: Postcolonial Approaches, edited by E. DeLoughrey, J. Didur and A. Carrigan, 1-32. New York: Routledge.

DeLoughrey, E.M., R.K. Gosson, and G.B. Handley. 2005. "Introduction", in Caribbean Literature and the Environment, edited by E.M. DeLoughrey, R.K. Gosson and G.B. Handley, 1-30. Virginia University of Virginia Press.

DeLoughrey, E.M., and G.B. Handley. 2011. "Introduction: Toward an Aesthetics of the Earth", in Postcolonial Ecologies: Literatures of the Environment, edited by E.M. DeLoughrey and G.B. Handley. Oxford: Oxford University Press.

Delpuech, A., and C.L. Hofman, eds. 2004. Late Ceramic Age Societies in the Eastern Caribbean. Paris Monographs in American Archaeology. Paris.

Denevan, W.M. 1992. "The pristine myth: the landscape of the Americas in 1492" Annals of the Association of American Geographers 82:369-385.

Department of Statistics & Economic Planning. 2001. St. Kitts Census. edited by the Commonwealth of St. Kitts and Nevis. Basseterre, St. Kitts.

Deppisch, S., and S. Hasibovic. 2013. "Socio-ecological resilience thinking as a bridging concept in transdisciplinary research on climate-change adaptation", Natural Hazards: Journal of the International Society for the Prevention and Mitigation of Natural Hazards 67 (1):117-127.

Descola, P. 2005. Beyond Nature and Culture. Translated by J. Lloyd. Chicago: University of Chicago Press.

Development Control Board and Planning, Department of Physical Planning and Environment, and Ministry of Sustainable Development. 2006. St. Christopher National Physical Development Plan. St. Kitts: Government of St. Kitts and Nevis.

Department of Energy and Environmental Protection. 2015. "Watershed Management" http://www.ct.gov/deep/cwp/view.asp?a=2719andq=325622anddepNav_GID=1654.

Diaz, S., S. Demissew, J. Carabias, C. Joly, M. Lonsdale, N. Ash, A. Larigauderie, J.R. Adhikari, S. Arico, and A. Baldi. 2015. "The IPBES Conceptual Framework: connecting nature and people", Current Opinion in Environmental Sustainability (14):1-16.

Diener, E. 2000. "Subjective well-being: the science of happiness and a proposal for a national index", American Psychology (26):34-43.

Digital Shoreline Analysis System (DSAS) Version 4.0 – An ArcGIS Extension for Calculating Shoreline Change. U.S. Geological Survey Open-File Report.

Dirks, N.B. 1992. "Introduction: colonialism and culture", in Colonialism and Culture edited by N.B. Dirks, 1-26. Anne Arbor, MI: University of Michigan Press.

Dockerty, T., A. Lovett, G. Sunnenberg, K. Appleton, and M. Parry. 2005. "Visualising the potential impacts of climate change on rural landscapes", Computer, Environment and Urban Systems 29:297-320.

Drayton, R. 2000. Nature's Government Science, Imperial Britain, and the 'Improvement' of the World. New Haven, CT: Yale University Press.

Duncan, S.L. 2006. "Mapping whose reality? Geographic information systems (GIS) and 'wild science'", Public Understanding of Science 15:411-434.

Dunn, C.E. 2007. "Participatory GIS a people's GIS?", Progressive Human Geography 31 (5):616-637.

DuTetre, J.B. 1667. Histoire Générale des Antilles habitées par les Francois. Paris: Jolly.

Dyde, B. 2005. Out of the Crowded Vagueness: A History of the Islands of St. Kitts, Nevis and Anguilla. Oxford: Macmillan Publishers Limited.

Edwards, A, and A. Jacque. 2007. "Alternatives to Sugar-Cane in St. Kitts: Competitiveness Studies of Four Crops in St. Kitts/Nevis", in Proceedings of the 26th West Indies Agricultural Economics Conference: Food Safety and Value Added Production and Marketing of Tropical Crops. Puerto Rico.

Elo, S., and H. Kyngäs. 2008. "The qualitative content analysis process", Journal of Advanced Nursing 62 (1):107-115.

Engelbrecht, H.J. 2009. "Natural Capital, subjective well-being, and the new welfare economics of sustainability: some evidence from cross-country regressions", Ecological Economics (68):380-388. Geospatial Hydrologic Modeling Extension (HEC-GeoHMS) 10.2.

Escobar, A. 1999. "After Nature: Steps to an Anti-essentialist Political Ecology", Current Anthropology 40:1-30.

Esri. 2017. "Geometric Correction". ESRI accessed 24/02/2017. http://support.esri.com/other-resources/gis-dictionary/term/geometric%20correction.

Europe, Council of. 2000. European Landscape Convention in Article 1 – Definitions, edited by the Council of Europe. Florence.

Fairhead, J., and M. Leach. 1996. Misreading the African Landscape. Cambridge: Cambridge University Press.

Fairhead, J., and M. Leach. 2003. Science, Society and Power: Environmental Knowledge and Policy in West Africa and the Caribbean. Cambridge: Cambridge University Press.

Fanon, F. 1963. The Wretched of the Earth. Translated by C. Farrington. New York: Grove Weidenfeld. Original edition, 1961.

Fanon, F. 1967. Black Skin, White Masks. New York, N.Y: Grove Press Inc. Original edition, 1952.

FAO. 2016. "Land degradation assessment", accessed 15/12/2016. http://www.fao.org/nr/land/ degradation/en/.

Farbotkoa, C., and H. Lazrus. 2012. "The first climate refugees? Contesting global narratives of climate change in Tuvalu", Global Environmental Change 22 (2):382-390.

Farina, A. 2000. "The cultural landscape as a model for the integration of ecology and economics", BioScience 50:313-20.

Faugier, J., and M. Sargeant. 1997. "Sampling hard to reach populations", Journal of Advanced Nursing (26):790-797.

Feagan, R. 2007. "The place of food: mapping out the 'local' in local food systems", Progress in Human Geography 31 (1):23-42.

Featherstone, D. 2003. "Spatialities of transnational resistance to globalization: the maps of grievance of the Inter-Continental Caravan", Transactions of the Institute of British Geographers (282):404.

Ferraz, S.F. de Barros, C.A. Vettorazzi, D.M. Theobald, and M.V. Ramos Ballester. 2005. "Landscape dynamics of Amazonian deforestation between 1984 and 2002 in central Rondônia, Brazil: assessment and future scenarios", Forest Ecology and Management 204 (1):69-85.

Fisher, B., R. Kerry Turner, and P. Morling. 2009. "Defining and classifying ecosystem services for decision making", Ecological Economics (68):643-653.

Fleming, P.H. 1987. "The Bitter of the Sweet: Sugar Production and Underdevelopment of St. Kitts". PhD Dissertation, Carleton University.

Fletcher, R., I. Johnson, E.Bruce, and K. Khun-Neay. 2007. "Living with heritage: site monitoring and heritage values in Greater Angkor and the Angkor World Heritage Site, Cambodia", World Archaeology 39 (3):385-405.

Fleuret, S., and S. Atkinson. 2007. "Wellbeing, health and geography: A critical review and research agenda",New Zealand Geographer (63):106-118.

Flora, C., and J. Flora. 2004. Rural Communities: Legacy and Change. 2nd ed. Boulder, CO: Westview Press.

Folke, C. 2006. "Resilience: the emergence of a perspective for socio-ecological systems analysis", Global Environmental Change 16:253-267.

Folke, C., S.R. Carpenter, B. Walker, M. Scheffer, T. Chapin, and J. Rockstrom. 2010. "Resilience Thinking: Integrating resilience, adaptability and transformability", Ecology and Society 15 (4):20.

Folke, C., and T. Hahn. 2003. "Socio-ecological Transformation for Ecosystem Management: the Development of Adaptive Co-management of Wetland Landscape in Southern Sweden", Ecology and Society 9 (4):2.

Ford, J. D., B. Smit, and J. Wandel. 2006. "Vulnerability to climate change in the Artic: A case study from Artic Bay, Canada", Global Environmental Change 16 (2):145-160.

Forte, M.C. 2006. Indigenous Resurgence in the Contemporary Caribbean: Amerindian Survival and Revival. Peter Lang.

Found, W., and M. Berbés-Blázquez. 2012. "The sugar-cane landscape of the Caribbean islands: Resilience, adaptation and transformation of the plantation socio-ecological system", in Resilience and the Cultural Landscape: Understanding and Managing Change in Human-Shaped Environments, edited by T. Plieninger and C. Bieling, 164-185. Cambridge, UK: Cambridge University Press.

Fowler, P. 2001. "Cultural landscape: great concept, pity about the phrase", in Planning for a sustainable partnership between people and place, Oxford, UK, May 1999.

Fox, J., J. Kummel, S. Yarnasarn, M. Ekasingh, and N. Podger. 1995. "Land-use and landscape dynamics in Northern Thailand: assessing change in three upland watersheds", Ambio (24):328-334.

Fox, J. 2011. "Siam Mapped and Mapping in Cambodia: Boundaries, Sovereignty, and Indigenous Conceptions of Space", Society and Natural Resources: An International Journal 15 (1):65-78.

Fox, J., K. Suryanata, and P. Hershock, eds. 2005. Mapping Communities Ethics, Values, Practice. The East West Center, Honolulu.

Frederick, H. 1981. "The Caribs and their colonizers: the problem of land", in The Rights of Indigenous People and their Land. Geneva.

Fridell, G. 2010. "The Case against Cheap Bananas: Lessons from the EU-Caribbean Banana Agreement", Critical Sociology 37 (3):285-307.

Furedi, F. 2007. "The changing meaning of disaster", Area (39):482-489.

Gadgil, M., P. Olsson, F. Berkes, and C.Folke. 2003. "Exploring the role of local ecological knowledge in ecosystem management: three case studies", in Navigating socio-ecological systems: building resilience for complexity and change, edited by F. Berkes, J. Colding and C. Folke:189-209. Cambridge: Cambridge University Press.

Galtung, J. 1969. "Violence, peace and peace research", Journal of Peace Research 6 (3):167-191.

Gamble, D.W., D. Campbell, T.L. Allen, D. Barker, S. Curtis, D. McGregor, and J. Popke. 2010. "Climate Change, Drought, and Jamaican Agriculture: Local Knowledge and the Climate Record", Annals of the Association of American Geographers 100 (4):880-893.

Garbach, K.M. 2012. Linking Social and Ecological Systems to Sustain Ecosystem Services in a Tropical Landscape. PhD Dissertation, University of California, Davis.

García-Colón, I. 2009. Land Reform in Puerto Rico: Modernizing the Colonial State, 1941-1969, New Directions in Puerto Rican Studies. Gainesville: University Press of Florida.

García-Nieto, A.P., C. Quintas-Soriano, M. García-Llorente, I. Palomo, C. Montes, and B. Martín-López. 2015. "Collaborative mapping of ecosystem services: The role of stakeholders' profiles", Ecosystem Services.

Gardner-Youden, H.L., C. Barbeau, D.D. McCarthy, V. Edwards, D. Cowan, and L.J.S. Tsuji. 2013. "Indigenous Mapping Technologies: the past, present and future of the collaborative geomatics web-based tool", Knowledge Management for Development Journal 7 (3):340-353.

Garrard, G. 2007. "Problems Concerning Islands", in "What is the Earthly Paradise?" Ecocritical Responses to the Caribbean, edited by C. Campbell and E. Somerville. Newcastle: Cambridge Scholars Publishing.

Gerbi, A. 1985. Nature in the New World: From Christopher Columbus to Gonzalo Fernández de Oviedo. Pittsburgh: University of Pittsburgh Press.

Gfeller, A.E. 2015. "Anthropologizing and indigenizing heritage: The origins of the UNESCO Global Strategy for a representative, balanced and credible World Heritage List", Journal of Social Archaeology 15 (3):366-386.

Giannecchini, M., W. Twine, and C. Vogel. 2007. "Land-cover change and human- environment interactions in a rural cultural landscape in South Africa" The Geographical Journal 173 (1):26-42.

Géigel, Antonio Gaztambide. 2000. "Identidades internacionales y cooperación regional en el Caribe." Revista Mexicana del Caribe V (9):6-38.

Géigel, Antonio Gaztambide. 2008. "La geopolítica del antillanismo en el Caribe del siglo XIX." Memorias. Revista Digital de Historia y Arqueología desde el Caribe 4 (8):1-35.

Gilmore, M.P., and J.C. Young. 2013. "The Use of Participatory Mapping in Ethnobiological Research, Biocultural Conservation, and Community Empowerment: A Case Study From the Peruvian Amazon", Journal of Ethnobiology 32 (1):6-29.

Glissant, E. 1989. Caribbean Discourse: Selected Essays. Charlottesville: University of Virginia.

Glissant, E. 1997. Poetics of Relation. Ann Arbor: University of Michigan Press.

Glotfelty, C, and H. Fromm, eds. 1996. The Ecocritical Reader: Landmarks in Literary Ecology. Athens, GA: University of Georgia Press.

Gohrisch, J., and E. Grünkemeier. 2013. "Introduction: Postcolonial Studies Across the Disciplines", in Postcolonial Studies Across the Disciplines, edited by J. Gohrisch and E. Grünkemeier. Amsterdam/ New York: Rodopi B.V.

Goldenberg, M. 2008. A review of rural and regional development policies and programs. Ottawa, ON: Canadian Policy Research Networks.

Goldstein, S., and R.B. Brooks. 2012. Handbook of resilience in children. Springer Science and Business Media.

González-Puente, M., M. Campos, M.K. McCall, and J. Munoz-Rojas. 2014. "Places beyond maps; integrating spatial map analysis and perception studies to unravel landscape change in a Mediterranean mountain area (NE Spain)", Applied Geography (52):182-190.

Goodman, N. 2003. Five kinds of capital: Useful concepts for sustainable development. Boston, MA: Tufts University.

Goodwin, R.C. 1978. "The Lesser Antilles Archaic: New Data From St. Kitts." Journal of the Virgin Islands Archaeological Society (5):6-16.

Goodwin, R.C. 1979. "Prehistoric Cultural Ecology of St. Kitts, West Indies: A Case Study in Island Archaeology." Ph.d. Dissertation, Department of Anthropology, Arizona State University.

Gosden, C.. 2004. Archaeology and Colonialism. Cambridge: Cambridge University Press.

Gossling, S. 2003. "Tourism and Development in Tropical Islands: Political Ecology Perspectives", in Tourism and Development in Tropical Islands: Political Ecology edited by S. Gossling, 1-37. Cheltenham: Edward Elgar.

Goudie, A.S. 2013. The Human Impact on the Natural Environment: Past, Present, and Future. 7th ed. Oxford, UK: Wiley-Blackwell.

Goveia, E. 1965. Slave Society in the British Leeward Islands at the End of the Eighteenth Century. New Haven, CT: Yale University Press.

Granderson, A.A. 2017. "Value conflicts and the politics of risk: challenges in assessing climate change impacts and risk priorities in rural Vanuatu", Climate and Development 1-14.

Gratani, M., E.L. Bohensky, J.R.A. Butler, S. G. Sutton, and S. Foale. 2014. "Experts' Perspectives on the Integration of Indigenous Knowledge and Science in Wet Tropics Natural Resource Management", Australian Geographer 45 (2).

Green, D., J. Billy, and A. Tapim. 2010. "Indigenous Australians' knowledge of weather and climate", Climatic Change 100 (2):337-354.

Green, N.. 1995. "Looking at the Landscape: Class Formation and the Visual", in The Anthropology of Landscape, edited by E. Hirsch and M. O'Hanlon. Oxford: Clarendon Press.

Greening, A. 2014. Understanding Local Perceptions and the Role of the Historical Context in Ecotourism Development: A Case Study of St. Kitts. Master of Science, Human Dimensions of Ecosystem Sciences and Management, Utah State University.

Gregoire, C., P. Henderson, and N. Kanem. 1996. "Karifuna: The Caribs of Dominica", in Ethnic Minorities in Caribbean Society, edited by Rhoda Reddock, 107-173. St. Augustine, Trinidad and Tobago: I.S.E.R., The University of the West Indies.

Groot, R. de, P.S. Ramakrishnan, A. van den Berg, T. Kulenthran, S. Muller, and D. Pitt. 2005. "Cultural and amenity services", in Ecosystems and human well-being: current state and trends, 455-476. Washington DC: Island Press.

Gross-Camp, N.D., A. Martin, S. McGuire, B. Kebede, and J. Munyarukaza. 2012. "Payments for ecosystem services in an African protected area: exploring issues of legitimacy, fairness, equity and effectiveness", Oryx 46 (24-33).

Grove, R. 1995. Green Imperialism: Colonial Expansion, Tropical Island Edens and the Origins of Environmentalism, 1600- 1860. Cambridge: Cambridge University Press.

Grove, R. 2002. "Climatic Fears: Colonialism and the History of Environmentalism", in Harvard International Review (Winter 2002).

Guimberteau, M., P. Ciais, A. Ducharne, J.P. Boisier, A.P.D. Aguiar, H. Biemans, H. De Deurwaerder, D. Galbraith, B. Kruijt, and F. Langerwisch. 2016. "Impacts of future deforestation and climate change on the hydrology of the Amazon basin: a multi-model analysis with a new set of land-cover change scenarios", in Hydrology and Earth System Sciences.

Gunderson, L.H., and C.S. Holling. 2002. Panarchy: Understanding transformations in human and natural systems. Washington DC: Island Press.

Guttmann-Bond, E. 2014. "Productive Landscapes: a Global Perspective on Sustainable Agriculture", Landscapes 15 (1):59-76.

Haas, P.M. 2016. Epistemic Communities, Constructivism, and International Environmental Politics. Abingdon: Routledge.

Haines-Young, R., and M. Potschin. 2010. "The links between biodiversity, ecosystem services and human well-being", in Ecosystem Services: A New Syndissertation, edited by D.G. Raffaelli and C.L.J. Frid, 111-139. New York, US: Cambridge University Press.

Haines-Young, R., and M. Postchin. 2011. Common International Classification of Ecosystem Services (CICES): 2011 Update, edited by the European Environment Agency. University of Nottingham, UK.

Harris, W. 1970. History, Fable, and Myth. Georgetown, Guyana: The National History and Arts Council Ministry of Information and Culture.

Harrison, J.L. 2014. "Neoliberal environmental justice: mainstream ideas of justice in political conflict over agricultural pesticides in the United States", Environmental Politics 23 (4):650-669.

Harrison, R., and L. Hughes. 2010. "Heritage, colonialism and postcolonialism", in Understanding the Politics of Heritage, edited by R. Harrison, 234-267. Manchester: Manchester University Press.

Hart, A.K., J.C. Milder, N. Estrada-Carmona, F.A. DeClerck, C.A. Harvey, and P. Dobie. 2015. "Integrated landscape initiatives in practice: assessing experiences from 191 landscapes in Africa and Latin America", in Climate Smart Landscapes: Multifunctionality in Practice, edited by P.A. Minang, M. van Noordwijk, O.E. Freeman, C. Mbow, J. de Leeuw and D. Catacutan, 89-101. Nairobi, Kenya: World Agroforestry Centre.

Hau'ofa, E. 1994. "Our Sea of Islands", in A New Oceania: Rediscovering Our Sea of Islands, edited by V. Naidu, E. Waddell and E. Hau'ofa. Suva: School of Social and Economic Development, The University of the South Pacific.

Hauser, M. 2015. "The Infrastructure of Nature's Island: Settlements, Networks and Economy of Two Plantations in Colonial Dominica." International Journal of Historical Archaeology 19 (3):601-622.

Hauser, M., and D. Hicks. 2007. "Colonialism and Landscape: Materiality and Scales of Analysis in Caribbean Historical Archaeology", in Envisioning Landscape: Situations and Standpoints in Archaeology and Heritage, edited by D. Hicks, L. McAtackney and G. Fairclough, 251-274. Walnut Creek, CA: Left Coast Press.

Heavyrunner, I., and K. Marshall. 2003. "'Miracle Survivors' Promoting Resilience in Indian Students" in Tribal College 14 (4):15.

Hegney, H. R., P. Baker, C. Rogers-Clark, C. King, E. Buikstra, A. Watson-Luke, K. McLachlan, and L. Stallard. 2008. Identification of personal and community resilience that enhance psychological wellness: a Stanthorpe study. Toowoomba, Australia: Centre for Rural and Remote Area Health, The University of Queensland and University of Southern Queensland.

Hegney, D., H. Ross, P. Baker, C. Rogers-Clark, C. King, and E. Buikstra. 2008. Building resilience in rural communities toolkit. Toowoomba, Australia: The University of Queensland and University of Southern Queensland.

Helliwell, J.F., and C.P. Barrington-Leigh. 2014. "Viewpoint: Measuring and understanding subjective well-being", Canadian Journal of Economics 43 (3):729-753.

Hengl, T., and D.G. Rossiter. 2002. "Supervised Landform Classification to Enhance and Replace Photo-Interpretation in Semi-Detailed Soil Survey", American Society of Agronomy 67 (6):1810-1822.

Herrington, S. 2010. "The Right to Landscape: Contesting Landscape and Human Rights". Cambridge Centre for Landscape and People (CCLP) Jesus College, Cambridge, UK December 8-10, 2008. Landscape Journal 29 (1):95-97.

Heuman, G. 2006. The Caribbean (Brief Histories). London: Hodder Arnold.

Hewitt, K., ed. 1983. Interpretations of Calamity from the Viewpoint of Human Ecology. London: Allen and Unwin.

Higman, B.W. 1995. "Small Islands, Large Questions: Post-Emancipation Historiography of the Leeward Islands." In Small Islands, Large Questions Society: Culture and Resistance in the Post-Emancipation Caribbean, edited by Karen Fog Olwig, 8-27. London: Frank Class.

Higman, B.W. 2010. A Concise History of the Caribbean. Cambridge: Cambridge University Press.

Hillstrom, K., and L.C. Hillstrom, eds 2004. Latin America and the Caribbean: A Continental Overview of Environmental Issues. Santa Barbara, CA: ABC CLIO.

Himmelstoss, E.A. 2009. " DSAS 4.0 Installation Instructions and User Guide" in Digital Shoreline Analysis System (DSAS) version 4.0 – An ArcGIS extension for calculating shoreline change: U.S. Geological Survey Open-File Report 2008-1278, edited by E.R. Thieler, E.A. Himmelstoss, J.L. Zichichi and A. Ergul.

Hoffman, C.A. 1973. "Archaeological Investigations on St. Kitts, WI", Caribbean Journal of Science 13:237-252.

Hofman, C.L., A.J. Bright, A. Boomert, and S. Knippenberg. 2007. "Island Rhythms: The Web of Social Relationships and Interaction Networks in the Lesser Antillean Archipelago Between 400 B.C. and A.D. 1492", Latin American Antiquity 18 (3):243-268.

Hofman, C.L., and M.L.P. Hoogland, eds. 2011. "Unravelling the Multi-Scale Networks of Mobility and Exchange in the Pre-Colonial Circum-Caribbean", in Communities in contact: essays in archaeology, ethnohistory and ethnography of the Amerindian circum-Caribbean, edited by C.L. Hofman and A. van Duijvenbode. Leiden: Sidestone Press. Hofman, C.L., and M.L.P. Hoogland. 2012. "Caribbean encounters: rescue excavations at the early colonial Island Carib site of Argyle, St. Vincent." Analecta Praehistorica Leidensia 63-76. Hofman, C.L.,

A. Mol, M.L.P. Hoogland, and R.V. Rojas. 2014. "Stage of encounters: migration, mobility and interaction in the pre-colonial and early colonial Caribbean." World Archaeology 46 (4).

Hofman, C.L., and M.L.P. Hoogland. 2015. "Beautiful Tropical Islands In The Caribbean Sea. Human Responses To Floods And Droughts And The Indigenous Archaeological Heritage Of The Caribbean", in Water and Heritage. Material, conceptual and spiritual connections, edited by W.J.H. Willems and H.P.J. van Schaik, 99-119. Leiden: Sidestone Press.

Hofman, C.L., M.L.P. Hoogland, and R. Grant Gilmore III. 2015. "Archaeological assessment at Bethlehem, St. Maarten, An early Valetta Treaty project in the Dutch Winward Islands." In Managing our past into the future: Archaeological heritage management in the Dutch Caribbean, edited by C.L. Hofman and J.B. Haviser, 217-232. Leiden: Sidestone Press Academics

Hofman, C.L., and M.L.P. Hoogland. forthcoming. "Arqueología y patrimonio de los Kalinago en las islas de San Vincente y Granada." In Indígenas e Indios en el Caribe: Presencia, legado y estudio edited by Roberto Valcárcel Rojas and Jorge Ulloa Hung. Santo Domingo: Instituto Tecnológico de Santo Domingo.

Hofman, C.L., M.L.P. Hoogland, A. Boomert, and A. Martin. forthcoming. "Colonial Encounters in the Southern Lesser Antilles. Indigenous resistance, material transformations, and diversity in an ever globalizing world." In Material Encounters and Indigenous Transformations in the Early Colonial Americas: Archaeological Case Studies, edited by Corinne L. Hofman and Floris Keehen. Leiden: Brill.

Holden, T., and L. Bourke. 2014. "Editorial: Rural community wellbeing", Rural Society 23 (3):208-215.

Holling, C.S. 1973. "Resilience and Stability of Ecological Systems", Annual Review of Ecology and Systematics 4:1-23.

Hong, S., P. Wehi, and H. Matsuda. 2013. "Island biocultural diversity and traditional ecological knowledge", Journal of Marine and Island Cultures 2 (2):57-58.

Honychurch, L. 1995. The Dominica Story: A History of the Island. Oxford: Macmillan Caribbean.

Hubbard, V.K. 2002. A History of St. Kitts: The Sweet Trade. Oxford: Macmillan Publishers Limited.

Huddell, A. 2010. "Effects of Neoliberal Reforms on Small-scale Agriculture in Brazil", Global Majority E-Journal 1 (2):74-84.

Huggan, G. 2008. Interdisciplinary measures. Literature and the Future of Postcolonial studies. University of Chicago Press.

Hughes, M.L., P.F. McDowell, and W.A. Marcus. 2006. "Accuracy assessment of geo-rectified aerial photographs: Implications for measuring lateral channel movement in a GIS", Geomorphology 74 (1-4):1-16.

Hulme, P. 1986. Colonial Encounters: Europe and the native Caribbean, 1492-1797. London: Methuen and Co.

Hulme, P. 2001. "Survival and Invention: Indigeneity in the Caribbean", in Postcolonial Discourses. An Anthology, edited by G. Castle, 293-307. Blackwell Publishers Ltd.: Oxford, UK.

Hulme, P., and N. Whitehead. 1992. Wild Majesty, Encounters with Caribs from Columbus to the Present Day. An Anthology. Oxford: Oxford University Press.

Hummel, D., S. Adamo, A. de Sherbinin, L. Murphy, R. Aggarwal, L. Zulu, J. Liu, and K. Knight. 2013. "Inter- and transdisciplinary approaches to population- environment research for sustainability aims: a review and appraisal", Population Environment (38):481-509.

Ianoş, I., I. Saghin, V.S. Ilinca, and D. Zamfir. 2013. "Perennial Values and Cultural Landscapes Resilience",2nd World Conference on Design, Arts and Education (DAE-2013), Romania, 19/3/2014.

IPCC. 2007. Contribution of Working Groups I, II and III to the Fourth Assessment Report of the Intergovernmental Panel on Climate Change, edited by Core Writing Team, R.K. Pachauri and A. Reisinger. Geneva, Switzerland.

Ireland, T. 2010. "Excavating Globalization from the Ruins of Colonialism: Archaeological Heritage Management Responses to Cultural Change" ICOMOS ScientificSymposium, Changing World, Changing Views of Heritage: The Impact of Global Change on Cultural Heritage, Dublin.

Ismail, M. H., and K. Jusoff. 2008. "Satellite Data Classification Accuracy Assessment Based from Reference Dataset", International Journal of Environmental, Chemical, Ecological, Geological and Geophysical Engineering 2 (3):23-29.

Jackson, P. 1989. Maps of Meaning: An Introduction to Cultural Geography. London: Unwin Hyman.

Jackson, S.E. 1995. "The water is not empty: cross-cultural issues in conceptualising sea space", Australian Geographer 26 (1):87-96.

Jácome, F. 2006. "Environmental Movements in the Caribbean", in Beyond sun and sand: Caribbean environmentalisms, edited by S.L. Baver and B.D. Lynch, 17-31. New Brunswick: Rutgers University Press.

Jaffe, R. 2006. "Urban Blight in the Caribbean City, Environment and Culture in Curaçao and Jamaica", Faculty of Anthropology, Leiden University.

Jaffe, R. 2007. "Global environmental ideoscapes, blighted cityscapes: city, island and environment in Jamaica and Curaçao", Etnofoor 19 (2):113-129.

Jaffe, R. 2008. "As lion rule the jungle, so man rule the earth: perceptions of nature and the environment in two Caribbean cities", Wadabagei 11 (3):46-49.

Jaffe, R. 2009. "Conflicting Environments: Negotiating Social and Ecological Vulnerabilities in Urban Jamaica and Curacao", in Global Change and Caribbean Vulnerability: Environment, Economy and Society at Risk?, edited by D. McGregor, D. Dodman and D. Barker, 317-335. Kingston: University of the West Indies Press.

Jaffe, R. 2013. "Unnatural Causes: Green Environmentalism, Urban Pollution and Social Justice in the Caribbean", in Environmental Management in the Caribbean Policy and Practice, edited by E. Thomas- Hope, 90-102. Kingston: University of West Indies.

Jolly, C.L. 1994. "Four theories of population change and the environment", Population Environment 16 (1):61-90.

Jones, M., P. Howard, K.R. Olwig, J. Primdahl, and I. Sarlov Herlin. 2007. "Multiple Interfaces of the European Landscape Convention", Norsk Geografisk Tidsskrift – Norwegian Journal of Geography 61:207-215.

Jong, R. de, S. de Bruin, M. Schaepman, and D. Dent. 2011. "Quantitative mapping of global land degradation using Earth observations", International Journal of Remote Sensing 32 (21):6823-6853.

Joshi, P.K., A.K. Jha, S.P. Wani, T.K. Sreedevi, and F.A. Shaheen. 2008. "Impact of Watershed Program and Conditions for Success: A Meta-Analysis Approach", in Global Theme on Agroecosystems: International Crops Research Institute for the Semi-Arid Tropics and National Centre for Agricultural Economics and Policy Research.

Kareiva, P., H. Tallis, T.H. Ricketts, G.C. Daily, and S. Polasky. 2011. Natural Capital: Theory and Practice of Mapping Ecosystem Services. Oxford: Oxford University Press.

Karrascha, L., T. Klenkea, and J. Woltjerb. 2014. "Linking the ecosystem services approach to social preferences and needs in integrated coastal land use management – A planning approach", Land Use Policy 38:522-532.

Keegan, B. 2004. "Islands of Chaos." In Late Ceramic Age Societies in the Eastern Caribbean, edited by A. Delpuech & C.L. Hofman, 33-44. Oxford: Archaeopress.

Keegan, W.F., S.M. Fitzpatrick, K.S. Sealey, M.J. LeFebvre, and P.T. Sinelli. 2008. "The Role of Small Islands in Marine Subsistence Strategies: Case Studies from the Caribbean", Human Ecology 36 (5):635-654.

Keegan, W.F., and C.L. Hofman. 2017. The Caribbean before Columbus. Oxford: Oxford University Press.

Kelman, I. 2010. "Hearing local voices from Small Island Developing States for climate change", Local Environment: The International Journal of Justice and Sustainability 15 (7).

Kelman, I. 2014. "No change from climate change: vulnerability and small island developing states", The Geographical Journal 180 (2):120-129.

Kelman, I. 2017. "How can island communities deal with environmental hazards and hazard drivers, including climate change?", Environmental Conservation:1-10.

Kelman, I., J.C. Gaillard, J. Mercer, J. Lewis, and A. Carrigan. 2015. "Island Vulnerability and Resilience Combining Knowledges for Disaster Risk Reducation, Including Climate Change Adaptation", in Global Ecologies and the Environmental Humanities Postcolonial Approaches, edited by E. DeLoughrey, J. Didur and A. Carrigan. New York: Routledge.

Kelman, I., J Lewis, J.C. Gaillard, and J. Mercer. 2015. "Island contributions to disaster research", Global Environment 8 (1):16-37.

Kincaid, J. 1988. A Small Place. New York: Farrar, Strauss and Giroux.

Kincaid, J. 1999. My Garden. New York: Farrar, Straus and Giroux.

King, A. 1995. "Avoiding ecological surprise: lessons from long-standing communities", Academy of Management Review (20):961-985. King, D. 2004. "Climate change science: adapt, mitigate, or ignore?", Science 303:176-177.

King, M.F., V.F. Renvo, and E.M.L.M. Novo. 2013. "The concept, dimensions and methods of assessment of human well-being within a socioecological context: a literature review", Social Indicators Research 116 (3):681-698.

Kjerfve, B. 1981. "Tides of the Caribbean Sea", Journal of Geophysical Research (86):C5.

Klak, T. 1998. "Thirteen Theses on Globalization and Neoliberalism", in Globalization and Neoliberalism: The Caribbean Context, edited by T. Klak, 3-23. Lanham, MD: Rowman and Littlefield Publishing Group.

Kohler, T. A. 1993. "Prehistoric human impact on the environment in the upland North American Southwest", Population and Environment 13 (4):255-268.

Kosiba, S., and A.M. Bauer. 2012. "Mapping the Political Landscape: Towards GIS Analysis of Environmental and Social Differences", Journal of Archaeology Method and Theory (20):61-101.

Kossek, B. 1994. "Land Rights, Cultural Identity and Gender Conflicts in the Carib Territory of Dominica", in Law and Anthropology, edited by R. Kuppé and R. Potz, 171-201. Dordrecht, the Netherlands: Martinus Nijhoff.

Krippendorff, K. 1980. Content Analysis: An Introduction to its Methodology. Newbury Park: Sage Publications.

Kulig, J., D. Edge, and J. Guernsey. 2005. "Community resiliency and health status: What are the links", Journal of Rural and Community Development 3 (3):76-94.

Kumar, M., and P. Kumar. 2008. "Valuation of the ecosystem services: a psycho-cultural perspective", Ecological Economics 69 (6):808-819.

Kyngas, H., and L. Vanhanen. 1999. "Content Analysis (Finish)", Hoitotiede (11):3-12.

Labat, J. 1970. The Memoirs of Père Labat 1693-1705. Translated and edited by J. Eaden. London: Frank Cass and Co. Ltd.

Laffoon, J.E., T.F. Sonnemann, T. Shafie, C.L. Hofman, U. Brandes, and G.R. Davies. 2017. "Investigating human geographic origins using dual-isotope ($87Sr/86Sr$, $\delta 18O$) assignment approaches." PloS O one 12 (2):e0172562.

Laidler, G.J. 2006. "Inuit and scientific perspectives on the relationship between sea ice and climate change: the ideal complement?", Climate Change (78):404-444.

Laird, S.G., A. Wardell-Johnson, and A.T. Ragusa. 2014. "Editorial: exploring the human- environment connection: rurality, ecology and social wellbeing", Rural Society 23 (2): 114-116.

Lal, R. 1997. "Deforestation effects on soil degradation and rehabilitation in western Nigeria. IV. Hydrology and water quality", Land Degradation and Development 8 (2):95-126.

Lamson, C. 1986. "Planning for resilient coastal communities: lessons from ecological systems theory", Coastal Zone Management Journal (13):249-254.

Lane, R., D. Lucas, F. Vanclay, S. Henry, and I. Coates. 2005. "'Committing to Place' at the Local Scale: the potential of youth education programs for promoting community participation in regional natural resource management", Australian Geographer 36 (3):351-367.

Larson, E.C., A.E. Luloff, J.C. Bridger, and M.A. Brennan. 2015. "Community as a mechanism for transcending wellbeing at the individual, social, and ecological levels", Community Development 46 (4):407-419.

Latta, A., and H. Wittman. 2012. "Citizens, Society and Nature: Sites of Inquiry, Points of Departure", in Environment and Citizenship in Latin America: Natures, Subjects and Struggles, edited by A. Latta and H. Wittman, 1-20. New York: Berghahn Books.

Latta, P.A. 2007. "Citizenship and the Politics of Nature: The Case of Chile's Alto Bío Bío", Citizenship Studies 11 (3):229-246.

Lawrence, K. 2014. Investigating the poverty reduction program of the organization of Eastern Caribbean States (OECS): Dominica, St. Kitts and Nevis, and St. Lucia. Master of Arts, Social Policy, Empire State College State University.

Layng, A. 1976. .The Carib Population of Dominica. PhD dissertation, Case Western Reserve University.

Layng, A. 1983. The Carib Reserve: Identity and Security in the West Indies. Washington DC: University Press of America.

Lazarus, N. 1999. Nationalism and Cultural Practice in the Postcolonial World. Cambridge: Cambridge University Press.

Lebel, L., J. M Anderies, B. Campbell, C. Folke, S. Hatfield-Dodds, T. P. Hughes, and J. Wilson. 2006. "Governance and the capacity to manage resilience in regional socio-ecological systems." Ecology and Society 11 (1):19.

Lee, D., M. Hampton, and J. Jeyacheya. 2014. "The political economy of precarious work in the tourism industry in small island developing states." Review of International Political Economy 22 (1).

Lehtinen, A. 2005. "Tracing environmental justice. On the associations of folk, justice and the environment. ." In Landscape, Law and Justice, edited by T. Peil and M. Jones, 81-91. Oslo: The Institute for Comparative Research in Human Culture.

Leifeld, P. 2012. Discourse Network Analyzer Manual.

Lemos, M.C., E. Boyd, E.L. Tompkins, H. Osbahr, and D. Liverman. 2007. "Developing adaptation and adapting development", Ecology and Society 12 (2):26.

Lennon, J.L. 2006. "Cultural Heritage Management", in Managing Protected Areas: A Global Guide, edited by M. Lockwood, G.L. Worboys and A. Kothari. London: Earthscan Publications Ltd.

Lennon, J.L. 2012. "Cultural landscape management", in Managing Cultural Landscapes, edited by K. Taylor and J.L. Lennon, 45-69. Oxon: Routledge.

Lenz, R., and D. Peters. 2006. "From data to decisions – steps to an application-orientated landscape research", Ecological Indicators (6):250-263.

Leonard, S., M. Parsonsa, K. Olawsky, and F. Kofoda. 2013. "The role of culture and traditional knowledge in climate change adaptation: Insights from East Kimberley, Australia", Global Environmental Change 23 (3):623-632.

Lewis, J., and I. Kelman. 2012. "The Good, The Bad and the Ugly: Disaster Risk Reduction (DRR) Versus Disaster Risk Creation (DRC)", PLOS Currents Disasters.

Lilley, Ian. 2009. "Strangers and brothers? Heritage, Human Rights, and Cosmopolitan Archaeology in Oceania." in Cosmopolitan Archaeologies, edited by L. Meskell, 48-67. Durham and London: Duke University Press.

Lindeström, P. 1925. Geographia America; with an account of the Delaware Indians, based on surveys and notes made in 1654-1656. Philadelphia: The Swedish Colonial Society.

Lipshultz, R.D. 2004. Global Environmental Politics: Power, Perspectives and Practice. Washington, DC: CQ Press.

Liu, J., and P. Opdam. 2014. "Valuing ecosystem services in community-based landscape planning: introducing a wellbeing-based approach", Landscape Ecology 29 (8):1347-1360.

Liverman, D.M. 1990. "Drought impacts in Mexico: Climate, agriculture, technology, and land tenure in Sonora and Puebla", Annals of the Association of American Geographers 80 (1):49-72.

Logan, W. 2012. "Cultural diversity, cultural heritage and human rights: towards heritage management as human rights-based cultural practice", International Journal of Heritage Studies 18 (3):231-244.

López-Marrero, T., K. Yamane, T. Heartsill-Scalley, and N. Villanueva-Colón. 2012. "The Various Shapes of the Insular Caribbean: Population and Environment." Caribbean Studies 40 (2):17-32. Lopez-Marrero, T., and B. Wisner. 2012. "Not in the same boat: disasters and differential vulnerability in the insular Caribbean", Caribbean Studies 40 (2):129-168.

López-Marrero, T., Hampton, E. Vergara, J. Quiroz, K. Simovic, and H. Arevalo. 2013. "Hazards and Disasters in the Insular Caribbean: A Systematic Literature Review." Caribbean Geography (18):84-104.

Lowitt, K., G.M. Hickey, A. Saint Ville, K. Raeburn, T. Thompson-Colón, S. Laszlo, and L. E. Phillip. 2015. "Factors affecting the innovation potential of smallholder farmers in the Caribbean Community", Regional Environmental Change (15):1367-1377.

Lu, F. 2010. "Patterns of indigenous resilience in the Amazon: A case study of Huaorani hunting in Ecuador", Journal of Ecological Anthropology (14):5-21.

Luginbühl, Y. 2006. "Landscape and Individual and Social Well-being", in Landscape and Sustainable Development: Challenges of the European Landscape Convention:. Council of Europe Publishing.

Luke, H. 1950. Caribbean Circuit. London: Nicholson and Watson.

Lynch, B.D. 2006. "Towards a Creole Environmentalism", in Beyond sun and sand: Caribbean environmentalisms, edited by S.L. Baver and B.D. Lynch. New Brunswick: Rutgers University Press.

Lyth, A., A. Hardwood, A.J. Hobday, and J. McDonald. 2016. "Place influences in framing and understanding climate change adaptation challenges", Local Environment: The International Journal of Justice and Sustainability 21 (6).

MA. 2003. Ecosystems and human well-being: a framework assessment. A report of the conceptual framework working group of the millennium ecosystem assessment, edited by Millennium Assessment. Washington DC: Island Press.

MA. 2005a. "Ecosystems and Human Well-being: Current State and Trends, Volume 1", in Millennium Ecosystem Assessment, edited by R. Hassan, R. Scholes and N. Ash. Washington DC.

MA. 2005b. Ecosystems and human wellbeing: biodiversity synthesis. Edited by Millennium Assessment. Washington DC: Island Press.

Mace, G.M., A. Balmford, and J.R. Ginsberg. 1998. Conservation in a changing world. Cambridge, UK: Cambridge University Press.

Madge, C. 1998. "Therapeutic landscapes of the Jola, The Gambia, West Africa", Health and Place 4 (4):293-311.

Madsen, D.L., ed. 1999. Post-Colonial Literatures: Expanding the Canon. London: Pluto Press.

Magis, K. 2010. "Community Resilience: An Indicator of Social Sustainability", Society and Natural Resources 23 (5):401-416.

Maguire, B., and P. Hagan. 2007. "Disasters and communities: understanding social resilience", The Australian Journal of Emergency Management 22 (2):16.

Mahler, V.A. 1981. "Britain, The European Community, and the developing Commonwealth: dependence, interdependence, and the political economy of sugar", International Organization 35:467-492.

Maida, C.A., ed. 2007. Introduction: Sustainability, Local Knowledge and the Bioregion. Edited by C. A. Maida, Sustainability and Communities of Place. New York: Berghahn.

Maloney, F.E., and R.C. Ausness. 1974. "The Use and Legal Significance of the Mean High Water Line in Coastal Boundary Mapping", North Carolina Law Revue (53):185.

Malpas, J. 2008. "New Media, Cultural Heritage and the Sense of Place: Mapping the Conceptual Ground", International Journal of Heritage Studies 14 (3):197-209.

Mans, J.L.J.A. forthcoming "Centros de conexión (heurísticos) indígenas en las Islas occidentales de Sotavento (1493-1631)." In Indígenas e indios en la reinvención del Caribe edited by R. Valcárcel Rojas and J. Ulloa Hung. Santo Domingo: INTEC.

Manyena, S. B. 2006a. "Rural local authorities and disaster resilience in Zimbabwe", Disaster Prevention and Management: An International Journal 15 (5):810-820.

Manyena, S.B. 2006b. "The concept of resilience revisited", Disasters 30 (4):434-450.

Martin, K. St., and M. Hall-Arber. 2008. "The Missing Layer: Geotechnologies, Communities, and Implications for Marine Spatial Planning", Marine Policy 32 (5):779-786.

Matthews, R., and P. Selman. 2006. "Landscape as a focus for integrating human and environmental processes", Journal of Agricultural Economics (57):199-212.

Mayring, P. 2000. "Qualitative content analysis", Qualitative Social Research 1 (2).

Mayring, P. 2014. Qualitative content analysis: theoretical foundation, basic procedures and software solution. AUT: Klagenfurt. http://nbn-resolving.de/urn:nbn:de:0168-ssoar-395173 (accessed 11/11/ 2015).

McGregor, D.F.M., D. Barker, and D. Campbell. 2009. "Environmental change and Caribbean food security: recent hazard impacts and domestic food production in Jamaica". in Global change and Caribbean vulnerability: environment, economy and society at risk?, edited by D.F.M. McGregor, D. Dodman and D. Barker, 197-217. Kingston: UWI Press.

McLain, R., M. Poe, K. Biendenweg, L. Cerveny, D. Besser, and D. Blahna. 2013. "Making sense of human ecology mapping: an overview of approaches to integrating socio-spatial data into environmental planning". Human Ecology 41 (5):651-655.

McLaren, D. 2003. Rethinking Tourism and Ecotravel. 2nd ed. Bloomfield, CT: Kumarian Press, Inc.

MEA. 2005. Ecosystems and human well-being: current state and trends. Washington DC: Island Press.

Medina, A. 1996. Recuentros y Figuarciones: Ensayos de Antropologia Mexicana. México: Instituto de Investigaciones Antropólogicas, Universidad Nacional Autónoma de México. Merriam-Webster. 2018. Environmentalism. In Merriam-Webster.

Mercer, J., D. Dominey-Howes, and K. Lloyd. 2007. "The potential for combining indigenous and western knowledge in reducing vulnerability to environmental hazards in small island developing states". Environmental Hazards (7):245-256.

Mercer, J., I. Kelman, B. Alfthan, and T. Kurvits. 2012. "Ecosystem-Based Adaptation to Climate Change in Caribbean Small Island Developing States: Integrating Local and External Knowledge". Sustainability 4 (8):1908-1932.

Milani, R. 2006. "Theorising Landscape European Cultural Identity, The Idea of Landscape and the Perspectives of a Common European Policy". in Landscape as Heritage: Negotiating European Cultural Identity, edited by M. Sassatelli. Badia. Fiesolana.

Milcu, A.I., J. Hanspach, D. Abson, and J. Fischer. 2013. "Cultural ecosystem services: a literature review and prospects for future research". Ecology and Society 18 (3):44.

Milder, J.C., A.K. Hart, P. Dobie, J. Minai, and C. Zaleski. 2013. "Integrated Landscape Initiatives for African Agriculture, Development, and Conservation: A Region-Wide Assessment". World Development 54:68-80.

Milikan, B.H. 1992. "Tropical Deforestation, Land Degradation, and Society". Latin American Perspectives 72 (19):45-72.

Mill, J.S. 1885. Principles of Political Economy with some of their Applications to Social Philosophy, edited by W.J. Ashley. London: Longmans, Green and Co.

Miller, D. 1994. Modernity: An Ethnographic Approach, Dualism and Mass Consumption in Trinidad. Oxford/London: Berg.

Mimura, N., L. Nurse, R.F. McLean, J. Agard, L. Briguglio, P. Lefale, R. Payet, and G. Sem. 2007. "Small Islands". Contribution of Working Group II to the Fourth Assessment Report of the Intergovernmental Panel on Climate Change, Cambridge.

Mintz, S.W. 1975. Slavery, Colonialism, and Racism: Eassys. New York: W. W. Norton & Company

Mintz, S. W. 1984. "From Plantations to Peasantries in the Caribbean." In Focus: Caribbean edited by Sidney W. Mintz & Sally Price. Washington D.C.: Woodrow Wilson International Center for Scholars.

Mitchell, W.J.T. 2002a. "Introduction", in Landscape and Power: Space, Place and Landscape, edited by W.J.T. Mitchell, 1-4. University of Chicago Press.

Mitchell, W.J.T. 2002b. "Imperial Landscape", in Landscape and Power: Space, Place and Landscape edited by W.J.T.Mitchell, 5-51. Chicago: University of Chicago Press. Moller, H., F. Berkes, P.O.B. Lyver, and M. Kislalioglu. 2004. "Combining science and traditional ecological knowledge: Monitoring populations for co-management", Ecology and Society 9 (3):2.

Moore-Colyer, R., and A. Scott. 2005. "What kind of landscape do we want? Past, present and future perspectives", Landscape Research (30):501-523.

Moore, J. W. 2003. "The Modern World-System as environmental history? Ecology and the rise of capitalism", Theory and Society 32 (3):307-377.

Moran, J. 2002. Interdisciplinarity. London/ New York: Routledge.

Mount, D., and S. O'Brien. 2013. "Postcolonialism and the Environment", in The Oxford Handbook of Postcolonial studies, edited by G. Huggan, 521-540. Oxford: Oxford University Press.

Mullaney, E. G.. 2009. "Carib Territory: Indigenous Access to Land in the Commonwealth of Dominica", Journal of Latin American Geography 8:71-96.

Myers, G. 2004. Banana Wars: the Price of Free Trade. London: Zed Books.

Mycoo, M.A., C. Griffith-Charles, and S. Lalloo. 2017. "Land management and environmental change in small-island-developing states: the case of St. Lucia." Regional Environmental Change 17 (4):1065-1076.

Nabhan, G. 2000. "Interspecific relationships affecting endangered species recognized by O'Odham and Comcaac cultures", Ecological Applications 10 (5):1288-1295.

Narchi, N. E. 2015. "Environmental Violence in Mexico. A Conceptual Introduction", Latin American Perspectives 42 (204):5-18.

Nelson, G.C., E. Bennett, A.A. Berhe, K. Cassman, R. DeFries, T. Dietz, A. Dobermann, A. Dobson, A. Janetos, M. Levy, D. Marco, N. Nakicenovic, B. O'Neill, R. Norgaard, G. Petschel-Held, D. Ojima, P. Pingali, R. Watson, and M. Zurek. 2006. "Anthropogenic Drivers of Ecosystem Change: an Overview", Ecology and Society 11 (2):29.

Nettley, A., C. Desilvey, K. Anderson, A. Wetherelt, and C. Caseldine. 2013. "Visualizing Sea-Level Rise at Coastal Heritage Site: Participatory Process and Creative Communication" ,Landscape Research 39 (6):637-667.

Ng, E.C.W, and A.T. Fisher. 2013. "Understanding Well-Being in Multi-Levels: A review", Health, Culture and Society 5 (1):308-323.

Nicholson, C.T.M. 2014. "Climate Change and the politics of casual reasoning: the case of climate change and migration", The Geographical Journal (180):151-160.

Nisbet, E.K., and J.M. Zelenski. 2013. "The NR-6: a new brief measure of nature relatedness", Frontiers in Psychology 4 (813).

Nisbett, M. 2008. "Saint Kitts and Nevis", in Africa and the Americas: Culture, Politics, and History, edited by R. M. Juang and N. Morrissette, 963. ABC CLIO: Santa Barbara, California.

Nixon, R. 2011. Slow violence and the environmentalism of the poor. Cambridge, MA: Harvard University Press.

Nkonya, E., J. von Braun, A. Mirzabaev, Q.B. Le, H. Kwon, and O. Kirui. 2016. "Concepts and Methods of Global Assessment of the Economics of Land Degradation and Improvement", in Concepts and Methods of Global Assessment of the Economics of Land Degradation and Improvement, edited by E. Nkonya, J. von Braun and A. Mirzabaev. New York: Springer International Publishing.

Norberg, J., and G. Cummings, eds. 2008. Complexity theory for a sustainable future. New York: Columbia University Press.

Norton, B.G., and D. Noonan. 2007. "Ecology and valuation: big changes needed", Ecological Economics 63 (4):664-675.

Nunn, P. D. 2009. "Responding to the challenges of climate change in the Pacific Islands: management and technological imperatives", Climate Research (40):211-231.

Nunn, P.D., K. Mulgrew, B. Scott-Parker, D.W. Hine, A.D.G. Marks, D. Mahar, and J. Maebuta. 2016. "Spirituality and attitudes towards Nature in the Pacific Islands: insights for enabling climate-change adaptation", Climate Change 136 (3):477-493.

Nurse, L., R. McLean, J. Agard, L.P. Briguglio, V. Duvat, N. Pelesikoti, E. Tompkins, and A. Webb. 2014. Contribution of Working Group II to the Fifth Assessment Report of the Intergovernmental Panel on Climate Change, in Climate change 2014: impacts, adaptation and vulnerability. Cambridge, UK/ New York, NY: Cambridge University Press.

Nurse, L., and R. Moore. 2005. "Adaptation to global climate change: an urgent requirement for Small Island Developing States", Review of European Community and International Environmental Law 14 (2):100-107.

Nys, P. 2009. "Landscape and Heritage- challenges of an environmental symbol", in Forward Planning: The Function of Cultural Heritage in a Changing Europe. Strasbourg: Council of Europe.

OECS. 2005 "St. Kitts and Nevis: retraining the sugar workers". St. Kitts: Organization of Eastern Caribbean States (OECS).

Oelschlaeger, M. 1991. The Idea of Wilderness. New Haven, CT: Yale University Press.

Okin, G.S., B. Murray, and W.H. Schlesinger. 2001. "Degradation of sandy arid shrubland environments: observations, process, modeling and management implications", Journal of Arid Environments (47):123-144.

Olsson, P., C. Folke, and F. Berkes. 2004. "Adaptive co-management for building social- ecological resilience", Environmental Management.

Olwig, K.F. 1980. "National Parks, Tourism, and Local Development: A West Indian Case", Human Organization 39 (1):22-25.

Olwig, K.F. 1995. "Introduction: Emancipation and its Consequences", in Small Islands, Large Questions: Society, Culture and Resistance in the Post-Emancipation Caribbean, edited by K. F. Olwig, 1-10. London: Frank Class.

Olwig, K.F. 1999. "Caribbean Place Identity: From Family Land to Region and Beyond", Identities 5 (4):435-467.

Olwig, K.R. 1993. "Sexual cosmology: nation and landscape at the conceptual interstices of nature and culture; or what does landscape really mean" in: Landscape Politics and Perspectives, edited by B. Bender. Oxford: Berg.

Olwig, K.R. 1996. "Recovering the Substantive Nature of Landscape", Annals of the Association of American Geographers 86 (4):630-653.

Olwig, K.R. 2002. Landscape, Nature and the Body Politic: From Britain's Renaissance to America's New World. Madison: University of Wisconsin Press.

Olwig, K.R. 2015. "Defining Landscape Democracy and its Antidissertation: Is Landscape the Spatial Meaning of Democracy?" Defining Landscape Democracy, Oscarsborg, Norway, 03/06/15-06/06/15.

Oomen, J., and L. Aroyo. 2011. "Crowdsourcing in the Cultural Heritage Domain: Opportunities and Challenges". International Conference on Communities and Technology, Brisbane, Australia.

Organization, United Nations Educational Scientific and cultural. 2005. Article 1-2, Basic Texts of the 1972 World Heritage Convention. Paris: UNESCO.

Organization, World Farmers'. 2013. "Black Sigatoka Disease threatens banana and plantain production", accessed 10/03/2017. http://www.wfo-oma.com/news/black-sigatoka-http://www.wfo-oma.com/news/black-sigatoka-disease-threatens-banana-and-plantain-production.html.

OSSIM. 2014. "Orthorectification" OSSIM Advanced image processing and geospatial data fusion, accessed 24/02/2017. https://trac.osgeo.org/ossim/wiki/orthorectification.

Oudenhoven, A.P.E. van, K. Petz, R. Alkemade, L. Hein, and R.S. de Groot. 2012. "Framework for systematic indicator selection to assess effects of land management on ecosystem services", Ecological Indicators (21):110-122.

Oudenhoven, F., D. Mijatovic, and P. Eyzaguirre. 2010. "Bridging managed and natural landscapes: the role of traditional (agri) culture in maintaining the diversity and resilience of socio-ecological system", in Sustainable use of biological diversity in socio-ecological production landscapes, edited by C. Belair, K. Ichikawa, B. Wong and B. Mulongoy, 8-21. Montreal.

Owen, N. 1974. Land and Politics in a Carib Indian Community: A Study of Ethnicity. PhD. University of Massachusetts.

Pagán -Jiménez, J.R. 2000. "La Antropología en Puerto Rico: Dictomía De Centro-Periferia", Boletín de Antropología Americana (36):193-202.

Pagán-Jiménez, J. R. 2004. "Is all archaeology at present a postcolonial one? Constructive answers from an eccentric point of view", Journal of Social Archaeology 4 (2):200-213.

Pagán Jiménez, J.R. 2007. De antiguos pueblos y culturas botánicas en el Puerto Rico indígena. El archipiélago borincano y la llegada de los primeros pobladores agroceramistas. Oxford: Archaeopress.

Pagán Jiménez, J.R., and R. Rodríguez Ramos. 2008. "Towards the Liberation of Archaeological Praxis in a 'Postcolonial Colony': The Case of Puerto Rico." In Archaeology and the Postcolonial Critique, edited by M. Liebmann & U. Rizvi, 53-71. Lanham: AltaMira.

Pagán Jiménez, J. R. 2009. El mundo vivido por los antiguos pobladores indígenas Huecoide en Las Antillas nororientale (circa 300 aC-500 dC). San Juan, Puerto Rico: Arqueología y democratización del conocimiento.

Pagán Jiménez, J.R. 2011. "Early Phytocultural Processes in the Pre-Colonial Antilles: A Pan-Caribbean Survey for an Ongoing Starch Grain Research." In Communities in Contact. Essays in Archaeology, Ethnohistory, and Ethnography of the Amerindian circum-Caribbean, edited by C.L. Hofman & A. van Duijvenbode, 87-116. Leiden: Sidestone Press.

Pajak, M.J., and S. Leatherman. 2002. "The high water line as shoreline indicator", Journal of Coastal Research 18 (2):329-337.

Paravisini-Gebert, L. 2005. "'He of the Trees': Nature, Environment, and Creole Religiosities in Caribbean Literature", in Caribbean Literature and the Environment, edited by E.M. DeLoughrey, R.K. Gosson and G.B. Handley, 182-199. Virginia: University of Virginia Press.

Parliaments, United Kingdom. 1833. An Act for the Abolition of Slavery throughout the British Colonies; for promoting the Industry of the manumitted Slaves; and for compensating the Persons hitherto entitled to the Services of such Slaves. Edited by United Kingdom Parliaments.

Pascua, P J.M.. 2015. I Ola Ka 'Aina, I Ola No Kakou: Place-Based and Indigenous Perspectives on Cultural Ecosystem Services In Hawaii. Master's Dissertation, University of Hawaii.

Patterson, T., and L. Rodriguez. 2004. "Political Ecology of Tourism in the Commonwealth of Dominica", in Tourism and Development in Tropical Islands: Political Ecology Perspectives, edited by S. Gossling, 1-28. Edward Elgar Publishers.

Pattullo, P. 1996. Last Resorts: The Cost of Tourism in the Caribbean. London: Cassell/Latin America Bureau.

Pelling, M., and D. Manuel-Navarrete. 2011. "From resilience to transformation: the adaptive cycle in two Mexican urban centers", Ecology and Society 16 (2):11.

Pelling, M., D. Manuel-Navarrete, and M. Redclift. 2012. "Climate change and the crisis of capitalism", in Climate Change and the Crisis of Capitalism: A chance to reclaim self, society and nature, edited by M. Pelling, D. Manuel-Navarrete and M.Redclift, 1-19. London/New York: Routledge.

Pelling, M., and J. I. Uitto. 2001. "Small island developing states: natural disaster vulnerability and global change", Environmental Hazards 3:49-62.

Perrings, C. 1998. "Resilience and sustainability", Environment and Development Economics (3):221-222.

Perrings, C., K.G. Mäler, C. Folke, C.S. Holling, and B.O. Jansson. 1995. Biodiversity loss: economic and ecological issues, edited by C. Perrings, K.G. Mäler, C. Folke, C.S. Holling and B.O. Jansson. Cambridge: Cambridge University Press.

Persoon, G.A., and R. Simarmata. 2014. "Undoing 'marginality': The islands of the Mahakam Delta, East Kalimantan (Indonesia)." Journal of Marine and Island Cultures 3 (2):43-53.

Pesoutouva, J., and C. Hofman. 2016. "La contribución indígena a la biografía del paisaje cultural de la República Dominicana. Una revisión preliminar", in Indigenas e Indios en el Caribe Presencia legado y estudio, edited by R.V. Rojas and J.U. Hung. Santo Dominigo, Dominican Republic: INTEC.

Pingali, P.L. 2012. "Green Revolution: Impacts, limits, and the path ahead", Proceedings of the National Academy of Sciences 109 (31):12302-12308.

Plieninger, T., D. van der Horst, C. Schleyer, and C. Bieling. 2014a. "Sustaining ecosystem services in cultural landscapes", Ecology and Society 19 (2):59.

Plieninger, T., S. Dijks, E. Oteros-Rozas, and C. Bieling. 2013. "Assessing, mapping, and quantifying cultural ecosystem services at community level", Land Use Policy (33): 118-129.

Plieninger, T., D. van der Horst, C. Schleyer, and C. Bieling. 2014. "Sustaining ecosystem services in cultural landscapes", Environment and Society 19 (2):59.

Plieninger, T., T. Kizos, C. Bieling, L. Le Du-Blayo, M. Budniok, M. Burgi, C.L. Crumley, G. Girod, P. Howards, J. Kolen, T. Kuemmerle, G. Micinski, H. Palang, K. Trommler, and P.H. Verburg. 2015. "Exploring ecosystem-change and society through a landscape lens: recent progress in European landscape research", Ecology and Society 20 (2):5.

Ploetz, R.C. 2001. "Black Sigatoka of Banana." APSNet, accessed 11/28/2016. http://www.apsnet.org/publications/apsnetfeatures/Pages/blacksigatoka.aspx.

Porter, R.W. 1984. History and Social Life of the Garifuna in the Lesser Antilles and Central America. PhD, Princeton University.

Postero, N.G. 2007. Now we are citizens: Indigenous Politics in Postmulticultural Bolivia. Stanford: Stanford University Press.

Potter, R., D. Barker, D. Conway, and T. Klak. 2004. The contemporary Caribbean. Harlow: Pearson/Prentice Hall.

Powell, K. 2010. "Making Sense of Place: Mapping as a Multisensory Research Method", Qualitative Inquiry 16 (7):539-555.

Pratt, M.L. 1992. Imperial eyes: travel writing and transculturation. New York: Routledge.

Premdas, R. R. 1996. Ethnicity and Identity in the Caribbean: Decentering a Myth, in Kellog Working Paper Series: Kellog Institute for International Studies.

Princen, T., and M. Finger. 1994. "Introduction", in Environmental NGOS in the World Politics: Linking the Local and the Global, edited by M. Finger and T. Princen. London/New York: Routledge.

Pulsipher, L.M. 1994. "The Landscapes and Ideational Roles of Caribbean Slave Gardens", in The Archaeology of Garden and Field, edited by N.F. Miller and K.L. Gleason, 202-220. Philadelphia, PA: University of Pennsylvania Press.

Pwiti, G. 1996. "Let the ancestors rest in peace? New challenges for cultural heritage management in Zimbabwe", Conservation and Management of Archaeological Sites 1 (3).

Ramirez-Gomez, S.O.I., G. Brown, and A.Tjon Sie Fat. 2013. "Participatory Mapping with Indigenous Communities for Conservation: Challenges and Lessons From Suriname" The Electronic Journal On Information Systems in Developing Countries 58 (2):1-22.

Ramirez-Gomez, S.O.I., C.A. Torres-Vitolas, K. Schreckenberg, M. Honzák, G.S. Cruz- Garcia, S. Willock, E. Palacios, E. Pérez-Minana, P.A. Verweij, and G.M. Poppy. 2015. "Analysis of ecosystem services provision in the Colombian Amazon using participatory research and mapping techniques", Ecosystem Services (13):93-107.

Ramos, R.R. 2011. "What is the Caribbean? An Archaeological Perspective." Journal of Caribbean Archaeology (Special Publication 3):19-51.

Raphaela, D., R. Renwick, I. Brown, B. Steinmetz, H. Sehdev, and S. Phillips. 2001. "Making the links between community structure and individual well-being: community quality of life in Riverdale, Toronto, Canada", Health and Place 7 (3):179-196.

Raudsepp-Hearne, C., G.D. Peterson, M. Tengö, E.M. Bennett, T. Holland, K. Benessaiah, G.K. MacDonald, and L. Pfeifer. 2010. "Untangling the Environmentalist's Paradox: Why Is Human Well-being Increasing as Ecosystem Services Degrade?", BioScience 60 (8):576-589.

Raymond, C.M, B.A. Bryan, D.H. MacDonald, A. Cast, S. Strathearn, A. Grandgirard, and T. Kalivas. 2009. "Mapping community values for natural capital and ecosystem services", Ecological economics 68 (5):1301-1315.

Reid, W.V., H.A. Mooney, D. Capistrano, S.R. Carpenter, K. Chopra, A. Cropper, P. Dasgupta, R. Hassan, R. Leemans, and R.M. May. 2006. "Nature: the many benefits of ecosystem services", Nature (443):749.

Reinar, D.A., and A.M. Westerlind. 2009. Urban Heritage Analysis. A handbook about Dive. Riksantivaren, Olso.

Relph, E. 1976. Place and placelessness. London: Pion.

Rhiney, K. 2016. "From Plantations to Services: A Historical and Theoretical Assessment of the Transition from Agrarian to Service-Based Industries in the Caribbean", in Globalization, Agriculture and Food in the Caribbean: Climate Change, Gender and Geography, edited by C.L. Beckford and K. Rhiney, 23-51. London: Palgrave Macmillan.

Rhiney, K. 2015. "Geographies of Caribbean Vulnerability in a Changing Climate: Issues and Trends", Geography Compass 9 (3):97-114.

Richardson, B.C. 1983. Caribbean migrants: Environment and human survival on St. Kitts. Knoxville: University of Tennessee Press.

Richardson, B.C. 1997. Economy and Environment in the Caribbean: Barbados and the Windwards in the 1800s. Barbados: The Press of the University of the West Indies.

Richardson, B.C. 1998. "The Contemporary Migration Cultures of St. Kitts and Nevis", in Blackness in Latin America and the Caribbean: Social Dynamics and Cultural Transformations, edited by A. Torres and N. E. Whitten, 375-395. Bloomington/ Indianapolis: Indiana University Press.

Richmond, C.A.M., and N.A. Ross. 2009. "The determinants of First Nation and Inuit health: A critical population health approach", Health and Place (15):403-411.

Ricketts, T.H. 2004. "Tropical forest fragments enhance pollinator activity in nearby coffee crops", Conservation Biology (18):1262-1271.

Rindfuss, R.R., and P.C. Stern. 1998. "Linking Remote Sensing and Social Science: The Need and the Challenge", in People and Pixels: Linking Remote Sensing and Social Science, edited by D. Liverman, E. F. Moran, R. R. Rindfuss and P. C. Stern. Washington DC: National Academy Press.

Ringel, G., and J. Wylie. 1979. "God's Work: Perceptions of the Environment in Dominica", in Perceptions of the Environment: A Selection of Interpretative Essays, edited by Y. Renard. Barbados: Caribbean Conservation Association/Association Carïbe pour l'Environment/Associacíon para la Conservación del Caribe.

Rishbeth, C. 2004. "Ethno-cultural representation in the urban landscape", Journal of Urban Design 9 (3):311-333.

Robinson, L. W, and F. Berkes. 2011. "Multi-level participation for building adaptive capacity: Formal agency-community interactions in northern Kenya", Global Environmental Change 21 (4):1185-1194.

Rocheleau, D. 2005. "Maps as Power Tools: Locating Communities in Space of Situating People and Ecologies in Place?", in Communities and Conservation Histories and Politics of Community-Based Natural Resource Management, edited by J. P. Brosius, A. Lowenthaupt Tsing and C. Zerner. Walnut Creek: AltaMira Press.

Rocheleau, D. B. Thomas-Slayter, and E. Wangari, eds. 1996. Feminist political ecology: global issues and local experiences. Abingdon: Routledge.

Rodrigues, K. 1984. "Old monkeys in the New World", New Scientist (1434):30-31.

Roebuck, L., J. Baehr, A. Fong, N. M. Ferris, and S. Zettle. 2004. Water Resources Assessments of Dominica, Antigua, Barbuda, St. Kitts and Nevis, edited by U.S. Army Corps of Engineers Mobile District and Topographic Engineering Center.

Roncoli, C., K. Ingram, and P. Kirshen. 2002. "Reading the rains: Local knowledge and rainfall forecasting in Burkina Faso", Society and Natural Resources (15):411-430.

Roos, B., and A. Hunt. 2010. "Narratives of Survival, Sustainability, and Justice", in Postcolonial Green: Environmental Politics and World Narratives, edited by B. Roos and A. Hunt, 1-17. Charlottesville/London: University of Virginia Press.

Rose, D.B., T. van Dooren, M. Chrulew, S. Cooke, M. Kearnes, and E. O'Gorman. 2012. "Thinking Through the Environment, Unsettling the Humanities", Environmental Humanities (1):1-5.

Ross, B., and A. Hunt, eds. 2010. Postcolonial Green: Environmental Politics and World Narratives. Charlottesville: University of Virginia Press.

Ross, H., and F. Berkes. 2014. "Research Approaches for Understanding, Enhancing, and Monitoring Community Resilience", Society and Natural Resources (27):787-804.

Rouse-Jones, M.D. 1977. St. Kitts, 1713-1763: A Study of the Development of a Plantation Colony. PhD Dissertation, Johns Hopkins University. Rouse, I.B. 1948. "The Carib" in Handbook of South American Indians, edited by J.H. Steward. Washington DC: Bureau of the American Ethnology.

Rowles, G. 1983. "Place and personal identity in old age: Observations from Appalachia", Journal of Environmental Psychology (3):299-313.

Rozenstein, O., and A. Karnieli. 2011. "Comparison of methods for land-use classification incorporating remote sensing and GIS inputs", Applied Geography 31 (2):533-544.

Ruggiero, P., M.G. Kratzmann, E. A. Himmelstoss, D. Reid, J. Allan, and G. Kaminsky. 2013. National Assessment of Shoreline Change: Historical Shoreline Change Along the Pacific Northwest Coast, in In Open-File Report 2012-2017, edited by U.S. Geological Survey Open-File Report. Reston, Virginia U.S. Geological Survey.

Ruiter, S. de. 2012. Mapping History. Master's Dissertation, Leiden University.

Rundstrom, A.R. 1990. "A Cultural Interpretation of Inuit Map Accuracy", Geographical Review 80 (2):155-168.

Russell, R., A.D. Guerry, P. Balvanera, R.K. Gould, K.M.A. Chan, S. Klain, J. Levine, and J. Tam. 2013. "Humans and nature: how knowing and experiencing nature affect well-being", Annual Review of Environment and Resources (38):473-502.

Ryden, K.C. 1993. Mapping the invisible landscape: Folklore, writing, and the sense of Place. University of Iowa Press.

Ryff, C.D., and C.L.M. Keyes. 1995. "The structure of psychological well-being revisited", Journal of Personal Social Psychology (69):719-727.

Saffache, P., and P. Angelelli. 2010. "Integrated Coastal Management in small islands: A comparative outline of some islands of the Lesser Antilles", Journal of Integrated Coastal Zone Management 10 (3):255-279.

Said, Edward. W. 1993. Culture and Imperialism. London: Random House.

Said, E.W. 1978. Orientalism. Western conceptions of the Orient. London: Routledge and Kegan Paul.

Saldana, J. 2013. The Coding Manual for Qualitative Researchers. London: Sage.

Samson, A.V.M., C.A. Crafword, M.L.P. Hoogland, and C.L. Hofman. 2015. "Resilience in Pre- Columbian Caribbean House-Building: Dialogue Between Archaeology and Humanitarian Shelter." Human Ecology 34 (2):323-337.

Samuel, T. 2011. "Planning Department Raises Awareness on Illegal Sand Mining" St. Kitts and Nevis Observer. http://www.thestkittsnevisobserver.com/2011/02/11/sand-mining.html.

Sanchez-Azofeifa, G.A., A. Pfaff, J.A. Robalino, and J.P. Boomhower. 2007. "Costa Rica's payment for environmental services program: Intention, implementation, and impact", Conservation Biology (21):1165-1173.

Sandström, K. 1995. Forests and Water-Friends or Foes?: Hydrological implications of deforestation and land degradation in semi-arid Tanzania. Linköping University Electronic Press.

Sapountzaki, K. 2003. "Social resilience to environmental risks: a mechanism of vulnerability transfer?", Management of Environmental Quality: An International Journal 18 (3):274-297.

Sassatelli, M. 2006. "Identities in Landscape: Constructed and Contested", in Landscape as Heritage: Negotiating European Cultural Identity, edited by M. Sassatelli. Badia Feisolana.

Sauer, C. 1925. "The Morphology of Landscape", University of California Publications in Geography 2 (2):19-54.

Sauer, P. 2007. "Reinhabitating Environmentalism: Picking up Where Leopold and Carson Left Off", in The Future of Nature: Writings on a Human Ecology from Orion Magazine, edited by B. Lopez. Minneapolis: Milkweed.

Schlosberg, D. 2013. "Theorising environmental justice: the expanding sphere of a discourse", Environmental Politics 22 (1):37-55.

Scholte, S.S.K., A.J.A. van Teefelen, and P.H. Verburg. 2015. "Integrating socio-cultural perspectives into ecosystem service valuation: A review of concepts and methods", Ecological Economics (114):67-78.

Scobie, M. 2016. "Policy coherence in climate governance in Caribbean Small Island Developing States", Environmental Science and Policy 58:16-28.

Scoones, I., and J. Thompson, eds. 1994. Beyond farmer first: rural people's knowledge, agricultural research and extension practice. London: Intermediate Technology Group.

Scullion, J., C.W. Thomas, K.A. Vogt, O. Perez-Maqueo, and M. Logsdon. 2011. "Evaluating the environmental impacts of payments for ecosystem services in Coatepec (Mexico) using remote sensing and on-site interviews", Environment Conservation (38):426-434.

Seamon, D. 1979. A geography of the lifeworld. New York: St. Martin's Press.

Shah, K.U., and H.B. Dulal. 2015. "Household capacity to adapt to climate change and implications for food security in Trinidad and Tobago",,Regional Environmental Change (15):1379-1391.

Sheller, M. 2003. Consuming the Caribbean From Arawaks to Zombies. London: Routledge.

Sheller, M. 2004. "Natural Hedonism: The Invention of Caribbean Islands as Tropical Playgrounds", in Tourism in the Caribbean: Trends, Development, Prospects, edited by D. T. Duval, 23-38. London: Routledge.

Sheng, T.C. 1990. Watershed management field manual. Edited by FAO Conservation Guide 13/6. Rome: Food and Agriculture Organization of the United Nations.

Sherbinin, A. de, L.K. VanWey, K. McSweeney, R. Aggarwal, A. Barbieri, and S. Henry. 2008. "Rural household demographics, livelihood and the environment", Global Environmental Change (18):38-53.

Sheridan, R.B. 1961. "The West India Sugar Crisis and British Slave Emancipation, 1830-1833", Journal of Economic History 21 (4):534-551.

Shiva, V. 1991. The Violence of the Green Revolution: Third World Agriculture, Ecology and Politics. London/New Jersey: Zed Books Ltd.

Siegel, P.E., C.L. Hofman, B. Berard, R. Murphy, J.U. Hung, R.V. Rojas, and C. White. 2013. "Confronting Caribbean heritage in an archipelago of diversity", Journal of Field Archaeology 38 (4):376-390.

Singh, V.P., and R.N. Yadava. 2003. "Watershed Management", in Proceedings of The International Conference on Water and Environment., Bhopal, India.

Skaria, A. 1999. Hybrid Histories: Forests, Frontiers, and Wilderness in Western India. Oxford, UK: Oxford University Press.

Smith, D.A., P.H. Herlihy, A.R. Viera, J.H. Kelly, A.M. Hilburn, M.A. Robledo, and J.E. Dobson. 2012. "Using Participatory Research Mapping and GIS to Explore Local Geographic Knowledge of Indigenous Landscapes in Mexico", Focus on Geography 55 (4).

Smith, M.K. 2003. Issues in Cultural Tourism Studies. London: Routledge.

Smith, L. 2006. The Uses of Heritage. London/ New York: Routledge

Smith, R.J., and K. Rhiney. 2016. "Climate (in)justice, vulnerability and livelihoods in the Caribbean: The case of the indigenous Caribs in northeastern St. Vincent", Geoforum (73):22-31.

Soini, K. 2001. "Exploring Human Dimensions of Multifunctional Landscapes through Mapping and Map-making", Landscape and Urban Planning 50 (4):443-476.

Soulis, K.X., and J.D. Valiantzas. 2012. "SCS-CN parameter determination using rainfall- runoff data in heterogeneous watersheds – the two-CN system approach", Hydrology and Earth System Sciences:1001-1015.

Spangenberg, J.H., and J. Settele. 2010. "Precisely incorrect? Monetising the value of ecosystem services", Ecological Complexity 7 (3):327-337.

Speranza, C. I., U. Wiesmann, and S. Rist. 2014. "An indicator framework for assessing livelihood resilience in the context of socio-ecological dynamics", Global Environmental Change:28.

Spradley, J.P. 1979. The Ethnographic Interview. New York: Holt, Rinehart and Winston.

Spradley, J. P. 1980. Participant Observation. Belmont: Wadsworth, Cengage Learning.

Stam, R., and E. Shohat. 2012. Race in Translation: Culture Wars and the Postcolonial Atlantic. New York City: NYU Press.

Stancioff, C.E., and C.L. Hofman. 2017. "Resilient Past Caribbean Communities: Using the archaeological record to investigate adaptability and heritage preservation in the Caribbean." European Association of Archaeologists, Maastricht.

Steckley, M. 2016. "Peasant balances, neoliberalism, and the stunted growth of non- traditional agro-exports in Haïti", Canadian Journal of Latin American and Caribbean Studies/Revue canadienne des études latino-américaines et caraïbes 1-22.

Stephenson, J. 2008. "The Cultural Values Model: An Integrated approach to values in landscapes", Landscape and Urban Planning (84):127-139.

Stock, P.V., J. Forney, S.B. Emery, and H. Wittman. 2014. "Neoliberal natures on the farm: Farmer autonomy and cooperation in comparative perspective", Journal of Rural Studies 36:411-422.

Stojanov, R., B. Duží, I. Kelman, D. Němec, and D. Procházka. 2016. "Local perceptions of climate change impacts and migration patterns in Malé, Maldives", The Geographical Journal

Strachan, I. 2002. Paradise and Plantation: Tourism and Culture. Charlottesville/London: University of Virginia Press.

Strecker, A. 2012. Landscape as Public Space: The Role of International and EU Law in the Protection of Landscape in Europe. PhD Dissertation, European University Institute.

Strecker, A. 2015. "Indigenous rights, cultural heritage and restitution in the Caribbean", Human Rights Defender 24 (2):23-25.

Strecker, A. 2016. "Revival, Recognition, Restitution: Indigenous Rights in the Eastern Caribbean", International Journal of Cultural Property (23):167-190.

Strecker, A. forthcoming. Landscape Protection in International Law. Oxford: Oxford University Press

Sumarauw, J., S. Frans, and K. Ohgushi. 2012. "Analysis on Curve Number, Land Use and Land Cover Changes and the Impact to the Peak Flow in the Jobaru River Basin, Japan", International Journal of Civil and Environmental Engineering 12 (2).

Summers, J.K., L.M. Smith, J.L. Case, and R.A. Linthurst. 2012. "A Review of the Elements of Human Well-Being with an Emphasis on the Contribution of Ecosystem Services", Royal Swedish Academy of Sciences (41):327-340.

Suneetha, M.S., and B. Pisupati. 2009. Learning from the Practitioners: Benefit Sharing Perspectives from Enterprising Communities. UNU-IAS and UNEP.

Symeonakis, E., N. Karathanasis, S. Koukoulas, and G. Panagopoulos. 2016. "Monitoring Sensitivity to Land Degradation and Desertification with the Environmentally Sensitive Area Index: the Case of Lesvos Island", Land Degradation and Development (27):1562-1573.

Tarraguel, A.A., B. Krol, and C. van Western. 2012. "Analysing the possible impact of landslides and avalanches on cultural heritage in Upper Svaneti, Georgia", Journal of Cultural Heritage (13):453-461.

Taylor, C. 2012. The Black Carib Wars, Freedom, Survival and the Marking of the Garifuna. Oxford: Signal Books.

Taylor, D.M. 1938. The Caribs of Dominica. Washington DC: Bureau of American Ethnology, Smithsonian Institution.

Taylor, K., and J.L. Lennon. 2012a. "Prospects and Challenges for cultural landscape management", in Managing Cultural Landscapes, edited by K. Taylor and J.L. Lennon, 345-364. Oxon: Routledge.

Taylor, K., and J.L. Lennon. 2012b. "Introduction: Leaping the fence", in Managing Cultural Landscapes, edited by K. Taylor and J.L. Lennon, 1-17. Oxon: Routledge.

Taylor, K.. 2012. "Landscape and meaning Context for a global discourse on cultural landscapes values", in Managing Cultural Landscapes, edited by K. Taylor and J.L. Lennon, 21-44. Oxon: Routledge.

Tebtebba. 2008. Indicators relevant for Indigenous Peoples: A Resource Book. Edited by the Indigenous Peoples International Centre for Policy Research and Education. Baguio City, Philippines: Tebtebba Foundation.

Tengberg, A., S. Fredholm, I. Eliasson, I. Knez, K. Saltzman, and O. Wetterberg. 2012. "Cultural ecosystem services provided by landscapes: Assessment of heritage values and identity", Ecosystem Services (2):14-26.

Thieler, E.R., E.A. Himmelstoss, J.L. Zichichi, andA. Ergul. 2008. "Digital Shoreline Analysis System (DSAS) Version 4.0 – An ArcGIS Extension for Calculating Shoreline Change." 1008-1278.

Thomas, J. 1993. "The Politics of Vision and the Archaeologies of Landscape", in Landscape – Meaning and Action, edited by B. Bender. Oxford: Berg.

Thomas-Hope, E. 2013a. "Introduction", in Environmental Management in the Caribbean: Policy and Practice, edited by E. Thomas-Hope, 3-10. Kingston: University of the West Indies Press.

Thomas-Hope, E. 2013b. "Conflicts and Contradictions in Environmental Policy and Practice in the Caribbean", in Environmental Management in the Caribbean: Policy and Practice, edited by E. Thomas-Hope, 11-27. Kingston: University of the West Indies.

Thompson, K.A. 2006. An Eye for the Tropics: Tourism, Photography, and Framing the Caribbean Picturesque. Durham: Duke University Press.

Tomer, M.D. 2004. "Watershed Management", in Encyclopedia of Soils in the Environment, edited by D. Hillel. Oxford, UK: Elsevier Ltd.

Tompkins, E.L. 2005. "Planning for climate change in small islands: Insights from national hurricane preparedness in the Cayman Islands", Global Environmental Change 15 (2):139-149.

Torres-Bennett, A. 2014. "Caribbean nations agree to seek slavery reparations from Europe". Reuters.

Trincsi, K., T. Pham, and S. Turner. 2014. "Mapping mountain diversity: Ethnic minorities and land use land cover change in Vietnam's borderlands", Land Use Policy (41):484-497.

Trouillot, M. 1992. "The Caribbean Region: An Open Frontier in Anthropological Theory", Annual Review of Anthropology 21:19-42.

Tsing, A.L., J.P. Brosius, and C. Zerner. 2005. "Introduction: Raising Questions about Communities and Conservation", in Communities and Conservation Histories and Politics of Community-Based Natural Resource Management, edited by J.P. Brosius, A.L. Tsing and C. Zerner, 1-34. Walnut Creek: AltaMira Press.

Turner, R.A., A. Cakacaka, N.A.J. Graham, N.V.C. Polunin, M.S. Pratchett, S.M. Stead, and S.K. Wilson. 2007. "Declining reliance on marine resources in remote South Pacific societies: ecological versus socio-economic drivers", Coral Reefs 26 (4):997-1008.

Turner, R. 2015. Travel and Tourism: Economic Impact 2015 Dominica. London: World Travel and Tourism Council.

United Nations. 1987a. Our Common Future – Brundtland Report. Oxford: Oxford University Press.

United Nations. 1987b. Report of the World Commission on Environment and Development: Our Common Future, in UN Documents: Gathering a Body of Global Agreements United Nations.

UN, and CEPAL. 2005 Restructuring Caribbean Industries to Meet the Challenge of Trade Liberalisation, edited by ECLAC. Port-of-Spain: ECLAC, Subregional Headquarters for the Caribbean.

UNU-IAS, Bioversity International, IGES, and UNDP. 2014. Toolkit for the Indicators of Resilience in Socio-ecological Production Landscapes and Seascapes (SEPLS).

VanPool, T. L., and R. D. Leonard. 2011. Quantitative Analysis in Archaeology. Sussex: Wiley-Blackwell.

Vayda, A. P. 1983. "Progressive contextualization: Methods for research in human ecology." Human Ecology 11 (3):265-281.

Vérin, P. 1961. " Les Caraïbes à Sainte Lucie depuis les contacts coloniaux", Nieuwe West-Indische Gids (41):66-80.

Vidal, A. 2003. "La región geohistórica del Caribe: tierra firme y cartagena de indias a cominezos del siglo XVI." Revista Mexicana del Caribe VIII (15):7-37.

Ville, A.S., G. Hickey, and L. Phillip. 2015. "Addressing food and nutrition insecurity in the Caribbean through domestic smallholder farming system innovation", Regional Environmental Change 15 (7):1325-1339.

Vogt, W.P. 1999. Dictionary of Statistics and Methodology: A Nontechnical Guide for the Social Sciences. London: Sage.

Wakefield, S., and C. McMullan. 2005. "Healing in places of decline: (re)imagining everyday landscapes in Hamilton, Ontario", Health and Place (11):299-312.

Walcott, D. 1990. Omeros. New York: Farrar, Strauss and Giroux.

Walker, B., L. Gunderson, A. Kinzig, C. Folke, S. Carpenter, and L. Shultz. 2006. "A handful of heuristics and some propositions for understanding resilience in socio-ecological systems", Ecology and Society 11:13.

Walker, B., and D. Salt. 2006. Resilience thinking: sustaining ecosystems and people in a changing world. Washington DC: Island Press.

Walker, B., C.S. Holling, S.R. Carpenter, and A. Kinzig. 2004. "Resilience, Adaptability and Transformability in Socio-ecological Systems", Ecology and Society 9 (2):5.

Wall, E., and T. Waterman, eds. 2018. Landscape and Agency: Critical Essays. Abingdon, United Kingdom: Routledge.

Wallerstein, I. 2011. The Modern World-System I: Capitalist Agriculture and the Origins of the European World-Economy in the Sixteenth Century. Berkeley: The Regents of the University of California.

Wani, S. P., T.K. Sreedevi, T.S.V. Reddy, B. Venkateswarlu, and C.S. Prasad. 2008. "Community watersheds for improved livelihoods through consortium approach in drought prone rain-fed areas", Journal of Hydrological Research and Development (23):55-77.

Wani, S.P., and K.K. Garg. 2009. "Watershed Management Concept and Principles". Best-bet Options for Integrated Watershed Management Proceedings of the Comprehensive Assessment of Watershed Programs in India, Andhra Pradesh, India, 25-27 July 2007.

Wani, S.P., P.K. Joshi, Y.S. Ramakrishna, T.K. Sreedevi, P. Singh, and P. Pathak. 2007. "A new paradigm in watershed management: A must for development of rain-fed areas for inclusive growth", in Conservation farming: Enhancing productivity and probability of rain-fed areas, edited by Swarup A., Bhan S. and Bali J.S., 39-60. Colombo, Sri Lanka: International Water Management Institute.

Warnes, C. 2009. "Introductory Address to the PSA Inaugural Conference", accessed 30/05/2015. http://www.postcolonialstudiesassociation.co.uk/assets/NewsDownloads/psanewsletterspecialissue.pdf.

Wasserman, S., and K. Faust. 1994. Social Network Analysis: Methods and Applications. Cambridge: Cambridge University Press.

Weis, T. 2007. "Small farming and alternative imaginations in the Caribbean today", Race Class 49 (2):112-117.

WHO. 2016. "Land degradation and desertification", accessed 15/12/2015. http://www.who.int/globalchange/ecosystems/desert/en/

Whyte, K.P. 2013. "On the role of traditional ecological knowledge as a collaborative concept: a philosophy study", Ecological Processes 2 (7):1-12.

Wiley, J. 1998. "The Banana Industries of Costa Rica and Dominica in a Time of Change", Tijdschrift voor Economische en Sociale Geografie 89 (1).

Wiley, J. 2008. The Banana Empires, Trade Wars, and Globalization. Lincoln/ London: University of Nebraska Press.

Wilke, S. 2010. "Performing Tropics: Alexander von Humboldt's Ansichten der Natur and the Colonial Roots of Nature Writing", in Postcolonial Green: Environmental Politics and World Narratives, edited by B. Roos and A. Hunt, 197-213. Charlottesville/ London: University of Virginia Press.

Williams, A. 2002. "Changing geographies of care: employing the concept of therapeutic landscapes as a framework in examining home space", Social Science and Medicine (55):141-154.

Willow, A.J. 2014. "The new politics of environmental degradation: un/expected landscapes of disempowerment and vulnerability", Journal of Political Ecology 21:237-257.

Willox, A. C., S.L. Harper, V.L. Edge, K. Landman, K. Houle, J.D. Ford, and the Rigolet Inuit Community Government. 2013. "'The land enriches the soul': On climatic and environmental change, affect, and emotional health and well-being in Nunatsiavut, Canada", Emotion, Space and Society (6):14-24.

Wilson, G.A. 2012. "Community resilience, globalization, and transitional pathways of decision-making", Geoforum 43 (6):1218-1231.

Wilson, G.A. 2014. "Community resilience: path dependency, lock-in effects and transitional ruptures",Journal of Environmental Planning and Management 57 (1):1-26.

Wilson, K. 2003. "Therapeutic landscapes and First Nations Peoples: An exploration of culture, health and place", Health and Place 9 (3):83-93.

Winterton, R., A.H. Chambers, J. Farmer, and S. Munoz. 2014. "Considering the implications of place-based approaches for improving rural community wellbeing: The value of a relational lens", Rural Society 23 (3):2.

Winthrop, R.H. 2014. "The strange case of cultural services: limits of the ecosystem services paradigm", Ecological Economics 108:208-214.

Wisner, B., J.C. Gaillard, and I. Kelman, eds. 2012. Handbook of Hazards and Disaster Risk Reduction. Abingdon: Routledge.

Wolf, J., and S.C. Moser. 2011. "Individual understandings, perceptions, and engagement with climate change: insights from in-depth studies across the world", Interdisciplinary Reviews: Climate Change 2 (4):547-569.

Wood, D. 1992. The Power of Maps. The Guilford Press.

Woodroffe, C.D. 2003. Coasts: Form, process and evolution. New York: Cambridge University Press.

Wortmann, C.S., M. Helmers, B. Gelder, L.W. Morton, D. Devlin, C. Barden, S. Anderson, R. Broz, T. Franti, T. Regassa, P. Shea, M. Tomer, L. Frees, and D. Griffith. 2008. Targeting of Watershed Management, Practices for Water Quality Protection, edited by the Heartland Regional Water Coordination Initiative.

Wu, J. 2013. "Landscape sustainability science: ecosystem services and human well-being in changing landscapes", Landscape Ecology 28 (6):999-1023.

Wylie, A. 2008. "The Integrity of Narratives: Deliberative Practice, Pluralism, and Multivocality", in Evaluating Multiple Narratives Beyond Nationalist, Colonialist, Imperialist Archaeologies, edited by J. Habu, C. Fawcett and J. M. Matsunaga. New York: Springer Science.

Wylie, J. 2007. Landscape. Abingdon/ New York: Routledge . Yang, W., T. Dietz, D.B. Kramer, X. Chen, and J. Liu. 2013. "Going Beyond the Millennium Ecosystem Assessment: An Index System of Human Well-Being", PLoS ONE 8 (5):1-7.

Yashar, D.J. 2005. Contesting Citizenship in Latin America: The Rise of Indigenous Movement and the Postliberal Challenge. New York: Cambridge University Press.

Young, J.C., and M.P. Gilmore. 2013. "The Spatial Politics of Affect and Emotion in Participatory GIS", Annals of the Association of American Geographers 103 (4):808-823.

Zimmerer, K.S., and T.J. Bassett. 2003. "Future directions in political ecology", in Political Ecology: An integrative approach to geography and environment-development studies, edited by K.S. Zimmerer and T.J. Bassett, 274-296. New York: The Guilford Press.A1. 2014. Sandy Point Town, St. Kitts, 20/1/2014.

Interviews

A2. 2014. Sandy Point Town, St. Kitts.
A3. 2014. Dieppe Bay, 22/1/2014.
A4. 2014. Fig Tree, St. Kitts.
A5. 2014. Palmetto Point, St. Kitts, 27/1/2014.
A6. 2014. Dieppe Bay, 30/1/2014.
A7. 2014. Basseterre, St. Kitts, 4/2/2014.
A9. 2014. Newton Ground, St. Kitts, 21/01/2014.
A10. 2014. Old, Road, St. Kitts, 30/1/2014.

A11. 2014. Basseterre, St. Kitts, 21/01/2014.
A12. 2014. Old Road Town, St. Kitts, 4/2/2014.
A13. 2014. Sandy Point Town, St. Kitts, 24/1/2014.
A14. 2014. Challengers, St. Kitts, 21/1/2014.
A15. 2014. Basseterre, St. Kitts, 28/1/2014.
A17. 2014. Old Road Town, St. Kitts, 24/1/2014.
A18. 2014. Halfway Tree, 27/1/2014.

B1. 2015. Salybia, 16/6/2015.
B3. 2016. Salybia, 21/06/2015.
B7. 2015. Bataca, 23/06/2015.
B8. 2015. Point, 24/06/2015.
B12. 2015. Salybia, 30/06/2015.
B15. 2015. Salybia, 01/07/2015.
B16. 2015. Salybia, 01/07/2015.
B20. 2015. Salybia, 17/06/2015.
B21. 2015. Salybia, 02/07/2015.
B22. 2015. Salybia, 02/07/2015.
B24. 2015. Crayfish River, 08/07/2015.
B25. 2015. Crayfish River, 08/07/2015.
B26. 2015. Salybia, 09/07/2015.
B28. 2015. Salybia, 10/07/2015.
B29. 2015. Crayfish River, 10/07/2015.
B30. 2015. Salybia, 14/07/2015.
B31. 2015. Monkey Hill, 15/07/2015.
B34. 2015. Salybia, 15/07/2015.
B36. 2015. St. Cyr, 16/07/2015.
B40. 2015. Salybia, 17/07/2015.
B47. 2015. Salybia, 17/07/2015.
B48. 2015. Salybia, 17/06/2015.
B49. 2015. St. Cyr, 18/07/2015.
B51. 2015. Crayfish River, 20/07/2015.
B55. 2015. St. Cyr, 24/07/2015.
B58. 2015. Salybia, 18/06/2015.
B60. 2015. Salybia, 20/06/2015.

Appendices

A

The interview questions and the analysis of the Socio-ecological Indicator

Landscape/Village changes
Can you describe how your village has changed over the years?
What brought about these changes?
Values in the landscape
What places in the environment, nature, town, or areas do people feel strongly about or identify with?
Why do people or you find these places important?
Who told you about these places?
Are these places also important for people outside the territory?
What is the feeling about these places in the community as a whole?
Are these places protected by the community or by the government or both?
Questions regarding the marine resources were
What is your relationship with the sea?
What are some activities that happen by the sea?
Do you and your friends hang out there?
Do you go fishing often?
Where does fishing happen?
Does everyone in the village go fishing?
What do you fish?
Has the amount changed over the years?
Where do you go fishing?
Has this changed?
Is fishing an important part of the territory? (specific to the Kalinago Territory)
Questions regarding the agricultural resources
Do you plant any vegetables or fruit?
Do you sell your crops in town or are they for your family only?
What are important plants?
What are the plants used for?

Table 33. Complete list of interview questions asked during both case studies. Continued on next page.

APPENDIX A | 245

What illnesses are the plants used for? (bush medicine)
Is there a special time to use them?
How do you pick them?
Are the important places that you mentioned above- are the plants found there?
Has this changed at all?
Questions regarding environmental degradation
The coastal Erosion on St. Kitts
In what respect has the coastline changed?
According to you, what are the causes behind these changes?
How has this impacted everyday life or other activities?
The soil erosion in the Kalinago Territory
Can you explain the soil erosion that has taken place?
According to you, what caused the soil erosion in the area?
How has this impacted everyday life or other activities?
Questions specific to the industrial agricultural production
The sugar cultivation on St. Kitts
How has the landscape changed since the end of sugar cultivation?
Did you or your family work in the sugar industry?
What has changed in the community or village since the end of sugar?
On the banana cultivation in the Kalinago Territory
How has the landscape changed since the end of bananas?
Did you grow bananas or figs?
Has this changed and what happened?
Questions specific to the Kalinago Territory concerning communal land:
How do you use the land in this territory?
Are there disputes over local land? What is their nature?
How do you know when the land/earth can be planted, must lie fallow, or needs nutrients?
Where did you learn this?
Are there ever problems with this education and planting?
How has this changed?

Table 33 (continued).

A.1 Defining the research focus of coastal villages of St. Kitts: the socio-ecological indicators

As discussed in chapter 3, understanding the links between ecology and society requires flexible methods, capable of merging qualitative and quantitative data. As stated in chapter 3 thirty semi-structured interviews were conducted on St. Kitts during fieldwork carried out between January 2014-February 2015 and April 2014-June 2014. They contain a wealth of data, but the qualitative nature of the information makes it difficult to compare with the land-change data and the subsequent survey analysis.

The preliminary interview data served to provide background information, or context, for the entire analysis. The main goal of this analysis was to understand the changes occurring within the landscape through the consideration of socio-ecological indicators as discussed in the methodology chapter (Oudenhoven

Main theme/ indicator	Sub Theme/ description	Interview quotes
Retention of local ecological knowledge (LEK)	Documentation of knowledge/acquisition of knowledge- education	Honestly, at school, they don't teach you about your island history, they teach you about American history or English history (A7 2014).
	Transmission of knowledge across generations	I tell them that their great great great grandmother used to work it (A12 2014).
Income diversity	Economic activity	So is it a real problem here, the jobs (A1 2014)
		That's a tough question. And the trick is to find a trickle down method that works, because unless, the man on the street, the fisherman, the farmer, the homemaker, sees the benefit of tourism they are not going to support it (A21 2014).
Demographics	Level of emigration	Remittances is how we have sustained ourselves (A25 2014).
	Interactions between groups	It is very hard to talk to young kids coming up today, it's very difficult. You try to tell them to right, and they feel like they minding their business (A7 2014).
	Number of generations interaction with the landscape	Quicker money, quicker money in the bush, quicker dead. But if you decide to work, you work in the sea. You couldn't work (A27 2014).
Cultural values	Important sites–buildings	But right down the other city, that wall, that old building. That was part of the French fort. You had two forts there. You had Two forts. Charles fort, no fort Charles (A4 2014).
	Important sites- natural	The island is very beautiful, naturally speaking, the backbone of mountains, I think, unlike some other islands, you know, we have a bit of everything here. We have volcanoes, we have coral reefs, we have beaches, because it is so small and in one day you can go to the top of the volcano, you can go to the depths of the sea, and to me, the diversity of natural end (A25 2014).
	Cultural practices- livelihoods	We would have a lot of fishery. Actually, my sons are fishing people. They still fish (A12 2014).
	Cultural practices- singing, dancing	Well, when I was in child, well young, they used to come out from Basseterre and go right around the island. They will play from shops to shops and shops. And wherever night meet them, if night meet them here, some will sleep (A5 2014).
	Persistence of history/heritage	And the history is so deep and so broad(A21 2014).
Food sovereignty and self-sufficiency	Availability traditional foods	And we roast bread fruit, potatoes, stuff like that, we still do those things (A22 2014).
	Availability of traditional medicine	You need to know what medication you are taking, you just can't use any kind of plant. Bush ain't really dangerous (sic) (A20 2014).
Multiple uses of land and plants	Diversity of planted crops, agriculture and cultivation in the past	Well, I have to think of the mountain area- where the people in the areas were amazing, They were farmers, farming, house, the non- sugar productive areas, more to the forests (A9 2014).
	Diversity of planted crops, agriculture and cultivation	The people have this thing in them that they look down on agriculture (A6 2014).
	Diversity of food sources- fishing	Yes, I do. I fish. and I dive. I do everything underwater. How is the fishing changed over the years? The fishing is actually not so much (A7 2014).

Table 34. Socio-ecological indicators: the main theme and sub theme, St. Kitts. Continued on next page.

Conservation of resources	Land degradation	So, I've always been thinking that, the whole coastline here needs to be reclaimed (A14 2014).
	Mechanisms for protection of habitats/species-fishing	You know, over-catching, right now, we are suffering. And this is what I think, the government here should step in. We want the fisherman (A7 2014).
	Conservation of natural places and biodiversity	But I know reefs sometimes die and when they die, they break apart (A7 2014).
	Conservation of built environment	You can see above here by the leper asylum that is Fort Charles, the government got some money from the city there and they did some work, stone work, but they didn't reach down this side.
Social-capital of landscape	Community development	This pavilion I think it is right not is not functioning. I think there is a playground, a playing field right here and the pavilion is on the grounds (A26 2014).
Complexity and intensity of interactions within ecosystems	Diversity of components in landscape used/maintained by communities	You also don't have that amount of pasture land because they had converted in recent years to cane fields and now that the sugar industry has gone out, there are not really used the lands, you know for, even for, a lot of the small farms and so on. More or less running wild bush and that kind of thing (A13 2014).
Customary laws, social institutions and autonomy	Practice of free and prior consent/involvement in development activities	Then, we ought to be part of that focus that must benefit what is happening in St. Kitts. The locals must (A9 2014).
	Recognition and respect of land and sites by governments, local communities, development industries	Problem is the government will talk of preservation, will talk of history but will do nothing to protect it (A10 2014).
	Levels of threat from the government, privatization or other	Of course, cause, they are selling out the land, which is not really a good land. You should more lease land (A3 2014).

Table 34 (continued). Socio-ecological indicators: the main theme and sub theme, St. Kitts.

et al. 2012; Oudenhoven *et al.* 2010). Applying these socio-ecological indicators as a guide, the interviews were coded with a main theme and sub theme. Table 34 describes the socio-ecological indicator of the main theme and sub themes with an example citation from relevant interviews. If participants did not want their names to be mentioned in their interview, a letter and number code were assigned.

A1.1 Percentages of the main and sub themes, the coastal villages of St. Kitts.

Each coded citation from the interviews has a main theme or sub theme (see Table 35). To visualize the connections between these themes related to the socio-ecological indicators, they can be imagined as a web. As discussed in chapter 3, this web can be imagined as the landscape. When applied to interview data, these indicators reveal community perceptions of the overall socio-ecological system (SES) or the landscape in the case study. In order to explore this socio-ecological relationship, first, the percentages of main themes and sub themes are presented (see Fig. 57). Hence, we observe that Cultural Values (37.50%) has the highest average, followed by customary laws and institutions (16.70%) and conservation of resources with (14.79%). Multiple uses of lands and plants has an average of (9.30%).

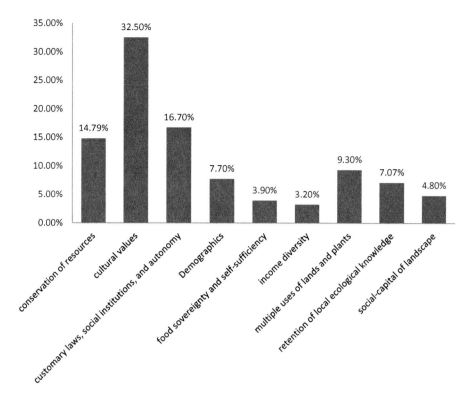

Fig. 56. Averages of the main themes, St. Kitts.

Next, to explore the web created through the connection of socio-ecological indictors, the data were exported to Visone (2011) in order to create visualization as well as an analysis in the form of an affiliation networks to compare relationships between main themes and sub themes.

Fig. 57 displays the percentage of sub themes encountered in the interview data, listed in alphabetical order. Here, the diversity of planted crops (10.3%), the important sites – buildings (7, 4%) the important sites – natural (10.1%), recognition and respect of land expressed by governments and local communities (9.6%) are the most frequently mentioned. Figs 57 and 58 illustrate that individuals consider the use of plants and lands as well as the conservation of resources (e.g., important sites – buildings, important sites – natural) to be extremely valuable and necessary. Furthermore, the land and political marginalization are connected, echoed by the strong appearance of the code customary laws and social institutions within the coded interview data.

To then visualize the connections between main indicators and sub indicators within the landscape of the St. Kitts case study area, the next step was to create an affiliation network comprising all codes and their links. Fig. 58 (see below) displays this network which is organized by means of a main theme compared to a sub theme, which is based on how interviewers assessed the relationship between the two as either negative or positive. Red lines indicate that interviewees generally speaking disagree about the fact that a connection between main themes (white nodes) and sub themes (blue nodes) still exists. Green lines indicate that participants mostly agree on the fact that there

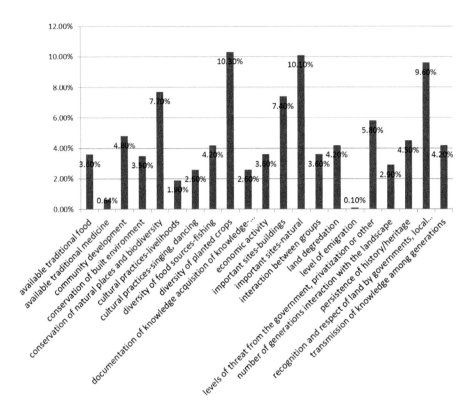

Fig. 57. Average percentages of the sub themes, St. Kitts.

is a connection between main themes and sub themes. Blue lines indicate that both an balanced mix of agreement and disagreement concerning the main theme and sub theme, or that both positive statements and negative statements have been made by individuals regarding the connection between main themes and sub themes.

It is important to note that a green line of agreement does not always indicate a positive relationship. For example, customary laws, social institutions and organizations are attached by means of a green line to levels of threat caused by the government or privatization. This may point at a strong level of threat brought about by these agencies directed against customary laws and social institutions located within the case study area. This phenomenon also occurs with the sub theme "Land degradation" which is also attached by means of a green link, suggesting that this type of degradation does indeed take place.

In the St. Kitts affiliation network (see Fig. 58) a red line indicates a negative relationship, a green line a positive relationship and a blue line a neutral relationship. We can now discern how to understand the relationships between the main and the sub themes, and how the majority of interviewees agree on the importance and value of cultural traditions (e.g., singing, dancing). For example, interviewee A7 was quick to note the significance of the contribution of her village, named Mansion, to Carnival, "Mansion Bull. At carnival, the red bull, he is from Mansion" (A7 2014). Additionally, the persistence of any history/heritage is

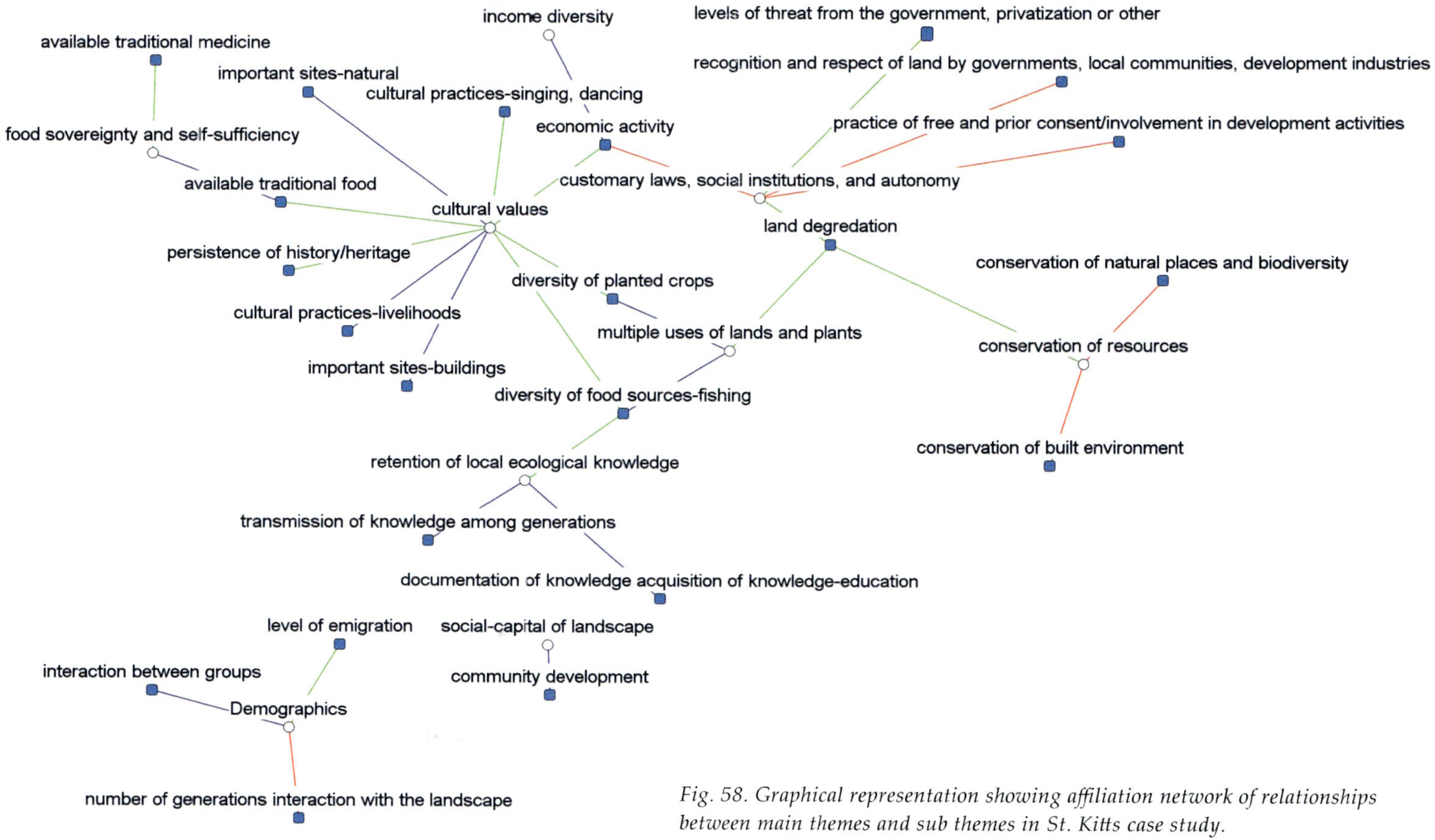

Fig. 58. Graphical representation showing affiliation network of relationships between main themes and sub themes in St. Kitts case study.

APPENDIX A | 251

clearly connected to the cultural values expressed in interviews. Most people knew of the Amerindians who lived on the island as well as of important events in local history. For example, one respondent refers to the petroglyphs in Bloody Ghaut and the lack of pictographs in his village, Half Way Tree as follows: "No drawings but they used live there. Dieppe Bay was one of the earlier towns. The main town was not the first. We had Dieppe Bay and Sandy Point Town" (A26 2014).

The negative relationship between the main and sub themes is present in categories such as the main theme "Customary laws, social institutions and autonomy" and the sub theme "Government respect and threat". This issue which concerns the role of politics and land access in the St. Kitts study area was discussed in chapter 4. The green line connecting "Customary laws, social institutions and autonomy" and "Levels of threat" sub theme represents the existence of a relationship, or that the government applies a high level of threat to land. For example, A1 discusses how the government affects any access to land or not, depending on which governmental party you support, "is like against them, you don't have no work, then your children have no more work" (A1 2014). This type of visualization serves to understand how individuals deal with the connections between the main themes and sub themes. Further, it highlights possible problematic developments in socio-ecological interactions.

A.2 Defining research focus of Kalinago Territory: socio-ecological indicators

As was the case on St. Kitts, following a familiarization with the location and an introduction to other members of the community, the informants in the Kalinago Territory were interviewed in for example Bataca, Cray Fish River, Point, St. Cyr, and Sineku where all in all, seventy interviews were conducted.

Socio-ecological indictors served to code the interview data (Oudenhoven *et al.* 2010) in order to enable a better understanding of the areas dealing with stress and disturbance affecting communities in the Kalinago Territory. For the defined socio-ecological indicators, descriptions and citations from interviews carried out in the course of the Kalinago Territory case study, see Table 35.

To explore the relationships present within this network, each main theme is then linked to a sub theme through an agreement of either the continuation or the disappearance of this relationship.

Firstly, the percentages of main themes, or main indicators, and sub themes, or sub- indicators, were calculated. This procedure provides a survey of the most commonly mentioned themes overall. For the "Percentage Occurrence of Main Themes", see Fig. 59. Here the categories "Main Theme of Cultural Values (20.60%), the "Multiple Uses of the Land and Plants" (18.18%) and the "Social Capital of the Landscape" (14.75%) are the most commonly mentioned.

The overall average occurrence of sub themes has also been calculated (see Fig. 60). The most frequently mentioned sub-themes concern the land tenure system (21%), the diversity of planted crops (10.75%), and the cultural practices – livelihoods (9.75%).

Following the coding of each interview, the results were visualized by using the software Visone (see Fig. 61). This tool reveals the variety of relationships created between

Main theme/ indicator	Sub theme/ description	Citation example
Retention of indigenous knowledge (TEK)	Documentation of knowledge/ acquisition of knowledge- education	" it's my dream to go to the school to start a program from the kindergarten, preschool, to start a language program" (B6 2015)
	Transmission of knowledge across generations	"I could give a contribution, pass the knowledge from my elderlies to the young children ,so that it could continue, so as I say, we have a strong culture, strong people, great warriors" (B6 2015)
Income diversity	Economic activity	"Everyone has become poor since bananas" (B8 2015)
	Employment available in the territory	"you really have to go out of the territory to work" (B40 2015)
Demographics	Level of emigration	"I work in Canada and then come back" (B59 2015)
	Interactions between groups	"Growing up, we had a lot more socialization" (B8 2015)
Cultural values	Important sites-buildings	"Well we had the old church, that would be a good thing if we could raise it, and we have some architect or something so we can remember what happened before" (B27 2015)
	Important sites- natural	"The centipede trail. The skeleton trail, we used to go to so often before, well there the nice places to go to" (B27 2015)
	Cultural practices- livelihoods	"the loss of agriculture is that also affect passing down heritage, or is something that most people did before" (B60 2015)
	Cultural practices- singing, dancing	"We celebrate culture through dance, because we have the cultural groups" (B6 2015)
Integration of social institutions	Use of traditional exchange and reciprocity systems	"And they only do it by koudemen, the koudemen, free labor"(B8 2015)
Food sovereignty and self-sufficiency	Availability of traditional foods	"You know normally you would have provisions for lunch, now you would have pasta. And our local drinks, you would find soda or things that you mix" (B60 2015)
	Availability of traditional medicine	"Well for medicine, for a headache or something, I make a local herbal tea"(B48 2015)
	Intensity of use of artificial fertilizers	"I market that, which is fertilizer thing, but for my home, I also have non-chemical. So, there is a big difference"(B8 2015)
Multiple uses of land and plants	Diversity of planted crops, agriculture and cultivation	"You more find that the younger generation they are not really keen into going back into agriculture"(B60 2015)
	Diversity of food sources- fishing	"Fishing is a big part, but before fishing, to go fishing down by the bay down there. Now, people don't really fish again" (B20 2015)
Conservation of resources	Land degradation	"It is not as good as before, no" (B3 2015)
	Conservation of natural places and biodiversity	"even if it is your land, we want to make you understand the watershed, we must preserve it because if climate change, next we may not have a river up in the trails" (B1 2015)
Social-capital of landscape	Community development	"That will help us now, to get those young people to learn a trade and make something for themselves"(B58 2015)
	Community engagement	"but you know they give back of their time, if their doctors, they do free clinics on Saturdays" (B40 2015)
Customary laws, social institutions and autonomy	Recognition of indigenous institutions-external members	"We can still not get money from the bank or nothing because they have some bad in between and we haven't got a title for our land, so that may cost some of us difficult for us" (B58 2015)
	Recognition of indigenous institutions-community members	"How are those things solved? The chief and council. So if you wanted some land, what would you do to get some? If I want land, like if my parents have a lot of land, then they would give me piece"(B20 2015)
	Levels of threat from government, privatization, or other	"Politics changed everything around. I can't remember anything you know"(B3 2015)

Table 35. Socio-ecological indicators and descriptions thereof, applied as codes for the interview analyses.

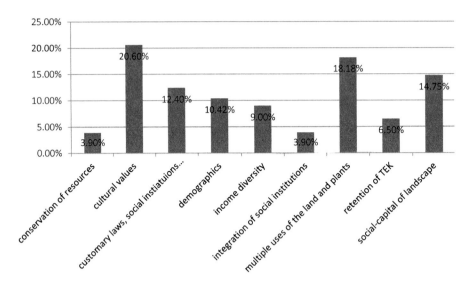

Fig. 59. Percentages of the main themes, the Kalinago Territory.

socio-ecological indicators, consequently, explaining the socio-ecological processes brought about occurring by means of a landscape change in the Kalinago Territory.

Fig. 61 displays an affiliation network which compares the main themes and the sub themes and is mutually connected by means of the type of agreement or disagreement. If statements are made in agreement, or if sub themes are connected to main themes, the line is green. If statements are made in disagreement, or if main themes and sub-themes are no longer linked, the line is red. In the case of an equal amount of disagreed and agreed statements, or if individuals agree or disagree on the fact that a main theme is still connected to a sub theme, the line is blue. This affiliation network is important when seeking to comprehend how disturbances (e.g., economic changes, land degradation) can influence a socio-ecological system through either a positive or a negative relationship.

The data reveal the importance of livelihood activities (e.g., agriculture, fishing) as a vehicle of transmission as well as an overall connector between socio-ecological indicators. Agriculture has formed the economic and social backbone of the Kalinago Territory because it shapes interactions. This fact is highlighted by the two most frequent and connective sub themes, the "Interaction between groups" and "Diversity of planted crops", emphasizing how agriculture has connected the community through land tenure systems, traditional foods and exchange between people.

Moving away from the central point, named the retention of TEK, in Fig. 61, we see the sub themes less interconnected to the main themes, for example, "the widespread use of language". It may be added here that the traditional Kalinago language had disappeared generations ago, according to many informants (A1 2015). Fig. 62 reveals how landscape-change resulted from a variety of factors, affecting socio-ecological indicators. This modification further implies the importance interviewees placed on the continuation of agriculture as this practice, or livelihood, creates links between the social, economic and environmental aspects of life.

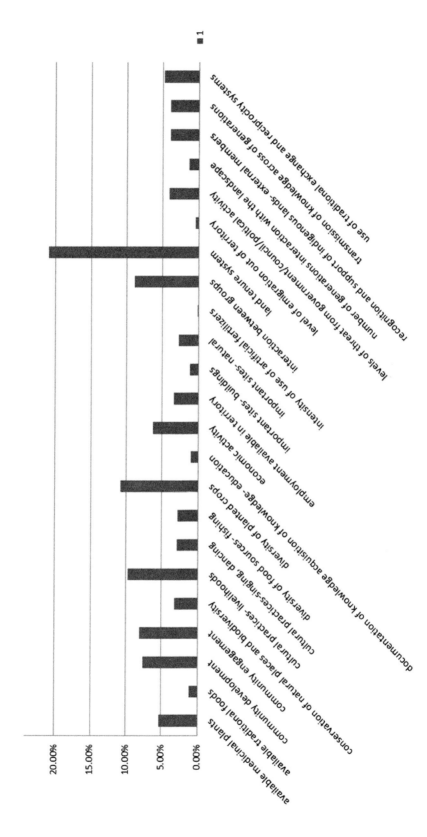

Fig. 60. Percentages of the sub themes, the Kalinago Territory.

APPENDIX A | 255

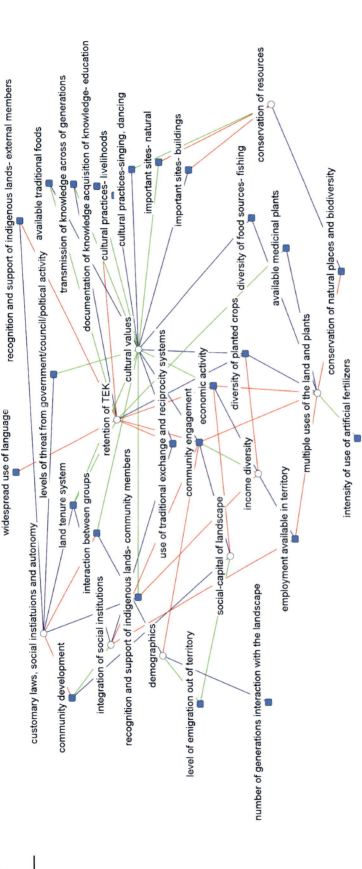

Fig. 61. Graphical representation showing affiliation network of relationships between main themes and sub themes in the Kalinago Territory case study.

Based on the results, perceived landscape changes and the effects on the social and ecological aspects of life in the Kalinago Territory can be visualized and analyzed with the help of socio-ecological indicators. Albeit preliminary, the present study reveals the value of ethnographic data in understanding socio-ecological systems. In addition, with the assistance of such visualization, the socio ecological relationships can be better understood and further investigated.

B

Land-use/land-change results

B.1 Land-use/land-cover change of the coastal villages, St. Kitts

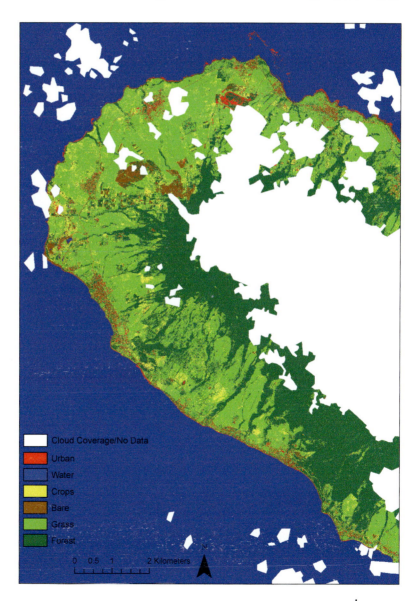

Fig. 62. ISO land-cover classification 2006, St. Kitts.

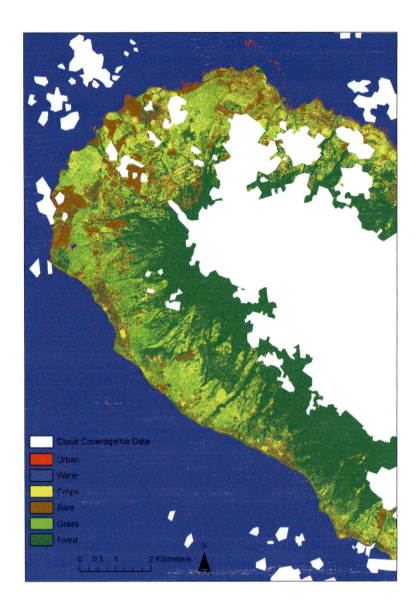

Fig. 63. ISO classification of the land cover 2015, St. Kitts.

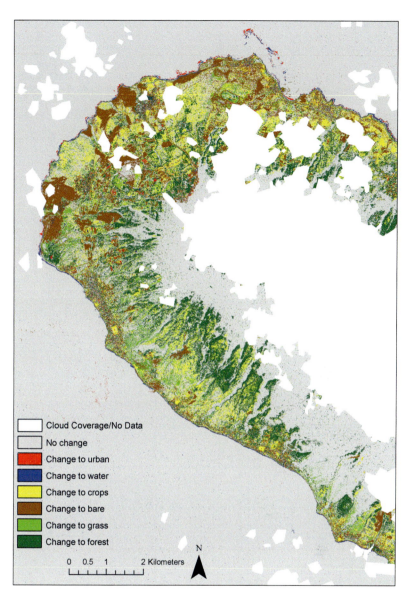

Fig. 64. ISO unsupervised classification of the land-changes 2006-2015, St. Kitts.

APPENDIX B

The ISO unsupervised classification Cross-Tabulation		Forest	Urban	Water	2015 Crops	Bare	Grass	TOTAL 2006	% in 2006
2006	Forest	16770348.82	103112.368	1113392.8135	1478770.824	999620.9742	1922798.17	21386043.96	0.182058
	Urban	182291.2398	186061.387	270438.6676	133192.5906	349548.1506	114035.386	1235567.422	0.010518
	Water	22140.94076	172611.445	65143967.54	4417.77977	63410.17402	10726.4155	65417274.3	0.556893
	Crops	1178847.524	55528.7161	34561.60953	999476.4134	895352.1198	1131824.77	4295591.151	0.036568
	Bare	405244.5573	65885.0559	182158.2438	276643.2195	601893.5814	259157.138	1790981.796	0.015247
	Grass	7243557.088	203165.827	85366.07688	6315337.612	3972387.771	5522970.65	23342785.02	0.198716
	TOTAL 2015	25802430.17	786364.799	65827884.96	9207838.439	6882212.771	8961512.52	117468243.7	
	% in 2015	0.219654516	0.00669428	0.560388773	0.078385768	0.058587858	0.07628881		

Table 36. ISO unsupervised classification Cross Tabulation Matrix 2006-2015, St. Kitts.

ML Supervised Classification Cross-Tabulation		Forest	Urban	Water	2015 Crops	Bare	Grass	TOTAL 2006	% in 2006
2006	Forest	216427.59	7949.43	203.4	24424.74	3272.13	48346.65	300625.074	0.351633242
	Urban	4907.07	13120.29	3095.19	4670.28	2654.46	6109.2	34556.82337	0.044420207
	Water	253.44	3782.88	42507.72	146.07	403.65	100.17	47194.00557	0.055201587
	Crops	30540.69	11998.89	296.01	32200.92	13177.44	75463.92	163678.6959	0.191450665
	Bare	4565.88	4671	552.87	7484.67	4964.67	13249.71	35489.05351	0.041510612
	Grass	35951.4	16164.99	259.65	58291.11	26132.13	136594.98	273395.6377	0.319783686
	TOTAL 2015	292646.07	57687.48	46914.84	127217.79	50604.48	279864.63	854939.29	
	% in 2015	0.342300411	0.067475528	0.054875054	0.148803303	0.05190729	0.327350296		

Table 37. Maximum Likelihood Classification Cross Tabulation Matrix 2006-2015, St. Kitts.

B.2 Land-use/land cover change analysis of the Kalinago Territory

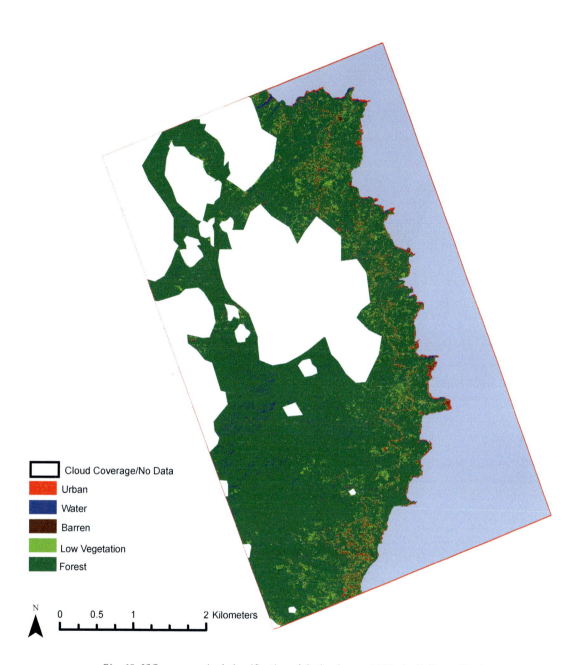

Fig. 65. ISO unsupervised classification of the land cover 2005, the Kalinago Territory.

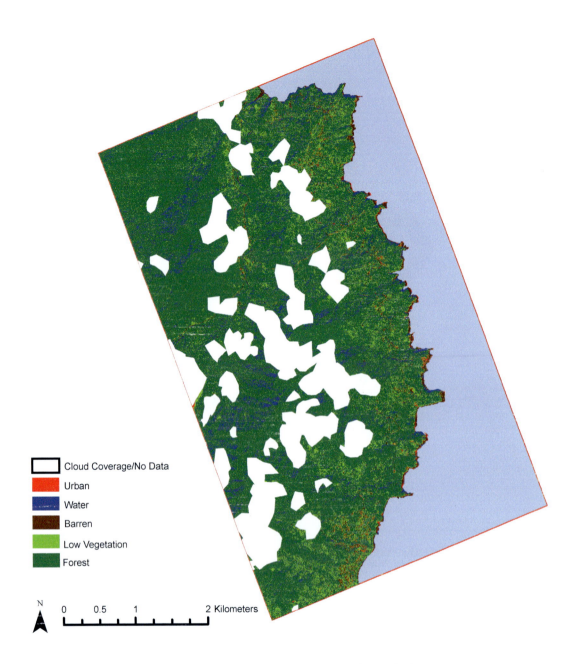

Fig. 66. ISO unsupervised classification of the land-cover 2014, the Kalinago Territory.

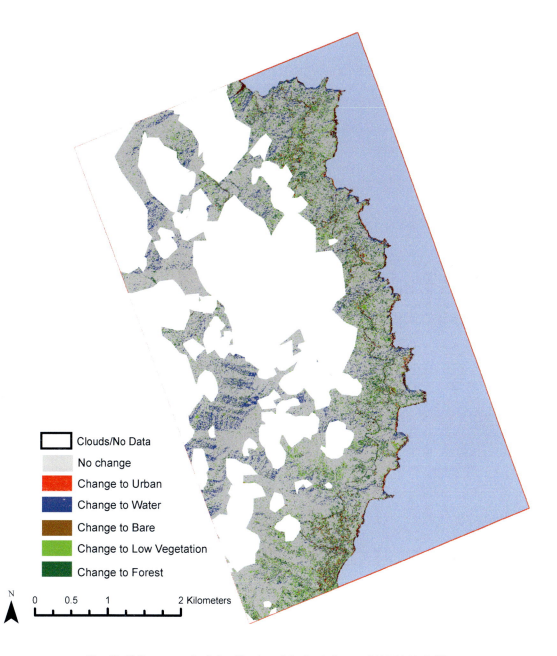

Fig. 67. ISO unsupervised classification of the land changes 2005-2014, St Kitts.

Table 38

The ISO unsupervised classification Cross-Tabulation		Low Vegetation	Forest	2014 Urban	Barren	Water	TOTAL 2005	% Total, 2005
2005	Low Vegetation	431297.28	911070.72	43585.92	79551.36	114877.4	**1580382.72**	0.0743933
	Forest	2044592.64	14778904.32	7780.32	1294376	247282.6	**18442955.52**	0.8681643
	Urban	88617.6	151395.84	55359.36	86682.24	132750.7	**514805.76**	0.0242334
	Barren	26300.16	271779.84	5287.68	118304.6	20119.68	**441792**	0.0207965
	Water	70652.16	8506.68	25839.36	15598.08	6653.76	**263687.04**	0.0124125
	TOTAL 2014	**2661459.84**	**16198214.4**	**207872.6**	**1594512**	**581564.2**	**21243623.04**	
	% Total, 2014	0.12528277	0.762497733	0.009785	0.075058	0.027376		

Table 38. ISO unsupervised classification Cross Tabulation Matrix 2005-2014, the Kalinago Territory.

Table 39

Maximum Likelihood Supervised Classification Cross-Tabulation		Low Vegetation	Forest	2014 Urban	Barren	Water	Total 2005	% Total, 2005
2005	Low Vegetation	1268421.12	1787368.32	130492.8	186474.24	172258.56	**3545015.04**	0.166848076
	Forest	2168570.88	13676365.44	121806.7	608388.48	227059.2	**16802190.72**	0.790980417
	Urban	61188.48	71758.08	60088.32	84142.08	36720	**313896.96**	0.014773732
	Barren	23489.28	88093.44	22371.84	77247.36	12061.44	**223263.36**	0.010508012
	Water	101479.68	107504.64	53187.84	41495.04	58930.56	**362597.76**	0.017065862
	TOTAL 2014	**3623149.44**	**15731089.92**	**387947.5**	**997747.2**	**507029.76**	**21246963.84**	
	% Total, 2014	0.170525514	0.74039237	0.018259	0.046959519	0.023863634		

Table 39. Maximum Likelihood Classification Cross Tabulation Matrix 2005-2014, the Kalinago Territory.

Land Class Type	2005 Area	Percentage	2014 Area	Percentage
Water	128.60 ha.	1.0%	574.70 ha.	4.6%

Table 40. Land class type: Water.

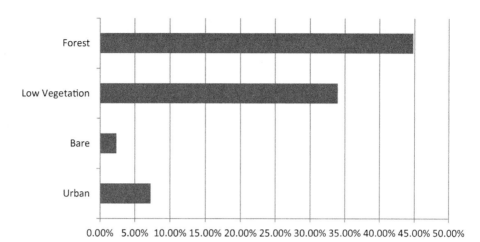

Fig. 68. Water gains: contributions from other land classes.

C

Micro factors methods applied to the coastal villages of St. Kitts

C.1 Survey questions, St. Kitts

	Demographic questions
1	Gender
2	Age
3	Village
4	Occupation
5	Family living situation
	Questions related to village changes, and to perceptions of landscape and society
6	Time span of living in a village
7	Personal knowledge of a village
8	Climate change effect on a village
9	Climate change effect on the quality of life
10	Coastal erosion effect on village
11	Coastal erosion effect on the quality of life
12	River or ghaut flooding effect on a village
13	River or ghaut flooding effect on the quality of Life
14	Sea level effect on a village
15	Sea level effect on the quality of life
16	New construction effect on a village
17	New construction effect on the quality of life
18	Other change effect on a village (individual gives change)
19	Other change effect on the quality of life (corresponds to question 18)
20	Attention to environment before the survey
21	Overall change in a village (has the village seen significant change over the years?)
22	Overall change effect on the quality of life (has the village changed for better or worse?)
23	Recommendations for changes in a village
24	Overall interest in supporting: education, tourism, agriculture, conservation, coastal development, urban development

Table 41. Survey questions asked on St. Kitts. Continued on next page.

	Questions regarding places and importance and values
25	What are places of importance to you?
26	Why are they important to you? What value do they have? (economic, social, historic, personal, natural, relaxation, Amerindian, fun, other)?
27	Are these places at risk, threatened or have they been degraded for any reason?

Table 41 (continued).

C.2 Data distribution provided by the survey respondents, St. Kitts

Age	
Mode	1
Range	5
Minimum	1
Maximum	6

Age		Frequency	%
Valid	15-20	57	32.8
	21-30	16	9.2
	31-40	34	19.5
	41-50	22	12.6
	51-60	32	18.4
	61 +	13	7.5
	TOTAL	174	100.0

Table 42. Age distribution.

Village Name	
Mode	13.0a
Range	16.0
Minimum	1.0
Maximum	17.0

Village Name	Frequency	%
Boyd's Village	1	.6
Challengers	18	10.3
Conyers	2	1.1
Fig Tree	10	5.7
Fortlands	1	.6
Frigate Bay	5	2.9
Goodwin Ghaut	1	.6
Halfway Tree	8	4.6
Lamberts	5	2.9
Middle Island	11	6.3
New Guinea	7	4.0
Newton Ground	4	2.3
Old Road	36	20.7
Sandy Point	36	20.7
St. Pauls	6	3.4
Stone Fort	3	1.7
Verchilds	20	11.5
TOTAL	174	100

Table 43. Village distribution.

Village Group	
Mode	2.0
Range	5.0
Minimum	1.0
Maximum	6.0

Village Group	Frequency	%
Sandy Point, Fig Tree	46	26.4
B. Goodwin Ghaut, Halfway Tree, New Guinea	20	11.5
C. Conyers, Lamberts, Middle Island	16	9.2
D. Old Road, Verchild	56	32.2
E. Boyd's Village, Challengers, Stone Fort	22	12.6
F. Fortlands, Frigate Bay, Newton Ground, St. Pauls	14	8.0
Total	174	100.0

Table 44. Village group distribution.

Occupation	
Mode	4
Range	6
Minimum	1
Maximum	7

Occupation	Frequency	%
Agriculture	19	10.9
Government	15	8.6
Tourism, commercial/retail, home keeper, retired	23	13.2
Education	45	25.9
Professional services	21	12.1
Merchant	27	15.5
Other	24	13.8
TOTAL	174	100.0

Table 45. Occupation distribution.

Family Living Situation	
Mode	4
Range	4
Minimum	1
Maximum	5

Family Living Situation		
Family	Frequency	%
Live alone	31	17.8
Couple with children	11	6.3
Couple without children	1	.6
Extended Family	128	73.6
Other	3	1.7
TOTAL	174	100.0

Table 46. Distribution of the family living situations.

D

The micro factors methods applied in the Kalinago Territory

D.1 Survey questions, Kalinago Territory

Demographic questions	
1	Village
2	Hamlet
3	Gender
4	Age
5	Name
The questions related to village changes, and on the perceptions of the landscape and society	
6	Crops planted
7	Hamlet changes
8	Territory-wide changes
9	Land-changes
10	Reasons behind answer
11	Water resources
12	Agricultural production
13	Soil fertility
14	Crop yield
15	Input amount
16	Explain
17	Fish yield
18	Coastal erosion affects
19	Beautiful/important sites in the Kalinago Territory
20	Location of these sites
21	Frequency of visit to sites
22	Community changes
23	Explain
24	Community activities
25	Attendance

Table 47. Survey questions asked in the Kalinago Territory. Continued on next page.

26	Education possibilities		
27	Political change		
28	Business opportunities		
29	Ease to start a business		
30	The Kalinago Territory should stay the same		
31	The Kalinago Territory needs more development		
32	The Kalinago Territory needs more agriculture		
33	The Kalinago Territory needs more nature		

Table 47 (continued).

D.2 Data distribution provided by the Kalinago Territory survey respondents

Gender		Frequency	%
	Male	43	60.6
	Female	28	39.4
	Total	**71**	**100.0**
Age	Age Group	Frequency	%
	20-30	30	42.3
	31-40	13	18.3
	41-50	11	15.5
	50-above	17	23.9
	Total	**71**	**100.0**
Hamlet	Name	Frequency	%
	Bataca	5	7.0
	Crayfish River	10	14.1
	Salybia/Point	33	46.5
	St. Cyr	13	18.3
	Mahaut River	3	4.2
	Gaulette River	3	4.2
	Sineku	4	5.6
	Total	**71**	**100.0**

Table 48. Data distribution of gender, age and hamlet.

	Territory		Land		Hamlet	
	Freq	%	Freq	%	Freq	%
1	13	18.3	23	32.4	16	22.5
2	26	36.6	26	36.6	32	45.1
3	28	39.4	14	19.7	23	32.4
Total	67	94.4	63	88.7	71	100.0
Missing	4	5.6	8	11.3		
	71	100.0	71	100.0		

Table 49. Distribution of the aggregated variables (recoded).

	Agriculture prod.		Soil		Crop yield		Input amount		Water res.	
	Freq.	%	Freq.	%	Freq.	%	Freq.	%	Freq.	%
1	40	58.8	24	36.9	34	49.3	7	10.6	54	78.3
2	18	26.5	20	30.8	20	29.0	11	16.7	13	18.8
3	10	14.7	21	32.3	15	21.7	48	72.7	2	2.9
Total	68	100.0	65	100.0	69	100.0	66	100.0	69	100.0
	3		6		2		5		2	
	71		71		71		71		71	

Table 50. Distribution of the aggregated variables (recoded).

	Community changes		Community activities		Education possibilities	
	Frequency	%	Frequency	%	Frequency	%
1	49	70.0	33	47.8	16	23.5
2	11	15.7	23	33.3	40	58.8
3	10	14.3	13	18.8	12	17.6
Total	70	100.0	69	100.0	68	100.0
	Political changes		Business possibilities		Ease to start a business	
	Frequency	%	Frequency	%	Frequency	%
1	39	54.9	47	66.2	45	63.4
2	26	36.6	14	19.7	15	21.1
3	6	8.5	10	14.1	11	15.5
Total		100.0		100.0	71	100.0

Table 51. Distribution of the aggregated variables (recoded).

E

Data results of the coastal villages of St. Kitts

E.1 Specific land class results of land-cover/land-change analysis

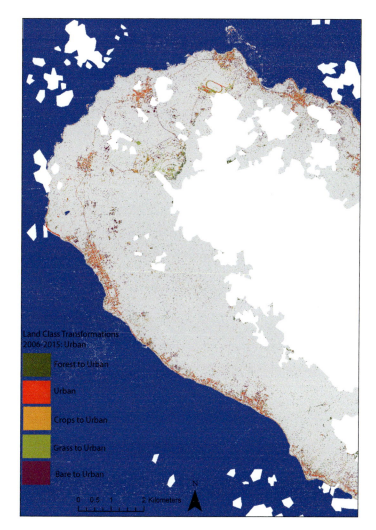

Fig. 69. Land-cover changes to Urban 2006-2015, St. Kitts.

APPENDIX E | 277

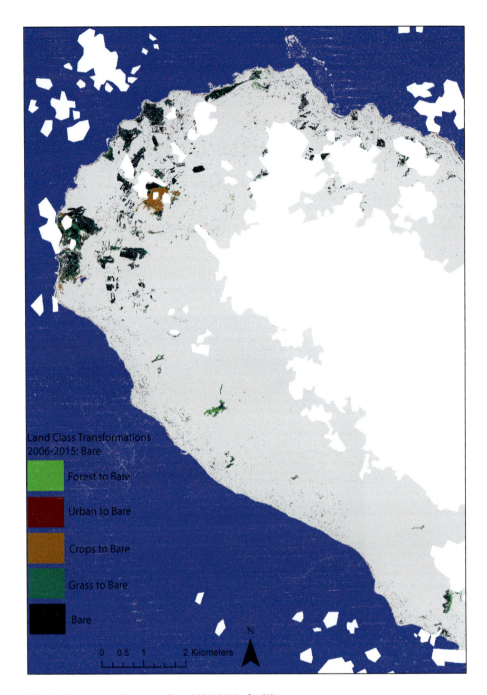

Fig. 70. Land-over changes to Bare 2006-2015, St. Kitts.

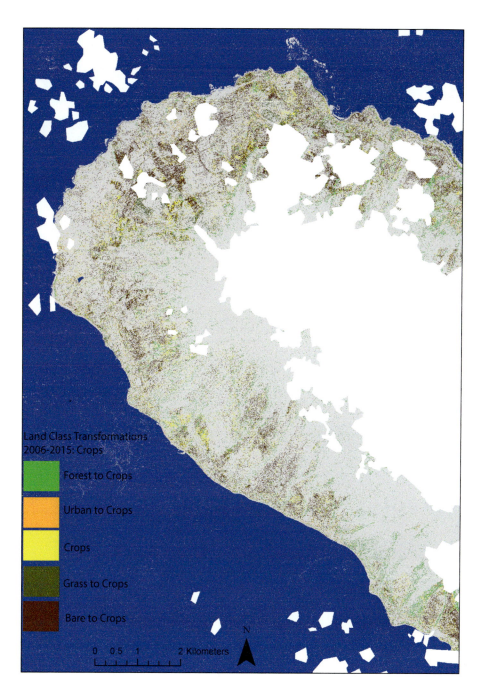

Fig. 71. Land-cover changes to Crops 2006-2015, St. Kitts.

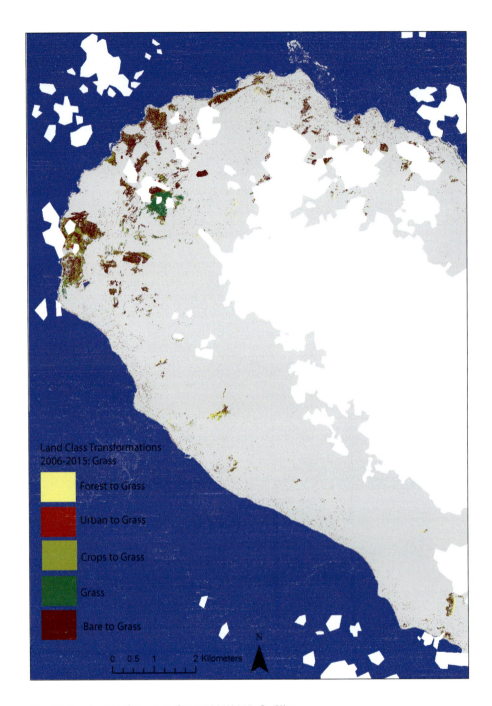

Fig. 72. Land-cover changes to Grass 2006-2015, St. Kitts.

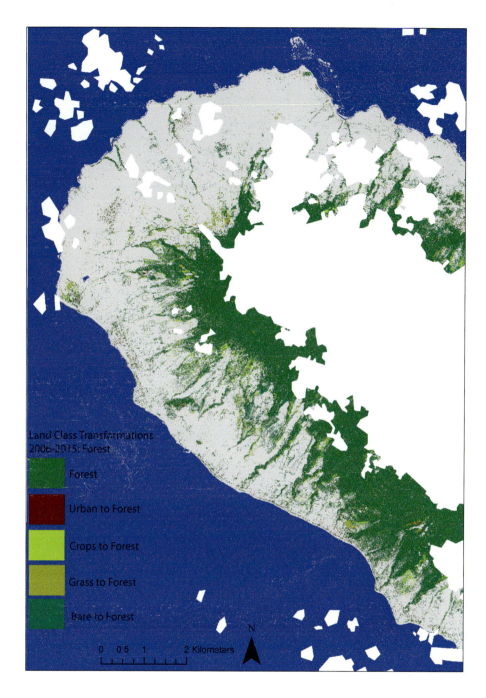

Fig. 73. Land-cover changes to Forest 2006-2015 St. Kitts.

E.2 Survey results of the coastal villages of St. Kitts

		Occupation									
		1	2	3	4	5	6	7	8	9	10
gender	Male	15	8	6	15	9	2	14	0	2	13
	Female	4	7	3	30	12	5	13	4	1	11
Total		19	15	9	45	21	7	27	4	3	24

	Value	Asymptotic Significance (2-sided)
Pearson Chi-Square	18.502a	.030
Likelihood Ratio	20.606	.015
Linear-by-Linear Association	.995	.319
N of Valid Cases	174	

*Table 52. Gender * Occupation Cross Tabulation*

Symmetric Measures		**Approximate Significance**
Ordinal by Ordinal	Kendall's Tau-b	.213
	Kendall's Tau-c	.213
	Spearman Correlation	.209c
Interval by Interval	Pearson's R	.320c
N of Valid Cases		

*Table 53. Gender * Occupation Chi-Square Test.*

	Sea Levels Changed				Total
	Very Negative	**Negative**	**Positive**	**Very Positive**	
Male	33	21	14	16	84
Female	40	31	15	4	90
Total	73	52	29	20	174

*Table 54. Gender * Sea Levels Change Cross tabulation.*

Chi-Square Tests

	Value	df	Asymptotic Significance (2-sided)
Pearson Chi-Square	9.633a	3	.022
Likelihood Ratio	10.145	3	.017
Linear-by-Linear Association	4.880	1	.027
N of Valid Cases	174		

		Value	Asymptotic Standardized Error	Approximate Tb
Ordinal by Ordinal	Kendall's Tau-b	-.124	.070	
	Kendall's Tau-c	-.146	.082	
	Spearman Correlation	-.134	.075	-1.771
Interval by Interval	Pearson's R	-.168	.073	-2.234
N of Valid Cases	174			

*Table 55. Gender * Sea Levels Chi-Square Test.*

	Coastal Erosion Effect				Total
Age Group	**Very Negative**	**Negative**	**Positive**	**Very Positive**	
10-20	42	7	4	4	57
21-30	10	4	0	2	16
31-40	16	9	0	9	34
41-50	11	7	0	4	22
51-60	17	7	0	8	32
61 and above	8	3	2	0	13
Total	**104**	**37**	**6**	**27**	**174**

*Table 56. Age (aggregated) * Coastal Erosion Effect on the Village Cross tabulation.*

	Value	Asymptotic Significance (2-sided)
Pearson Chi-Square	27.672	.024
Likelihood Ratio	30.399	.011
Linear-by-Linear Association	2.851	.091
N of Valid Cases	174	

Symmetric Measures					
		Value	Asymptotic Standardized Error	Approximate Tb	Approximate Significance
Ordinal by Ordinal	Kendall's Tau-b	.130	.061	2.118	.034
	Kendall's Tau-c	.116	.055	2.118	.034
N of Valid Cases		174			

Table 57. Age (aggregated) * Coastal Erosion Effect on the Village Chi-Square Test.

	Coastal Erosion Impact on the quality of life				
Age group	Very negative	Negative	Positive	Very positive	Total
10-20	40	9	5	3	57
21-30	9	5	0	2	16
31-40	19	6	3	6	34
41-50	7	12	0	3	22
51-60	18	5	2	7	32
61 and above	6	4	2	1	13
Total	99	41	12	22	174

Table 58. Age (aggregated) * Coastal Erosion Effect on the quality of life Cross tabulation.

Chi-Square Tests	Value	df	Asymptotic significance (2-sided)
Pearson Chi-Square	26.971a	15	.029
Likelihood Ratio	27.681	15	.024
Linear-by-Linear Association	4.633	1	.031
N of Valid Cases	174		

Symmetric Measures					
		Value	Asymptotic Standard Error	Approximate Tb	Approximate Significance
Ordinal by Ordinal	Kendall's Tau-c	.137	.057	2.409	.016
N of Valid Cases		174			

Table 59. Age (aggregated) * Coastal Erosion Effect on the quality of Life Chi-Square Test.

E.3 Coastal erosion of coastal villages, St. Kitts

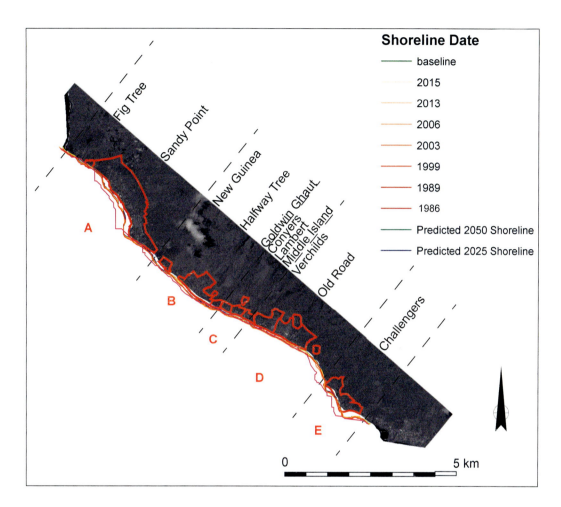

Fig. 74. Extracted shorelines 1986-2015.

F

Data results of the Kalinago Territory

F.1 Specific land class results of the land-use/land-change analysis

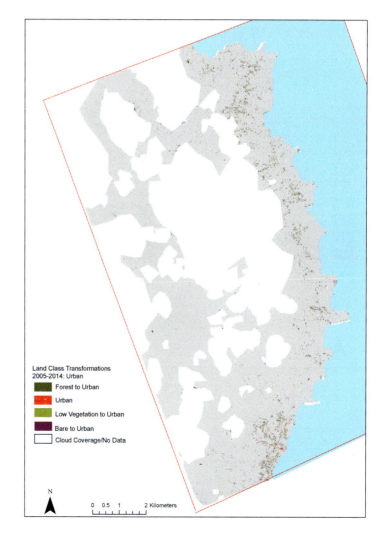

Fig. 75. Land-cover changes to Urban 2005-2014, the Kalinago Territory.

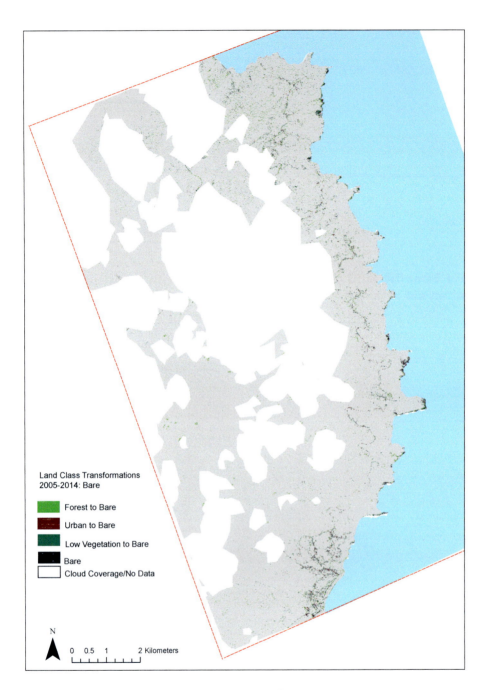

Fig. 76. Land-cover changes to Bare 2005-2014, the Kalinago Territory.

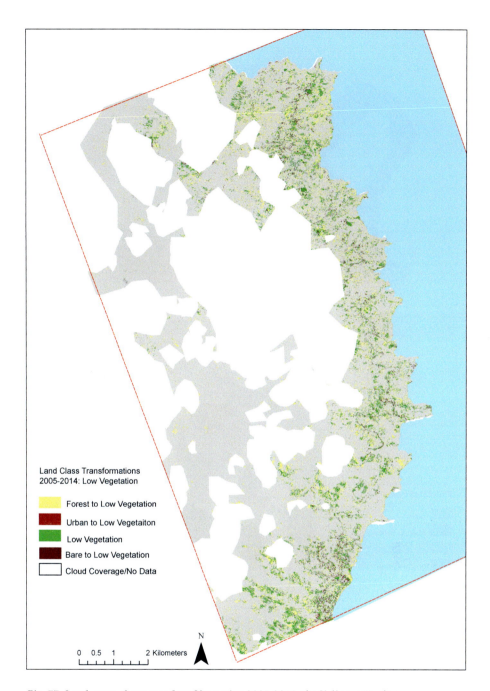

Fig. 77. Land-cover changes to Low Vegetation 2005-2014, the Kalinago Territory.

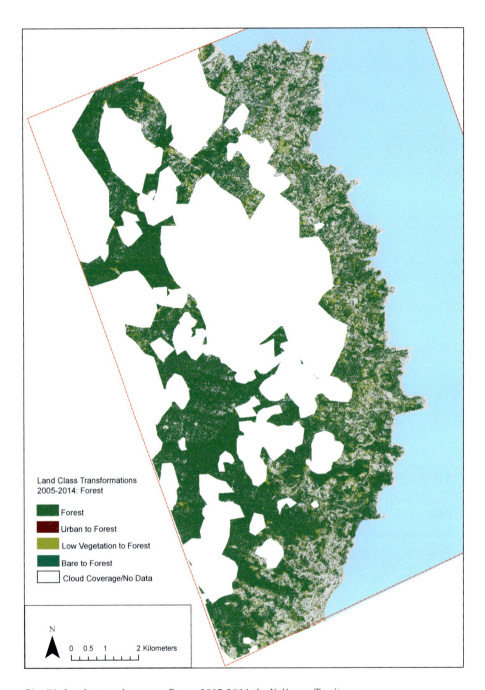

Fig. 78. Land-cover changes to Forest 2005-2014 the Kalinago Territory

F.2 Kalinago Territory survey results

N	Valid	69
	Missing	2
Mean		1.04
Median		1.00
Std. Deviation		.268
Range		2
Minimum		1
Maximum		3

Table 60. Descriptive statistics of water resources.

Perception of changes to the water resources	Frequency	Cumulative Percentage
Negative	67	97.1
No change	1	98.6
Positive	1	100.0
Total	69	
Total	71	

Table 61. Overall perception of changes to water resources.

	Water resources			
Age Group	Negative	No Change	Positive	Total
10-20	29	0	0	29
21-30	12	0	0	12
31-40	11	0	0	11
41-50	15	1	1	17
51-60	67	1	1	69
61 +above	29	0	0	29
Total	**12**	**0**	**0**	**12**

*Table 62. Water Resources * Age Cross-Tabulation*

Chi-Square Tests	Value	df	Asymptotic significance (2-sided)
Pearson Chi-Square	6.300a	6	.390
Likelihood Ratio	5.790	6	.447
Linear-by-Linear Association	3.767	1	.052
N of Valid cases	69		

Symmetric measures		Value	Asymptotic Standard Error	Approximate Tb	Approximate Significance
Ordinal by Ordinal	Kendall's tau-c	.066	.045	1.472	.141
N of Valid Cases		69			

*Table 63. Water resources * Age Chi-Square Test.*

		Gender		Total
		Male	Female	
WaterResources	Negative	40	27	67
	No Change	1	0	1
	Positive	1	0	1
Total		42	27	69

*Table 6. Water resources * Gender Cross-Tabulation.*

Chi-Square Tests	Value	df	Asymptotic Significance (2-sided)
Pearson Chi-Square	1.324a	2	.516
Likelihood Ratio	2.024	2	.363
Linear-by-Linear Association	1.171	1	.279
N of Valid Cases	69		

Symmetric Measures		Value	Asymptotic Standard Error	Approximate Tb	Approximate Significance
Ordinal by Ordinal	Kendall's Tau-c	-.045	.031	-1.445	.149
N of Valid Cases		69			

*Table 65. Water resources * Gender Chi-Square Test.*

Water Resources	Hamlet Frequency						
	Bataca	Crayfish River	Salybia/Point	St. Cyr	Mahaut River	Gaulette River	Sineku
Negative	5	9	30	13	3	3	4
No change	0	1	0	0	0	0	0
Positive	0	0	1	0	0	0	0
Total	**5**	**10**	**31**	**13**	**3**	**3**	**4**

*Table 66. Water resources * Hamlet Cross-Tabulation.*

Chi-Square Tests			
	Value	df	Asymptotic Significance (2-sided)
Pearson Chi-Square	7.202a	12	.844
Likelihood Ratio	5.541	12	.937
Linear-by-Linear Association	.424	1	.515
N of Valid Cases	69		

Symmetric Measures					
		Value	Asymptotic Standard Error	Approximate Tb	Approximate Significance
Ordinal by Ordinal	Kendall's tau-c	-.035	.030	-1.183	.237
N of Valid Cases		69			

*Table 67. Water resources * Hamlet Chi-Square Test.*

F.3 Watershed management of the Kalinago Territory

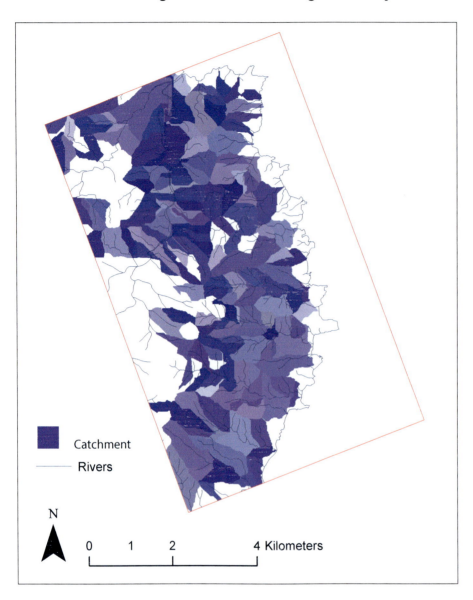

Fig. 79. Watershed catchments, the Kalinago Territory.

Summary

This thesis focuses on landscape change caused by natural and anthropogenic factors and the subsequent effects on community well-being on the Caribbean islands of St. Kitts and Dominica.

As a first step, both studies trace the use of the landscape. From the early indigenous inhabitants, to the foreign colonizers, to modern Caribbean independence, the land use continually reflects the values and constraints of the local societies. However, as landscapes are dynamic, in order to understand the layers of history, society and environment, each case study relies on collaboration with local partners. To illustrate the interactions between community and ecology within rural island areas, the analysis has focused on land-use, land-cover change, land and water management and community views. Through a community response to a shifting environment, fresh outlooks are created from the consideration of the effects of landscape change on community well-being.

The methodology in each case study begins with interviews with community members. After coding to specific socio-ecological indicators, the interviews in each case study expose the main topic of focus. Subsequent methods can be broken down into segments that address macro factors and micro factors. Macro factors clarify methods completed in both case studies. This would include preliminary interviews. A second method in this category is the classification of land use/land cover using satellite imagery. In each case study, classified images from two different dates reveal the modifications that have taken place through time. Micro factors require the collaboration of each community in each case study as they focus on analyzing landscape transformations described by community members. Both qualitative and quantitative methods complement the analysis, creating a holistic investigation, sensitive to the local and cultural context.

As one of the first islands colonized by the British in the Lesser Antilles, the island of St. Kitts was almost entirely cultivated with sugar cane until 2006. Even following the nationalization of the sugar cane industry and the eventual collapse of the sugar cane production on the island, much of the fertile lands remain fallow to this day. The land use/land cover analysis affirms a decline in crops and an increase in grasslands during the period of 2006-2015 throughout the study area. Interviewees further illuminate such land conversion by describing how despite its nationalization, land has yet to be re-distributed. The overgrowth of the land has reached such an extent, that individuals can no longer access their mountain fields, important for not only cultural and historical reasons but also for food security and self-sufficiency. Interviews throughout the study area further exposed that the local coastline had eroded dramatically in recent years. The sea endures as a collective cultural space for many Kittitians. For fishermen, the sea and the coast continue to be connected to their livelihoods that is increasingly put in jeopardy due to the erosion. Working together with local partners at the St. Kitts and Nevis Coast Guard and the Department of Physical Planning and Environment. Ministry of Sustainable Development (DPPE)-, we conducted a coastal survey. This included analyzing the changing shoreline between 1986 and 2015 in order to determine the amount of coastline that had already eroded away. Finally, an implemented household survey investigated how the changing landscape and coastline alters communities and their livelihoods. Results demonstrate not only an expected negative perception of climate-related environmental conversion, such as increased hurricanes or coastal erosion, but also a negative perception of societal transformations. Individuals often related such loss of community engagement to a transition in one's relationship with the land.

In the Kalinago Territory, the banana export market connected a rural and isolated indigenous community with the global market. The Kalinago Territory rapidly modernized in a period of twenty years. During the mid-2000's, the WTO ended preferential trading, ultimately ending the economic viability of banana cultivation throughout the Caribbean, and the Kalinago Territory. Without bananas, stable incomes disappeared, terminating not only much food security but also a rich cultural heritage tied to agriculture. Again, using land use/land cover analysis, the results of the analysis for the period of 2005-2014 describes an increase of low vegetation and a decline in forest. Such a result is further explained by interviewees, considering the rapid decline in agriculture as a toll of the lack of available markets and high prices of inputs. Therefore, land has become fallow and overgrown. Interviewees also report reduced water resources, again linking the increase in current deforestation to the decline in agriculture throughout the Kalinago Territory. Rivers and streams remain important cultural sites for the Kalinago because of their mythical and historical significance as well as their commonality in daily recreational activities and daily chores. Working together with the Ministry of Kalinago Affairs and the Chief and Council of the Kalinago Territory, we investigated the changing curve numbers, or potential for run-off in the watershed area between 2005 and2014. Results illustrate a higher increase for run-off potential in stream areas, supporting the decrease in forested areas and increase in low vegetation. Finally, a household survey sought to reaffirm much of the collected interview and GIS/Remote Sensing data. Again, individuals reported a decline in agriculture and water resources. Such aspects negatively impact Kalinago cultural life as so much of the rural society remained based around the land.

Such drastic landscape changes in such a relatively short period of time of course are not only related to the environment but a reflection of larger socio-economic and political influences. However, such types of landscape conversions rarely transform only the natural ecology, leading to implications in the customary practices and traditions that play an integral part in the fabric of communities, the heritage, or more specifically, perceived well-being.

Samenvatting

Dit proefschrift richt zich op veranderingen in het landschap veroorzaakt door zowel natuurlijke als antropogene factoren, en de daaropvolgende effecten op het welzijn van de gemeenschap op de Caraïbische eilanden St. Kitts en Dominica. Hier, als een eerste stap, traceren twee studies het gebruik van het landschap. Vanaf de vroege, inheemse bewoners tot aan de buitenlandse kolonisten, en tot aan de moderne Caraïbische onafhankelijkheid, weerspiegelt het gebruik van land voortdurend niet alleen de waarden maar ook de beperkingen van de plaatselijke samenlevingen. Echter daar landschappen dynamisch zijn, vertrouwt elke case study op het samenwerken met plaatselijke partners om de gelaagdheid van de geschiedenis, de maatschappij en het milieu te begrijpen. Om de interacties tussen de gemeenschap en de ecologie binnen de landelijke eilandgebieden aan te tonen, is de analyse gericht op het gebruik van het land, op de transformaties in de bodem bedekking, op het land- en waterbeheer, en op meningen geuit door de gemeenschap. Naar aanleiding van de reactie van de gemeenschap op een veranderende omgeving komen er nieuwe perspectieven tot stand die zijn gebaseerd op de afweging van de effecten van wijzigingen in het landschap op het welzijn van de gemeenschap.

De methodologie in elke case study begint met het interviewen van leden van de gemeenschap. Na het coderen van specifieke sociaalecologische indicatoren, leggen de interviews in elke case study het voornaamste onderwerp van de focus bloot. De hierop volgende methodes kunnen worden verdeeld in segmenten die zich zowel op macrofactoren als op microfactoren richten. Macrofactoren verklaren de methoden die in beide case studies zijn toegepast en zouden ook voorlopige interviews betreffen. Een tweede methode in deze categorie behelst de indeling van het gebruik van land en de verandering in de bodem bedekking met behulp van satellietbeelden. In elke case study onthullen geclassificeerde beelden verkregen met behulp van twee verschillende datums de wijzigingen die in de loop der tijd hebben plaatsgevonden. Microfactoren vereisen de samenwerking met iedere gemeenschap in elke case study, aangezien deze factoren zich richten op het analyseren van veranderingen in het landschap die door gemeenschapsleden worden beschreven. Zowel kwalitatieve als kwantitatieve methoden complementeren deze analyse, waarbij een holistisch onderzoek wordt gecreëerd, dat sterk rekening houdt met de lokale en culturele context.

St. Kitts, een van de eerste eilanden die door de Britten in de Kleine Antillen werd gekoloniseerd, was tot 2006 bijna volledig beplant met suikerriet. Zelfs na de nationalisering van de suikerriet industrie en de uiteindelijke ineenstorting van de productie hiervan op het eiland, liggen vele vruchtbare gebieden op St. Kitts nu nog braak. Wat betreft het tijdvak 2006-2015 bevestigt de analyse van zowel het grondgebruik en de bodem bedekking zowel een afname van de gewassen als een toename van de graslanden binnen het gehele studiegebied. Geïnterviewden lichten deze transformatie van het land verder toe door te beschrijven hoe, ondanks de nationalisering, er nog land moet worden herverdeeld. De overgroei op het land is zodanig toegenomen, dat individuen geen toegang meer hebben tot hun op bergen gelegen velden, die niet alleen om cultuur-historische redenen, maar ook in verband met de voedselzekerheid en zelfvoorziening belangrijk zijn. Interviews afgenomen in het studiegebied onthulden verder dat de kustlijn aldaar in de afgelopen jaren dramatisch geërodeerd was. De zee blijft in stand als een collectieve culturele ruimte voor vele inwoners van St. Kitts. Voor vissers zijnde zee en de kust nog steeds verbonden met hun levensonderhoud, dat meer en meer gevaar loopt ten gevolge van erosie. In samenwerking met lokale partners gelieerd aan de St. Kitts and Nevis Coast Guard en aan het Department of Physical Planning and Environment (DPPE) werd een kust survey uitgevoerd. Deze omvatte het analyseren van de veranderende kustlijn tussen 1986 en 2015 met de bedoeling de hoeveelheid reeds verdwenen kustlijn vast te stellen. Tenslotte werd, middels een geïmplementeerd onderzoek naar huishoudens, research verricht naar de wijze waarop het veranderende landschap en de kust zowel de gemeenschappen als hun levensonderhoud wijzigden. Resultaten tonen vervolgens niet alleen een verwachte negatieve perceptie van klimaat gerelateerde veranderingen in het milieu aan, zoals bijvoorbeeld meer orkanen of een toenemende kust erosie, maar ook een negatieve perceptie van maatschappelijke transformaties. Individuen koppelden een dergelijk verlies van gemeenschapsverband aan een wijziging in de relatie met het land.

In de Kalinago Territory verbond de bananen exportmarkt een landelijke, geïsoleerde inheemse gemeenschap met de wereldmarkt. Dit deel van Dominica is binnen twintig jaar snel gemoderniseerd. Halverwege het eerste decennium van de 21e eeuw beëindigde de WTO de preferentiële handel, waardoor de economische levensvatbaarheid van de bananenteelt in het Caraïbisch gebied inclusief de Kalinago Territory tenslotte verdwijnt. Zonder bananen was er van stabiele inkomsten geen sprake, waardoor er niet alleen een eind kwam aan veel zekerheid in verband met de voedselvoorziening maar ook aan een rijk cultureel erfgoed verbonden met de landbouw. Na een analyse van het gebruik van het land/de verandering in de bodem bedekking, duiden de resultaten van dit onderzoek met betrekking tot het tijdvak 2005-2014 nogmaals op een toename van het lage vegetatie dek en op een daling wat betreft de bebossing. Een dergelijke uitkomst wordt nader beschreven door de geïnterviewden, waarbij zij de snel krimpende landbouw beschouwen als een tol van het gebrek aan beschikbare markten en de hoge prijzen van inputs. Daarom ligt het land braak en is het overgroeid. De geïnterviewden melden ook een afname wat betreft het aantal waterbronnen, waardoor de toename van de huidige ontbossing opnieuw wordt gekoppeld aan de tanende landbouw in het hele Kalinago Territory. Rivieren en beken blijven belangrijke culturele plekken voor het Kalinago volk vanwege hun mythische en historische betekenis, en hun dagelijks gemeenschappelijkheid met betrekking tot zowel recreatieve activiteiten als dagelijkse taken. Samen met het Ministry of Kalinago Affairs en de Chief and Council of the Kalinago Territory, hebben wij de veranderende curvegetallen, oftewel de potentiële afstroming, in de stroomgebieden onderzocht wat betreft het tijdvak 2005-2014. De uitkomst hiervan illustreert een grotere toename van het afstroom potentieel in stroomgebieden, die de afname van de beboste gebieden en de toename van de lage vegetatie onderbouwen. Ten slotte tracht een onderzoek naar huishoudens veel van de middels interviews verzamelde informatie en de GIS/Remote Sensing data te bevestigen. Nogmaals meldden individuen een afname wat betreft de landbouw en de waterbronnen. Dergelijke factoren hebben een negatief effect op het culturele leven van het Kalinago volk, aangezien een groot deel van de plattelandsgemeenschappen rond het land gevestigd bleven.Zulke drastische wijzingen in het landschap gedurende een dergelijk korte periode zijn natuurlijk niet alleen gerelateerd aan het milieu, maar vormen ook een weerspiegeling van grotere sociaaleconomische en politieke invloeden. Dergelijke vormen van veranderingen wat betreft het landschap transformeren zelden slechts de natuurlijke ecologie, hetgeen leidt tot implicaties met betrekking tot de gebruikelijke praktijken en tradities die een wezenlijke rol spelen binnen het weefsel van gemeenschappen en het erfgoed, of in meer specifieke zin, het waargenomen welzijn.

Curriculum vitae

Charlotte Eloise Stancioff is a Bulgarian-American GIS and Ecosystem services specialist. Born in Washington, DC but residing in the Netherlands, She holds a a BA in International Relations and Geography at the University of Chapel Hill in North Carolina and a MSc in Geoinformatics at the University of Toulouse-Jean Jaurès/ École Nationale Supérieure Agronomique in Toulouse, France.

Through both her research and professional experiences, she has pursued her goal of developing collaborative mixed methods while leveraging her knowledge of GIS/remote sensing and international relations to achieve sustainable results in the domain of ecosystem services, sustainable development and well-being. As she is well-versed in working with community partners and multiple stakeholder partners, she has conducted numerous on-site trainings and workshops as well as provided impact modeling assessments and technical support in environmental, disaster management, digital heritage and media domains At ease in culturally diverse settings, she has gained experience through similar projects in international setting such as Brazil, Crete and Bulgaria. Throughout her PhD research within the ERC-Synergy NEXUS1492 project at Leiden (2013-2017), she worked directly with different Caribbean island governmental ministries on a variety of environmental and social projects, producing tangible results combining environmental and social data. Her work included providing on-site trainings, environmental impact modeling and technical support to community partners and stakeholders by using mixed methods of community participation, GIS, ethnographic, and environmental data. Such collaborative partnerships produced holistic and sustainable efforts as watershed management plans, GIS database and Land survey for the Kalinago Territory and coastal prediction model and land use/land cover change analysis for St. Kitts. Furthermore, she has also advised and developed digital medias in the cultural domain for the Ministry of Culture St. Kitts and the Museo de Altos de Chavon in the Dominican Republic since 2014. She presented her work at various conferences throughout Europe, the US and the Caribbean. Furthermore, she has published the result of the collaborative efforts made throughout the research in variety of multidisciplinary journals.